Food Shortage, Climatic Variability, and

Epidemic Disease in Preindustrial Europe

ALSO BY JOHN D. POST

The Last Great Subsistence Crisis in the Western World

Food Shortage, Climatic Variability, and
Epidemic Disease in Preindustrial Europe

THE MORTALITY PEAK IN THE EARLY 1740s

—————————————————————— JOHN D. POST

Cornell University Press   ITHACA AND LONDON

First published 1985 by Cornell University Press.

International Standard Book Number 0-8014-1773-2
Library of Congress Catalog Card Number 85-4684
Printed in the United States of America
Librarians: Library of Congress cataloging information
appears on the last page of the book.

The paper in this book is acid-free and meets the guidelines for
permanence and durability of the Committee on Production Guidelines
for Book Longevity of the Council on Library Resources.

To the memory of Andrew B. Appleby,
whose ideas and work have informed
the pages that follow

Contents

Tables

Preface

When harvests have failed in Europe, epidemic disease has invariably followed. This book attempts to advance understanding of the relationships between food shortages and epidemic mortality in preindustrial societies. My principal concern is to assess the relative influence of climatic variability, nutritional status, and such remedial measures as public welfare programs on morbidity and mortality rates. The basic methodological approach adopted to establish the chain of causation running from harvest shortfalls to epidemic diseases is to trace through the dynamics of a preindustrial subsistence crisis. Famine mortality has been accounted for by the widely accepted hypothesis of a synergistic relationship between nutritional deficiency and infection. At the same time, we know that epidemics in preindustrial societies can be promoted by environmental stress and social disarray as well. Accordingly, this book seeks to discover whether the epidemic mortality that coincided with preindustrial food shortages derived predominantly from prolonged malnutrition or from environmental deprivations.

Because nutritional and social inadequacies were interwoven in preindustrial subsistence crises, it is difficult to assess the relative demographic impact of the two variables. A wide-scale cross-national investigation seemed the most appropriate strategy to ease this methodological problem. If nutritional stress provoked epidemic mortality, for example, the magnitude of national increases in food prices should correspond in some measure with the amplitude of national mortality peaks. The European subsistence crises and mortality peak of the years 1740–1742 constitute a most suitable case for such a comparative study. The fact that a shortage of food and a wave of communicable diseases spread simultaneously over the British Isles, Scandinavia, France, the Low Countries, the German-language states, Switzerland, and Italy

11

permits an analysis of the national variants in food prices, welfare policies, prevailing epidemics, and demographic outcomes. The critical tasks prove to be the working out of the functional relationships that could connect the complex of historical events to the specific infections that predominated during the early 1740s and the identification of the networks and pathways that could spread contagion in preindustrial Europe.

No researcher can presume to undertake such a wide-ranging investigation without depending on and being indebted to the hypotheses, data, and findings of other scholars. I am indebted, first of all, to the studies, suggestions, and critical analysis of Steven L. Kaplan of Cornell University. For the Scandinavian evidence, I owe a large debt to the magisterial monograph of Arthur E. Imhof, *Aspekte der Bevölkerungsentwicklung in den nordischen Ländern, 1720–1750* (Bern, 1976). For much of the Swiss agricultural and meteorological data, I am indebted to the unstinting generosity of Christian Pfister of the University of Bern, whose seminal investigations and findings appear in *Das Klima der Schweiz von 1525 bis 1860 und seine Bedeutung in der Geschichte von Bevölkerung und Landwirtschaft* (Bern, 1984). Roger S. Schofield of the Social Science Research Council's Cambridge Group for the History of Population and Social Structure kindly provided monthly mortality figures for England, in advance of the publication of E. A. Wrigley and R. S. Schofield, *The Population History of England, 1541–1871* (Cambridge, Mass., 1981), which furnished the remaining demographic data for England. For Ireland, I owe a debt of gratitude to the study of Michael Drake, "The Irish Demographic Crisis of 1740–41," *Historical Studies* 6 (1968). For France, I am indebted to the work of Professor Kaplan and also to the joint study of Michel Bricourt, Marcel Lachiver, and Denis Queruel, "La Crise de subsistance des années 1740 dans le ressort du Parlement de Paris," *Annales de Démographie Historique* (1974). The demographic data for Scotland derive principally from the definitive work of Michael Flinn and others, *Scottish Population History* (Cambridge, England, 1977). As always, I have benefited from the critical evaluation and encouragement of Herbert Moller of Boston University. The list of debts could be extended. They are acknowledged in the text and in the references.

For the invaluable assistance provided, I am especially appreciative of the service rendered by Jeanne K. Siracco and her staff at the Interlibrary Loan Division of Dodge Library, Northeastern University. I am also indebted to Robin Price, deputy librarian, and the staff of the Wellcome Institute for the History of Medicine, and to the staff of the Rare Book

Division, Countway Library, Harvard Medical School. I owe an eternal debt of gratitude to my wife, Ruth, for her unfailing understanding and sympathy, which have lightened the tasks.

JOHN D. POST

Boston, Massachusetts

Food Shortage, Climatic Variability, and
Epidemic Disease in Preindustrial Europe

1. *Introduction*

The second half of the eighteenth century saw the passing of the old demographic regime in western Europe. Mortality crises began to subside, and death rates no longer reached the drastic peaks registered in the seventeenth century. Fernand Braudel has called this momentous change the shattering of the old biological order.[1] The mortality wave of the early 1740s marked the last occasion when a surge in the number of burials simultaneously reduced population growth in all regions of western Europe. As in seventeenth-century crises, the elevated mortality resulted from the coincidence of famine conditions and widespread epidemics of fatal diseases. The decade of the 1740s accordingly represents one of the turning points in the population history of Europe. To account for the retreat of the old demographic regime, it is necessary to understand not only the preindustrial subsistence crisis in all of its facets but also its antecedents and sequelae.

The syndrome of a preindustrial subsistence crisis is well known. The lines of causation from food shortage to mortality, however, present historical and theoretical problems that have not been completely resolved. What was the sequence and the pattern of the climatic, biological, economic, and demographic events? What independent role, if any, did the antecedent unfavorable weather play in the elevated morbidity rates associated with harvest failures? Can the established hypothesis of a synergistic relationship between nutritional deficiency and infection adequately explain the subsequent epidemic diseases? Or did the epidemics emerge primarily from endemic diseases whose morbidity and mortality rates were driven up by the intensification of human deprivations and the dilution of the normal components of community resistance? The

1. Fernand Braudel, *Capitalism and Material Life, 1400–1800,* trans. Miriam Kochan (New York, 1973), 37.

17

paramount issue becomes, it would seem, whether the recurrent coincidence of prolonged food shortage and epidemic mortality derived from the biological interaction of undernutrition and infection or resulted more from the environmental, ecological, and social changes provoked by the harvest shortfalls.

Because the essential eighteenth-century data are still too sketchy to permit a conclusive analysis, and because present-day epidemiological knowledge has not resolved every aspect of the interaction of nutrition and infection, historical investigations of preindustrial epidemics may not always provide definitive answers. But the comparative medical and demographic evidence that exists for the mortality waves that swept over western Europe can compensate in part for the unavailable data. In the European subsistence crises and mortality peak of 1740–1742, economic and demographic statistics together with clinical medical records are available to some measure for thirteen countries or locations. The advantage of a comparative approach is that it permits an analysis of the national variants in food shortage, mortality, and epidemic disease. The surviving clinical evidence, informed and supplemented by medical and epidemiological findings, makes it possible to identify the prevailing epidemics with a sufficient degree of accuracy. It should be stressed at this point that the ability to assess the relative incidence of the specific fatal diseases at the national and provincial levels is critical to the methodological solution.

The passing of the old demographic regime raises a related yet distinct problem: the identification of the circumstances that intervened in the course of the eighteenth century to check European mortality crises. After the disappearance of bubonic plague from western Europe, preindustrial mortality crises were touched off chiefly by famine, with the death rate climbing from some combination of prolonged hunger and epidemic disease. It is not clear, however, to what extent the leveling of mortality peaks in the eighteenth century resulted from the abatement of famines and "famine fevers," as opposed to the decline of epidemic diseases due to other causes. As a consequence, the ability to specify the conditions and to describe the networks that spread contagion in preindustrial Europe is indispensable to the answer. There is general agreement that eighteenth-century medicine and public health methods could not have made a key contribution. There is also general agreement as to the catalogue of improvements that led to the disappearance of famine, but the relative contribution of the several variables involved is still being debated.

Recent historical research has demonstrated that a series of economic advances and political innovations eased crisis mortality in the eighteenth century. The combined benefits of an expanded international trade in food, new crop mixes better insulated against the weather, and the growth of emergency grain stocks moderated the impact of subsistence crises. In the more favored countries of western Europe, famines were eliminated. Public administrations, but not in all locations, became more effective in delivering food, fuel, shelter, and rudimentary health care to the needy during those years in which the level of distress mounted sharply. European societies learned to insulate their working populations against the potential calamities that extreme weather events could still trigger. But not all societies proved equally successful in adapting to climatic shocks.

The identification of the decisive changes that brought about a decline of epidemic mortality in the wake of harvest shortfalls will resolve in large measure the two main questions posed. A brief review of the findings of the studies concerned with the passing of the old demographic regime in Europe will further clarify the issues and will also place the mortality peak of the early 1740s in perspective. Karl Helleiner found that, in the years 1740–1741, death and disease still engendered acute distress in most countries of Europe, even though mortality no longer assumed quite the disastrous proportions it had reached in earlier centuries. In 1742 Norway could still record a national death rate of 52 per 1,000, and the Swedish county of Värmland a catastrophic rate in excess of 100 per 1,000, yet this crisis was a far cry from those experienced by several European regions during the 1690s. Helleiner agreed with Pierre Goubert's observation that after 1741 the old demographic regime seemed defunct.[2]

The study of Old Regime mortality crises has secured most attention in France, owing to the success that regional demographic history has enjoyed there. The findings of the regional studies have been synthesized in a definitive work.[3] In Goubert's contribution to the work, he suggested that seventeenth- and eighteenth-century French mortality crises can usefully be classified into three general types: those occasioned by war, by plague, and by subsistence crises. He has concluded that modern French population growth began in the course of the eighteenth century as the result of the retreat of plague and military crises after 1715 and the

2. Karl L. Helleiner, "The Population of Europe from the Black Death to the Eve of the Vital Revolution," in *The Cambridge Economic History of Europe*, vol. IV: *The Economy of Expanding Europe in the 16th and 17th Centuries* (Cambridge, 1967), 92–93.
3. Fernand Braudel and Ernest Labrousse, eds., *Histoire économique et sociale de la France: 1660–1789* (Paris, 1970).

pronounced weakening of subsistence crises in subsequent decades. "It is commonly taught and surely true in a good part of the kingdom, that the fearful demographic crises of 1693–1694 and 1709–1710 were the last that the Old Regime knew." But this generalization was qualified, for around 1725 and later still, in 1741 and 1771, genuine dearths of cereal grains produced locally and even regionally authentic mortality peaks in France. Moreover, population growth was rarely visible in France before 1750. Goubert believes that population growth would have appeared sooner in the absence of the return of crisis mortality between 1739 and 1743.[4]

The French mortality peak, as elsewhere in western Europe around 1740, succeeded a decade of relatively low mortality levels. Climatic conditions improved in the 1730s, following the unfavorable weather that had predominated during the second half of the 1720s. For a period of ten years, and in some locations for fifteen years, the French population suffered neither severe food shortages nor widespread epidemics. In the course of the next fifteen years, however, and particularly during the 1740s, the French demographic experience reverted to the Old Regime pattern, in which the accumulated surplus of a decade was nearly wiped out in a few years. The conspicuous rise in the number of death was due to a succession of fevers, dysenteries, mediocre or bad harvests, and the great dearth of 1741. It was only after 1750 that a positive demographic balance reappeared throughout France.[5]

Mortality crises began to weaken and the population began to increase almost everywhere in western Europe after 1750: the automatic progression from dearth to higher death rates was blocked. Explanations for this demographic reversal have focused on the economic and political changes that lowered mortality levels in the eighteenth century. Goubert has attributed the improvement to increased production, more efficient methods of transportation, and more effective governmental policies. Public administration, once having controlled the problem of hunger, now directed its attention to infectious disease, with attempts to isolate, treat, and prevent epidemics.[6] Louis Henry also has recognized the 1740s as a demographic turning point. Although there continued to be bad years, epidemics, and food shortages in France from 1750 to the end of the century, they no longer reached the extent nor the intensity of the earlier

4. Ibid., 60–62.

5. Ibid., 75.

6. Pierre Goubert, "Historical Demography and the Reinterpretation of Early Modern French History: A Research Review," in T. K. Rabb and R. I. Rotberg, eds., *The Family in History* (New York, 1973), 40–42.

crises. Henry, by contrast, is not at all certain of the reasons for the improvement and suggests that perhaps "it was just a piece of good luck, the continuation of which was made possible by the undeniable progress of a later period."[7] Braudel likewise remains unconvinced of the validity of Goubert's explanation for the reduction of mortality. He has put forth the possibility that the change after 1750 may have been largely fortuitous, since "every disease has its own autonomous life, independent of the endless correlations" advanced by historians. Furthermore, even correlations with economic crises are "at most only accidents in a history linked with other factors: rodents, parasites, bacilli, viruses, or some form of merchandise."[8] The critical issue of the present study of course is the degree to which every disease has an autonomous life of its own and the degree to which epidemics are promoted by environmental stress and prolonged food shortage.

Michael Flinn's investigation of the stablization of death rates in preindustrial Europe found that demographic crises could be broken down into discrete types, which shed light on the progressive leveling of mortality peaks in the eighteenth century. He discovered three types, similar to but more comprehensively delineated than those put forth by Goubert: (1) crises induced by military activity or possibly major civil unrest; (2) crises induced by famine, with the majority of deaths resulting from disease; (3) crises provoked by epidemic disease not associated with food shortage. Flinn found a generally downward trend in western European death rates starting in the second quarter of the eighteenth century, which was interrupted by the severe crisis around the years 1740–1742.

The military mortality crisis, in which military destructiveness exacted a large human toll, essentially ended in the seventeenth century. Although it is true that armies continued to march through Europe, as in the War of the Austrian Succession (1740–1748), their operations led to strikingly few civilian casualities. In addition, as measured by demographic consequences, this type of crisis had been the least significant. The second type of crisis, severe and widespread famine, disappeared from Europe after the 1690s. Flinn does not deny that famine continued into the eighteenth century, citing, for example, the fact that the years 1740–1742 produced lethal famine in Ireland and Scandinavia and drove death rates in some French districts close to the peaks reached in the 1690s. But in the majority of western European countries, the loss of life

---

7. Louis Henry, "The Population of France in the Eighteenth Century," in D. V. Glass and D. E. C. Eversley, eds., *Population in History* (London, 1965), 447–48.

8. Braudel, *Capitalism*, 51.

during eighteenth-century food shortages did not match the demographic catastrophes of the seventeenth century.

Flinn concluded that mortality began to stabilize in eighteenth-century Europe both because military mortality crises had vanished and because the destructive subsistence crisis was being progressively tamed by the improved transportation of food supplies, by economic development, and by the growing rationalization of public administration. No longer was it necessary, in an increasing number of regions in Europe, for one locality to be exposed to a mortality crisis from starvation while a neighboring region suffered scarcely at all. The improved ability to transport grain was reflected in the steady decline of the disparate movements of regional grain prices, so visible still in the seventeenth century. The improvements in transportation were powerfully supplemented by the more successful efforts of both central and local public authorities to organize and distribute food supplies to the destitute and the helpless in years of scarcity and high cereal prices.

Yet in spite of economic and administrative advances, mortality levels remained high and continued to fluctuate during the eighteenth century. As Flinn put it, instability was merely reduced, not eliminated. The continuing instability derived from the third type of mortality crisis, the epidemic owing "nothing to military or economic circumstances," which continued to recur. If improved social organization prevented the destitute from actually dying of hunger in the event of a severe subsistence crisis, neither the level of economic development nor rationalized public administration could alleviate their more permanent state of undernourishment, which in turn left the poor vulnerable to both endemic and epidemic disease.[9]

To what extent are the conclusions reached in Flinn's investigation confirmed by the events that unfolded in the 1740s? Despite a degree of empirical validity, the model of discrete mortality crises fails first of all to account for the total aspects of the mortality peak of 1740–1742. The mortality wave corresponded to his crisis induced by famine, with the majority of deaths resulting from disease. Scandinavia and Ireland were the only regions where mass famines occurred. Elsewhere, however, the ability of public welfare and relief programs to prevent crisis mortality in the face of food shortages and elevated cereal prices stands out from the evidence. The differential national mortality peaks registered in the 1740s indicate that rationalized public administration could protect the

9. Michael W. Flinn, "The Stabilisation of Mortality in Pre-industrial Western Europe," *Journal of European Economic History* 3 (Fall 1974), 292–96; Flinn, *The European Demographic System, 1500–1820* (Baltimore, 1981), 47–64.

working population from epidemics to a significant extent. The shortage of food and prolonged undernutrition, moreover, were not entirely responsible for the climbing mortality.

The climatic variability that led to the harvest shortfalls influenced the rise in death rates over and above the impact of higher food prices. The winter of 1739–1740 proved the longest and coldest in modern western European history. The autumn months of 1740 and the early winter months of 1740–1741 were marked by excessive precipitation in the form of heavy rains and early snowfalls, which produced destructive floods over most of the region. Droughtlike springs and summers predominated each year from 1740 to 1742. The winter of 1741–1742 turned out to be nearly as cold as the arctic winter of 1740. The pronounced climatic variability not only delayed the ripening of crops and prejudiced the survival of animals. The extreme weather events also proved detrimental to human health. The severe and protracted cold seasons lengthened the period of time people spent in close, indoor personal contact and as a consequence intensified the risks of louse-borne and respiratory diseases. The extended droughts during the warm seasons facilitated the diffusion of the bacteria that cause such enteric diseases as dysentery and typhoid fever. Because the mortality peak of 1740–1742 coincided with an almost uninterrupted series of climatic shocks, it is necessary to explore the relationship between environmental stress and epidemic diseases if all the potential lines of causation are to be traced.

As in the mortality crises of the 1690s, a shortage of food and high cereal prices constituted the proximate problem in the early 1740s. But the mortality wave did not originate exclusively in the subsistence crises. The combined consequences of climatic shock, social disarray, prolonged undernutrition, and military operations brought about the crisis mortality. The medical evidence shows that epidemics of typhus, dysentery, typhoid fever, smallpox, and influenza made up the mass infections of 1740–1742. The smallpox and influenza epidemics can be categorized in part as fortuitous, in that neither nutritional status nor environmental stress appears to determine their incidence. Needless to say, there is no method that allows the precise ranking of the independent variables in the order of their impact on the mortality peak. It is by working out the functional relationships that connect such variables to epidemic mortality that it becomes possible to asses their relative influence in the respective countries of western Europe. It is also necessary to discover and describe the pathways along which contagion spread in preindustrial societies.

Some connection between famine and infection has been postulated throughout history, even if it has not been possible to specify the causative links. Jean Meuvret first noted that the study of the demographic effects of epidemics was bedeviled by the fact that outbreaks of disease coincided with famines, which were killers themselves. Seeing people die from infectious disease who were also starving, preindustrial writers seized upon an oversimplified view that failed to distinguish between the two causes. As late as the twentieth century, in fact, physicians and historians alike believed that prolonged undernutrition lowered resistance of humans to virtually all infectious disease. In all probability, bubonic plague was the original disease that inspired the older view, which was summed up in the expression "first dearth and then plague." But the position that undernutrition or malnutrition inevitably promotes infection is no longer the majority medical viewpoint.

Meuvret arrived at the conclusion that famine conditions favored the spread of an epidemic. The principal "vectors" who diffused infection were the beggars, vagrants, and day laborers forced into temporary migration; these groups abandoned the countryside to seek work and food in the towns. Meuvret believed that townspeople were prudent in closing their gates to the destitute from the villages. The record shows that the proliferation of beggars often preceded outbreaks of epidemic disease. Goaded by hunger, the unemployed and helpless deserted their homes and wandered in search of relief, which was available, if at all, in the towns. Although famine years did not always produce widespread epidemics, endemic infections were nevertheless liable to be generalized by itinerant groups, who could cover considerable distances while incubating a disease.[10]

Because mass vagrancy has not always been present when epidemics have broken out in the midst of food shortages, Meuvret expanded his explanation by adopting the finding that emerged from Goubert's pioneering demographic study of the Beauvaisis in northern France. Goubert discovered that elevated mortality persisted for a year or two after dearth conditions disappeared. He concluded that the death rate was influenced by the aftereffects of a food shortage; he considered disease propagated, even engendered, by undernourishment to be the immediate cause.[11] Meuvret agreed with this hypothesis and suggested further that malnutrition could have played a similar role. Death from starvation remained the extreme case, but hunger could bring about the same end by a roundabout means. Bad food, even more dangerous than no food, could be fatal. In

10. Jean Meuvret, "Demographic Crises in France from the Sixteenth to the Eighteenth Centuries," in Glass and Eversley, *Population,* 510–12.

11. Pierre Goubert, *Beauvais et le Beauvaisis de 1600 à 1730,* 2 vols. (Paris, 1960).

preindustrial famines, the most wretched commonly eased their hunger by turning to substitutes for cereals, such as mixtures of grain and tree bark, or worse still, the decomposing flesh of carrion animals. Meuvret also pointed out that the fatal diseases of crisis years struck chiefly among the poor classes, unlike the great epidemics of plague and smallpox which spared no one.[12]

Meuvret's observations are supported by the sequence of food shortage, itinerant vagrancy, and the outbreak of "famine fevers" in the early 1740s. His hypotheses, however, fail to account for all variants of the progression from harvest shortfalls to epidemic mortality. The English population, for example, suffered severe epidemics of "fever" and dysentery from 1740 to 1742, yet England experienced no more than a moderate dearth, with only a slight increase in the scale of vagrancy. Moreover, there is no evidence of widespread hunger or the consumption of unwholesome foods. Prussia, by contrast, registered a sharper increase in cereal prices, passed through a more pronounced dearth, and, also unlike England, became a theater of war. Yet Prussia experienced no more than a moderate rise in mortality, with no mass infections.

These examples of a lack of correspondence between the degree of food shortage and the morbidity and mortality rates of infectious diseases point out the fact that epidemics cannot be approached as entities. Each contagion has its own etiology and its own epidemiology. The connection with prolonged undernutrition must be demonstrated infection by infection. Not only should an approximate statistical correlation exist between the trend of food prices and the changing incidence of an infection. The epidemiology of a communicable disease also must be reconciled with the prevailing environmental, ecological, and social conditions; that is to say, it should be possible to set forth the functional relationship with the respective independent variables. The execution of the procedure may entail taking account of the weather, nutritional status, clothing, housing conditions, personal hygiene, environmental sanitation, behavorial changes, alterations in community spacing arrangements, exposure to disease vectors, and the previous prevalence of an infection.

The methodological problems are apparent. To begin with, it is difficult to assess the causal relationship of nutritional status and infection in populations whose living conditions also involve a pronounced deficiency in housing amenities, personal hygiene, and environmental sanitation. This enigma exists even in the absence of famine conditions.

12. Meuvret, "Demographic Crises," 518–19.

It is well known that the biological and environmental handicaps that together lead to infection and malnutrition are inextricably interwoven in conditions of poverty and distress.[13] The methodological dilemma, as well as the decisive issue, has been summed up in the observation made by two medical practitioners with clinical experience in the African famines of the 1970s. "Once famine is shorn of antecedent catastrophe and its inevitable results of poor hygiene, inadequate sanitation, and overcrowding, what is its effect on the resistance of the organism to infection?"[14]

Previous studies have demonstrated the difficulty in arriving at valid statistical relationships between the shortage of food and the incidence of epidemic diseases.[15] Yet a repeated association between subsistence crises and epidemics is found in the historical record, and it seems almost certain that the connection goes beyond a fortuitous coincidence in time and space. The methodological solution is advanced by the current medical knowledge that not all common infections are influenced to the same degree by nutritional status. Some infections are so virulent that they produce disease regardless of human differences in resistance. Smallpox, bubonic plague, influenza, typhoid fever, typhus, and malaria, epidemics of which broke out in the early 1740s, are diseases either slightly or not at all influenced by nutrition. By contrast, dysentery and diarrheal diseases, and a number of respiratory diseases, which also became epidemic during 1740–1741, are among the common infections believed to be definitely influenced by nutritional deficiency, in that the outcome of infection can be determined by nutritional status.[16] Accordingly, if a synergistic relationship between undernutrition or malnutrition and infection was primarily responsible for the mortality wave of the early 1740s, and if no complicating variables influenced death rates, we would anticipate a significant degree of correspondence between the magnitude of the national increases in food prices and in mortality from those epidemic diseases strongly influenced by undernutrition.

---

13. Sidney L. Kark, *Epidemiology and Community Medicine* (New York, 1974), 249.

14. John Murray and Anne Murray, "Suppression of Infection by Famine and Its Activation by Refeeding—A Paradox?" *Perspectives in Biology and Medicine* 20 (1977), 471.

15. See, for example, Andrew B. Appleby, "Nutrition and Disease: The Case of London, 1550–1750," *Journal of Interdisciplinary History* 6 (Summer 1975), 1–22. Appleby found no correspondence between bread prices and death rates in the London bills of mortality apart from typhus and the classification "ague and fever."

16. "The Relationship of Nutrition, Disease, and Social Conditions: A Graphical Presentation," *Journal of Interdisciplinary History* 14 (Autumn 1983), 503–506. The Autumn number is entirely devoted to the topic of hunger and history.

The European mortality wave of 1740–1742 originated for the most part in epidemics of dysentery and "continued fever," infections that are associated with the intensification of human deprivations. No region of western Europe suffered crisis mortality in the absence of widespread epidemics of dysentery or continued fever or commonly both. As for the epidemics of continued fever, the clinical evidence discloses that they were made up of the louse-borne infections of typhus and relapsing fever, mixed together with the enteric disease typhoid fever. Altogether the evidence indicates that the subsistence crises and the increase in the number of deaths from epidemic disease were causally connected, though not necessarily as a consequence of the interaction of nutrition and infection. Food shortage and disease did not march in lockstep from inception to diffusion, but the subsistence crises nonetheless invoked a related series of phenomena that transformed endemic infections into epidemic diseases.

Apart from the shortage of food, the weather conditions could trigger epidemics of louse-borne fever in preindustrial Europe. Both typhus and relapsing fever are transmitted by the human body louse. The long cold seasons of the early 1740s fostered louse infestation by prolonging the time spent in indoor confinement, mostly in wretched and unventilated living quarters. Epidemics of typhus and relapsing fever result from the breakdown of personal hygiene. The increase in the scale of unemployment and itinerant vagrancy in the early 1740s promoted the spread of louse-borne fevers. In the case of dysentery, the dry springs and summers that stretched from 1740 to 1743 enhanced the environmental preconditions for the explosion of morbidity rates. The beggars and vagrants set afoot by joblessness and climbing food prices were capable of transforming the infection into lethal national epidemics. The public welfare installations that were set up or expanded to meet the increasing needs of the poor ironically became networks for spreading infection. Typhoid fever, because of its etiology and epidemiology similar to dysentery, also became more prevalent in the environmental and social conditions that marked the early 1740s. The case-fatality rate of dysentery is prejudiced by undernutrition or malnutrition, but typhoid fever is influenced by nutritional status only slightly if at all.

Not all epidemics that become rife in the early 1740s can be traced to the consequences of climatic variability or the shortage of food. The dramatic outbreak of bubonic plague that claimed some 47,000 lives in Sicily and Calabria during 1743 was in all probability part of the epidemic that had raged in the Balkans, Hungary, the Ukraine, and the

Ottoman empire since 1738.[17] Because plague is so virulent and produces disease regardless of nutritional status, the epidemic has been deemed beyond the scope and concerns of the investigation. The influenza pandemic that swept over Europe during 1742–1743 likewise seems unrelated either to nutrition or the food shortages.[18] The numerous smallpox epidemics that erupted in the early 1740s owed more to the previous prevalence of the disease and the number of new susceptible human hosts than to the subsistence crises. The historical record shows that plague, influenza, and smallpox have produced mortality crises without preying on malnourished populations.[19] Because the victims of influenza and smallpox swelled the number of burials recorded in western European parish registers, however, it is still necessary to assess their relative demographic impact.

Although documentary sources of information do not always yield final answers, it is possible to deduce several conclusions from the evidence. To anticipate the findings, the connecting link between the subsistence crises and epidemic mortality proved to be more social than physiological; that is to say that the rising incidence of infectious disease derived more from social disarray and dysfunctional behavior than from dangerously lowered human resistance to pathogenic microorganisms. The evidence also indicates that climatic variability could drive up death rates independently of food shortages. This relationship held true in the more environmentally sheltered societies as well as those located at the subarctic margins of Europe. The evidence suggests that the most effective method of minimizing epidemics of fever and dysentery was to preempt the dysfunctional changes in behavior and in community spacing. Public policies that constrained the inevitable rise in unemployment, work migrations, vagrancy, and begging tended to reduce the risk of epidemics. As a consequence, the differential national mortality peaks of 1740–1742 can be accounted for in a large part by the relative ability of public administrations to cope with the welfare crises.

The seven chapters that follow present the evidence that bears on the question of the relationship of food shortage and epidemic disease. Chapter 2 examines the available demographic data for the ten-year

17. Jean-Noël Biraben, *Les Hommes et la peste en France et dans les pays européens et méditerranéens*, 2 vols. (Paris, 1975), I, 399–400, 429, 435, 446–47; Georg Sticker, *Die Pest: Die Geschichte der Pest* (Giessen, 1908), 240–44.

18. For discussion of this pandemic, see W. I. B. Beveridge, *Influenza: The Last Great Plague* (London, 1977), 27–28.

19. Ann Carmichael, "Infection, Hidden Hunger, and History," *Journal of Interdisciplinary History* 14 (1983), 252, 257.

period from 1735 to 1744. The dependent variable of the investigation is the annual movement of the number of deaths recorded in thirteen western European locations. The annual number of births and marriages have been calculated also, in order to measure the degree to which the demographic fluctuations conformed to the so-called "triple distortion" created by preindustrial subsistence crises. The years of severe food shortage saw the burial curve rise while the baptismal and nuptial curves fell. Chapter 3 reconstructs the weather during the period 1735–1744, assesses the significance of climatic variability and extreme weather events, and discusses the impact of climatic shock on the demographic crisis. Chapter 4 surveys the consequences of the weather patterns for grain harvest yields and the survival of livestock. Chapter 5 displays the course of cereal prices during the period 1735–1744, to measure the relative severity of the national food shortages. Chapter 6 documents the scope of the national welfare and relief programs in order to asses their relative ability to inhibit the rise in death rates. The chapter also examines the national subsistence crises to determine the scale of the increase in the incidence of begging, vagrancy, rioting, and social turbulence. Chapter 7 attempts to measure the proportion of excess deaths that were traceable to hunger and hypothermia rather than to epidemic disease.

Chapter 8 focuses on the resolution of the principal issue, the question of whether the epidemic mortality derived from the biological interaction of undernutrition and infection or was the consequence of environmental, ecological, and social changes. The basic methodological approach is to correlate the fluctuations in the number of deaths and the series of independent variables (weather, crop yields, cereal prices, social disorder, welfare programs, and random epidemics). The application of present-day medical knowledge to the information found in the historical documents, together with the demographic evidence, makes it possible to advance the solution to the question posed.

2. The European Mortality Peak of 1740–1742

The mortality peak of the early 1740s is an outstanding fact of European demographic history. The magnitude and the geographical scope of the rise in mortality levels remain to be established. The first concern is to measure the annual number of deaths during the years 1735–1744, so that the course of European mortality can be determined. The mortality trends have been derived, to the degree of accuracy that the available demographic evidence permits, from the annual movement of the number of deaths recorded in thirteen western European countries during the ten-year period under study.

The relative severity of a mortality peak is ideally measured by a comparison of annual crude death rates with the average death rate experienced over a selected base period. The crude death rate is determined by calculating the number of deaths per 1,000 population during a given year. Such statistical precision is not possible for the first half of the eighteenth century. True vital statistics, that is to say accurate national totals of births, deaths, and marriages, are not available for any European country prior to 1750. The Scandinavian countries possess the most complete record of burials and baptisms in the eighteenth century, beginning in 1735. The research of the Social Science Research Council (SSRC) Cambridge Group for the History of Population and Social Structure has provided estimated monthly vital statistics for England beginning with 1541.[1] For the remainder of the European countries, the systematic records of burials and baptisms that are available from 1735 must serve as indexes of annual mortality and fertility trends.

Because not all deaths and births were registered, parish records of burials and baptisms prove to be defective substitutes for true vital

1. E. A. Wrigley and R. S. Schofield, *The Population History of England, 1541–1871* (Cambridge, Mass., 1981), 503–26.

statistics. Religious minorities often escaped parochial registration. Certain classes of deaths, such as those of infants, young children, vagrants, and paupers, were inconsistently recorded. It should also be recognized that the underregistration of these groups often worsened during years of crisis mortality. Moreover, the number of deaths among infants, paupers, and vagrants rose out of proportion during subsistence crises. As a consequence, the parish registers and bills of mortality have invariably understated the magnitude of mortality crises.[2] In spite of these deficiencies, the surviving records of burials are adequate for the restricted purpose of following short-term mortality trends. Although it is true that the underregistration of children's deaths can be a particular problem in a mortality crisis caused by severe epidemics of childhood diseases, the elevated incidence of infectious disease in the early 1740s did not conform to that pattern.

Parish registers that have become lost or were never drawn up present a more intractable problem. In the case of Ireland, for example, where parochial records are extremely scarce, the researcher is forced to rely either on impressionistic accounts or on estimates deduced from fiscal records. The state of Ireland's parish registers is particularly unfortunate. The impressionistic and fiscal evidence suggests that the mortality crisis of 1740–1741 may have been as severe as in the Great Famine of the 1740s, after adjustment for the smaller population of the earlier century. The parochial records of France are sufficiently comprehensive to permit estimates of national mortality trends and of the annual number of deaths beginning with 1740. Elsewhere in western Europe, the parochial records yield figures that are adequate to follow the annual fluctuations of mortality.

The Annual Movement of Western European Deaths, 1735–1744

Table 1 displays indexes of the annual movement of the number of deaths recorded in thirteen European locations during the ten-year period from 1735 to 1744. The indexes found in the last line of the table show the average year-to-year fluctuations in European mortality and also disclose the amplitude of the mortality peak of 1740–1742. The index numbers indicate that the death rate in the eighteenth century, unlike that of today, was quite unstable. The year 1735 was marked by low

2. For discussion of the parish register deficiencies, see L. M. Cullen and T. L. Smout, eds., *Comparative Aspects of Scottish and Irish Economic and Social History, 1600–1900* (Edinburgh, 1977), 21–22.

Table 1. Indexes of annual number of deaths in Europe, 1735–1744 (1735–1744 = 100)

Location	1735	1736	1737	1738	1739	1740	1741	1742	1743	1744
England	89	94	102	92	93	106	118	124	98	85
Scotland	88	96	109	88	93	122	116	107	90	91
Ireland (Dublin)	93	89	94	106	93	140	119	99	93	72
France	80	93	93	96	109	123	116	111	94	83
Low Countries	83	95	102	93	97	99	149	98	98	84
Germany	84	116	114	99	98	112	110	96	92	78
Austria (Vienna)	88	112	108	118	98	111	105	105	87	69
Switzerland	86	100	115	84	85	108	100	123	112	87
Italy	94	115	96	87	86	100	107	112	108	95
Sweden[a]	70[b]	82	102	92	93	108	98	118	131	76
Finland	64	75	104	85	97	157	95	136	112	74
Norway	68	74	88	83	83	92	149	187	112	76
Denmark	81	102	114	100	96	114	112	103	100	83
Unweighted averages	82	96	103	94	94	115	115	117	101	81

[a]Base period 1736–44.

[b]Index number derived from Stockholm and nine Swedish counties.

Reprinted from John D. Post, "Climate Variability and the European Mortality Wave of the Early 1740s," *The Journal of Interdisciplinary History* 15 (1984), 10, table 1, with permission of the editors of The Journal of Interdisciplinary History and The MIT Press, Cambridge, Massachusetts. Copyright © 1984 by the Massachusetts Institute of Technology and the editors of *The Journal of Interdisciplinary History*.

SOURCES: SSRC Cambridge Group for the History of Population and Social Structure (personal communication, Roger S. Schofield); Michael Flinn et al., *Scottish Population History from the Seventeenth Century to the 1930s* (Cambridge, 1977), 483–88; John Rutty, M.D., *A Chronological History of the Weather and Seasons, and of the Prevailing Diseases in Dublin* (London, 1770), xiv, 45, 61, 69, 80, 84, 98, 125, 130; M. Messance, *Recherches sur la population des généralités d'Auvergne, de Lyon, de Rouen, et de quelques provinces et villes du royaume* (Paris, 1766), 315–26; E. Charlot and J. Dupâquier, "Mouvement annuel de la population de la ville de Paris de 1670 à 1821," *Annales de démographie historique* (1967), 511–14; François Lebrun, *Les Hommes et la mort en Anjou aux 17e et 18e siècles* (Paris, 1971), 509; M. Lachiver, "Une Etude et quelques esquisses," *Annales de démographie historique* (1969), 234; Ph. Wiel, "Tamerville," ibid., 188; J. Lelong, "Saint-Pierre-Eglise," ibid., 125–35; M.-H. Jouan, "Les Originalités démographiques d'un bourg artisanal normand au XVIIIe siècle, Villedieu-les-Poeles, 1711–1790," ibid., 122; Hubert Charbonneau, *Tourouvre-au-Perche aux XVIIe et XVIIIe siècles (1668–1819)* (Paris, 1970), 260; Etienne Gautier and Louis Henry, *La Population de Crulai, paroisse normande* (Paris, 1958), 243–44; Jean Ganiage, *Trois Villages d'Ile-de-France: Etude démographique* (Paris, 1963), 131; M. Frésel-Lozey, *Histoire démographique d'un village en Béarn: Bilhères-d'Ossau au XVIIIe–XIXe siècles* (Bordeaux, 1969), 242, 246; Michel Morineau, *Les Faux-semblants d'un démarrage économique: Agriculture et démographie en France au XVIIIe siècle* (Paris, 1970), 309–13 367–70; Mohamed El Kordi, *Bayeux aux XVIIe et XVIIIe siècles* (Paris, 1970), 115, 167; Jean-Claude Perrot, *Genèse d'une ville moderne: Caen au XVIIIe siècle*, 2 vols. (Paris, 1975), II, 958–62; A. Lefèbvre-Teillard, *La Population de Dôle au XVIIIe siècle* (Paris, 1969), 75–76; Thomas F. Sheppard, *Lourmarin in the Eighteenth Century* (Baltimore, 1971), 227–29; Raymond Deniel and Louis Henry, "La Population d'un village du Nord de la France, Sainghin-en-Melantois, de

mortality levels in every region of western Europe. Beginning in 1736, an increase in the number of deaths in every country (except Ireland) resulted in a minor mortality peak. The west-central lands of Germany, Austria, Switzerland, and Italy, however, registered a sharper rise in mortality than occurred in northwestern Europe. The rise in the number of deaths peaked in 1737, after the mortality wave intensified in the Scandinavian countries. The years 1738 and 1739 proved, on balance, to be a period of lower European death rates, with the exception of France, where the number of deaths rose noticeably in 1739. The onset of the major mortality peak in 1740 is unmistakable; the number of deaths climbed in each of the thirteen countries.

Table 1 shows that the level of European mortality rose 22 percent from 1739 to 1740. Finland and Ireland passed through mortality crises, defined in this study as an increase of 30 percent or more above the average number of deaths during the ten-year base period. In Finland, the number of deaths increased by 62 percent in 1740; in Ireland, the increase amounted to 51 percent. European mortality remained at the same elevated level in 1741, with Ireland, Norway, and the Low Countries suffering mortality crises. In Norway, the number of deaths climbed 62 percent in 1741; in the Low Countries, the increase amounted to 51 percent. The European mortality wave peaked in 1742, when the number of deaths rose 24 percent above the level of 1739, and 43 percent above the low death rates of 1735. A pronounced increase in Scandinavian death rates was responsible for the higher mortality in 1742. Norway registered a more severe mortality crisis than in 1741; the number of deaths climbed 26 percent above the previous year, and 125 percent above the mortality level of 1739. Finland also passed through a second mortality crisis in 1742, though less severe than in 1740. The number of deaths in Sweden increased 20 percent in 1742, in line with the Scandinavian mortality trend. The number of deaths in England and Switzerland also peaked in 1742. At the same time, the mortality levels in Ireland, Scotland, the Low Countries, and Germany had already significantly declined by 1742.

In 1743, the number of deaths fell in all countries except Sweden, where mortality rose 11 percent above the elevated death rate of the previous year to reach a peak 41 percent above the figure of 1739. The European mortality wave had essentially passed by 1743, however, even though elevated death rates persisted in Sweden, Finland, and Switzerland. The European mortality peak disappeared in 1744, when the number of deaths fell sharply to a level slightly below the low level of mortality that prevailed in 1735.

1665 à 1851,'' *Population* 20 (July–August, 1965), 597; J. Canard, ''Les Mouvements de population à Saint-Roman d'Urfé de 1612 à 1946,'' *Bulletin de la Diana* 29 (1945), 151–53; R. Beaudry, ''Alimentation et population rurale en Périgord au XVIIIe siècle,'' *Annales de démographie historique* (1976), 56–57; Marcel Lachiver, *La Population de Meulan du XVIIe au XIXe siècle* (Paris, 1969), 80–81, 198; Yves Blayo, ''Mouvement naturel de la population française de 1740 à 1829,'' *Population* 30, special no. (November 1975), 52–56; Nicolaas Duyn, *Historische aanmerkingen van drie strenge winters (1709, 1740, 1742)* (Haarlem, 1746), 185, 193–94; G. T. Mentink and A. M. van der Woude, *De demografische ontwikkeling te Rotterdam en Cool in de 17e en 18e eeuw* (Rotterdam, 1965), 104, 126–27, 170; A. M. van der Woude, *Het Noorderwertier*, 3 vols. (Wageningen, 1972), III, 634–37; G. van Houtte, *Leuven in 1740, ein krisisjaar: Ekonomische, sociale en demografische aspekten* (Brussels, 1964), 226–29; D. Dalle, *De Bevolking van Veurne-Ambacht in de 17e en de 18e eeuw* (Brussels, 1963), 284, 288, 350, 354, 371–74; De Brouwer, ''De demografische evolutie in de meierij Erembodegem en de heerlijkheid Oordegem gedurende de XVIIe en XVIIIe eeuw,'' in *Cinq études de démographie locale, XVIIe–XVIIIe siècles* (Brussels, 1963), 98–115; J. De Vos, ''De omvang en de evolutie van het Eeklose Bevolkingscijfer tijdens de XVIIe en de XVIIIe siècles (Louvain, 1977), 638–41, 663–68, 668–70, 733–37; Johann Peter Süssmilch, *Die göttliche Ordnung in den Veränderungen des menschlichen Geschlechts*, 4th ed., 3 vols. (Berlin, 1775), I, 15, 24, 26, 48–49, 85, 92–93, 100–101, 104–105, 110, 114, 118, 121–24; Berlin, *Statistisches Jahrbuch der Stadt Berlin* 34 (1915–19), 67, 101; Arthur E. Imhof, ''Die nicht-namentliche Auswertung der Kirchenbücher von Giessen und Umgebung,'' in Imhof, ed., *Historische Demographie als Sozialgeschichte* (Darmstadt, 1975), 119–24; François G. Dreyfus, ''Prix et population á Trèves et à Mayence au XVIIIe siècle,'' *Revue d'histoire économique et sociale* 34 (1956), 244–46; Otto Roller, *Die Einwohnerschaft der Stadt Durlach im 18. Jahrhundert* (Karlsruhe, 1907), 46–53, 64–67, 94–97, 110; A. Schreiber, ''Die Entwicklung der Augsberger Bevölkerung vom Ende des 14. Jahrhunderts bis zum Beginn des 19. Jahrhunderts,'' *Archiv für Hygiene* 123 (1939–40), 166; Stephan Glonner, ''Bevölkerungsbewegung von Sieben Pfarreien im Kgl. Bayerisches Bezirksamt Tölz seit Ende des 16. Jahrhunderts,'' *Allgemeines Statistisches Archiv* 4 (1896), 264; D. G. Bäumler, ''Medizinalstatistische Untersuchungen über Weiden (Oberpfalz) von 1551 bis 1800,'' *Archiv für Hygiene* 120 (1938), 226; Wilhelm Ehrhart, ''Die Sterblichkeit in der Reichstadt Kempten (Allgäu) in den Jahren 1606–1624 and 1686–1870,'' *Archiv für Hygiene und Bakteriologie* 116 (1936), 125; E. François, ''La Population de Coblence au XVIIIe siècle,'' *Annales de démographie historique* (1975), 335–36; François, ''La Mortalité urbaine en Allemagne au XVIIIe siècle,'' ibid. (1978), 124; Karl Kisskalt, ''Epidemiologisch-statistische Untersuchungen über die Sterblichkeit von 1600–1800,'' *Archiv für Hygiene und Bakteriologie* 137 (1953), 38; Franz Schmölz and Therese Schmölz, ''Die Sterblichkeit in Landsberg am Lech von 1585–1875,'' ibid. 136 (1952), 527; W. Jungkunz, ''Die Sterblichkeit in Nürnberg, 1714–1850,'' *Mitteilungen des Vereins für Geschichte der Stadt Nürnberg* 42 (1951), 304–305; Jean-Paul Lehners, ''Die Pfarre Stockerau im 17. und 18. Jahrhundert,'' in Heimold Helczmanovszki, ed., *Beiträge zur Bevölkerungs- und Sozialgeschichte Österreichs* (Vienna, 1973), 398–99; A. Burckhardt, *Demographie und Epidemiologie der Stadt Basel während der letzten drei Jahrhunderts, 1601–1900* (Basel, 1908), 90, 95, 98; E. Olivier, *Médecine et santé dans le pays de Vaud*, 2 vols. (Lausanne, 1962), II, 1,227; Silvio Bucher, *Bevölkerung und Wirtschaft des Amtes Entlebuch im 18. Jahrhundert* (Luzern, 1974), 16, 19; Edouard Mallet, ''Recherches historiques et statistiques sur la population de Genève; Son mouvement annuel et sa longévité depuis le XVIe siècle jusqu'à nos jours (1549–1833),'' *Annales d'hygiène publique et de médecine légale* (1837), 44; M. Schürmann, *Bevölkerung, Wirtschaft, und Gesellschaft in Appenzell-Innerrhoden im 18. und frühen 19. Jahrhundert* (Appenzell, 1974), 319–25; Hans-Rudolf Burri, *Die Bevölkerung Luzerns im 18. und frühen 19. Jahrhundert* (Luzern, 1975), 182–83; Daniele Beltrami, *Storia della popolazione di Venezia dalla fine del secolo XVI alla caduta della repubblica* (Padova, 1954), 112–27, 151–53; U. Tucci, ''Innesto del vaiolo e società nel Settecento veneto,'' *Annales cisalpines d'histoire sociale* 1 (1973), 206; P. Donazzolo and M. Saibante, ''Lo sviluppo demografico di Verona e della sua provincia dalla fine del sec. XV ai nostri giorni,'' *Metron* 6 (1926), 79–84; Salvatore Fedele, ''Strutture e movimento della popolazione in una parrocchia della Capitanata, 1711–1750,'' *Quaderni Storici* 17 (1971), 475; Fiorenzo Rossi, ''Storia della popolazione di Adria dal XVI al XIX secolo,'' *Genus* 26 (1970), 119; Giuseppe Ferrario, *Statistica medica di Milano dal secolo XV fino ai nostri giorni*, 2 vols. (Milan, 1838–50), II, 200, 378; Arthur E. Imhof, *Aspekte der Bevölkerungsentwicklung in den nordischen Ländern, 1720–1750*, 2 vols. (Bern, 1976), I, 76–78, 140, 167–68; Michael Drake, *Population and Society in Norway, 1735–1865* (Cambridge, 1969), 169–75, 182; Sweden, Statistika Centralbyrän, *Historisk Statistik för Sverige*, I, *Befolkning, 1720–1967* (Stockholm, 1969), 86.

It should be noted that the shape of the European mortality peak as shown in table 1 is not exact. As already stated, the index numbers, with the exception of the Scandinavian countries, represent estimates based on incomplete data, which may not always reflect national trends. The index numbers for England are based on the national mortality estimates compiled by the SSRC Cambridge Group from an aggregative sample of 404 parish registers, approximately 4 percent of the 10,000 English parishes.[3] It is apparent from the index numbers of table 1 that the annual fluctuations of English mortality determined by the Cambridge Group paralleled the European trends during the years 1735–1744. It is possible, however, that the Cambridge Group's sample parishes, which are not totally representative of the national distribution of the population, understate the rise in the number of English burials during 1740-1741.

The Cambridge Group's 4 percent aggregative sample underrepresents the southwestern counties. Out of the total of 1,712 southwestern parishes, only 31 are included in the sample, or 1.8 percent. The weighting procedures reduced the percentage share of southwestern parishes still further, to 1.2 percent. Because the southwestern counties of Devonshire, Dorset, Somerset, Wiltshire, and Cornwall suffered disproportionately more from harvest shortfalls and fever epidemics during 1740–1741, the increase of mortality in this region was greater than the national average.

The county of Devonshire experienced a true mortality crisis during the years 1740–1742.[4] In 1740, the city of Plymouth and the towns of Tavistock, Honiton, and Totnes registered twice the number of annual average burials recorded during the period 1728–1752. Apart from Plymouth, the peak mortality in the Devon towns occurred in 1741 rather than 1740. The industrial town of Tiverton passed through crisis mortality in 1741, when 650 burials took place, which constituted a fourfold increase over the long-term average. The city of Exeter registered a crude death rate of 52 per 1,000 in 1741. The towns of Crediton, South Molton, Colyton, Ottery St. Mary, Dartmouth, and Ilfracomb also experienced crisis mortality in 1741, with the number of burials reaching twice or three times the average of 1728–1752. They year 1742 brought peak mortality to such other Devon towns as Barnstaple, Bideford, and Northam, where the number of burials amounted to more than double the long-term average. The Devon towns registered a total of 4,753 peak-year burials during the years 1740–1742, compared with an average of

3. Wrigley and Schofield, *Population History,* 38–43.
4. N. C. Oswald, "Epidemics in Devon, 1538–1837," *Devonshire Association* 109 (1977), 102–104.

2,047 annual burials from 1728 through 1752, or an increase of 132 percent. The greatest increase in burials, 145 percent, took place in 1741. Nor did the villages of Devonshire escape crisis mortality during the years 1740–1742, as the sharp rise in the number of rural burials indicates.[5]

Crisis mortality was not restricted to the southwestern counties of England. The localities represented by Thomas Short's aggregate mortality series, which he identifies inadequately as "market towns" (located presumably in the Midlands), show the same pattern as Devonshire, with more extreme mortality peaks. Altogether in these market towns the number of burials rose from 704 in 1739 to 1,940 in 1740, peaked at 6,205 in 1741, declined to 3,345 in 1742, and then collapsed to 201 in 1743.[6] Although not too much weight can be attached to such untypical mortality fluctuations, it is true that the continued fever epidemics of the early 1740s were primarily an urban phenomenon. The figures are also further evidence that English mortality may have peaked in 1741 rather than in 1742.

The index numbers for Scotland found in table 1 derive from the regional mortality indexes computed by the authors of *Scottish Population History*. It should be noted that the availability of Scottish parish registers remains limited. In addition, there exist significant variations in the extent to which the surviving registers serve the different regions of Scotland. Out of the total of 115 usable burial registers or comparable parochial sources, 48 are located in the eastern lowlands but only 8 in the far north. The number of available registers for the other regions falls between these two extremes, with the Highlands and Hebrides not represented at all in the ten-year period under study.[7]

The Scottish demographic evidence clearly indicates that mortality peaked in 1740 and then declined in both 1741 and 1742. The parish registers indicate that Scotland escaped a national mortality crisis, that is, the increase in the number of deaths recorded during 1740–1741 remained less than 30 percent above the ten-year average. The level of mortality, however, may have increased more than the available burial registers show. The impressionistic evidence suggests that a sharp rise in the number of deaths occurred in the extensive region of the Highlands during 1741. This remote area suffered from a shortage of food and fodder, as well as from epidemics of dysentery and fever.[8]

5. Ibid.

6. Thomas Short, *New Observations on City, Town, and Country Bills of Mortality* (London, 1750), 88–89.

7. Michael Flinn et al., *Scottish Population History* (Cambridge, 1977), 98–101, 483–88.

8. See, for example, M. M. Mackay, "A Highland Minister's Diary," *Cornhill Magazine* 152 (November 1935), 570–80.

The mortality indexes for Ireland are based on the number of burials recorded at Dublin, owing to the almost total unavailability of parish burial registers. The critical question becomes the degree to which the 50 percent increase of Dublin burials in 1740 represented the change in national mortality levels. According to the estimates of firsthand observers in the early 1740s, the number of excess deaths (i.e., the natural decrease of the population) ranged from 80,000 to 400,000 during the two-year period 1740–1741. Michael Drake's investigation of the Irish demographic crisis concluded that the crude death rate reached between 50 and 70 per 1,000 during 1740–1741,[9] which would imply a mortality increase in excess of 50 percent.

The recent studies of Stuart Daultrey, David Dickson, and Cormac Ó Gráda indicate "an excess death rate well above 50 per 1,000 in each of the two years of famine epidemic."[10] Estimates of crude death rates depend on sound estimates of national population totals. The high death rate suggested in this study derives in part from the finding that the population of Ireland was smaller in the 1740s than previous estimates had concluded. The proposed revision of the population total is based on the investigation of the movement in the number of taxed houses in Ireland. The number of taxed houses declined between 1732 and 1744 mainly as a consequence of the mortality crisis of 1740–1741.

The investigation of taxed houses disclosed that the Irish mortality crisis was more a southern and western than a northern and eastern phenomenon. The population of the southwestern province of Munster may have fallen by as much as 20 percent during 1740–1741. Munster's six counties may have accounted for almost half of the total excess mortality.[11] Dickson has computed mortality indexes from parish burial registers located in the provinces of Munster and Ulster. In rural Munster, the level of mortality (1701–1775 = 100) rose from 114 in 1739 to 187 in 1740, increased further to 278 in 1741, and then declined to 82 in 1742. In urban Munster, the level of mortality rose from 90 in 1739 to 133 in 1740, increased to 253 in 1741, and then declined to 110 in 1742. In Ulster, the level of mortality rose from 105 in 1739 to 161 in 1740, increased to 166 in 1741, and then declined to 86 in 1742.[12] In all

9. For a discussion of Irish mortality estimates during 1740–41, see Michael Drake, "The Irish Demographic Crisis of 1740–1741," *Historical Studies* 6 (1968), 120–22.

10. Stuart Daultrey, David Dickson, and Cormac Ó Gráda, "Eigthteenth-Century Irish Population: New Perspectives from Old Sources," *Journal of Economic History* 41 (September 1981), 601–28.

11. Cormac Ó Gráda, Eighteenth-Century Irish Population: Old Sources and New Speculations, unpublished manuscript, 1980.

12. David Dickson, "Famine in Ireland, 1700–1775: A Review," paper presented at the Famine in History Symposium, Vevey, Switzerland, July 1981, app. 3.

likelihood, the indexes of table 1 based on the number of burials at
Dublin understate the percentage rise in mortality that occured in Ireland
during 1740–1741, significantly so for 1741. It seems certain that the
national death rate rose considerably above 50 per 1,000.[13]

The mortality indexes for France require discussion to clarify the
shape of the national mortality peak of the early 1740s. The demographic evidence suggests that two somewhat distinct mortality patterns—one
essentially urban and northern, the other rural and southern—developed
in France. The mortality indexes of table 1 could not be based on the
results of the study of French population movements carried out by the
Institut National d'Etudes Démographiques (INED), which goes back
only as far as 1740.[14] As a consequence, the indexes covering the
ten-year period beginning with 1735 had to be computed from the
aggregate totals of the demographic studies that have exploited French
parish registers. Because such studies have centered on the population
movements of the Paris region and other northern urban locations, the
indexes reflect mortality trends that were not always typical of national
demographic patterns.

The index numbers of table 1 indicate that the course of mortality in
France during the period 1735–1744 paralleled the general European
trends, except that the mortality peak first materialized in 1739 rather
than in 1740. A recent survey of the number of deaths that occurred in
rural France before 1740 found the same lower mortality in the 1730s
and also confirmed the fact that the mortality peak developed in 1739.[15]
The investigation is based on a cross-section sample of fifty-one villages. The study found unusually low mortality from 1735 to 1738,
followed by a sharp rise in the number of deaths in 1739. The pronounced increase in mortality was primarily the result of a steep rise in
the number of burials in northern France, where the deaths in 1739
nearly tripled the number recorded in 1738.

The INED's study shows, however, that the mortality indexes of table
1 are biased on the upward side in 1740 and 1741. During those two
years, both urban and northern rural death rates rose higher than the
national average. The INED investigation also reveals that while urban
mortality peaked during 1741–1742, the number of deaths recorded in
the villages peaked in 1741 and 1743. The national level of mortality

13. Ó Gráda, "Irish Population," 38.

14. For these results, see Yves Blayo, "Mouvement naturel de la population française de
1740 à 1829," *Population* 30, special no. (November 1975), 15–64.

15. Danièle Rebaudo, "Le Mouvement annuel de la population française rurale de 1670 à
1740," *Population* 34 (May–June 1979), 590–97.

peaked in 1741. The elevated rural mortality of 1743 was primarily a southern phenomenon. The INED study confirms the fact that mortality declined sharply everywhere in France during 1744. In sum, the curve of the national mortality peak in France departed somewhat from the general European pattern, in contrast to the indications of table 1. The number of deaths rose more moderately in 1740 and climbed again in 1743. But mortality in France peaked in 1741, as it did generally elsewhere in Europe.[16]

The mortality indexes for the Low Countries are based on the burials in three Dutch towns and on a small number of parish registers located in the southern Netherlands. The index for 1740, for example, is derived from a total of 3,815 deaths. The index numbers for 1740 and 1741 indicate that, contrary to the European trend, the death rate in the Low Countries did not become elevated until 1741. In all likelihood the mortality index for 1740 is biased on the downward side by the small sample. Owing to the absence of complete time series, neither the burials recorded in Amsterdam nor those of the large town of Haarlem are included in table 1. If the number of deaths at those two urban locations were factored into the indexes, the year 1740 would show a significant increase in mortality. At Amsterdam, the number of burials rose from 7,507 in 1739 to 10,056 in 1740, an increase of 34 percent. At Haarlem, the number rose form 1,117 in 1739 to 1,544 in 1740, an increase of 38 percent. The burial figures for Amsterdam and Haarlem would also lower the index number for 1741 to some degree. Although mortality remained elevated at both Amsterdam (9,864 burials) and Haarlem (1,282 burials), the number of deaths declined at each location in 1741.[17]

The mortality indexes computed for Germany are based on a considerably larger number of deaths—67,964 in 1740, for example. At the same time, some 95 percent of the burials were registered in Prussia. This circumstance tends to exaggerate the amplitude of the German mortality peak of 1736–1737 and possibly to understate the increase of German mortality during 1740–1741. The German mortality peak of 1736–1737 reflects the undue statistical influence of a mortality crisis that beset the large northeastern administrative region of "Prussia and Lithuania." The total number of burials recorded in this east Elbian province make up 22 percent of the deaths on which the mortality indexes for Germany are based.

16. Blayo, "Mouvement naturel," 52–56.
17. Nicolas Duyn, *Historische aanmerkingen van drie strenge winters (1709, 1740, 1742)* (Haarlem, 1746), 185, 193–94.

The statistical influence of the deaths that occurred in Prussia and Lithuania can be seen in the three sets of index numbers that appear in table 2. The mortality crisis that erupted in Prussia and Lithuania during

Table 2. Indexes of annual number of deaths in all Germany and in Prussia and Lithuania, 1735–1744 (1735–1744 = 100)

Year	All Germany[a]	Prussia and Lithuania[b]	Germany exclusive of Prussia and Lithuania
1735	84	96	81
1736	116	156	104
1737	114	144	105
1738	99	93	101
1739	98	94	100
1740	112	91	118
1741	110	90	116
1742	96	83	100
1743	92	78	96
1744	78	75	78

[a]From table 1.
[b]Computed from the burials recorded.
SOURCE: Indexes computed from Johann Peter Süssmilch, *Die göttliche Ordnung in den Veränderungen des menschlichen Geschlects,* 4th ed., 3 vols. (Berlin, 1775), I, 15, 24, 26, 48-49, 85, 92-93, 100-101, 104-105, 110, 114, 118, 121-24.

1736–1737 is apparent in the figures. The untypically low mortality in Prussia and Lithuania during the European mortality peak of 1740–1742 is also apparent. The explanation for the ability of the northeastern region of Germany to avoid the elevated death rates of the early 1740s will illuminate the relationships among food shortage, climatic variability, and epidemic disease in preindustrial Europe. The recomputed index numbers also show that when the deaths registered in Prussia and Lithuania are removed, the mortality curve for the remainder of Germany more nearly parallels the European demographic pattern of the early 1740s.

No firm conclusions can be drawn from the index numbers computed for Austria (table 1), which represent only the deaths recorded at Vienna and the nearby town of Stockerau. The onset of elevated mortality in 1740 and the continuation of high death rates through 1742 are nonetheless also apparent in the demographic pattern of urban Austria. In addition, the limited Austrian burial figures reflect the west-central European mortality peak of 1736–1737.

The mortality indexes for Switzerland are based on a more varied sample than are those for Austria. The number of available burial registers, however, constitutes too small a percentage of the presumed number of deaths in Switzerland during the period 1735–1744, and thus the figures should be interpreted with caution. Bearing the limitations in mind, the index numbers of table 1 indicate that the mortality curve in Switzerland corresponded to the annual movement of European death rates, with a mortality peak in 1736–1737 and elevated mortality each year from 1740 to 1743.

The mortality indexes for Italy, as in the case of France, are based to a disporportionate degree on northern urban burials. They are derived from a sample of some 22,000 deaths recorded each year. The indexes show that the number of burials in Italy climbed noticeably in 1740 and then increased each year to reach a peak in 1742, in conformity with the general European pattern. The west-central European mortality peak of 1736 is also reflected in the indexes for Italy.

In Scandinavia, the record of burials became substantially complete in 1735, and thus the mortality indexes of table 1 portray the annual movement of death rates in the four Scandinavian countries with a high degree of accuracy. The abrupt onset of elevated mortality in 1740 is apparent in the figures, but it is also evident that the four countries exhibited variations in annual mortality trends.

Finland, then a part of the Swedish monarchy, suffered a severe mortality crisis in 1740. The number of burials recorded that year jumped 62 percent above the total of the previous year, to reach a level 145 percent above the low mortality of 1735. At the same time, the number of deaths in Sweden, Norway, and Denmark rose only moderately in 1740. In 1741, however, the number of burials recorded in Norway (then a part of the Danish monarchy) rose 62 percent above the total of 1740, to reach a level 119 percent above the low mortality of 1735. The Norwegian death rate climbed higher still in 1742, reaching a level 26 percent above the elevated rate of 1741 and 103 percent above the rate of 1740. Death rates in Finland, Sweden, and Denmark, by contrast, declined in 1741. The year 1742, however, brought higher death rates to Sweden and Finland as well to Norway. Finland endured a second mortality crisis in 1742, when the number of deaths increased 43 percent above the total of 1741. Sweden, in contrast to the general European pattern, suffered crisis mortality in 1743, when the death rate climbed 87 percent above the low mortality of 1735. Elsewhere in Scandinavia, the level of mortality declined in 1743. In 1744, death rates fell sharply everywhere in Scandinavia.

Because national population totals are known for the four Scandinavian countries, it is possible to compute crude death rates.[18] If a mortality

18. Arthur E. Imhof, *Aspekte der Bevölkerungsentwicklung in den nordischen Ländern, 1720–1750* (Bern, 1976), 76–78.

crisis is defined as a year in which the crude death rate exceeds 40 per 1,000, then a global Scandinavian mortality crisis occurred only in 1742, when the death rate reached 40.7 per 1,000. At the national level, however, each year of the European mortality peak of the early 1740s saw crisis mortality somewhere in Scandinavia: Finland in 1740 (52.0 per 1,000), Norway in 1741 (40.8 per 1,000), both Finland (45.6 per 1,000) and Norway (52.2 per 1,000) in 1742, and Sweden in 1743 (43.7 per 1,000). As the indexes of table 1 show, national mortality crises were uncommon elsewhere in Europe. Ireland passed through crisis mortality in both 1740 and 1741, and the Low Countries endured a mortality crisis in 1741.

At the same time, national death rates in preindustrial Europe mask the large variance in mortality that could occur at the provincial and county level. It is the process of accounting for the differential regional mortality that took place within the western European countries during the early 1740s that sheds the most light on the relationship between food shortage and the incidence of epidemic disease. The Scandinavian burial records reveal that severe local mortality crises occurred in years when death rates rose only moderately in other provinces and counties. In addition, the same local region did not necessarily experience the highest death rate in a successive year of peak mortality. In the Norwegian mortality crisis of 1741, for example, the southwestern coastal diocese of Kristiansand registered the highest regional death rate, 66.0 per 1,000, while none of the other three dioceses recorded a death rate above 45.0 per 1,000. In the Norwegian mortality crisis of 1742, the central diocese of Akershus recorded the highest regional death rate, 67.3 per 1,000. Neither the western diocese of Bergen nor the northern diocese of Trondheim, however, experienced an annual death rate in excess of 45.0 per 1,000 in any year from 1735 to 1744.[19] These examples of regional mortality fluctuations are taken from Scandinavia because of the availability of local crude death rates. The regional variations of mortality in the majority of the western European countries also are of critical importance in explaining the course of the mortality peak of the early 1740s, even though the lack of local demographic data renders the task of measurement more difficult.

The national and regional demographic fluctuations of the early 1740s give rise to a series of questions that can be resolved only by an examination of all the variables capable of influencing the level of mortality. Previous historical investigations concluded that the mortality wave originated in a subsistence crisis. In order to guage the total

19. Ibid., 170–78.

demographic impact of elevated food prices, it is also necessary to establish the annual movement of the number of births and marriages and to correlate the fluctuations with the mortality trends. Moreover, the movement of the three demographic variables offers clues as to the circumstances and events that led to the increase in the number of deaths during the early 1740s. Finally, the failure of the demographic variables to fluctuate in accordance with the predicted pattern of a subsistence crisis would seem to rule out food shortage as the primary explanation for the mortality peak of 1740–1742.

The Annual Movement of Western European Births and Marriages, 1735–1744

Pierre Goubert has written that preindustrial mortality peaks habitually produced a "triple distortion" of the parish demographic curves, influencing the number of marriages and births as well. When the burial curve shot up, the nuptial and baptismal curves collapsed nearly together. When the crisis passed, the number of burials fell off momentarily, the number of marriages and baptisms increased, and the demographic variables soon returned to their normal fluctuating state of equilibrium. Goubert prefers to call this historical phenomenon a "demographic crisis of the *ancien* type" rather than a mortality crisis, even though it was the dramatic rise in the number of burials that riveted attention. He defends the more general term on the basis that it preserves the complexity of the demographic events and avoids prejudging the causes of the fluctuations.

Goubert's investigations discovered two essential causes of the demographic crises of the former type. The principal cause turned out to be the high price of grains, which produced dearth or famine, that is to say, "economic crises of the *ancien* type." The second cause proved to be epidemic disease, which generally was associated with a shortage of food. He found that epidemic diseases rarely acted alone in a "pure state"—that is, they rarely operated at random.[20]

If the mortality peak of 1740–1742 was primarily the result of elevated grain prices, then a triple distortion of the parish demographic curves in the early 1740s would be anticipated, in conformance with Goubert's model. In addition, the number of deaths, births, and marriages should then move inversely before the middle of the decade. But the fact that the three demographic variables move in the directions laid down by Goubert does not preclude the possibility that epidemic disease

20. Pierre Goubert, *Cent Mille Provinciaux au XVIIe siècle* (Paris, 1968), 69–70.

acting in a "pure state" was also responsible for the mortality crisis or that such complicating variables as climatic stress and warfare influenced the annual fluctuations.[21]

The mortality indexes of table 1 have shown that the level of European mortality rose in 1736, declined in 1738–1739, climbed sharply in 1740, remained elevated through 1742, and fell off noticeably in 1743 and precipitously in 1744. For the most part, preindustrial demographic crises lasted no more than two years. The fact that the mortality peak that erupted in 1740 persisted for three years, and in some regions four years, suggests that Goubert's model may not fully account for the crisis. Nonetheless, it is safe to conclude that harvest shortfalls and dearth conditions must be numbered among the major variables if the parish register curves exhibit the pattern expected in the wake of a subsistence crisis.

Table 3 displays index numbers representing the annual births that were recorded during the period 1735–1744. Table 3 differs from table 1 in that figures for Scotland and Ireland are missing, owing to the paucity of fertility records. A comparison of the indexes of births and deaths in the five years from 1735 through 1739 discloses no apparent inverse movement between the two variables:

Year	1735	1736	1737	1738	1739
Births	103	102	103	103	107
Deaths	82	96	103	94	94

Moreover, no trend in the annual movement of the birth rate is discernible. The minor European mortality peak of 1736–1737 failed to provoke any distortion in the fertility curve during 1737–1738. The comparison of the fertility and mortality index numbers during the five-year period 1735–1739 does not suggest that the mortality peak of 1736–1737 was touched off by food shortage. Tables 1 and 3, however, make evident an inverse relationship between fertility and mortality for Germany in 1737. As will be seen below, the price of grain did become elevated in Prussia during 1736–1737.

The comparison of the fertility and mortality indexes for the five years from 1740 through 1744, by contrast, discloses the demographic movements that would be anticipated in the event of a subsistence crisis. The inverse relationship between the two variables is apparent in the figures that follow:

21. For discussion of preindustrial mortality crises, see John D. Post, *The Last Great Subsistence Crisis in the Western World* (Baltimore, 1977), 108–22.

Year	1740	1741	1742	1743	1744
Births	100	94	92	95	100
Deaths	115	115	117	101	81

The birth rate exhibited a downward trend in 1740 and fell uninterruptedly to a low point in 1742 before an inverse movement between the number of births and deaths set in again during 1743. The depth of the fertility trough remained moderate, however, compared with the amplitude of the mortality peak. Fertility declined 14 percent from 1739 to 1742, the extreme year for both births and deaths, whereas mortality rose 24 percent. In correspondence with Goubert's model, the birth and death rates began to move in opposite directions in 1743, and then in 1744 the number of births returned to "normal" levels, while the number of deaths fell off sharply. In sum, the inverse relationship between the fertility and mortality trends during the five-year period 1740–1744 indicates that the rise in mortality was influenced by food shortage. At the same time, the moderate decline in the number of births suggests that famine conditions did not become common.

The annual movement of the number of European marriages also strongly suggests that the mortality peak of 1740–1742 was touched off by elevated food prices. Marriage rates even more than birth rates reflect adjustments to economic prospects. If the economic horizon begins to darken, marriage plans may be put off till more propitious times. The harvest shortfalls and rising cereal prices of 1739–1740 did not promise an optimistic economic future. The grain harvest was the heartbeat of the preindustrial economy and economic prospects were perceived largely in terms of food prices. Marriages might also be postponed because of pestilence, but epidemics are difficult to anticipate.

Table 4 displays index numbers representing the annual marriages that were recorded in western Europe during the ten-year period 1735–1744. Time series of marriages are fewer than those for deaths and births during this period. Table 4 lacks figures for Scotland, Ireland, Austria, Sweden, Norway, and Denmark. As the available statistics show, the number of marriages began to fall in 1739 and remained depressed until 1742. The decline in nuptiality was even more moderate than the decline in fertility. Measured from 1738 to 1741, the year in which marriages fell to their lowest number, the fall in nuptiality amounted to 10.8 percent. In addition, the marriage rate recovered more decisively than the birth rate in 1743. Allowing for the nine-month gestation period, it appears that the marriage rate also recovered more strongly than the "conception rate" in 1743. In 1744, European marriage and birth rates

Table 3. Indexes of annual number of births in Europe, 1735–1744 (1735–1744 = 100)

Location	1735	1736	1737	1738	1739	1740	1741	1742	1743	1744
England	105	103	101	103	105	100	93	91	99	100
France	100	101	106	100	105	99	99	95	96	99
Low Countries	106	105	106	105	102	97	88	94	101	95
Germany	103	100	93	97	104	96	91	99	108	109
Austria (Vienna)	114	110	111	109	120	106	81	78	84	88
Switzerland	106	99	106	103	102	97	100	94	96	97
Italy	99	93	100	101	102	101	99	103	98	103
Sweden[a]	99[b]	92	94	104	113	100	99	98	92	107
Finland	105	111	110	113	112	104	98	74	78	96
Norway	100	105	105	97	108	103	95	90	95	102
Denmark	101	99	96	102	102	99	94	97	103	106
Unweighted averages	103	102	103	103	107	100	94	92	95	100

[a]Base period, 1736–1744.

[b]Index number derived from Stockholm and nine Swedish counties.

SOURCES: E. A. Wrigley and R. S. Schofield, *The Population History of England, 1541–1871* (Cambridge, Mass., 1981), 495–99; E. Charlot and J. Dupâquier, "Mouvement annuel de la population de la ville de Paris de 1670 à 1821," *Annales de démographie historique* (1967), 511–14; François Lebrun, *Les Hommes et la mort en Anjou aux 17e et 18e siècles* (Paris, 1971), 509; M. Lachiver, "Une Etude et quelques esquisses," *Annales de démographie historique* (1969), 234; Ph. Wiel, "Tamerville," ibid., 188; J. Lelong, "Saint-Pierre-Eglise," ibid., 125–35; M.-H. Jouan, "Les Originalités démographiques d'un bourg artisanal normand au XVIIIe siècle, Villedieu-les-Poeles, 1711–1790," ibid., 122; Hubert Charbonneau, *Tourouvre-au-Perche aux XVIIe et XVIIIe siècles (1668–1819)* (Paris, 1970), 260; Étienne Gautier and Louis Henry, *La Population de Crulai, paroisse normande* (Paris, 1958), 243–44; Jean Ganiage, *Trois Villages d'Île-de-France: Etude démographique* (Paris, 1963), 131; M. Frésel-Lozey, *Histoire démographique d'un village en Béarn: Bilhères-d'Ossau au XVIIIe–XIXe siècles* (Bordeaux, 1969), 242, 246; Michel Morineau, *Les Faux-semblants d'un démarrage économique: Agriculture et démographie en France au XVIIIe siècle* (Paris, 1970), 309–13, 367–70; Mohamed E. Kordi, *Bayeux aux XVIIe et XVIIIe siècles* (Paris, 1970), 115, 167; A. Lefebvre-Teillard, *La Population de Dôle au XVIIIe siècle* (Paris, 1969), 75–76; Thomas F. Sheppard, *Lourmarin in the Eighteenth Century* (Baltimore, 1971), 227–29; Raymond Deniel and Louis Henry, "La Population d'un village du Nord de la France, Sainghin-en-Melantois, de 1665 à 1851," *Population* 20 (July–August, 1965), 597; J. Canard, "Les Mouvements de population à Saint-Roman d'Urfé de 1612 à 1946," *Bulletin de la Diana* 29 (1945), 151–53; Marcel Lachiver, *La Population de Meulan du XVIIe au XIXe siècle* (Paris, 1969), 80–81; G. T. Mentink and A. M. van der Woude, *De demografische ontwikkeling te Rotterdam en Cool in de 17e en 18e eeuw* (Rotterdam, 1965), 104, 126–27, 170; Etienne Hélin, *La Démographie de Liège aux XVIIe et XVIIIe siècles* (Brussels, 1963), 256–57; F. Blockmans, "De Bevolkingscijfers te Antwerpen in de XVIIIe eeuw," in *Antwerpen in de XVIIIe eeuw* (Antwerp, 1952), 402–407; Hans van Werveke, "De Curve van het Gentse Bevolkingscijfer in de 17e en de 18e eeuw," *Verhandelingen van de Koninklyke Vlaamse Academie voor Wetenschappen, Letteren en Schone Kunsten van Belgie*

10 (1948), 23, 34; A. M. van der Woude, *Het Noorderwerrier*, 3 vols. (Wageningen, 1972), III, 624–31; G. van Houtte, *Leuven in 1740, ein krisisjaar: Ekonomische, sociale, en demografische aspekten* (Brussels, 1964), 226–29; D. Dalle, *De Bevolking van Veurne-Ambacht in de 17e en de 18e eeuw* (Brussels, 1963), 284; De Brouver, "De demografische evolutie in de meierij Erembodegem en de heerlijkheid Oordegen gedurende de XVIIe en XVIIIe eeuw," in *Cinq Etudes de démographie locale (XVIIe–XVIIIe siècles)* (Brussels, 1963), 98–115; J. De Vos, "De omvang en de evolutie van het Eeklose Bevolkingscijfer tijdens de XVIIe en de XVIIIe eeuw," in ibid., 137; Johann Peter Süssmilch, *Die göttliche Ordnung in den Veränderungen des menschlichen Geschlechts*, 4th ed., 3 vols. (Berlin, 1775), I, 15, 24, 26, 48–49, 85, 92–93, 100–101, 104–105, 110, 114, 118, 121–24; Arthur E. Imhof, "Die nichtnamentliche Auswertung der Kirchenbücher von Giessen Umgebung," in Imhof, ed., *Historische Demographie als Sozialgeschichte* (Darmstadt, 1975), 119–24; François G. Dreyfus, "Prix et population à Trèves et à Mayence au XVIIIe siècle," *Revue d'histoire économique et sociale* 34 (1956), 246; Stephan Glonner, "Bevölkerungsbewegung von Sieben Pfarreien im Kgl. Bayerisches Bezirksamt Tölz seit Ende des 16. Jahrhunderts," *Allgemeines Statistisches Archiv* 4 (1896), 264; Otto Roller, *Die Einwohnerschaft der Stadt Durlach im 18. Jahrhundert* (Karlsruhe, 1907), 46–53; 64–67, 94–97, 110; A. Schreiber, "Die Entwicklung der Augsburger Bevölkerung vom Ende des 14. Jahrhunderts bis zum Beginn des 19. Jahrhunderts," *Archiv für Hygiene* 123 (1939–40), 166; D. G. Bäumler, "Medizinalstatistische Untersuchungen über Weiden (Oberpfalz) von 1551 bis 1800," ibid. 120 (1938), 226; Wilhelm Ehrhart, "Die Sterblichkeit in der Reichstadt Kempten (Allgäu) in den Jahren 1606–1624 und 1686–1870," ibid 116 (1936), 125; E. François, "La Population de Coblence au XVIIIe siècle," *Annales de démographie historique* (1975), 335–36; Franz and Therese Schmölz, "Die Sterblichkeit in Landsberg am Lech von 1585–1875," *Archiv für Hygiene und Bakteriologie* 136 (1952), 527; W. Jungkunz, "Die Sterblichkeit in Nürnberg, 1714–1850," *Mitteilungen des Vereins für Geschichte der Stadt Nürnberg* 42 (1951), 304–305; Jean-Paul Lehners, "Die Pfarre Stockerau im 17. und 18. Jahrhundert," in Heimold Helczmanovszki, ed., *Beiträge zur Bevölkerungs- und Sozialgeschichte Österreichs* (Vienna, 1973), 398–99; A. Burckhardt, *Demographie und Epidemiologie der Stadt Basel während der letzten drei Jahrhunderts, 1601–1900* (Basel, 1908), 90, 95, 98; E. Olivier, *Médecine et santé dans le pays de Vaud*, 2 vols. (Lausanne, 1962), II, 1,227; Silvio Bucher, *Bevölkerung und Wirtschaft des Amtes Entlebuch im 18. Jahrhundert* (Luzern, 1974), 16, 19; Edouard Mallet, "Recherches historiques et statistiques sur la population de Genève: Son mouvement annuel et sa longévité depuis le XVIe siècle jusqu'à nos jours (1549–1833)," *Annales d'hygiène publique et de médecine légale* (1837), 44; M. Schürmann, *Bevölkerung, Wirtschaft, und Gesellschaft in Appenzell-Innerrhoden im 18. und frühen 19. Jahrhundert* (Appenzell, 1974), 319–25; Hans-Rudolf Burri, *Die Bevölkerung Luzerns im 18. und frühen 19. Jahrhundert* (Luzern, 1975), 182–83; Daniele Beltrami, *Storia della popolazione di Venezia dalla fine del secolo XVI alla caduta della repubblica* (Padova, 1954), 112–27, 151–53; Athos Belletini, *La popolazione di Bologna dal secolo XV all'unificazione italiana* (Bologna, 1961), 94; P. Donazzolo and M. Saibante, "Lo sviluppo demografico di Verona e della sua provincia dalla fine del sec. XV ai nostri giorni," *Metron* 6 (1926), 79–84; Salvatore Fedele, "Strutture e movimento della popolazione in una parrocchia della Capitanata, 1711–1750," *Quaderni Storici* 17 (1971), 475; Arthur E. Imhof, *Aspekte der Bevölkerungsentwicklung in den nordischen Ländern, 1720–1750* (Bern, 1976), 76–78, 167–68.

Table 4. Indexes of annual number of marriages in Europe, 1735–1744 (1735–1744 = 100)

Location	1735	1736	1737	1738	1739	1740	1741	1742	1743	1744
England	104	95	100	100	103	98	88	97	107	107
France	93	94	99	101	97	96	96	101	122	101
Low Countries	108	107	101	99	103	86	90	107	102	99
Germany	97	93	97	99	104	88	101	115	109	97
Switzerland	102	99	102	105	96	99	88	97	114	98
Italy	99	93	101	104	101	99	97	92	104	111
Finland	105	106	105	103	95	93	78	75	101	140
Unweighted averages	101	98	101	102	100	94	91	98	108	108

SOURCES: E. A. Wrigley and R. S. Schofield, *The Population History of England, 1541–1871* (Cambridge, Mass., 1981), 495–99; E. Charlot and J. Dupâquier, "Mouvement annuel de la population de la ville de Paris de 1670 à 1821," *Annales de démographie historique* (1967), 513; Ph. Wiel, "Tamerville," ibid. (1969), 188; François Lebrun, *Les Hommes et la mort en Anjou aux 17e et 18e siècles* (Paris, 1971), 509; M. Lachiver, "Une Etude et quelques esquisses," *Annales de démographie historique* (1969), 234; J. Lelong, "Saint-Pierre-Eglise," ibid., 125–35; M.-H. Jouan, "Les Originalités démographiques d'un bourg artisanal normand au XVIIIe siècle, Villedieu-les-Poeles, 1711–1790," ibid., 122; Hubert Charbonneau, *Tourouvre-au-Perche aux XVIIe et XVIIIe siècles (1668–1819)* (Paris, 1970), 260; Etienne Gautier and Louis Henry, *La Population de Crulai, paroisse normande* (Paris, 1958), 243–44; Jean Ganiage, *Trois Villages d'Ile-de-France: Etude démographique* (Paris, 1963), 131; M. Frésel-Lozey, *Histoire démographique d'un village en Béarn: Bilhères-d'Ossau au XVIIIe–XIXe siècles* (Bordeaux, 1969), 242, 246; Michel Morineau, *Les Faux-semblants d'un démarrage économique: Agriculture et démographie en France au XVIIIe siècle* (Paris, 1970), 309–13, 367–70; Mohamed El Kordi, *Bayeux aux XVIIe et XVIIIe siècles* (Paris, 1970), 115, 167; A. Lefebvre-Teillard, *La Population de Dôle au XVIIIe siècle* (Paris, 1969), 75–76; Thomas F. Sheppard, *Lourmarin in the Eighteenth Century* (Baltimore, 1971), 227–29; Raymond

Deniel and Louis Henry, "La Population d'un village du Nord de la France, Sainghin-en-Melantois, de 1665 à 1851," *Population* 20 (July–August 1965), 597; J. Canard, "Les Mouvements de population a Saint-Roman d'Urfé de 1612 à 1946," *Bulletin de la Diana* 29 (1945), 151–53; Marcel Lachiver, *La Population de Meulan du XVIIe au XIXe siècle* (Paris, 1969), 80–81; G. T. Mentink and A. M. van der Woude, *De demografische ontwikkeling te Rotterdam en Cool in de 17e en de 18e eeuw* (Rotterdam, 1965), 104, 126–27; D. Dalle, *De Bevolking van Veurne-Ambacht in de 17e en de 18e eeuw* (Brussels, 1963), 350; J. De Vos, "De omvang en de evolutie van het Eeklose Bevolkingscijfer tijdens de XVIIe en de XVIIIe eeuw," in *Cinq Etudes de démographie locale (XVIIe–XVIIIe siècles)* (Brussels, 1963), 137; Hans van Werveke, "De curve van het Gentse Bevolkingscijfer in de 17e en de 18e eeuw," *Verhandelingen van de Koninklyke Vlaamse Academie voor Wetenschappen, Letteren en Schone Kunsten van Belgie* 10 (1948), 34; Johann Peter Süssmilch, *Die göttliche Ordnung in den Veränderungen des menschlichen Geschlechts*, 4th ed., 3 vols. (Berlin, 1775), I, 15, 24, 26, 48–49, 85, 92–93, 100–101, 104–105, 110, 114, 118, 121–24; Arthur E. Imhof, "Die nicht-namentliche Auswertung der Kirchenbücher von Giessen Umgebung," in Imhof, ed., *Historische Demographie als Sozialgeschichte* (Darmstadt, 1975), 119–24; Stephan Glonner, "Bevölkerungsbewegung von Sieben Pfarreien im Kgl. Bayerisches Bezirksamt Tölz seit Ende des 16. Jahrhunderts," *Allgemeines Statistisches Archiv* 4 (1896), 264; Otto Roller, *Die Einwohnerschaft der Stadt Durlach im 18. Jahrhundert* (Karlsruhe, 1907), 46–53; 64–67, 94–97, 110; A. Schreiber, "Die Entwicklung der Augsburger Bevölkerung vom Ende des 14. Jahrhunderts bis zum Beginn des 19. Jahrhunderts," *Archiv für Hygiene* 123 (1939–40), 166; G. Baümler, "Medizinalstatistische Untersuchungen über Weiden (Oberpfalz) von 1551 bis 1800," ibid. 120 (1938), 226; E. François, "La Population de Coblence au XVIIIe siècle," *Annales de démographie historique* (1975), 335–36; Silvio Bucher, *Bevölkerung und Wirtschaft des Amtes Entlebuch im 18. Jahrhundert* (Luzern, 1974), 16, 19; Hans-Rudolf Burri, *Die Bevölkerung Luzerns im 18. und frühen 19. Jahrhundert* (Luzern, 1975), 182–83; Edouard Mallet, "Recherches historiques et statistiques sur la population de Genève: Son mouvement annuel et sa longévité depuis le XVIe siècle jusqu'à nos jours (1549–1833)," *Annales d'hygiène publique et de médecine légale* (1837), 44; M. Schürmann, *Bevölkerung, Wirtschaft, und Gesellschaft in Appenzell-Innerrhoden im 18. und frühen 19. Jahrhundert* (Appenzell, 1974), 319–25; Salvatore Fedele, "Strutture e movimento della popolazione in una parrocchia della Capitanata, caduta della repubblica (Padova, 1954), 112–27, 151–53; Daniele Beltrami, *Storia della popolazione de Venezia dalla fine del secolo XVI alla 1711–1750," *Quaderni Storici* 17 (1971), 475; Arthur E. Imhof, *Aspekte der Bevölkerungsentwicklung in den nordischen Ländern, 1720–1750* (Bern, 1976), 140.

were both buoyant. In sum, the trough in marriages that extended from 1740 to 1742 paralleled the fall in birth rates, the demogràphic pattern that would be anticipated in the event of a subsistence crisis.

Altogether, the trends and the annual movements of European death, birth, and marriage rates indicate rather decisively that the demographic fluctuations of the early 1740s reflected an "economic crisis of the *ancien* type." At the same time, the untypical demographic trends that occurred in several countries and regions suggest that conditions and events other than elevated grain prices influenced the mortality peak. The succeeding chapters will examine the relative demographic significance of such "complicating variables" as climatic variability, social disorder, war, welfare crises, and the changing incidence of epidemic disease as well as the impact of grain harvest outcomes and cereal prices. The chapter that follows begins the investigation with an analytical survey of the weather conditions that predominated in western Europe during the late 1730s and early 1740s.

3. *Weather Patterns*

The unfolding European mortality peak coincided with the long, severe winter of 1739–1740, which was followed by a frosty and dry spring and a cool and dry summer. The year 1740 then concluded with a frosty and extremely wet autumn and early winter. The spring months of 1741 turned out raw and dry; the summer was drought-ridden; the winter of 1741–1742 proved nearly as frigid as the arctic winter of 1739–1740; and then the summer of 1742 brought another dry season. By 1742, the regions of western and northern Europe had passed through three consecutive years punctuated by climatic stress.

In what measure did these extreme weather events contribute to the increased number of deaths recorded in the early 1740s? The question must be considered from three different perspectives. First of all, such anomalous weather patterns commonly reduce the yield of cereal crops and bring about elevated food prices, which in preindustrial societies have also correlated with higher death rates, the consequence in part of prolonged undernutrition and an increased incidence of infectious diseases. Second, abnormally low temperatures and cold, dense atmospheres can result in deaths from the process of hypothermia, almost certainly facilitate the spread of respiratory infections, and probably lead to changes in the number of deaths from heart attacks and strokes. Third, the persistence of extreme atmospheric conditions can promote the diffusion of selected pathogenic microorganisms and disease vectors, giving rise to such infections as dysentery, typhus, and typhoid fever. The paramount question becomes whether or not a significant functional relationship obtained between the weather patterns of 1739–1742 and the rising death rates of the early 1740s.

The economic and demographic impact of the extended period of climatic stress was intensified by the factor of climatic variance. Before the cold season of 1739–1740, a succession of moderate winters had dominated the first four decades of the eighteenth century. By 1740, the consciousness of "great winters" was reduced to the indelible memory of the winter of 1708–1709. In northwestern Europe, the severe winter of 1739–1740 was preceded by almost a half century of predominantly milder climate; the period from 1700 to 1740 proved a moderate interval in the secular "little ice age" that stretched to 1850. The winter seasons of the decade 1730–1739 were the mildest of the first half of the eighteenth century, averaging 1.1°F (0.6°C) above normal in England, and a still milder +2.3°F (+1.3°C) in Holland. By contrast, the cold season of 1740 was characterized by below-normal mean temperatures that set in as early as October 1739 and persisted until August 1740, with strikingly low winter readings. At London, Paris, Berlin, and Utrecht, locations for which temperature records are available, the annual mean temperature of 1740 averaged 4.1°F (2.3°C) below normal. For the first six months of 1740 the mean temperature at these same four locations fell 6.1°F (3.4°C) below the long-term normal mean.[1] The low atmospheric temperatures delayed the grain and grape harvests throughout western Europe. The grape harvests in northeastern France, the south Rhenish region, and western Switzerland, for example, did not take place, on average, until October 14; thus the vintage of 1740 was the second latest from 1675 to 1879.[2]

The significance of the climatic variability of the 1730s and 1740s can best be illustrated by a brief description of the climatic regime of western Europe. The climate of western Europe has alternated between the dominance of "maritime" and "continental" patterns. Maritime climate is characterized, on balance, by a westerly atmospheric circulation that produces mostly mild, damp winters and cool, dry summers. Continental climate is dominated by frontal systems, with north–south circulation and a high frequency of blocking anticyclones, which produce mostly cold, dry winters, and hot, dry summers.

Mild winters predominate when air masses reach western Europe after traveling over the long track of the Atlantic Ocean, the more common European weather pattern. Arctic winter weather occurs in western Europe when air masses arrive over continental tracks from northern Russia. The severe winters ensue when blocking anticyclones reverse the direction of the prevailing winds from the usual southwesterly to easterly

1. Hans von Rudloff, *Die Schwankungen und Pendelungen des Klimas in Europa seit dem Beginn der regelmässigen Instrumenten-Beobachtungen* (*1670*) (Braunschweig, 1967), 89–119.

2. Micheline Baulant, E. Le Roy Ladurie, and Michel Demonet, "Une Synthèse provisoire: Les Vendanges du XVe au XIXe siècle," *Annales: Economies, Sociétés, Civilisations* 33 (July–August 1978), 765.

flows. Anticyclones over northern Europe are extensions of the semiper-manent high-pressure region near the North Pole. They generally occur in the form of separate cells in the latitudes of the subpolar zone of prevailing low pressure and are relatively common over Iceland, Scandinavia, and northern Russia. In severe European winters, the easterly air masses of the continental arctic type cross the Russian frontier with temperature reading close to or below zero degrees Fahrenheit. As the easterly airstream mixes with warmer air in western Europe, the atmospheric temperatures rise, but the readings may still stand close to zero when the air mass reaches Holland and eastern France. Strong easterly winds generally accompany this arctic weather pattern; thus the wind-chill factor adds considerably to the discomfort. Such severe weather conditions can last from a few days to several weeks.[3] The winter of 1740 witnessed a series of extended cold spells with easterly and northeasterly winds.

The evidence shows that the weather of northwestern Europe began to conform to the continental model in late 1739. Hans von Rudloff has computed the monthly departures from long-term mean temperatures for the year 1740, which are displayed in table 5.[4] The table discloses that all monthly temperature departures at the four European locations remained negative until September, with the exception of the Paris region. The January and February departures of more than $-10°F$ ($-6°C$) represent extraordinary negative values, as the long-term record of temperatures in England and Holland demonstrates.

The central England temperature series compiled by Gordon Manley and the Holland meteorological series assembled by Aart Labrijn make it possible to reconstruct the weather patterns for the early 1740s at two key locations. Table 6 displays the monthly mean temperatures (Celsius scale) representative of central England for the ten-year period 1735–1744. The standard thirty-year mean temperatures for the twentieth century are included for the purposes of comparison. The abnormally low tempera-tures of 1740 stand out in the table: the annual mean temperature of 6.8°C proved the lowest value for the entire observation period from 1659 to 1973, falling 2.8°C or 5.0°F below the standard mean. The May 1740 mean temperature of 8.6°C was the lowest for that month during the series, also falling 2.8°C below the standard mean. The same was true for the October 1740 mean of 5.3°C, which constituted a larger

---

3. H. H. Lamb, *Climate: Present, Past and Future*, vol. II: *Climate History and the Future* (New York, 1978), 440–541; Lamb, *The English Climate* (London, 1964), 9–56; Gordon Manley, *Climate and the British Scene* (London, 1952), 79–80, 233–34.

4. Rudloff, *Schwankungen*, 112. Rudloff includes in the table uncertain values for Uppsala, Sweden, which I have not reproduced here.

Table 5. Monthly departures from mean temperature in four European locations, 1740

Location	Jan.	Feb.	Mar.	Apr.	May	June	July	Aug.	Sept.	Oct.	Nov.	Dec.	Year
Berlin	-7.0	-6.1	-3.2	-3.1	-3.9	-2.1	-2.2	-0.9	+3.0	-3.9	-2.0	+1.2	-2.5°C
Holland (De Bilt)	-6.3	-5.0	-2.7	-2.7	-4.6	-3.1	-1.8	-1.1	+0.8	-3.5	-1.7	-0.1	-2.5°C
Central England	-6.5	-5.7	-1.5	-1.6	-2.5	-1.4	-0.6	-0.9	+0.7	-4.3	-2.7	-2.0	-2.5°C
Paris	-7.4	-7.7	-2.9	-0.5	-2.0	+0.8	+0.4	+0.7	+2.4	+0.8	-0.9	+1.9	-1.2°C

SOURCE: Hans von Rudloff, *Die Schwankungen und Pendelungen des Klimas in Europa seit dem Beginn der regelmässingen Instrumenten-Beobachtungen (1670)* (Braunschweig, 1967), 112.

Table 6. Monthly means for air temperature, central England, 1735–1744 (°C)

Year	Jan.	Feb.	Mar.	Apr.	May	June	July	Aug.	Sept.	Oct.	Nov.	Dec.	Year
1735	4.4	4.0	5.8	8.9	10.9	13.3	14.8	16.2	14.2	10.3	6.3	5.4	9.6
1736	6.4	3.1	6.9	8.6	10.6	15.7	16.4	17.8	14.4	10.4	6.9	6.4	10.3
1737	6.2	4.2	6.1	8.8	12.5	15.9	17.4	13.8	14.2	8.9	6.1	4.9	9.9
1738	4.6	4.6	5.5	9.9	11.4	14.2	16.4	16.0	12.5	10.2	6.3	6.1	9.8
1739	4.0	6.8	5.8	6.7	11.6	15.2	16.0	14.7	13.1	9.6	3.7	3.2	9.2
1740	-2.8	-1.6	3.9	6.4	8.6	12.8	15.3	14.7	14.0	5.3	3.3	2.2	6.8
1741	1.7	4.4	4.2	7.1	9.3	15.2	15.6	16.7	14.7	11.0	7.8	3.9	9.2
1742	1.9	3.6	4.1	6.6	10.6	15.0	15.8	15.8	12.2	9.2	4.4	1.1	8.4
1743	3.6	5.4	5.3	5.4	13.3	15.6	14.9	16.9	14.2	8.9	9.3	4.9	9.8
1744	1.4	2.9	4.8	6.7	10.8	14.4	16.4	15.4	12.8	9.4	6.9	3.5	8.8
1931–1960	3.4	3.9	5.9	8.4	11.4	14.6	16.2	16.0	13.7	10.1	6.7	4.7	9.6

SOURCE: Gordon Manley, "Central England Temperatures: Monthly Means 1659 to 1973," *Quarterly Journal of the Royal Meteorological Society* 100 (July 1974), 389–98.

negative departure of 4.8°C. The table also reveals that the extended period of below-normal mean temperatures began in August 1739 and continued without interruption until September 1740, with the most anomalous negative departures occurring in January (-6.2°C or -11.7°F) and February (-5.2°C or -9.4°F). Finally, the table discloses the period of abnormally cold weather that predominated from January to May 1742.

Labrijn's Holland series of monthly mean temperatures reveals similar weather patterns for the northwestern region of the continent. Table 7 sets out the mean temperatures (Celsius scale) by month, season, and year for the ten-year period 1735–1744. As in central England, the 1740 annual mean temperature of 6.5°C proved the lowest of the observation period from 1735 to 1944, falling 2.5°C or 4.5°F below the normal mean for the 210-year period. The 1740 mean spring temperature of 5.0°C constituted a low for that season during the observation period, falling 3.1°C or 5.6°F below the 210-year mean. In Holland, the change to abnormally cold weather occurred during October 1739. The factor of climatic variance can be seen in the winter and spring mean temperatures. From 1735 to 1739, all ten seasonal values remained above the 210-year means, whereas from 1740 to 1744 the five spring means and three of the five winter means stayed below the long-term mean. The extremely cold period from January to May 1742 is also apparent from the table.

The year 1740 also initiated a trend to lower precipitation amounts and a tendency to droughtlike conditions in northwestern Europe, which persisted into 1743. Table 8 displays the measured seasonal and annual precipitation at Zwanenburg, in Holland, during the ten-year period 1735–1744, together with the long-term averages for the 210-year period 1735–1944. As can be seen, precipitation amounts were normal or above normal each year from 1735 to 1739 but thereafter fell considerably below normal each year from 1740 to 1743. The first eight months of 1740 stand out as a particularly dry period, when precipitation measured only 321mm. The excessively wet autumn of 1740 also stands out in the record. The most damaging period of drought in the Low Countries occurred during the spring and summer of 1741, when measured precipitation fell below the low values recorded in the same seasons of 1740. Not until the summer of 1742 did measured rainfall return to more normal values. In England, the sharp change to drier conditions is reflected in the record of measured precipitation at Kew, in the southeastern county of Surrey. Over the 270-year period from 1701 to 1970, the annual precipitation has averaged 23.91 inches. The record of the annual

Table 7. Monthly, annual, and seasonal means of air temperature, Zwanenburg-Utrecht-De Bilt 1735-1744 (°C)

Year	Jan	Feb	Mar	Apr	May	Jun	Jul	Aug	Sep	Oct	Nov	Dec	Year	Wi	Sp	Su	Au
1735	4.1	3.7	6.1	9.3	12.3	15.5	16.5	17.7	15.4	8.2	5.5	4.8	9.9	3.4	9.2	16.6	9.7
1736	3.1	1.9	4.1	9.3	12.3	15.2	17.5	18.2	15.2	10.3	7.5	5.5	10.1	3.3	8.6	17.0	11.0
1737	6.0	4.5	5.6	8.2	13.3	15.8	16.6	14.6	15.3	9.7	5.7	2.7	9.8	5.3	9.0	15.7	10.2
1738	0.9	3.4	5.4	9.2	12.4	15.0	16.5	16.1	13.3	10.6	2.8	5.8	9.2	2.3	9.0	15.9	8.9
1739	3.1	6.0	5.7	6.1	13.2	14.8	17.0	15.6	14.0	7.7	0.9	3.7	9.0	5.0	8.3	15.8	7.5
1740	-4.5	-2.5	2.0	5.5	7.5	12.2	15.1	15.4	14.8	6.2	3.5	2.5	6.5	-1.1	5.0	14.2	8.2
1741	1.0	3.5	3.2	5.9	9.8	13.9	17.0	16.4	14.2	11.6	7.9	2.6	8.9	2.3	6.3	15.8	11.2
1742	-1.0	4.8	2.9	5.4	9.5	14.7	16.4	14.9	12.1	9.1	5.0	-2.4	7.6	2.1	5.9	15.3	8.7
1743	1.8	4.4	4.3	4.9	11.6	15.9	15.7	17.1	14.3	7.3	7.9	2.5	8.0	1.3	7.0	16.2	9.8
1744	-0.1	-0.4	3.5	7.2	11.2	14.8	15.8	15.3	13.7	10.7	6.4	3.1	8.4	0.7	7.3	15.3	10.3
1735-1944	1.1	2.4	4.4	7.9	12.1	15.1	16.7	16.5	14.1	9.8	5.3	2.5	9.0	2.0	8.1	16.1	9.7

SOURCE: Aart Labrijn, *Het klimaat van Nederland gedurende de laatste twee en een halve eeuw* (Schiedam, 1945), 89–93.

Table 8. Seasonal amounts of precipitation, Zwanenburg, Holland, 1735–1744 (in millimeters)

Year	Winter	Spring	Summer	Autumn	Year
1735	210	81	216	250	723
1736	185	81	163	259	741
1737	263	163	261	205	828
1738	107	134	316	197	734
1739	148	149	269	232	849
1740	106	135	112	267	598
1741	132	65	116	194	470
1742	75	61	220	239	566
1743	57	147	152	157	541
1744	43	137	110	329	629
1735–1944	153	130	219	230	742

SOURCE: Aart Labrijn, *Het klimaat van Nederland de laatste twee en een halve eeuw* (Schiedam, 1945), 95–99.

precipitation amounts from 1735 to 1744, shown in table 9, indicate the abrupt change in 1740. The rain that fell in the summer months (i.e., June, July, and August) of 1741 and 1742 was markedly deficient, amounting to 4.56 and 4.14 inches for the two years, respectively.

The time series shown in tables 5–9 do not of course fully document the sequence of extreme weather events and abnormal seasons in all regions of Europe. The surviving fragmentary data and impressionistic sources, however, indicate that like weather conditions predominated throughout western, central, and northern Europe. The sources also disclose the economic losses and human distress that ensued in the years from 1740 to 1743. A concise survey of the regions under study will demonstrate the nature of the climatic stress and its relative intensity from location to location.

The temperature and precipitation time series for England are fairly representative of the weather conditions that prevailed throughout the

Table 9. Annual precipitation in Kew, Surrey, 1735–1744 (in inches)

Year	Precipitation	Departure
1735	23.02	− 0.89
1736	25.17	+ 1.26
1737	26.56	+ 2.65
1738	26.61	+ 2.70
1739	30.73	+ 6.82
1740	20.82	− 3.09
1741	19.60	− 4.31
1742	19.08	− 4.83
1743	16.72	− 7.19
1744	25.57	+ 1.66

SOURCE: E. G. Wales-Smith, "Monthly and Annual Totals of Rainfall Representative of Kew, Surrey, from 1679 to 1970," *Meteorological Magazine* 100 (1971), 355–58.

British Isles. As table 6 shows, the change to below-normal temperatures began in the second half of 1739. This period was characterized by excessive rather than deficient precipitation. Measured rainfall at Kew accumulated to 16.17 inches during the last six months of 1739, an amount that approached the total of 20.82 inches that fell during all of 1740.[5] In East Anglia, a deep frost set in as early as November 5.[6] In the southwestern English county of Devonshire, a "rainy and cold September" resulted in "Great Quantaties of Corn" being "quite destroyed." October continued cold, with constant northeast winds.[7] The northern region of England passed through an excessively wet and frosty autumn, with damage to the cereal crops, there being "much Corn, and the greatest Part of Barley lost." But in the Midlands the grain harvests were completed before the bad weather became installed.[8] North Wales also encountered frosty autumn weather that reduced crop yields in 1739.[9] In Scotland, the grain harvests were delayed by the cold and wet weather in 1739 and yielded a relatively light crop.[10] On balance, Britain experienced wet, late harvests; the excessive rainfall and autumn storms caused considerable damage to cereal crops.[11] In Ireland, the weather conditions of the last half of 1739 proved somewhat worse. September turned out "very wet"; October was dry and cold; and November brought "rain, frost, and stormy" weather.[12] Although the potato crop escaped with little damage, the wet summer and autumn of 1739 reduced grain harvest yields.[13]

The meteorological time series for Holland are less representative of the weather conditions that prevailed on the Continent. Contrary to the satisfactory harvest outcomes elsewhere in western Europe, the provinces located to the west of Paris, in particular Maine, Touraine, and

5. E. G. Wales-Smith, "Monthly and Annual Totals of Rainfall Representative of Kew, Surrey, from 1697 to 1970," *Meteorological Magazine* 100 (1971), 358.

6. T. Southwell, "An Account of the Severe Winter of 1739–40 and of Its Effects in the County of Norfolk in the Year Following," *Norfolk and Norwich Naturalists Society, Transactions* 2 (1875), 125.

7. John Huxham, *Observations on the Air, and Epidemic Diseases from the Beginning of the Year 1738, to the End of the Year 1748*, trans. from Latin by John Corham Huxham, 2 vols. (London, 1759–67) II, 43–45.

8. Thomas Short, *A General Chronological History of the Air, Weather, Seasons, Meteors, etc.* (London, 1749), 252.

9. K. L. Gruffydd, "The Vale of Clwyd Corn Riots of 1740," *Flintshire Historical Society Publications* 27 (1975–76), 37.

10. Michael Flinn et al., *Scottish Population History* (Cambridge, 1977), 216.

11. E. L. Jones, *Seasons and Prices* (London, 1964), 137; J. M. Stratton, *Agricultural Records, A.D. 220–1968*, ed. Ralph Whitlock (London, 1969), 74.

12. John Rutty, M.D., *A Chronological History of the Weather and Seasons, and of the Prevailing Diseases in Dublin* (London, 1770), 74–76.

13. Michael Drake, "The Irish Demographic Crisis of 1740–41," *Historical Studies* 6 (1968), 106–107.

Anjou, suffered deficient cereal harvests in 1738. Grain yields also turned out somewhat deficient in the provinces of Berry and Poitou, to the south. Even central France experienced disappointing harvests, especially the Bourbonnais and Auvergne, whereas the Ile-de-France reported mostly average yields.[14] The combination of low spring and summer temperatures and excessive precipitation was responsible for the low grain yields in 1738. The provinces of northwestern France are dominated by maritime climatic patterns and as a consequence always run a higher risk of cool and damp summers. In 1739, all the provinces in the northern half of France experienced the same cold and wet autumn months that unfolded in the British Isles. Although the cereal crops in France were safely stored by October, the poor autumn weather set back the sowing of winter grains and led to reduced grain yields in 1740.[15]

The southern Netherlands and the German states encountered autumn weather patterns similar to those recorded in Holland. The Belgian region was struck by heavy rains that rendered it difficult to bring in the cereal crops.[16] The rivers in Germany were already frozen by the first of November. The early winter weather put an end to Baltic shipping at the end of October. Plowing and other critical agricultural routines could not be completed before the early frosts set in, so that the winter grain yields of 1740 were compromised.[17] In Switzerland, the cold and wet weather arrived during October.[18] In Sweden, according to Anders Celsius, the

14. Michel Bricourt, Marcel Lachiver, and Denis Queruel, "La Crise de subsistance des années 1740 dans le ressort du Parlement de Paris," *Annales de Démographie Historique* (1974), 284–87; Jean-Michel Desbordes, ed., *La Chronique villageoise de Varreddes (Seine-et-Marne): Un Document sur la vie rurale des XVIIe et XVIIIe siècles* (Paris, 1969), 24–25; François Lebrun, *Les Hommes et la mort en Anjou aux 17e et 18e siècles* (Paris, 1971), 138.

15. E. J.-F. Barbier, *Journal historique et anecdotique du règne de Louis XV,* 4 vols. (Paris, 1847–56), II, 254.

16. Etienne Hélin, "La Déroulement de trois crises à Liège au XVIIIe siècle," in Paul Harsin and Etienne Hélin, eds., *Problèmes de mortalité* (Liège, 1963), 490–91; G. van Houtte, *Leuven in 1740, ein krisisjaar: Ekonomische, sociale, en demografische aspekten* (Brussels, 1964), 11–21, 245.

17. Friedrich Samuel Bock, *Versuch einer wirtschaftlichen Naturgeschichte von dem Königreich Ost- und Westpreussen,* 5 vols. (Dessau, 1782–85), I, 766–68; Johann Christoph Becmann, *Historische Beschreibung der Chur und Mark Brandenburg,* ed. B. L. Bekmann, 2 vols. (Berlin, 1751–53), 541; Johann Christian Kundmann, *Die Heimsuchungen Gottes in Zorn und Gnade über das Herzogthum Schlesien in Müntzen* (Leipzig, 1742), 243; Heinrich C. F. Schenck, *Die Wunder Gottes im Winter* (Arnstadt, 1741), 18; Christian Heinrich Pfaff, *Über die strengen Winter, vorzüglich des 18. Jahrhunderts* (Kiel, 1809–10), 100; Curt Weikinn, *Quellentexte zur Witterungsgeschichte Europas,* 5 vols. (Berlin, 1958–67), IV, 243–45.

18. G. Walser, *Appenzeller-Chronik,* pt. 3 (*1732–1772*), ed. G. Nuesch (Trogen, 1830), 163–64; Anne-Marie Piuz, "Climat, récoltes, et vie des hommes à Genève, XVIe–XVIIIe siècles," *Annales: Economies, Sociétés, Civilisations* 29 (May–June 1974), 615; Christian Pfister, CLIMHIST data bank, 236. This last reference is drawn from a meteorological computer data bank, which Dr. Pfister has kindly made available, and which is scheduled for publication in 1985.

year 1739 concluded with four months of cool, cloudy, and wet weather.[19] The same unpropitious weather patterns dominated Norway as early as the summer months and reduced the grain yields.[20] In Finland, a snowstorm on the first day of autumn buried the unharvested rye in the large northern county of Österbotten and occasioned a severe harvest failure. Snow also covered the crops in the fields of southern Finland.[21] In sum, the cold and wet autumn of 1739 reduced the yields of the European cereal harvests to some degree and in addition set back the sowing of winter grains, which in turn resulted in lower harvest yields in 1740.

The arctic-like airflows arrived in central and western Europe during the first week of January (the last week of December 1739 in the British Isles, where the old calendar was still in force). The distress caused by the low atmospheric temperatures was compounded by a strong and bitter east wind that continued to blow at gale velocity for a week. The Marsham phenological journal indicates that *indoor* temperature readings fell below 30°F in East Anglia.[22] Thomas Short's indoor thermometer in Sheffield fell to 26°F; and in Rutland Thomas Barker's thermometer registered 23°F.[23] These three indoor readings were recorded in substantially built homes of the propertied classes. We can only speculate as to the temperatures that prevailed in the cottages, huts, and hovels of Europe's working population during the intense cold spells. Moreover, it is difficult to imagine the possible impact of indoor temperatures below the freezing point when we are told that temperatures no lower than 60°F can threaten the elderly, the undernourished, and the chronically ill with death from accident hypothermia. As for outdoor minimum temperatures in England, Gordon Manley has cited a single reading near zero degrees Fahrenheit.[24] It might be noted that Fahrenheit's mercury thermometer, which was perfected at Amsterdam in 1714, supposedly adopted the benchmark of zero because nature never produced readings below that point.

Temperatures moderated in England after the first great easterly storm passed, but successive cold waves brought abnormally low readings for a

19. M. de Réaumur, "Observations du thermomètre faites en 1740," *Histoire de l'Académie royale des sciences* (Paris, 1742), 564–66.

20. Arthur E. Imhof, *Aspekte der Bevölkerungsentwicklung in den nordischen Ländern, 1720–1750* (Bern, 1976), 727.

21. Eino Jutikkala, *Die Bevölkerung Finnlands in den Jahren 1721–1749* (Helsinki, 1945), 39.

22. Southwell, "Severe Winter," 125.

23. Gordon Manley, "The Great Winter of 1740," *Weather* 13 (1958), 13–14.

24. Ibid., 14–15.

period of more than eleven weeks. The ice on Norfolk ponds remained thick enough for skating from Christmas 1739 to March 2, 1740, or for sixty-nine consecutive days.[25] The low temperatures and high winds created economic disruption as well as personal hardship. At London, where shipping constituted a major source of income and employment, the combination of wind, tide, and ice drove hundreds of lighters, barges, and boats from their fastenings in the Thames River. Ships at sea were driven to shore and smashed to pieces. All navigation became obstructed at the end of December and remained so until the end of February.[26] The interruption of London's coal shipments proved a social calamity, since coal was the principal fuel used for home heating. Deaths from exposure and accident hypothermia multiplied in England through the winter months, the result of both the shortage of fuel and the inadequacies of the welfare system. The vagrants and the destitute who died in the streets of London and other English towns during the frigid winter of 1740 were for the most part adults who did not belong to the urban parishes and thus found themselves outside the regular welfare system. The press focused public attention on the defects of the parish relief organization in failing to meet the emergency welfare needs. "Such Swarms of miserable Objects as now fill our Streets are shocking to behold; many of these having no legal Settlements, have no Relief from the Parish; but yet our fellow Creatures are not to be starved to Death; yet how are they drove about by inhuman Wretches from Parish to Parish, without any Support."[27] London's welfare crisis was eventually eased after the Thames became free of ice and employment opportunities returned.[28]

All regions of England suffered human and economic losses from the winter weather of 1740. At Plymouth in Devonshire, where the climate is invariably more moderate than the eastern counties, John Huxham noted on December 31, "Coldest Day in the Memory of Man." His meteorological observations indicate the dominance of high atmospheric pressure and easterly winds throughout March, suggestive of the persistent influence of blocking anticyclones.[29] Manley believes that the cold winter of 1740 has never been surpassed in Devonshire. Myrtles and less hardy trees were killed to the roots at Penzance, in Cornwall,[30] where

25. Southwell, "Severe Winter," 125–26.
26. *Gentleman's Magazine* 10 (January 1740), 34–35; *London Daily Post,* March 1, 1740.
27. *London Advertiser,* February 15, 1739/40; also see *London Daily Post,* January 5 and January 8, 1740; *London Advertiser,* January 3 and January 8, 1739/40.
28. *London Daily Post,* March 1, 1740; *London Advertiser,* February 19, 1739/40.
29. Huxham, *Observations,* II, 48–54.
30. Manley, "Great Winter," 14.

travelers today are surprised to find palm trees flourishing. In northwestern England, William Stout of Lancashire wrote, all living creatures suffered from the frost. "Sheep starved, the ground being covered with frozen snow a month together," and "Many trades men frozen out of their trades and imploy, and starved for want of fire; Coles and turfe being at double prices."[31] Accounts originating in the Midlands related similar hardships. According to Thomas Short, "The great Frost began December 25, and continued eight Weeks with some Relents, but was not out of the Earth before June '40."[32] But his summary statement of human casualties seems more pessimistic than the weight of the evidence warrants: "Multitudes of poor people were lost, both in Houses and Fields by the Severity of the Cold. Many horses and much cattle were lost. Great was the Misery and Necessity of the Poor."[33] Accounts less somber in tone can be multipled for all regions of England.[34] The suffering endured by the unemployed poor called for and elicited emergency municipal campaigns to collect funds for those unable to cope with the "climatic shock," and the success of those measures reduced the potential number of deaths.[35]

Scotland, unlike England, was buffeted by large amounts of snowfall as well as by low temperatures and high winds. The snowstorms, however, proved a mixed calamity, for an added grim feature of the winter of 1740 was the lack of a protective snow cover for the winter grains over most of western Europe. The January snowstorms in Scotland produced drifts twenty-four feet high in some districts of the eastern lowlands.[36] Heavy snowfalls in eastern Scotland are consistent with a weather map that shows an anticyclone extending from Scandinavia over Scotland. The blocking high-pressure cells would in such a case force the Atlantic depressions to follow a more southerly course, resulting in a cold easterly airstream and frequent snowfalls along the eastern region of

31. *Autobiography of William Stout of Lancaster, 1665–1752,* ed. J. D. Marshall (Manchester, 1967), 227–28.

32. Thomas Short, *A Comparative History of the Increase and Decrease of Mankind in England and Several Countries Abroad* (York, 1767), 93.

33. Short, *Chronological History,* 255; also see Short, *New Observations on City, Town, and Country Bills of Mortality* (London, 1750), 344.

34. For Kent and Essex, see *London Daily Post,* January 4, 1740; for Cumberland, see ibid., January 10, 1740; Manley, "Great Winter," 15; for Salisbury, see *London Advertiser,* January 18, 1739/40; for Bristol, see *London Daily Post,* January 29, 1740; for Gloucester, see ibid., January 24, 1740; and for other locations, see *London Advertiser,* February 21, 1739/40; *London Daily Post,* February 7, 1740.

35. See *London Advertiser,* January 18, January 22, and February 21, 1739/40; *London Daily Post,* January 24, January 29, February 7, and February 28, 1740.

36. Ebeneezer Henderson, ed., *The Annals of Dunfermline* (Glasgow, 1879), 434.

Britain.[37] The combination of intense winter cold and successive snow-storms stilled most Scottish economic activity by mid-January, shutting down mills and interfering with the delivery of coal. The Edinburgh press reported "the most bitter frost ever known (or perhaps recorded) in this part of the World, a piercing Nova Zembla Air, so that poor Tradesmen could not work . . . ; so that the Price of Meal, etc. is risen as well as that of Coals."[38] An indoor temperature reading of 20°F was recorded at Aberdeen on January 18.[39] The chilling cold waves that blanketed Scotland created a shortage of food and water for livestock, which perished in large numbers.[40] If western Scotland escaped the full brunt of the wintry blasts from the east, this region nonetheless witnessed a critical shortage of food and also was plagued by an unusually large number of vagrants roving through the countryside.[41]

In Ireland, where a mortality crisis unfolded during 1740, the winter was somewhat less severe than in Britain. Dr. John Rutty recorded the onset of the frigid easterly airstream on December 27, "intolerably piercing at S.E. and E."[42] The Dublin press reported that the severe frost "continued for 7 weeks almost without a break."[43] At Cork, the river Lee "was frozen up towards the end of the year, by the hardest frost in the memory of man, after which a great scarcity followed."[44] As in England, droughtlike conditions dominated in Ireland, particularly in the southern counties. Measured precipitation at Cork amounted to slightly more than 21 inches in 1740, in contrast to 54 inches in both 1738 and 1739.[45] The intense frost curtailed employment in most trades, and the price of coal rose sharply in Dublin.[46] The cold and dry weather continued into the spring months.[47] The extended period of frost led to the

37. D. D. Kemp, "Winter Weather in West Fife in the Eighteenth Century," *Weather* 31 (December 1976), 402–403.

38. *Caledonian Mercury*, January 17, 1740.

39. M. G. Pearson, "The Winter of 1739/40 in Scotland," *Weather* 28 (January 1973), 20–24.

40. *Caledonian Mercury*, January 21, 1740.

41. Sir John Sinclair, *The Statistical Account of Scotland*, 21 vols. (Edinburgh, 1791–98), IV, 39, 300; VI, 29, 252; *Caledonian Mercury*, February 25, 1740; *London Daily Post*, December 19, 1740.

42. Rutty, *Chronological History*, 77.

43. *Faulkner's Dublin Journal*, January 8–12, January 22–26, and February 5–9, 1740.

44. Charles Smith, *The Antient and Present State of the County and City of Cork*, 2 vols. (Dublin, 1750), II, 229.

45. Ibid., 398.

46. *Faulkner's Dublin Journal*, January 5–8, January 8–12, and January 19–22, 1740; *London Advertiser*, January 9 and January 15, 1739/40; Drake, "Demographic Crisis," 103–105.

47. Rutty, *Chronological History*, 77–80.

death of "a vast number of sheep," which perished "for want of fodder."[48] But the most fateful consequence of the deep frost proved to be the destruction of the potato crop. The practice had become customary either to leave the potatoes undug or to store them in shallow pits until the Christmas season. A few inches of soil, however, afforded little protection against the intense frost that set in at the end of December. The bulk of the potato harvest was said to have been destroyed in a single night.[49]

The winter weather on the Continent north of the Alps closely paralleled the patterns of the British Isles and can be documented in less detail. The winter cold of 1740 prompted comparisons with the famous arctic winter of 1709. René de Réaumur, whose thermometer was now in wide use, believed that "the name of the great winter has become appropriate to 1709, the one of the long winter is deservedly due to 1740."[50] This generalization was valid for France (especially the southern half), Italy, and the Mediterranean lands, but the evidence clearly shows that the winter of 1740 was colder in the British Isles, Scandinavia, the Baltic region, the Low Countries, and Germany. Théodore Augustin Mann's compilation of the minimum temperatures recorded in 1740 indicates that readings fell to $-2°F$ in the Low Countries, $-10°F$ in Germany, $-18°F$ at Uppsala, and $-26°F$ at Warsaw. At the same time, the lowest temperature recorded at Venice was 3°F, and at Montpellier, in southern France, the temperature did not fall below a relatively balmy 29°F.[51] In the winter of 1740, unlike that of 1709, neither the lagoons in Venice nor the shores of the Mediterranean froze over. Christian Heinrich Pfaff's investigation of severe European winters concluded that the intensity of the cold had been greater in 1740 than in 1709 in the regions that included Sweden, Britain, Poland, Holland, Prussia, and the remaining German states.[52]

Even in France, according to Réaumur, the winter of 1740 brought the longest uninterrupted cold season in memory.[53] From October 1739 to March 1740, a total of seventy-five days of frost was recorded at Paris.[54]

48. *London Advertiser,* March 4, 1739/40.

49. Drake, "Demographic Crisis," 106–107; *Faulkner's Dublin Journal,* January 8–12 and January 12–15, 1740.

50. Réaumur, "Observations," 539.

51. Théodore Augustin Mann, *Mémoires sur les grandes gelées et leur effets* (Ghent, 1792), 71.

52. Pfaff, *Über die strengen Winter,* 106 and end tables.

53. Réaumur, "Observations," 539.

54. *Mercure de France,* February 1740, 379; Fr. Arago, *Oeuvres,* 17 vols. (Paris, 1858), VIII, 286.

By March, the long winter in Paris had created "a great dearth of all provisions."[55] At nearby Varreddes, the land did not thaw until March 9, and the frost "caused illnesses as much in this country as the great amount elsewhere and from which a great many people died."[56] The winter in Burgundy has been described as "cruel from mid-December to the end of May; the cold killed a third of Volnay's vines."[57] To the east in Lorraine, the ice on the Moselle River reached "up to 27 inches thick," and the temperature fell lower by "a degree than in 1709," but the snow that fell earlier "preserved the crops."[58] In the provinces west of Paris, the frost "still made itself felt up to the end of May, so that no hope was seen for the winter grains."[59] The grain fields of northwestern France lacked the snow cover that was more common in northeastern France.

The winter season in the Low Countries was more severe than in France. At Haarlem, Nicolaas Duyn counted sixty-seven days on which the temperature fell below freezing, compared with sixty-one days during the winter of 1708–1709. On January 11, his thermometer registered a low of $-2°F$ at the morning reading, $0°F$ at midday, and a daily mean of $6°F$; a strong northeast wind blew for the duration of the cold spell. The Dutch Republic received little snow cover in 1740, in marked contrast to the heavy snowfalls of 1709.[60] The Zeider Zee froze over completely. The Haarlem-Leiden canal was frozen a total of eighty days during the winter of 1739–1740, whereas not a single day of freezing had occurred during the winter of 1738–1739. The winter of 1740 put an end to a consecutive series of thirty-one years during which even moderately severe winters in Holland had been rare. Afterward, the winters of both 1741 and 1742 proved colder than normal, particularly the latter, when the canal remained frozen for twenty-seven days.[61] The Belgian region of the Netherlands endured nine weeks of frost, followed by cold spring months. Flanders, unlike Hainaut and Lorraine, received little snow cover. But even where the fields were covered with snow

55. Barbier, *Journal*, II, 254.
56. Desbordes, *Chronique*, 25.
57. P. de Saint-Jacob, *Les Paysans de la Bourgogne du nord au dernier siècle de l'ancien régime* (Dijon, 1960), 295.
58. Jacques Baltus, *Annales de Baltus (1724–1756)*, ed. Abbé E. Paulus (Metz, 1904), 94.
59. Quoted in Lebrun, *Anjou*, 138.
60. Nicolaas Duyn, *Historische aanmerkingen van drie strenge winters (1709, 1740, 1742)* (Haarlem, 1746), 6–13, 81, 180; for a similar account, see J. H. Hering, *Tafereel van harde winters* (Amsterdam, 1784), 88–93.
61. Jan de Vries, "Histoire du climat et économie: Des faits nouveaux, une interprétation différente," *Annales: Economies, Sociétés, Civilisations* 32 (March–April 1977), 199–201, 222.

until May, "the inopportune weather with now thaw, now rain, now snow, now frost, had caused most of the harvest to be spoiled."[62]

The intense cold spell that gripped Germany during January 1740 resulted in some deaths from exposure hypothermia and led to a large number of deaths among farm animals.[63] The populations of Berlin, Wittenberg, Weimar, Göttingen, and Danzig all complained of piercing northeast winds.[64] The frost lasted almost without respite until mid-March, and a cold spring season with nighttime frosts followed.[65] In the Habsburg monarchy, the low temperatures and harsh winds led to enormous animal losses, primarily from a shortage of fodder. Reportedly, some million head of sheep perished in Bohemia; while "forage is so scarce in Hungary, that it has occasion'd a great Mortality among the Cattle."[66] The winter of 1739–1740 was less severe in Switzerland except for the month of February, which was as frigid as in Germany.[67] In the northern half of the Italian peninsula, the weather patterns were similar to those in Switzerland, with February a colder month than January. Temperature readings at Pavia fell below the freezing point every day in February, with a low of 3°F. But the harshness of the winter season in Italy derived more from the duration than from the intensity of the cold.[68]

In the Scandinavian region, the months of January and May 1740 were the most severe, measured by the negative departures from normal mean temperatures. After May, all monthly mean temperatures remained below normal for the balance of the year.[69] Anders Celsius wrote that February was colder than January, but he communicated identical low temperature

62. Quoted in T. Bernier, "Notice sur l'origine et la tenue des anciens registres d'état civil dans la province de Hainaut," *Mémoires de la Société des sciences, des arts, et des lettres du Hainaut,* 4th ser., 9 (1887), 567–68; see also Emile Vanderlinden, "Chronique des événements météorologiques en Belgique jusqu'en 1834," *Mémoires de l'Académie royale de Belgique, Classe des Sciences,* 2d ser., 6 (1924), 187–88.

63. Kundmann, *Schlesien,* 246; Vincent P. Sonderland, *Die Geschichte von Barmen im Wupperthale* (Elberfeld, 1821), 80; Becmann, *Chur und Brandenburg,* I, 542; Bock, *Ost- und Westpreussen,* I, 769–70.

64. Pfaff, *Über die strengen Winter,* 90–101.

65. Schenck, *Winter,* 20, 58; Bock, *Ost- und Westpreussen,* I, 777–80; Kundmann, *Schlesien,* 246–47; Becmann, *Chur und Brandenburg,* I, 554.

66. *London Advertiser,* May 7, 1740; see also Schenck, *Winter,* 31–32, 42, 58; Bock, *Ost- und Westpreussen,* I, 793; Kundmann, *Schlesien,* 274.

67. Pfister, CLIMHIST data bank, 237–38; Walser, *Appenzeller-Chronik,* 163–66; Piuz, "Climat," 615–16; Christoph Trümpi, *Neuere Glarner Chronik* (Winterthur, 1774), 559.

68. Alfonso Corradi, *Annali delle epidemie occorse in Italia dalle prime memorie fino al 1850,* 8 vols. (Bologna, 1865–94), IV, 1,402; Giuseppe Ferrario, *Statistica medica di Milano dal secolo XV fino ai nostri giorni,* 2 vols. (Milan, 1838–50), II, 129, 137, 143; Pfaff, *Über die strengen Winter,* 99–100.

69. Rudloff, *Schwankungen,* 112.

readings of $-9°F$ for both months. It is clear, however, that the Uppsala-Stockholm district experienced fourteen consecutive weeks of frost during the cold season of 1739–1740, with bitter easterly winds dominating into the spring months, and that temperatures again fell below the freezing point as early as September 6.[70] The entire Baltic region suffered from the winter cold more than in 1709. In Sweden, hundreds of persons froze to death, as apparently did considerably more horses.[71] The Denmark Sound froze as solidly in 1740 as in the celebrated frost of 1658; sleds passed from Elsinore to Sweden in February. The Baltic Sea between Stockholm and Abo, in Finland, also froze over. The winter season was nearly as severe in Norway as in Sweden and Finland.[72]

To sum up, the abnormally low winter temperatures of 1740 brought most industrial and commercial activity to a standstill for extended periods of time in northwestern Europe and as a consequence propelled unemployment rates in urban locations to elevated levels. Because of the inadequate public welfare systems of the 1740s, the diminished employment opportunities and the climatic shocks created considerable distress, resulting in the death of an undetermined number of persons from exposure and accident hypothermia. In the agricultural sector, the extreme weather events and the shortage of fodder led to the death or slaughtering of millions of sheep, cattle, and horses. The decline in the livestock population not only represented a loss of real capital and wealth for the economy but also meant ruin for some farmers and peasants. The reduction in the number of farm animals, together with the damaging low atmospheric temperatures, prejudiced the grain harvest yields in 1740 and beyond. Although the moderating temperatures of the spring months eased the distress of the human population, the stress on domestic animals and the threat to growing crops continued as long as precipitation and temperatures remained significantly below normal.

An extended period of cool and dry spring–summer weather in Europe deepened the shortage of fodder and heightened concern for the success of the cereal harvests. In the British Isles, the spring season was both abnormally cold and drought-ridden. The Marsham phenological time series in East Anglia shows that spring warmth arrived at its latest

---

70. Réaumur, "Observations," 564–66; Pfaff, *Über die strengen Winter,* 89–90, end tables; Mann, *Mémoires,* 71.

71. Schenck, *Winter,* 26–27; Réaumur, "Observations," 566; Pfaff, *Über die strengen Winter,* 100.

72. *London Daily Post,* February 16, 1740; Réaumur, "Observations," 566; Pfaff, *Über die strengen Winter,* 100–101; Imhof, *Bevölkerungsentwicklung in den nordischen Ländern,* 727, 732; Jutikkala, *Bevölkerung Finnlands,* 39; Weikinn, *Witterungsgeschichte,* IV, 246–48.

date in 1740.[73] The wind direction settled in east and northeast "and continued so with little change till the middle of June; the Weather, especially at Night, very cold all the while, and little or no rain."[74] Cold northeast winds were common throughout the months of April and May. Snow fell in London as late as May 17; and a heavy frost struck northern Yorkshire on May 30.[75] The drought continued through the month of June in Britain, with southwestern England experiencing the driest conditions. According to John Huxham, "the Springs were quite shut up, and even Rivers became intirely dry."[76] In the Midlands, Short recorded that the "cold continued till June 21, a few Days excepted. June and July colder than ordinary. A great Drought till August."[77] In Scotland, the planting of spring crops was delayed because the earth remained "hard frozen till far in April. And the frost continued in the air till well in summer."[78] A tendency to drought dominated Scotland throughout the first half of 1740.[79] In Ireland, Dr. Rutty wrote that spring was "six weeks more backward than usual," with a persistent disposition to drought.[80] By May, the damage to pasture and growing crops was in part irreparable: "Grass and Corn were all burnt up, and the Fields looked as red as Foxes."[81] By the end of May 1740, "a great Mortality amongst the Cattle" had already taken place, and "many thousands of Families" found themselves "in the utmost Distress."[82]

The mid-summer months brought the return of more normal temperatures and timely precipitation. Although harvest outcomes varied in the British Isles, the late-summer weather removed the threat of drastically deficient grain harvests in Britain.[83] In southwestern England, however,

73. J. A. Kington, "An Application of Phenological Data to Historical Climatology," *Weather* 29 (September 1974), 326–27. The record shows that the flowering dates of the hawthorn have varied over a range of 55 days extending from April 16 (day 106), 1779, to June 8 (day 160), 1740. Over the entire series, the average date of that flowering event fell on May 12, the 132d day of the year. For a comprehensive understanding of phenological principles, see Helmut Lieth, ed., *Phenology and Seasonality Modelling* (New York, 1974).

74. Southwell, "Severe Winter," 128.

75. Stratton, *Agricultural Records*, 74.

76. Huxham, *Observations*, II, 56–60.

77. Short, *Comparative History*, 94; for a similar account, see Short, *Chronological History*, II, 256.

78. A. Allardyce, ed., *Scotland and Scotsmen in the Eighteenth Century from the MSS of John Ramsay of Ochtertyre*, 2 vols. (Edinburgh, 1888), II, 211–12; also see, William Kennedy, ed., *Annals of Aberdeen* (Edinburgh, 1818), 291.

79. *Caledonian Mercury*, April 21, 1740; *Scots Magazine*, May 1740, 237, P.S. dated June 12.

80. Rutty, *Chronological History*, 80; *Faulkner's Dublin Journal*, April 22–26, 1740.

81. *London Advertiser*, May 24, 1740.

82. *London Advertiser*, May 29, 1740; also see *Faulkner's Dublin Journal*, May 3–6, May 31–June 5, and June 21–24, 1740; Drake, "Demographic Crisis," 113.

83. Manley, "Great Winter," 16; Stratton, *Agricultural Records*, 74; Jones, *Seasons*, 137.

the dry conditions changed to excessive precipitation, which "occasioned a very bad Harvest, spoiled almost all the Corn."[84] Crop yields also proved deficient in Scotland, but not to the degree experienced in Devonshire.[85] In Ireland, where a subsistence crisis had already become a reality early in 1740, the wet weather pattern that set in at the end of August and lasted through the first half of September occasioned the same poor harvests as in southwestern England.[86]

On the Continent, the cool, dry spring months in conjunction with the wet late-summer months both delayed the harvests and reduced grain yields. The period from March to May in northern France brought a succession of frosts and thaws that may have compromised the harvest outcomes more than the extreme winter cold spells.[87] In the Paris region, "the rye did not come into ear at mid-May and as far as the wheat was concerned ears appeared only on June 15, and the harvest was made very late."[88] The weather changed for the worse at the beginning of the harvest period.[89] Cold and wet weather prevailed in northern France during the first week of August; frost and ice were noted as early as August 3 in much of the region.[90] Beginning on August 11, an almost unbroken period of cold rain lashed the provinces of northern France for thirteen consecutive days.[91] Although the grape harvests were irreparably damaged, the cereal yields turned out less deficient than was anticipated, particularly in the case of the barley crop.[92] Nonetheless, in September 1740 the Paris administration began to take steps to counter a developing dearth.[93] In the Low Countries, the drought was absolute until July. The trees in Belgium were still not in full leaf as late as June. The harvests were begun only at the end of August and could not be completed until

84. Huxham, *Observations,* II, 82–84.

85. *Caledonian Mercury,* June 30, 1740, August 22, 1740; Allardyce, *Scotland,* II, 212.

86. Rutty, *Chronological History,* 81–82.

87. Bricourt et al., "Crise," 306–308; Réaumur, "Observations," 549–52; M. Maraldi, "Observations météorologiques faits à l'Observatoire royal pendant l'année 1740," in *Histoire de l'Académie royale des sciences* (Paris, 1742), 613; Barbier, *Journal,* II, 256.

88. Desbordes, *Chronique,* 25–26.

89. Réaumur, "Observations," 552–53.

90. Pierre de Narbonne, *Journal des règnes de Louis XIV et Louis XV de l'année 1701 à l'année 1744 par P. Narbonne, premier commissaire de police de la ville de Versailles,* ed. J.-A. Le Roi (Versailles, 1866), 476; Bricourt, Lachiver, and Queruel, "Crise," 308; Réaumur, "Observations," 553; M. du Hamel, "Observations botanico-météorologiques pour l'année 1740," in *Histoire de l'Académie royale des sciences* (Paris, 1744), 164.

91. Bricourt et al., "Crise," 308; Narbonne, *Journal,* 476; Réaumur, "Observations," 553.

92. Réaumur, "Observations," 554; Narbonne, *Journal,* 477, 483; Desbordes, *Chronique,* 26; Baltus, *Annales,* 94–95; Lebrun, *Anjou,* 138.

93. Barbier, *Journal,* II, 261–62; *London Advertiser,* September 18, 1740; Bricourt, Lachiver, and Queruel, "Crise," 312–17.

October. On October 9, a severe frost destroyed the grapes and other late fruits. A small number of poor people had already been forced to fall back on eating nettles as a substitute for vegetables.[94]

The spring months in the German states also remained colder than normal, with the prevailing winds blowing from the north and northeast. At the beginning of May, the ground was still frozen and the pastures were still not green. Frosts in May damaged the winter grains and the garden vegetables. From August to the first week in October the weather turned cold and wet. The vintage was ruined and grain yields fell off.[95] In several Swiss cantons, the prolonged snow cover damaged the grape vines and created a shortage of hay and fodder. A biting northeast wind called the *Bise* dominated the spring weather. A dearth of bread grains developed in the eastern cantons, where mills were brought to a halt by frozen rivers. But in the majority of the Swiss cantons the months of May and June were warm, with normal amounts of precipitation. In Switzerland as elsewhere, however, the weather turned cold and wet during August and delayed all harvests.[96] Spring in Italy likewise proved colder than normal, and the summer months remained cool. But the weather patterns caused less agricultural damage in Italy than in northwestern Europe.[97]

In Sweden, by contrast, the backward spring season created a shortage of food and fodder in several counties. The extremely cold spring of 1740 is reflected in the ice-melting dates of the Mälarsee, a large lake near Stockholm. This time series also discloses the change of the Scandinavian climatic regime from moderate winters during the 1720s and 1730s to prolonged cold seasons in the 1740s. In the 1720s, the average ice-melting date of the Mälarsee fell on April 14. In the 1730s, the average date was April 16; but in the 1740s, on average, the ice did not melt until May 2. In 1740, the ice did not break up until May 10, the latest date ever recorded. Spring in Sweden was, on balance, extraordinarily dry. At the same time, several southeastern counties experienced excessively wet spring weather. In the southwestern region, the grain harvests were ruined by cold summer rains. In almost all counties, the

94. Vanderlinden, "Chronique," 187–88; Hélin, "Crises à Liège," 491; Houtte, *Leuven,* 11–21; Bernier, "Hainaut," 567–68.

95. Schenck, *Winter,* 20, 58; Bock, *Ost- und Westpreussen,* I, 781–83; Kundmann, *Schlesien,* 248–52; Karl Müller, *Geschichte des badischen Weinbaus,* 2d ed. (Lahr, 1953), 210.

96. Pfister, CLIMHIST data bank, 238–42; Trümpi, *Neuere Glarner Chronik,* 560–62; Piuz, "Climat," 616; Walser, *Appenzeller-Chronik,* 166–69; Jurg Bielmann, *Die Lebensverhältnisse im Urnerland während des 18. und zu Beginn des 19. Jahrhundert* (Basel, 1972), 79; Hans-Rudolf Burri, *Die Bevölkerung Luzerns im 18. und frühen 19. Jahrhundert* (Luzern, 1975), 78; Christian Pfister, "Central European Thermal and Wetness Indices for Spring and Summer from 1525 to 1825," *Journal of Interdisciplinary History* 9 (Autumn 1978), 9–13.

97. Corradi, *Annali,* IV, 1,402.

anomalous spring and summer weather destroyed the hay crop. Moreover, the summer season was tryingly short in every region of Scandinavia. As a consequence of the unfavorable weather patterns of 1740, the grain harvest yields were reduced almost everywhere in Scandinavia.[98] In summary, the combination of cool, dry spring and summer seasons and excessively wet periods from August to October damaged the European grain, grape, and hay crops, resulting in elevated cereal prices and, in some regions, a shortage of food and fodder.

The frosty and wet autumn and early winter of 1740–1741 produced another extended period of climatic stress. In the British Isles, the autumn of 1740 was probably the coldest in two centuries.[99] According to Thomas Short, the time from August 20 to December 27 "was one continued Shift of Rains and Frost."[100] The autumn was intemperately cold and wet in every region of England.[101] The excessive precipitation is documented by the 7.32 inches measured at Kew for the combined months of November and December.[102] Temperature readings remained considerably below normal during November, December, and January.[103] Some English districts suffered hardship from heavy precipitation and inundations, while frost and ice caused the chief damage elsewhere. The Newcastle district, in the northeast, for example, was struck by a deep frost in mid-December, which froze over the major rivers and led to a shortage of food and fodder.[104] Floods caused most of the distress in the east Midlands, as was also the case on the Continent. According to Short, "the great Floods in Russia, Sweden, Denmark, Germany, France, and Britain, did prodigious Mischief; these Countries were greater Sufferers by the Last, than by the great Frost."[105] Scotland witnessed similar early autumn frosts, with large amounts of snowfall. In the second week of October, "the Snow was upwards of a foot deep, in so much that it was not possible for the Reapers to cut down the standing Corn."[106] The autumn also brought "excessive rains in harvest," which "did material damage" to the grain crops in Scotland.[107] At the end of December, a destructive snowstorm swept through northern Scotland,

98. Imhof, *Bevölkerungsentwicklung in den nordischen Ländern,* 136, 727–28.
99. Manley, "Great Winter," 16.
100. Short, *Chronological History,* II, 257–28.
101. Huxham, *Observations,* II, 85; Stratton, *Agricultural Records,* 74; Short, *New Obervations,* 345.
102. Wales-Smith, "Rainfall," 358.
103. Manley, "Central England Temperatures," 394, 398; see table 6.
104. *London Daily Post,* December 25, 1740.
105. Short, *Chronological History,* 257–63; also see Huxham, *Observations,* II, 86–90; *London Daily Post,* February 18 and March 25, 1741.
106. *London Advertiser,* October 14, 1740.
107. Allardyce, *Scotland,* II, 212.

leaving snow drifts of ten feet or more, and occasioned the death of "a vast Number of Cattle."[108] The severity of the winter of 1740–1741 was perceived to be "not many degrees milder than the preceding one."[109] Food riots became endemic in Scotland at the end of the winter.[110] In Ireland, the autumn months were punctuated by frequent frosts, snow and sleet.[111] A foot of snow fell in central Ireland on December 13, 1740.[112] Bread riots had broken out in Dublin as early as May 1740, and by January 1741 the shortage of food coincided with epidemics of dysentery and fevers.[113]

On the Continent, the excessive precipitation that fell in the autumn months of 1740 caused widespread flooding in December and January. In France a week of constant rain during early December triggered inundations that swamped arable fields, drowned livestock, swept away mills, and flooded parts of Paris and other major towns. The Seine's high water marks exceeded by eleven inches the record set in the floods of 1711.[114] "All the country from Tours as far as Nantes," as well as "all the country" that the Rhone and Saone rivers "run through," was drowned.[115] In Grenoble, the floods left the wells contaminated with "a black Slime," which raised fears of "epidemical Distempers."[116] The inundations were responsible for "an infinite number of individuals suffering immense property losses."[117] The floodwaters in France finally receded in February 1741. The balance of the winter was cold and brisk.[118] In the Low Countries as well, "the rain and snow did not cease the entire month of December which caused the greatest inundations."[119] The heavy precipitation that fell during the last three months of 1740 led to the rising and the overflowing of the large rivers. Dikes broke in Holland, where entire districts were under water. The floodwaters invaded the towns of Holland and Gelderland; Arnheim and Nimegan were

108. *London Daily Post,* December 30, 1740.

109. Allardyce, *Scotland,* II, 212.

110. *London Daily Post,* March 31, 1741; see also *Caledonian Mercury,* October 30, 1740, and March 17, 1741.

111. Rutty, *Chronological History,* 82; *Faulkner's Dublin Journal,* October 25–28, 1740; Drake, "Demographic Crisis," 112.

112. *London Daily Post,* December 23, 1740.

113. *Faulkner's Dublin Journal,* May 31–June 3, 1740; *London Advertiser,* January 24, 1740/41.

114. Narbonne, *Journal,* 486; Barbier, *Journal,* II, 278–80; *Mercure de France,* December 1740, 2,950; Réaumur, "Observations," 554–55; Bricourt et al., "Crise," 321–22.

115. See letters from Paris in *London Daily Post,* January 7, 1741.

116. *London Daily Post,* February 13, 1741.

117. *Mercure de France,* December 1740, 2,952.

118. Barbier, *Journal,* II, 286; Desbordes, *Chronique,* 26; Bricourt et al., "Crise," 322–23.

119. Vanderlinden, "Chronique," 187–88; Hélin, "Crises à Liège," 491; Houtte, *Leuven,* 11–21.

totally inundated.[120] The rising of the Meuse and Sambre rivers in Belgium flooded the town of Namur. The overflowing of the Meuse also inundated Liège, where dikes, bridges, and mill leets were carried away. As in the previous winter, the subfreezing temperatures paralyzed the mills.[121]

The same weather patterns predominated in the German states during the last three months of 1740. The excessive precipitation brought about widespread flooding in December and January.[122] In the Swiss cantons, Geneva, St. Blaise, St. Gall, Appenzell, Basel and Winterthur all reported frost damage to the grapevines in October. The weather in November turned raw, cold, and snowy.[123] The heavy precipitation of December caused floods in the towns of Zürich and Geneva and created extensive damage in the canton of Appenzell. Measured precipitation at Zürich accumulated to 300mm for the months of December and January, in contrast to a combined mean of 126mm.[124] The months of December and January also brought heavy precipitation to Italy, with rising river levels and floods. Florence was especially hard hit, while the overflowing of the Tiber damaged the countryside surround Rome.[125] In Scandinavia, excessive precipitation is the southern counties of Sweden inflicted additional damage to the cereal crops. The early and long winter of 1740–1741 drove food prices still higher in both Sweden and Norway.[126]

By spring 1741, the succession of extreme weather events had driven up food prices everywhere in western, central, and northern Europe (which will be discussed in a later chapter), and authentic subsistence crises predominated in most regions. The suffering of the working population was compounded by the hardships created by climatic stress. Short summed up the conditions prevailing in England: "Miserable was

120. Louis Torfs, *Fastes des calamités publiques survenues dans les Pays-Bas*, 2 vols. (Paris, 1859–62), I, 316; *London Daily Post*, January 2, 1741; *London Advertiser*, January 12, 1741; for a comprehensive summary of the pan-European floods of 1740, see *Gentleman's Magazine* 10 (1740), 621; for an exhaustive account of the flooding and freezing of European rivers during 1740–41, see Weikinn, *Witterungsgeschichte*, IV, 243–68.

121. Hélin, "Crises à Liège," 491; Vanderlinden, "Chronique," 188; Bernier, "Hainaut," 568.

122. Bock, *Ost- und Westpreussen*, I, 784–87; Kundmann, *Schlesien*, 252–55; Müller, *Weinbaus*, 210; Weikinn, *Witterungsgeschichte*, IV, 251–52; *London Advertiser*, December 27, 1740 and January 2, 1741.

123. Pfister, CLIMHIST data bank, 241–42; Piuz, "Climat," 615; Walser, *Appenzeller-Chronik*, 167–68; Trümpi, *Neuere Glarner Chronik*, 562.

124. Pfister, CLIMHIST data bank, 242–43; Trümpi, *Neuere Glarner Chronik*, 562–63; Walser, *Appenzeller-Chronik*, 171.

125. Corradi, *Annali*, IV, 1,402; Giovanni Targioni-Tozzetti, *Lettera* (Florence, 1741), 5–6; *London Daily Post*, January 7, 1741.

126. Imhof, *Bevölkerungsentwicklung in den nordischen Ländern*, 728–40; Réaumur, "Observations," 564–66; Pfaff, *Über die strengen Winter*, 89–90, end tables; Mann, *Mémoires*, 71.

the State of the Poor of the Nation from the two last severe Winters: Scarcity and Dearth of Provisions, Want of Trade and Money, a Spanish War remisely prosecuted.''[127] The distress among the poor in England was concentrated in urban locations and in the western and northern counties, where the prolonged environmental stress had been most damaging to agriculture and had reduced employment opportunities.[128] In Scotland, because of the two consecutive poor harvests of 1739 and 1740, subsistence conditions reached an acute stage in the spring of 1741.[129] Multitudes of poverty-stricken persons crowded into Edinburgh seeking food and employment.[130] By late winter 1741, the population of Aberdeen County was reported to be ''in extreme want.''[131] Also by late winter, ''mobs'' in many regions of Scotland ''robb'd, plunder'd or destroy'd whatever Granaries of Meal they could find.''[132] In Ireland, the working population was desperately short of food by the spring of 1741 and was also racked by epidemics of fever and dysentery.[133] Everywhere on the Continent north of the Alps, elevated food prices prevailed; with a rising incidence of epidemic diseases.[134]

Extreme weather events continued to dominate in most European regions during 1741 and carried over into 1742. The spring and summer months of 1741 and 1742 were, on balance, excessively dry. In England, the drought was virtually absolute from January to June 1741. Rainfall at Kew for the first six months of 1741 measured a total of 7.68 inches. The drought was more marked in the northern and western counties. The English cereal harvests, nonetheless, turned out favorably in 1741 and also in 1742.[135] Scotland in large measure escaped the droughtlike

127. Short, *Chronological History,* 262–63.

128. For press accounts of dearth in the west and north, see *London Daily Post,* February 18, March 25, and April 16, 1741.

129. *Caledonian Mercury,* October 30, 1740.

130. *London Daily Post,* December 30, 1740.

131. *Caledonian Mercury,* March 17, 1741.

132. *London Daily Post,* March 31, 1741.

133. *Faulkner's Dublin Journal,* July 28–August 1 and August 1–4, 1741; Drake, ''Demographic Crisis,'' 116–18; Rutty, *Chronological History,* 86–87.

134. Jean-Pierre Goubert, *Malades et médecins en Bretagne, 1770–1790* (Paris, 1974), 329–30; Claude Bruneel, *La Mortalité dans les campagnes: Le Duché de Brabant aux XVIIe et XVIIIe siècles* (Louvain, 1977), 212–16, 638–41, 649–62, 663–68, 668–70; Heinrich Haeser, *Lehrbuch der Geschichte der medizin und der epidemischen Krankheiten,* 3d ed. (3 vols.; Jena, 1875–82), III, 468–79; Karl Kisskalt, ''Epidemiologisch-statistische Untersuchungen über die Sterblichkeit von 1600–1800,'' *Archiv für Hygiene und Bakteriologie* 137 (1953), 37–41; E. Olivier, *Médecine et santé dans le pays de Vaud,* 2 vols. (Lausanne, 1962), II, 667–69, 1,144–50, 1,192–99, 1,227; Jutikkala, *Bevölkerung Finnlands,* 38–41; Imhof, *Bevölkerungsentwicklung in den nordischen Ländern,* 641–49.

135. Wales-Smith, ''Rainfall,'' 358; Manley, ''Great Winter,'' 16; Stratton, *Agricultural Records,* 75; Huxham, *Observations,* II, 93–102; Marshall, *Stout of Lancaster,* 230–31; Short, *Comparative History,* 94; Short, *New Observations,* 345; Short, *Chronological History,* II, 263; Jones, *Seasons,* 139.

conditions, as beneficial rains fell early in June and removed the threat of a third consecutive poor harvest. The grain harvests in Scotland turned out successfully both in 1741 and 1742.[136] In Ireland, the spring and summer of 1741 remained cool and dry, and the autumn was frosty; but as in Britain, the cereal harvests fell out favorably.[137] The dry weather that predominated in the British Isles during the spring and summer of 1741 had little adverse impact on grain yields. The question remains, however, to what extent the excessively dry conditions fostered the epidemic levels of dysentery that had developed by that time.

In France, the spring and summer months were likewise unusually dry. La Mettrie noted that the summer was "very hot and very dry"; he attributed the intestinal illnesses that appeared in August to the sequence of weather patterns.[138] In Belgium and in Holland, the summer months of 1741 were also extremely dry. Epidemic dysentery became rife in the provinces of the southern Netherlands and northern France in August of that year.[139] In Germany, the period from March to July 1741 proved so dry as to reduce the quantity of the wine harvest. The droughtlike conditions extended into the spring and summer of 1742.[140] The spring, summer, and autumn of 1741 were warm and dry in Switzerland, but the winter of 1741–1742 proved abnormally severe again, and shortages of food and fodder in some cantons persisted into a third year.[141] In Europe generally, the winter of 1741–1742 turned out to be one of the most severe of the century. Great amounts of snow fell that winter, and the weather continued raw and cold until May.[142]

On the Scandinavian peninsula, the weather remained abnormally cold through 1741 and 1742. The anomalously low atmospheric temperatures were echoed in the late ice-melting dates of the Mälarsee—on April 27, 1741, and April 30, 1742. Snow fell in the southern Swedish county of Skaraborg as late as June 4, 1742. In Sweden, the cereal harvests were deficient both in 1741 and 1742; the counties of Uppsala and Blekinge, among others, suffered three consecutive poor grain harvests. In Norway,

---

136. *Scots Magazine*, October 1741, 475; *London Daily Post*, June 30, 1741.

137. Rutty, *Chronological History*, 84; *Faulkner's Dublin Journal*, August 1–4 and September 15–18, 1741.

138. Julien Offray de La Mettrie, *Oeuvres de médecine* (Berlin, 1755), 269; also see Desbordes, *Chronique*, 26.

139. Bernier, "Hainaut," 568; Houtte, *Leuven*, 245.

140. Bock, *Ost- und Westpreussen*, I, 780–83; Müller, *Weinbaus*, 210; Herbert Zielinski, "Klimatische Aspekte Bevölkerungsgeschichtlicher Entwicklung," in Arthur E. Imhof, ed., *Historische Demographie als Sozialgeschichte* (Darmstadt, 1975), 959–60.

141. Walser, *Appenzeller-Chronik*, 172; Bielmann, *Urnerland*, 73, 79; Piuz, "Climat," 615; Burri, *Luzern*, 78; Silvio Bucher, *Bevölkerung und Wirtschaft des Amtes Entlebuch im 18. Jahrhundert* (Luzern, 1974), 90–91, 234.

142. Easton, *Hivers*, 130.

the unfavorable weather reduced grain yields in 1741; and then in 1742 the combination of late-summer frosts and prolonged rainfall during the harvest period produced harvest failures. By 1742, famine conditions gripped Norway and were common in several Swedish counties.[143]

Altogether, the evidence indicates that the extended period of extreme weather events form 1739 to 1742 prejudiced the well-being of the European working population. The sequence of anomalous seasons gave rise to the threat of hypothermia, elevated food prices, hunger, the loss of farm animals, unemployment, the destruction of property, and large-scale destitution. It seems certain that the three-year period of climatic stress was in part implicated in the European mortality wave of the early 1740s, albeit to an extent that cannot readily be measured. The evidence suggests three possible functional relationships that connect the cumulative stress with the mortality peak of 1740–1742. First, the low temperatures and cold, dense atmospheres led to deaths from the process of hypothermia, elevated the incidence of fatal respiratory diseases, and provoked deaths from cardiovascular diseases. Second, the extreme atmospheric conditions that comprised lengthy, frigid winter seasons and prolonged spring–summer dry periods facilitated the diffusion of the disease vectors and pathogenic microorganisms that give rise to epidemic fevers and diarrheal disease. Third, the weather-induced decline in grain yields created subsistence crises that led to deaths from hunger and at the same time promoted a higher incidence of epidemic disease, the so-called famine fevers.

In order to determine the relative significance of these three possible functional relationships, it is necessary to assess the degree of national food shortages, to trace the course of national cereal prices, to compare the levels of social turbulence, and to measure the effectiveness of welfare and relief programs in the locations under study. It is also necessary to identify the mechanisms that could account for a connection between climatic stress and infectious disease and to specify the pathways and networks that spread infections in preindustrial Europe. The next chapter focuses on the detrimental impact that the weather patterns of 1739–1742 had on grain harvest yields and on animal husbandry.

143. Imhof, *Bevölkerungsentwicklung in den nordischen Ländern,* 728–40.

4. *Cereal Harvest Outcomes*

Climatic variability can have a direct effect on the biophysical processes of the growth of plants and the survival of farm animals, which were critical for the well-being of preindustrial societies. Even a marginal decrease in the harvest volume of cereals brought about a pronounced rise in prices in preindustrial Europe. The higher food costs led in turn to nutritional deficiencies in the diets of the working population, and on occasion this deprivation progressed to hunger.

The social consequences of high food prices can be devastating, whatever the cause. In preindustrial Europe, however, the specific nature as well as the severity of harvest shortfalls modulated the influence of dearth on mortality and epidemics. Genuine food shortages tended to maximize the scale of social disorder, which in turn hindered the attempts of public authorities to carry out remedial measures. Food riots and related popular disturbances complicated public and voluntary endeavors to maintain minimum standards of welfare. The fear of hunger understandably produced personal anxiety and public turbulence.

The nature of the harvest deficiencies—that is, whether the winter or spring grains fell off in yields—was likewise critical, because this fact often determined the scale of the consequent distress. For the same reason it also mattered which of the winter cereals, wheat or rye, and which of the spring cereals, barley or oats, proved deficient in volume. Rye rather than wheat among the winter cereals was the basic bread grain of the working population. Therefore a significant decline in the seed-yield ratio of rye brought about a more severe subsistence problem than a similar drop in wheat yields. On the other hand, the availability and price of barley and oats commonly governed the ability of a region to avoid famine conditions, as the work of Andrew Appleby has shown.[1] In the process of tracing the relationship between food shortage and epidemic disease, it is accordingly not sufficient to rely exclusively on the price of cereals, even though prices are a good indicator of the supply of food actually available for consumption. It becomes possible to arrive at a clearer understanding of the nutritional consequences of crop failures if the harvest outcomes are known for each of the principal grains.

The price of food can be driven up by speculative market practices, by trade restrictions, by wartime conditions, and by monetary inflation as well as by deficient harvest yields. The mere threat of a weather-induced crop failure drove up grain prices in preindustrial Europe, as the anticipation of rising prices motivated producers and dealers to withhold cereals from the market and also multiplied the number of hoarders purchasing food against future needs. In times of shortage or threatened shortage, governments at both the national and the local level attempted to restrict the trade in foodstuffs, in particular to prevent the export of grains seeking higher prices in other lands. During times of war (both the War of the Austrian Succession and the war between Russia and Sweden-Finland broke out in the early 1740s), military and naval commissary purchases also put upward pressure on food prices, as did the trade restrictions and economic uncertainties associated with the waging of war. The present chapter, however, will examine only the degree to which the weather conditions reduced grain output; I shall consider the course of cereal prices in the following chapter.

It is not unreasonable to expect that the series of inclement seasons that predominated in western Europe from 1739 to 1742 should have lowered grain yields. The growth of all cereal plants depends, of course, on weather conditions. But the individual grains exhibit varying atmospheric sensitivities, which must also be considered in light of the microenvironment of an agricultural location. Although both temperature and precipitation are decisive variables in the regulation of plant growth, the mean temperature and the length of the growing season disproportionately govern the grain harvest outcomes in Scandinavia, Scotland, and the upland districts of western Europe. In the lowland regions of western Europe, on the other hand, the timing and amount of precipitation exercise a more considerable influence on crop yields. Much of the essential precipitation is provided by summer thunderstorms, which occur fairly reliably each year. It should be noted, therefore, that the

---

1. See Andrew B. Appleby's pathbreaking article "Grain Prices and Subsistence Crises in England and France, 1590–1740," *Journal of Economic History* 39 (1979), 865–87.

sharp decrease in annual measured rainfall that often takes place during periods in which western Europe's climatic regime is dominated by continental rather than maritime flows, which was the case in the early 1740s, turns out to be less crucial for cereal culture in northern regions than the low annual totals imply.[2]

The relationship between weather conditions and plant growth is particularly complex in the case of the winter grains. Three rather than two atmospheric variables govern the growth of plants: temperature, precipitation, and the intensity of light. Each of the three factors is required in varying degrees during the course of the growth phases, of which a total of eight can be distinguished in the cultivation of winter grains. Either too much or not enough of the needed factor at any time can be detrimental to the development of the plant. Slicher van Bath has proposed a model of ideal weather conditions for the cultivation of winter wheat in the temperate zone.[3] Although the model assumes the availability of monthly values of the three atmospheric variables, a stipulation that cannot be made good for most regions in the 1740s, the application of the model to the surviving evidence makes it nonetheless possible to "improve" the historical knowledge of harvest outcomes.

The most critical winter grain harvest during the decade under study took place during the crop year 1739–1740. Slicher van Bath's model indicates that the weather conditions of the first six growth phases of the crop year 1739–1740 were detrimental rather than beneficial to the growth of winter grains. This was particularly true for phases 3, December 21 through February, and 4, the month of March. It will be recalled that the weather conditions from the end of December until March were dominated by temperatures close to 0°F, deep frosts, and strong northeasterly winds. The ideal weather called for by the model is, by contrast, "fairly dry conditions, a little snow, never more than 10°C of frost, no hard winds." The ideal weather for the month of March involves "no frost after grain has resumed growth." March 1740 in western Europe turned out cold and dry, with recurrent frosts and thaws. For April, the model calls for weather that is "sunny, slight rainfall at regular intervals." But the weather of April 1740 was again cold and dry, with recurrent frosts and thaws.

During the course of the eighth phase, however, the decisive late-

---

2. For a discussion of the relationship between weather conditions and plant growth in Scandinavia and northern Europe, see Gustaf Utterström, "Climatic Fluctuations and Population Problems in Early Modern History," *Scandinavian Economic History Review* 3 (1955), 5–41.

3. B. H. Slicher van Bath, "Agriculture in the Vital Revolution," in *Cambridge Economic History of Europe* (Cambridge, 1977), V, 57.

summer period from the end of July to the beginning of September, the majority of agricultural regions enjoyed beneficial weather conditions, "dry, warm and sunny, no heat wave." In some regions, by contrast, the weather turned wet and frosty at the end of August and prejudiced harvest yields where the inclement conditions set in before the crops could be safely gathered and stored. According to the model, the European wheat harvests should have been deficient in 1740, but the severity of the shortfalls would vary from region to region with the timing of the late-summer precipitation and the spring frosts. The evidence indicates, as will be shown, that the model "retrodicts" the harvest outcomes of 1740 with some degree of accuracy and also accounts for the more favorable yields than the anomalous weather patterns implied.[4]

Wheat, at the same time, was not an important bread grain in the food budget of Europe's working population. The other cereal grains, rye in particular, however, react to weather conditions along more or less the same lines as wheat. Rye plants, in fact, survive better than wheat in colder regions, being more "winter proof."[5] But the maturity of rye is particularly controlled by the temperatures of late spring and early summer. Christian Pfister has shown that the most deferred rye harvests in Switzerland between 1525 and 1880 took place in years dominated by abnormally low late-spring and early-summer temperatures—1542, 1879, 1740, 1816, 1698, 1555, 1628, and 1573, ranked in order of the length of the delay.[6] In 1740, all winter grain harvests were delayed. Thus the longer the harvests had to be deferred, the more likely that the plants would be damaged by the heavy precipitation and frosts that arrived at the end of August. As a consequence, the superior ability of rye to withstand low atmospheric temperatures was offset by the delayed harvests that exposed the plants to untimely precipitation and resulted in lower yields in some European locations both in 1739 and in 1740.

The spring grains barley and oats made up an indispensable component of the food supply of the working poor in the northern regions of Europe. Barley, like rye, withstands low atmospheric temperatures more successfully than wheat, but the plants are especially vulnerable to wet summers. Oats not only exhibit less resistance to night frosts but also require a longer growth period than barley.[7] As a consequence, the frosts that occurred in the late spring and early autumn of 1740 would have

4. Ibid.
5. Ibid.
6. Christian Pfister, "The Little Ice Age: Thermal and Wetness Indices for Central Europe," *Journal of Interdisciplinary History* 10 (Spring 1980), 672–74.
7. Slicher van Bath, "Agriculture," 57.

reduced the yields of the oat crops more significantly than those of the barley crops. Thus the model of ideal weather conditions indicates that wheat and oat yields would have suffered more than rye and barley yields in 1740, and this is the outcome that the evidence discloses.

Seed-yield ratios are a quantitative measure of the volume output of the cereal harvests. The final quantity of food produced and the market price, however, are governed in part by the relative quality of a cereal crop. The succession of spring frosts and thaws in 1740, for example, not only would reduce the volume of grain harvested but also would lower the quality of the grain. Low-quality grain translated into both less flour and poorer flour for the baking of bread. Because poor-quality flour absorbs less water, kneads less well, and proofs less successfully, such flour also produces less bread per measure. In addition, grain that has been damaged by wet weather at harvesttime, as much of it was in both 1739 and 1740, is difficult to store and does not keep well. As Steven Kaplan has summarized the quantity—quality relationship, a deficient cereal yield produced a multiplying downward impact on food supplies. The end result was to cause the price of food to rise out of proportion to the magnitude of the decline in the gross physical volume of the crops harvested.[8]

The detrimental weather conditions of 1739–1742 also reduced cereal harvest volumes by contributing to the reduction in the number of farm animals as a result of starvation, exposure, and distress slaughtering. Livestock, besides being a source of milk, butter, cheese, and meat, was indispensable for plowing, harrowing, harvesting, and the supply of fertilizer. Normal arable routines could not be carried out in the absence of a sufficient number of farm animals. Deficient crops of hay and oats as well as bread grains, therefore, produced a downward effect on the supply of food. Scant hay harvests and poor oat yields meant less fodder and a lower level of animal health and energy. The deficiency of fodder also dictated that fewer animals could be kept and fed over the winter. A decline in the number of farm animals resulted in a reduction in the area sown with cereals, a reduced supply of fertilizer, a smaller volume of dairy products, and thus in a further decline in the available supply of food.[9]

8. For a discussion of net grain yields, flour content, and the multiplying effects, see Steven L. Kaplan, *Bread, Politics, and Political Economy in the Reign of Louis XV,* 2 vols. (The Hague, 1977), I, 253–54, 373; for a discussion of these issues in the case of the pan-European harvest failures of 1816, see John D. Post, *The Last Great Subsistence Crisis in the Western World* (Baltimore, 1977), 40–41.

9. For an illuminating discussion of these relationships, see Arthur E. Imhof, *Aspekte der Bevölkerungsentwicklung in den nordischen Ländern, 1720–1750* (Bern, 1976), 716–17, 810, 1,071.

Arthur E. Imhof's study of Scandinavia found, for example, that the prolonged inclement weather of the early 1740s reduced the food supply through its detrimental impact on the health of farm animals. Because of the reduction in pasture, the livestock required extended stall feeding, which proved dangerous to their health. For both animals and humans, the long, cold winters lengthened the period of time spent crowded into small, poorly heated, poorly ventilated living spaces. Livestock were confined in narrow, stuffy stalls in which standards of hygiene were problematical. The same environmental conditions that promoted epidemic disease in human communities fostered a higher incidence of infections among farm animals. Because of the lack of spring and summer grazing opportunities, the same cereal supplies also had to be stretched for both human and animal subsistence. It should be borne in mind that, because cattle, horses, and sheep represented large capital investments and real wealth, a decrease in their numbers lowered the general standard of living and thereby enlarged the size of the "harvest-sensitive" fraction of the population, as well as lowering the volume of food production.[10]

To sum up, the cumulative detrimental effect of an extended series of poor agricultural seasons on total food production was the function of a sequence of reinforcing events. The long severe winters and delayed springs reduced both winter grain yields and the quantity of spring grass or pasture. The need to extend the stall feeding of livestock aggravated the shortage of fodder. The long severe winters and cold springs, as in 1740, also reduced the acreage sown to barley and oats. The wet autumns and early winters, as in 1739 and 1740, likewise reduced the area sown to wheat and rye and cut into the yields of all cereals. The shortage of fodder not only led to higher mortality among the livestock but also meant less productive surviving animals; both outcomes translated into a reduction in the area sown to cereals.

Because not all agricultural regions fared equally badly from the inclement weather conditions of the early 1740s, it is necessary to survey the regional grain harvest outcomes. Knowledge of national harvest yields is needed to determine the extent to which the sharp rise in food prices during 1739–1740 ensued from food shortages and also to correlate crop yields and mortality trends. Knowledge of the yields of the individual cereals is needed to understand the impact of crop deficiencies in specific agricultural regions. Grain harvest outcomes for the entire ten-year period 1735–1744 must be surveyed to ascertain the influence of food shortage on death rates.

10. Ibid., 785–86, 810–12.

1735–1738

The evidence indicates that European cereal harvests from 1735 to 1738 turned out, on balance, successfully. Although no precise measures of national grain yields are available, several studies have evaluated harvest volumes from the combination of impressionistic evidence and price data. According to the investigations of W. G. Hoskins, England did not experience a "bad" harvest from 1735 to 1738, though neither were grain yields "good."[11] The weight of the impressionistic evidence confirms his findings.[12] In the case of Scotland, firsthand evidence pertaining to harvest outcomes is virtually absent for the years 1735–1738. If the trend of cereal prices is an approximate index of harvest yields, however, Scotland escaped bad harvests during these four years.[13] The lack of complaint or comment also suggests satisfactory crop yields. Knowledge of crop yields in Ireland is equally difficult to obtain. John Rutty is silent on harvest outcomes for 1735–1738 in his chronological history of the seasons. In view of his subsequent notice of extreme harvest outcomes, the lack of comment suggests that crop yields were neither abundant nor deficient.[14]

Several regions on the Continent proved exceptions to the satisfactory harvest yields from 1735 to 1738. In France, the northwestern provinces suffered poor cereal harvests in 1738. Grain prices began to climb that year, and a marked fall in prices did not set in until 1742.[15] Harvest yields were most deficient in the provinces to the west of Paris, particularly in Maine and Touraine but also in Anjou. Grain volumes also fell off in the provinces of Berry and Poitou. A few provinces in central France likewise experienced poor cereal harvests, in particular the Bourbonnais and Auvergne. The deficient crops in the provinces

11. For the concern of this study, see W. G. Hoskins, "Harvest Fluctuations and English Economic History, 1620–1759," *Agricultural History Review* 16, pt. 1 (1968), 15–31.

12. See J. M. Stratton, *Agricultural Records, A.D. 220–1968,* ed. Ralph Whitlock (London, 1969), 72–73; E. L. Jones, *Seasons and Prices* (London, 1964), 137–38; T. S. Ashton, *Economic Fluctuations in England, 1700–1800* (London, 1959), 19.

13. Michael Flinn et al., *Scottish Population History* (Cambridge, 1977), 216, 494–95; Henry Hamilton, *An Economic History of Scotland in the Eighteenth Century* (London, 1963), 5, 397–98.

14. John Rutty, *A Chronological History of the Weather and Seasons and of the Prevailing Diseases in Dublin* (London, 1770); Rutty, *An Essay Towards a Natural History of the County of Dublin,* 2 vols. (Dublin, 1772).

15. E. Labrousse, *Esquisse du mouvement des prix et des revenus en France au XVIIIe siècle* (Paris, 1932), 183; Labrousse et al., *Le Prix du froment en France au temps de la monnaie stable, 1726–1913* (Paris, 1970), 9.

west of Paris were compounded by the fact that only mediocre volumes had been gathered in 1737.[16]

In the Low Countries, grain harvest volumes were satisfactory from 1735 to 1738. Winter grain prices remained relatively low both in the Dutch Republic and in the southern Netherlands but began to rise in 1738.[17] At the same time, crop yields varied from cereal to cereal and from district to district. G. van Houtte has shown that at Seraing-le-Château, near Liège, a progressive decline in rye harvests from 1735 to 1738 combined with lower spelt yields in 1737 to explain the rising cereal prices in 1738.[18] F. Daelemans found, however, that wheat yields rose from 1735 to 1738 at several villages in South Brabant.[19] Grain yields in the Basse-Meuse region of the southern Netherlands also remained satisfactory from 1735 to 1738, falling only marginally below the long-term (1620–1750) average in 1738.[20]

In the lands of eastern Germany, by contrast, grain yields fell off markedly in 1736. Harvest failures were common in east Elbian Prussia. The crop deficiencies prompted Friedrich Wilhelm I to place an embargo on the export of cereals in 1736. A shortage of grain developed in the province of Prussia and Lithuania during 1737. When prolonged drought conditions raised the possiblity of another harvest shortfall in 1738, the Prussian king authorized the purchase of cereals abroad. But in fact the harvest yields of 1738 turned out successfully.[21] As a consequence of the poor grain yields of 1736, cereal prices rose in most German markets.[22]

The mortality indexes of table 1 indicate that Germany passed through

16. Michel Bricourt, Marcel Lachiver, and Denis Queruel, "La Crise de subsistance des années 1740 dans le ressort du Parlement de Paris," *Annales de Démographie Historique* (1974), 284–90; François Lebrun, *Les Hommes et la mort en Anjou aux 17e et 18e siècles* (Paris, 1971), 131, 138; Jean-Michel Desbordes, ed., *La Chronique villageoise de Varreddes (Seine-et-Marne): Un Document sur la vie rurale des XVIIe et XVIIIe siècles* (Paris, n.d. [1969]), 24–25.

17. G. van Houtte, *Leuven in 1740, ein Krisisjaar: Ekonomische, sociale, en demografische aspekten* (Brussels, 1964), 210–11; Nicolaas W. Posthumus, *Inquiry into the History of Prices in Holland*, 2 vols. (Leiden, 1946–64), II, 415.

18. Houtte, *Leuven*, 210–16.

19. F. Daelemans, "Tithe Revenues in Rural South West Brabant, Fifteenth to Eighteenth Century," in Herman van der Wee and Eddy van Cauwenberghe, eds., *Productivity of Land and Agricultural Innovation in the Low Countries (1250–1800)* (Leuven, 1978), 29–30, 33, 36–41.

20. Myron P. Gutmann, *War and Rural Life in the Early Modern Low Countries* (Princeton, 1980), 84–90.

21. Acta Borussica, *Denkmäler der preussischen Staatsverwaltung im 18. Jahrhundert: Getreidehandelspolitik*, vol. III: W. Naudé, *Die Getreidehandelspolitik und Kriegsmagazinverwaltung: Brandenburg-Preussens bis 1740* (Berlin, 1901), 251, 289.

22. Ibid., 543–48; Moritz J. Elsas, *Umriss einer Geschichte der Preise und Löhne in Deutschland vom ausgehenden Mittelalter bis zum Beginn des 19. Jahrhunderts*, 2 vols. (Leiden, 1936–49), II, B, 105, 122, 126; Wilhelm Abel, *Massenarmut und Hungerkrisen im vorindustriellen Europa* (Hamburg, 1974), 180.

a minor mortality peak during the years 1736–1737, principally in the province of Prussia and Lithuania. Mortality, moreover, became slightly elevated elsewhere in Germany and in central Europe during those two years. The elevated German death rates of 1736–1737 have been attributed to smallpox epidemics and other infectious diseases rife in central Europe,[23] but it appears that high food prices also influenced mortality levels. Knowledge of grain yields in Austria and the Habsburg monarchy is scant. The trend of cereal prices, however, suggests that Austrian harvests were also deficient in 1736.[24]

The research of Christian Pfister has provided systematic estimates of grain harvest yields in the Swiss cantons. His findings indicate that harvest outcomes in the state of Bern, on the western Swiss plateau, were successful each year from 1735 to 1738 but with a downward trend starting in 1738. Grain yields were less favorable in the northern canton of Zürich, particularly in the years 1735 and 1738.[25] On balance, the evidence does not show deficient harvests in Switzerland from 1735 to 1738, though grain prices began to rise in 1738.[26] Insofar as Italy is concerned, the evidence fails to disclose any significant harvest failures during the years 1735–1738.[27]

The cereal harvest outcomes in Scandinavia also were successful from 1735 to 1738. Harvest outcomes on the Scandinavian peninsula are known at the county level. Annual cereal harvests were of course not uniform in a region as vast as Scandinavia, with its varying climatic regimes, environmental differences, and regional reliance on varieties of bread grains. On balance, however, Scandinavian cereal harvests were "good" to "abundant" each year from 1735 to 1738 except in Denmark, which shared the central European tendency to deficient grain yields in 1736.[28] But not every Scandinavian county enjoyed favorable harvests each year from 1735 to 1738. The counties of Malmöhus and Östergötland, for example, in southern Sweden, experienced deficient harvests in

23. Johann Peter Süssmilch, *Die göttliche Ordnung in den Veränderungen des menschlichen Geschlechts*, 4th ed., 3 vols. (Berlin, 1775), I, 70.

24. Alfred F. Pribram, *Materialen zur Geschichte der Preise und Löhne in Österreich* (Vienna, 1938), 371, 381, 386–87, 391, 396, 405–406, 409–410, 434, 441–42, 531, 534.

25. Christian Pfister, personal communication, August 9, 1979.

26. S. Bucher, *Bevölkerung und Wirtschaft des Amtes Entlebuch im 18. Jahrhundert* (Luzern, 1974), 234.

27. Alfonso Corradi, *Annali delle epidemie occorse in Italia dalle prime memorie fino al 1850*, 8 vols. (Bologna, 1865–94), IV, 1,400–402; Aldo de Maddalena, *Prezzi e mercedi a Milano dal 1701 al 1860*, 2 vols. (Milan, 1974), I, 98–128, 378–84.

28. Imhof, *Bevölkerungsentwicklung in den nordischen Ländern*, 723–25; Gustaf Utterström, "Some Population Problems in Pre-industrial Sweden," *Scandinavian Economic History Review* 2 (1954), 126–27; Astrid Friis and Kristof Glamann, *A History of Prices and Wages in Denmark, 1660–1800* (London, 1955), 154.

1735.[29] Nonetheless, in light of the moderate, maritime weather regime that predominated in the 1730s, Scandinavian cereal harvests can be expected to have turned out successfully during that decade.[30]

Altogether, European cereal harvests turned out satisfactorily during the years from 1735 to 1738. The deficient harvests of 1736 in central Europe and the harvest shortfalls of 1738 in northwestern France were the major exceptions to this generalization. European death rates remained relatively low form 1735 to 1738, with the pronounced exception of the mortality peak that developed in the German lands during 1736–1737, marked by crisis mortality in the east Elbian province of Prussia and Lithuania. In 1739, however, European cereal harvests were deficient, grain prices rose noticeably, and the extended period of cheap food supplies came to an end.

1739–1741

Cereal prices are the function not only of the current harvests but also of the crop yields of the preceding year or two and, in some years, of the anticipated yields of an impending harvest. Under more normal market conditions, the price of cereals during the first seven or eight months of 1740 would be determined mainly by the harvest outcomes of 1739. But because of the abnormal weather conditions that predominated during the first half of 1740, market prices reflected the anticipated harvest failures of that year. The evidence shows that the dearth-level grain prices that prevailed during 1740–1741 were the function of weather-related crop deficiencies in 1739, 1740, and, in some regions, also in 1741.

European cereal harvests were deficient almost without exception in 1739. G. W. Hoskins has classified the English crop yields of 1739 as "deficient" and as "worst in the West." In England, the price of cereals in 1739 climbed 23.6 percent above the thirty-one-year moving average.[31] The impressionistic evidence indicates that the harvests were delayed and then damaged by September storms.[32] John Huxham's account of the severe damage sustained by the wheat crop in Devonshire supports the

---

29. Imhof, *Bevölkerungsentwicklung in den nordischen Ländern*, 723–25; Eino Jutikkala, *Die Bevölkerung Finnlands in den Jahren 1721–1749* (Helsinki, 1945), 28–29; Friis and Glamann, *Prices*, 154.

30. Utterström, "Climatic Fluctuations," 8, 19; Imhof, *Bevölkerungsentwicklung in den nordischen Ländern*, 789–809; Jutikkala, *Bevölkerung Finnlands*, 28–32.

31. Hoskins, "Harvest Fluctuations," 23, 31.

32. See Stratton, *Agricultural Records*, 74; Jones, *Seasons*, 138.

view that harvest outcomes were worse in western England.[33] Harvest yields were also poor in the northern counties of England; according to Thomas Short, "much Corn, and the greatest Part of Barley lost." But harvests proved successful in the Midland counties.[34] For Scotland, the evidence discloses both a late harvest and a light crop.[35] One commentator traced the scarcity of food in late 1740 to the failure of the 1739 crop.[36] Some Scottish locations, such as the Orkney Islands and the counties of the far north, may have suffered harvest failures in 1739,[37] but outcomes generally were not so severe. In Ireland, the grain harvest outcomes were less than satisfactory in 1739. Although Rutty is silent on the question, the inclement weather recorded in his history of the seasons, in particular the wet spell in late August and September, suggests that crop damage was inescapable.[38] Michael Drake concluded that the wet summer and autumn of 1739 reduced cereal yields.[39] L. M. Cullen has written that Ireland in fact experienced a poor grain harvest in 1739.[40] Harvest outcomes were more satisfactory, however, in Ulster.[41]

In northern France, crop yields proved more successful in 1739 than in 1738. Although harvests were still somewhat deficient in 1739, the cereal crops were for the most part safely stored before the cold and wet weather became established in the late summer. Nonetheless, the inclement weather interrupted the sowing of winter grains and contributed to the smaller crop volumes of 1740. By the end of 1739, moreover, the cumulative harvest shortfalls of 1737, 1738, and 1739 produced dearth conditions in northern France. The shortage of cereals began to prompt references in the correspondence of local public administrators to the famine of 1709–1710. The combined effect of imported grain supplies and a more favorable harvest outlook in the summer months of 1739 eased food prices somewhat. But because cereal stocks had become so

33. John Huxham, *Observations on the Air, and Epidemic Diseases from the Beginning of the Year 1738 to the End of the Year 1748,* 2 vols. (London, 1759–67), II, 38–42.

34. Thomas Short, *A General Chronological History of the Air, Weather, Seasons, Meteors, etc.* (London, 1749), 252.

35. Flinn et al., *Scottish Population History,* 216, 494–95; Hamilton, *Economic History,* 5, 397–98.

36. *Caledonian Mercury,* October 30, 1740.

37. Sir John Sinclair, *The Statistical Account of Scotland,* 21 vols. (Edinburgh, 1791–98), XIV, 319.

38. Rutty, *Chronological History,* 74–76.

39. Michael Drake, "The Irish Demographic Crisis of 1740–41," *Historical Studies* 6 (1968), 106–107.

40. L. M. Cullen, *An Economic History of Ireland since 1660* (London, 1972), 69.

41. Drake, "Demographic Crisis," 106–107.

depleted in northern France, prices failed to fall to the levels of 1736–1737 even after the harvests were gathered.[42]

The grain producers in the Low Countries were less fortunate in 1739; they were forced to harvest their crops during a period of heavy rain. Both the reaping and the storage of cereals were delayed. Seed–yield ratios fell off, but the harvest volumes in the southern Netherlands have been described as no worse than "mediocre."[43] The fact that grain and legume prices rose sharply in 1739 suggests, however, that cereal yields were poorer than mediocre in 1739. The limited evidence on seed–yield ratios does not permit a satisfactory resolution of this question. Grain production did not decline at Seraing-le-Château[44] or in the Basse-Meuse district, but seed–yield ratios fell off noticeably in the sample of South Brabant villages.[45] It is clear, however, that the supply of food in the Austrian Netherlands was perceived to be deficient after the 1739 harvests. The exportation of grain was prohibited from all provinces by decrees issued on September 16, October 19, and November 28, 1739, citing the recent harvest shortfalls.[46] Rye prices at the sensitive Amsterdam market began to rise immediately after the 1739 harvests, indicating that crop yields in western Europe were disappointing and that the supply of cereals had become tight.

In Germany, as in northern France, the rye and wheat crops were reaped and stored before the inclement weather of 1739 became installed. But spring grains and vegetables suffered from the hot, dry weather in August and cold, wet conditions in September and October.[47] The subsistence crisis that confronted Frederick the Great in 1740 has been traced to the unseasonable weather that "completely ruined the harvests of 1739 in many parts of the state."[48] The price of cereals in Germany rose sharply at the end of 1739.[49] Grain prices in Austria also

42. Bricourt et al., "Crise," 290–304.
43. Etienne Hélin, "Le Déroulement de trois crises à Liège au XVIIIe siècle," in Paul Harsin and Etienne Hélin eds., *Problèmes de mortalité*, Actes du Colloque International de Démographie Historique (Liège, 1963), 490–91.
44. Houtte, *Leuven*, 210–16.
45. Daelemans, "Tithe Revenues," 36–41; Gutmann, *War and Rural Life*, 87.
46. Hubert van Houtte, "La Législation annonaire des Pays-Bas à la fin de l'Ancien Régime et la disette de 1789 en France," *Vierteljahrschrift für Sozial- und Wirtschaftsgeschichte* 10 (1912), 102.
47. Heinrich C. J. Schenck, *Die Wunder Gottes im Winter* (Arnstadt, 1741) 18; Friedrich Samuel Bock, *Versuch einer wirtschaftlichen Naturgeschichte von dem Königreich Ost- und Westpreussen*, 5 vols. (Dessau, 1782–85), I, 766–67.
48. Walther Hubatsch, *Frederick the Great of Prussia: Absolutism and Administration*, trans. Patrick Doren (London, 1975), 58.
49. Elsas, *Preise*, I, 588, 672; II, A, 467–68; II, B, 105, 122; Dietrich Ebeling and Franz Irsigler, eds., *Getreideumsatz, Getreide- und Brotpreise in Köln, 1368–1797*, pt. 2: *Brotgewichte und Brotpreise: Wochen-, Monats-, und Jahrestabelle Graphiken* (Cologne, 1977), xxxiv, 256, 267.

began to rise during the second half of 1739.[50] An isolated record of rye
seed–yield ratios in Slovakia shows a drop from 6.8 in 1738 to 5.7 in
1739,[51] or a decline of 16 percent. Swiss grain yields, on the other hand,
were favorable in 1739. Pfister's harvest volume index shows above-
average values for both Bern and Zürich.[52] Cereal harvests also turned
out successfully in Italy.[53]

On the Scandinavian peninsula, however, crop yields fell off in 1739,
particularly in the northern counties of Sweden-Finland. The months of
August, September, and October were dominated by cool, cloudy and
wet weather, the opposite of the ideal dry, warm, and sunny conditions
called for to maximize grain yields. In Finland, the rye crops were
damaged by a severe frost on August 10–11; reportedly the winter grain
harvests in the northern county of Österbotten yielded no more than a
fourth of a normal volume.[54] Cereal yields were deficient to a lesser
degree in the central and southern counties of Sweden-Finland. Crop
yields in Norway have been described as below average in the harvests
of 1739.[55]

To sum up, the grain yields of 1739 fell off in western and northern
England, Scotland, southern Ireland, northern France, the southern
Netherlands, Germany, the Habsburg monarchy, and the Scandinavian
peninsula. Harvest shortfalls were most pronounced in western England,
northern Scotland, northern Germany, and the northern counties of
Sweden-Finland. Grain prices at the same time moved sharply upward in
all regions, suggesting that the supply of cereals was perceived to be
deficient. In northern France and to some degree in Prussia the shortage
of cereals was traceable in part to the poor harvest outcomes of earlier
years. Cereal prices were already elevated and food supplies already
short when the severe weather conditions of 1740 set in.

Famine conditions developed in only a limited number of European
regions during the years 1740–1742, in spite of the cumulative harvest
shortfalls and the extremely detrimental weather of 1740. Harvest
volumes fell off less in 1740 than might be anticipated from the
atmospheric conditions. In the case of England, Hoskins assigned the
harvest outcomes his lowest classification, "dearth." He has written of

50. Pribram, *Preise*, 371, 381, 386–87, 391, 396, 405–406, 409–10, 434, 441–42, 531,
534.
51. Abel, *Massenarmut*, 181.
52. Pfister, personal communication.
53. Maddalena, *Prezzi*, I, 98–128, 378–84; Corradi, *Annali*, IV, 1,401–1,402.
54. Jutikkala, *Bevölkerung Finnlands*, 93; Imhof, *Bevölkerungsentwicklung in den nordischen
Ländern*, 725–26.
55. Imhof, *Bevölkerungsentwicklung in den nordischen Ländern*, 725–27; Utterström,
"Population Problems," 127.

"the great dearth of 1740."[56] The evidence indicates that the western region of England suffered the worst agricultural effects from the weather of 1739–1740 but that harvest outcomes varied considerably from region to region. According to Thomas Tooke, the winter of 1739–1740 was followed by a "very deficient harvest."[57] T. S. Ashton has written of the "great famine of 1740."[58] J. D. Chambers reported a "bad" harvest in Nottinghamshire.[59] The deficient harvests in northern Wales in both 1739 and 1740 have been described.[60] The weight of historical opinion has concluded that the English grain harvests of 1740 were late and markedly deficient.[61] Gordon Manley's study of the winter of 1740 found, however, that except for the western region of the country, the grain harvest "was fairly satisfactory."[62]

The weight of the firsthand observations suggests that Manley's less pessimistic account is closer to the mark. The press printed surprisingly few comments about the state of English cereal crops in 1740. A summary account appeared in late August: "From most of the Counties in England we have advice that the Corn in general is in good Order, and that we are like to have a plentiful Harvest."[63] As we know, however, optimistic reports in the face of deficient harvests were common in the eighteenth century, because of both reluctance to encourage speculative practices and a desire to avoid providing fuel for grain riots. Still, the English press had no hesitation in reporting dearth and hunger in many regions of England, primarily in the western counties.[64]

The evidence indicates that although harvest yields were deficient in the western and northern counties, the crop volumes proved adequate in the south Midlands, East Anglia, and southern England. Huxham wrote that in Devonshire the weather "spoiled almost all the Corn."[65] Moreover, "almost all the vegetables were destroyed."[66] In northwestern

56. Hoskins, "Harvest Fluctuations," 23.

57. Thomas Tooke and William Newmarch, *A History of Prices and of the State of Circulation from 1792 to 1856*, 6 vols. (New York, 1838–57), I, 43.

58. T. S. Ashton, *An Economic History of England: The Eighteenth Century* (London, 1955), 53.

59. J. D. Chambers, *Nottinghamshire in the Eighteenth Century*, 2d ed. (New York, 1966), 284.

60. K. L. Gruffydd, "The Vale of Clwyd Corn Riots of 1740," *Flintshire Historical Society Publications* 27 (1975–76), 36–37.

61. See also Stratton, *Agricultural Records*, 74–75; Jones, *Seasons*, 138–39.

62. Gordon Manley, "The Great Winter of 1740," *Weather* 13 (1958), 14–15.

63. *London Advertiser*, August 29, 1740.

64. See *London Daily Post*, January 19, June 21, July 3, September 30, October 18, December 12, and December 25, 1740, and February 18, 1741; *London Advertiser*, February 15, May 10, August 22, and November 18, 1740.

65. Huxham, *Observations*, II, 82.

66. M. Dunsford, *Historical Memoirs of Tiverton* (Exeter, 1790), 227–28.

England, Stout wrote that "much of the wheat sown was killed in the ground, and it proved at most half a crop." In addition, "the coldness of the spring and late seeding made a failure in oats and barley."[67] The press accounts of 1740 report poor harvests in the western counties of Somerset, Herefordshire, Gloucestershire, and Staffordshire.[68] Short's accounts of harvest outcomes make it clear that crop yields varied from region to region.[69] Short states, however, that the wheat, oats, and vegetable crops turned out badly almost everywhere, and that "Barley and Malt . . . was indeed all the Nation had to depend on."[70] English farmers planted a larger than usual crop of barley in the spring of 1740, convinced that the winter frosts had destroyed much of the wheat crop. According to the Marsham journal, this conclusion was too pessimistic: "Many farmers in divers parts of the kingdom, despairing of a crop, plowed their lands for barley; but the event showed they were greatly mistaken in their judgment, for the crop of winter corn, particularly in Norfolk, proved as plentiful as ever was known." But the Marsham journal also mentions deficient harvests in most western counties, "where the crop quite failed" and farmers "had not so much wheat to reap as they sowed," so that "the poor almost starved." Apparently the county of Norfolk enjoyed a brisk export sale of grain to "the West and the North."[71]

In summary, the evidence discloses that English cereal harvests turned out to be seriously deficient in the West, somewhat deficient in the North, satisfactory in the southern Midlands and in southern England, and successful in East Anglia. The more favorable outcomes are consistent with the large number of dry, warm days and the absence of heavy rainfall in eastern and southern England from the middle of June until the beginning of September. A study of English wheat harvests in the nineteenth century corroborates the fact that such a weather pattern is beneficial for grain yields.[72]

The severe winter cold and the dry winter and spring months of 1740 nonetheless caused a critical shortage of fodder and occasioned large

67. J. D. Marshall, ed., *Autobiography of William Stout of Lancaster, 1665–1752* (Manchester, 1967), 228–29.

68. *London Advertiser,* September 23, 1740; *London Daily Post,* September 30, November 23, and December 12, 1740, and February 24, 1741.

69. Thomas Short, *New Observations on City, Town, and Country Bills of Mortality* (London, 1750), 344.

70. Short, *Chronological History,* 256, 278.

71. T. Southwell, "Account of the Severe Winter of 1739–40 and of Its Effects in the County of Norfolk in the Year Following," *Norfolk and Norwich Naturalists Society, Transactions* 2 (1875), 128–29.

72. Jones, *Seasons,* 55–56.

losses among the European animal herds. A reduction in the number of farm animals would also result in a dropoff in the supply of food. With fewer animals, the area sown to cereals would have to be cut back, arable productivity would decline, and the supply of fertilizer would decrease. In England, according to Ashton, the weather during the years 1738 and 1739 had been kind to livestock, but then "two barren winters in succession swept away half of the sheep; the starving cattle were unable to produce calves; and the oxen were so weak that it was only with difficulty that the seed was got into the ground." The scarcity of hay and roots, moreover, meant that large numbers of cattle were driven to the slaughterhouses. Another consequence was a steep rise in the price of dairy produce.[73] If large numbers of horses, cattle, and sheep perished during 1740, it is clear that some adverse impact on the grain harvest volumes of 1740, 1741, and 1742 should be anticipated.

Although the evidence is not conclusive, it seems doubtful that Ashton's statements reflect the national experience in England. It is true that the supply of dairy products fell off and that the price of cheese and butter rose sharply.[74] But the press carried virtually no accounts of high livestock mortality in England during the early 1740s. Stout's account, on the other hand, is similar to Ashton's pessimistic generalizations. "Sheep starved" and many cattle were slaughtered "for fear of winterage."[75] Short reported high mortality among the farm animals in the Midlands. "Many horses and much Cattle were lost," with hay still scarce and expensive in 1741.[76] According to Marsham journal, "The flocks in the champaign country, and in most other places, were half destroyed, and most of the lambs died, purely for want of sustenance, there being no grass at all, either in the meadows or on the heaths."[77]

Apparently large numbers of sheep starved to death in England, but it may be questioned whether half the sheep population perished during the early 1740s. Even if cattle herds had to be reduced because of inability to stall-feed animals over the winter, the evidence fails to suggest that great numbers of cattle died of starvation.[78] If the reduction in numbers of draft animals interfered with the planting of cereals, such losses were not reflected in the more than ample harvest volumes gathered in 1741. Wheat yields were high in 1741 in spite of an absolute drought from

73. Ashton, *Economic fluctuations,* 19–20.
74. Ibid., 15–16.
75. Marshall, *Stout of Lancaster,* 227–34.
76. Short, *New Observations,* 344–46.
77. Southwell, "Severe Winter," 128.
78. See Stratton, *Agricultural Records,* 75; Jones, *Seasons,* 138; Ashton, *Economic Fluctuations,* 20.

January to June. Because midsummer rainfall was timely and adequate, and because August brought warm and dry days, these favorable harvest outcomes would be anticipated both from Slicher van Bath's model[79] and from the experience of the nineteenth century.[80] Devonshire,[81] Lancashire,[82] and the Midlands all reaped a "plentiful grain harvest" in 1741.[83] The press carried numerous accounts of the favorable wheat yields of 1741. By August, the dearth that had prevailed in the western counties was over.[84] The evidence discloses that the English cereal harvests of 1741 turned out "good" to "abundant."

The mortality figures of table 1 show that English death rates peaked in 1742 rather than in 1741, an indication that nutritional deprivation alone is not an adequate explanation for the prolonged mortality peak. The demographic outcome is not inconsistent, however, with Pierre Goubert's finding that dearths produce a higher case-fatality rate in reigning infectious diseases for a year or two after a food shortage disappears.[85] The resolution of this question will be taken up in the final chapter.

The Scottish cereal harvests of 1740 turned out badly in every region of the country. According to Henry Hamilton, the deficient harvests of 1739 were followed by the late and the "most disastrous one of 1740," and a great dearth of provisions ensued.[86] The barley crop, as was the case in England, fared better than the oat crop.[87] But on balance, the spring grains were deficient in 1740. In the northeastern lowlands, "the crop was stunted, almost useless, and hardly fit to sustain cattle."[88] The spring grains rather than winter grains supplied the bulk of the cereals in Scotland. Oatmeal occupied first place in the popular diet, followed by barley and beans; all three foods were commonly found in "meal." Wheat was not a major source of bread, and the cultivation of potatoes was still virtually unknown. As a consequence, any moderate decrease in the supply of oatmeal could cause a serious food shortage.[89]

The Scottish press tended to issue optimistic reports on the growing

79. Slicher van Bath, "Agriculture," 57.
80. Jones, *Seasons,* 56.
81. Huxham, *Observations,* II, 99–102.
82. Marshall, *Stout of Lancaster,* 230–34.
83. Short, *Chronological History,* 263, 278.
84. *London Daily Post,* August 13, 1741.
85. Pierre Goubert, *Beauvais et la Beauvaisis de 1600 à 1730,* 2 vols. (Paris, 1960).
86. Hamilton, *Economic History,* 7, 375.
87. Flinn et al., *Scottish Population History,* 216–17.
88. K. Walton, "Climate and Famines in Northeast Scotland," *Scottish Geographical Magazine* 68 (1952), 1–6.
89. For a discussion of cereals and subsistence in eighteenth-century Scotland, see Hamilton, *Economic History,* 375; Walton, "Climate and Famines," 13–19.

crops in 1740,[90] and such reports continued to appear throughout the summer,[91] despite the detrimental weather conditions. The press accounts, in part, were attempts to persuade farmers and dealers who had grain to bring their supplies to the markets in order to avoid food riots.[92] According to the majority of writers, the harvest shortfalls were severe in 1740. A Highland minister wrote: "Famine is threatened by the Severity of the Season."[93] John Ramsay of Octertyre noted "an excessive bad crop."[94] The comment of the *Annals of Aberdeen* "that the grain did not yield one half of the usual quantity of meal" is probably an exaggeration but indicates a poor harvest outcome.[95] Robert Maxwell, the agricultural improver, referred to the "bad crop" of 1740.[96] The *Old Statistical Account* contains several references to the deficient grain harvests of 1740. The parish of Abernyte, in the county of Perth, related that Scotland "produced a much smaller quantity of grain" in 1740.[97] The parish of Montquhitter, in the county of Aberdeen, reported "another season of scarcity."[98] The parish of Speymouth, in the county of Moray, traced the high death rates of 1741–1742 "in some measure, from the great failure in crop 1740."[99] The parish of Fearn, in the Highland county of Ross, noted that "many starved."[100]

The late-spring frosts of 1740 delayed the sowing of oats and barley. The oat harvests were then delayed by the cool summer weather. Oats do not resist late-spring night frosts so well as barley, and they also require a longer growing period than barley.[101] It should be noted that the common varieties of both oats and barley cultivated in the first half of the eighteenth century ripened later than present-day plants.[102] Frosts were common in Scotland during the months of April, May, and June 1740.[103] When Highland reapers arrived in the Lothians at the end of

90. *Caledonian Mercury,* June 9, 1740.

91. For example, see ibid., June 30 and August 22, 1740.

92. Flinn et al., *Scottish Population History,* 217–18.

93. M. M. Mackay, "A Highland Minister's Diary," *Cornhill Magazine* 152 (November 1935), 572.

94. A. Allardyce, ed., *Scotland and Scotsmen in the Eighteenth Century from the MSS of John Ramsay of Ochtertyre,* 2 vols. (Edinburgh, 1888), II, 211–12.

95. W. Kennedy, *Annals of Aberdeen* (Edinburgh, 1818), 290.

96. Robert Maxwell, ed., *Select Transactions of the Honourable the Society of Improvers* (Edinburgh, 1743), v.

97. Sinclair, *Statistical Account,* IX, 151.

98. Ibid., VI, 133.

99. Ibid., XIV, 378.

100. Ibid., XXXIX, 300.

101. Slicher van Bath, "Agriculture," 57.

102. Walton, "Climate and Famines," 19.

103. *Caledonian Mercury,* April 21, 1740; Allardyce, *Scotland,* II, 211–12; Kennedy, *Aberdeen,* 291.

August, they found that the oat crop was not yet ready to be cut.[104]
Subsequently rainfall caused material damage to the oat crops before the
harvest could be completed.[105] A snowstorm in the first week of October
buried the oats that were still standing in the fields.[106] The shortage of
food in Scotland at the end of 1740 was compounded by the deficient
crops of 1739.[107] But the harvest shortfalls were "not so severe as to
lead the peasantry into eating their seed corn."[108]

The combination of the severe weather and the shortage of fodder
produced a hazard for the survival of livestock in Scotland. Blackface
sheep, however, have demonstrated the ability to survive low temperatures and deep snow cover. The late-spring snowstorms presented the
greatest danger, because the food supply is at its lowest ebb and sheep
are less resilient at lambing time, and also because the lambs themselves
are fragile.[109] The cattle seem to have suffered heavier losses than sheep;
the prolonged drought and scarce fodder in 1740 were the principal
hazard.[110] It should be noted, however, that reports of enforced liquida-
tion sales and mass autumnal slaughter of cattle in Britain have been
commonly exaggerated.[111] Nonetheless, the evidence indicates that the
long winter and the late spring of 1740 led to significant cattle losses
from the lack of pasture in northern Scotland.[112] There were new reports
of "vast" cattle losses when heavy snowstorms blanketed Scotland again
in the winter of 1740–1741.[113] Although the animal deaths contributed to
the grave distress that prevailed in the Highlands during 1740–1741,[114]
the national loss of livestock does not seem to have reached crisis levels.

Nor does the evidence suggest that the animal losses of 1740 reduced
the supply of food to a critical degree in Scotland, with the exception of
the Highland regions. Scottish crop yields proved ample in 1741; cereal
prices returned to "normal" levels following the successful harvests.[115]
As in England, elevated food prices in Scotland persisted for only a year
or so.[116] The Edinburgh press[117] and John Ramsay agreed that "the

104. Flinn et al., *Scottish Population History,* 217.
105. Allardyce, *Scotland,* II, 212.
106. *London Advertiser,* October 14, 1740 [datelined Edinburgh, October 7, 1740].
107. *Caledonian Mercury,* October 30, 1740.
108. Flinn et al., *Scottish Population History,* 217.
109. For an extended discussion of British sheep production and the impact of severe winters
and drought, see Jones, *Seasons,* 78–86, 92–98.
110. *Caledonian Mercury,* January 21, 1740.
111. Jones, *Seasons,* 99–102.
112. Flinn et al., *Scottish Population History,* 217.
113. *London Daily Post,* January 3, 1741.
114. Kennedy, *Aberdeen,* 294.
115. Flinn et al., *Scottish Population History,* 217.
116. Hamilton, *Economic History,* 7.
117. *Scots Magazine,* October 1741, 475.

sufferings of the poor were soon compensated by the universal plenty and cheapness of the very next season.''[118] In summary, Scottish cereal yields were somewhat deficient in 1739, noticeably deficient in 1740, and then relatively abundant in 1741. The dearth in Scotland, as in England, ended during the second half of 1741. The trend of mortality in Scotland, however, followed a somewhat different course. As table 1 shows, the number of deaths peaked in 1740 and then declined both in 1741 and in 1742. The Scottish mortality curve paralleled the rise and fall of cereal prices, and therefore the mortality peak was consistent with the demographic effects of a subsistence crisis.

In Ireland also the winter grains did not constitute the principal source of food for the laboring population. Oatmeal was a primary food source, but in Ireland, unlike Scotland, potatoes had become an important component of the food supply, particularly in the southwestern province of Munster. Ireland also produced a surplus of barley in years of successful harvests.[119] The loss of a substantial proportion of the potato crop of 1739 during a cold wave was largely responsible for the severe subsistence crisis that developed in Ireland during 1740.[120] Although contemporary writers assumed that the laboring poor were dependent on the potato crop for subsistence, it is difficult, as Michael Drake has cautioned, to assess the degree to which the crop had become indispensable to the national food supply. The evidence discloses, however, that potatoes had become indispensable to the population of Munster. A resident physician was of the opinion that those who tended cattle in Munster subsisted "upon an acre or two of potatoes and a little skimmed milk."[121] The well-known letter of "Publicola" claimed that "potatoes had long been the principal if not the only subsistence of the poor of the province."[122] The loss of the potato crop in turn created upward pressure on grain prices in 1740, as people who normally ate potatoes were now forced to purchase cereals.[123]

The detrimental weather conditions of 1740 reduced both the cereal yields and the volume of the potato crop.[124] Even apart from the weather, lower harvest volumes would have been the rule because the

118. Allardyce, *Scotland,* II, 212.

119. For a discussion of Ireland's grain production, grain consumption, and food exports and imports, see Cullen, *Economic History,* 68–69.

120. Drake, "Demographic Crisis," 106–107; K. H. Connell, *The Population of Ireland, 1750–1845* (London, 1950), 144; *Faulkner's Dublin Journal,* January 8–12 and January 12–15, 1740; Rutty, *Natural History,* II, 350.

121. Quoted in Drake, "Demographic Crisis," 108.

122. Ibid.

123. Ibid., 110.

124. Rutty, *Chronological History,* 80–83.

loss of the potato stores made it necessary to consume a portion of the seed potatoes and seed grain reserved for planting.[125] The press carried anxious reports about the harvest outcomes as early as April, believing that the spring drought had destroyed the grain "in the ground."[126] The climbing cereal prices also derived from the practice of withholding grain from the market in anticipation of still higher prices.[127] Sheriffs' inventories of stored grain disclosed that considerable quantities were being held off the market in the counties of Dublin and Wexford.[128]

Although it is clear that both the cereal and potato crops were deficient in 1740,[129] the subsistence crisis and famine conditions resulted more from dependence on potatoes in southwestern Ireland and failure to import food supplies than from drastic harvest shortfalls. Famine in Ireland during 1740–1741 ensued in part from the fact that harvests were deficient in Britain and elsewhere in Europe. As L. M. Cullen has noted, when harvest outcomes were unsatisfactory again in 1744, the favorable grain yields in England made it possible to pour cereals into Ireland in the spring and summer of 1745 to provide subsistence for the population, which again had exhausted the food supplies.[130] Heavy livestock mortality also reduced the food supply in Ireland during 1740–1741. The evidence indicates that large numbers of animals died from hunger as a result of the shortage of pasture, but evidence of the consequences for arable farming is lacking. Both sheep[131] and cattle[132] perished during the cold and dry winter and spring seasons of 1740, while a fatal epizootic disease killed numerous horses during the winter of 1740–1741.[133]

The Irish subsistence crisis came to an end with the successful cereal and potato harvests of 1741. The cereal harvests in northern Ireland were described as "very good,"[134] while the oat harvest in county Roscommon was believed to be the "finest crop" in many years.[135] In addition to the more favorable yields of 1741, more land appears to have been cultivat-

125. Drake, "Demographic Crisis," 112; Charles Creighton, *A History of Epidemics in Britain*, 2 vols. (Cambridge, 1891–94), II, 241.

126. *Faulkner's Dublin Journal*, April 22–26, 1740.

127. See *Faulkner's Dublin Journal*, June 10–14, June 17–21, June 21–24, August 30–September 2, and October 4–7, 1740.

128. Drake, "Demographic Crisis," 115; *Faulkner's Dublin Journal*, January 3–6, October 11–14, and November 25–29, 1740, and February 17–21, 1741.

129. Rutty, *Chronological History*, 82–83; Cullen, *Economic History*, 69.

130. Cullen, *Economic History*, 68–69.

131. *Faulkner's Dublin Journal*, February 23–26 and April 22–26, 1740; *London Advertiser*, March 4, 1739/40; Rutty, *Natural History*, II, 349–50.

132. *London Advertiser*, May 29, 1740.

133. *Faulkner's Dublin Journal*, February 17–21, 1741; Drake, "Demographic Crisis," 117.

134. *Faulkner's Dublin Journal*, August 1–4, 1741.

135. Quoted in Drake, "Demographic Crisis," 117.

ed than in 1740. The supply of potatoes became abundant and remained so for the balance of the eighteenth century.[136]

To sum up, a scarcity of food and high grain prices predominated in Ireland from the beginning of 1740 until the autumn of 1741, with the province of Munster experiencing famine conditions. Mortality trends in Ireland were similar to those in Scotland. Table 1 shows, however, that the number of deaths rose more sharply in Ireland during 1740, 50 percent or more, and then fell more precipitously in 1742. The mortality curve in Ireland traced a pattern consistent with the anticipated demographic effects of a subsistence crisis.

In northern France, the winter grains were partially destroyed in the ground by the deep frosts of 1740, particularly in those areas where there was a lack of protective snow cover. The wheat losses were replaced in part by barley planted in March, a countermeasure learned from the tragic experience of 1709–1710. But the succession of spring frosts and thaws further reduced cereal yields. Fears for the success of the grain harvests were widespread by June.[137] The wet and cold weather of early August worsened the outlook.[138] The winter grain harvests were delayed. Réaumur reported that no rye had been cut in the Paris region as late as the first week of August, though the cutting normally began in the first week of July.[139] Also, the excessive precipitation that fell in August caused the wheat to germinate (i.e., to sprout) and to rot. Observers predicted no better than a "half-harvest" for winter grains. The cereal harvests in northern France were not completed until a month later than usual; in normal years, the harvest was stored by mid-September and the fall planting of winter grains was begun in the first week of October. The late-summer rains not only delayed the cereal harvests of 1740 but also set back the sowing of the next crop of winter grains.[140]

The evidence indicates that the early-autumn warm spell proved sufficient to bring the spring crops to maturity but that the aggregate degree of warmth in 1740 was insufficient for high wheat yields and inadequate to ripen grapes. This generalization is supported by the systematic study of French harvest outcomes in 1740 carried out by

136. Rutty, *Chronological History,* 98, 107; Drake, "Demographic Crisis," 118, 123; *Faulkner's Dublin Journal,* September 15–18, 1741.

137. E. J.-F. Barbier, *Journal historique et anecdotique du règne de Louis XV,* 4 vols. (Paris, 1847–56), II, 256.

138. See M. de Réaumur, "Observations du thermomètre faites en 1740," *Histoire de l'Académie royale des sciences* (Paris, 1742), 552–53; and Pierre de Narbonne, *Journal des règnes de Louis XIV et Louis XV de l'année 1701 à l'année 1744 par P. Narbonne, premier commissaire de police de la ville de Versailles,* ed. J.-A. Le Roi (Versailles, 1866), 476.

139. Réaumur, "Observations," 552–53.

140. Bricourt et al., "Crise," 310–11; Réaumur, "Observations," 554.

Michel Bricourt, Marcel Lachiver, and Denis Queruel. The area investigated encompasses the large region of France that was subject to the jurisdiction of the Parlement de Paris, essentially the northern half of France excluding the provinces of Brittany and Normandy and the provinces of eastern France. The relative harvest yields in 1740 could be determined because of the fact that crop volumes were used to decide whether the rents would be paid in cash or in kind. In brief, in the years in which harvest yields were normal, the existing lease agreements were executed in accordance with their terms. In years in which yields turned out to be deficient, however, the local agents of the Parlement were authorized to prescribe payments in money rather than in grain. In the harvests of 1740, rent payments in money were more common for winter grains and payments in kind more common for spring grains. It should be noted that the winter grains (Wheat, rye, maslin) supplied the large measure of bread cereals in France.[141]

The investigation by Bricourt and his colleagues disclosed that seven different methods of payment were employed for the crops of 1740, which could be translated into the following classifications according to yields:

Payment in kind	good harvest
Three-quarters in kind, one-quarter in money	good harvest
Two-thirds in kind, one-third in money	good harvest
One-half in kind, one-half in money	average harvest
Two-thirds in money, one-third in kind	poor harvest
Three-quarters in money, one-quarter in kind	poor harvest
Payment in money	poor harvest

The authors were of the opinion that the decree setting out the methods of payment was based on too optimistic a view of the winter grain yields. Local officials often rented out land, and it was in their self-interest to perceive higher yields than in fact were the case. It is naturally preferable to be paid in kind rather than in money when grain supplies are short and prices are rising.[142]

According to the methods of payment stipulated in the decree, the harvest results of 1740 fell into three zonal outcomes: first, a western and southern zone, essentially the provinces of Maine, Anjou, Touraine, Poitou, Marche, Berry, Bourbonnais, and also some departments located in the Centre, where good or average yields were the rule (this zone,

141. Bricourt et al., "Crise," 311. Information as to the methods of payment that were carried out in 1740 is found in a decree of the Parlement de Paris issued on December 14, 1740.
142. Ibid., 311–12.

which was relatively spared in 1740, had suffered the poorest harvests in 1738); second, a northern and eastern zone, essentially the provinces of Artois, Picardy, and Champagne, where mainly good or average yields were most common; and third, an intermediate zone, made up of the territory within a ring of 100 kilometers drawn around Paris, where mostly deficient harvests were the rule. The harvest outcomes for the three zones can be summarized by distributing the percentages of good, average, and poor yields experienced in each region:[143]

Zone	Good	Average	Poor
1 (west and south)	29%	35%	35%
2 (north and east)	25	50	25
3 (Paris region)	14	38	48
Average	23	40	37

The figures show that while zones 1 and 2 witnessed, on balance, more satisfactory harvest outcomes than the Paris region, nonetheless all regions suffered a high percentage of poor harvests.

The poor yields in the Paris region, and the fact that winter grains sustained more damage than spring grains in 1740, are corroborated in a report to the Academy of Sciences.[144] The improved weather of September benefited the spring grains but proved of little help to the winter grains. In the Paris region, the cereal harvests were completed between September 20 and September 25, whereas usually all grain was stored by mid-August. In some districts grain still lay ungathered in the fields when the first snow fell at the beginning of November. The crops germinated in the fields. The author estimated that the winter grains harvested in 1740 produced one-quarter less flour than the crop of the previous year, which meant that the supply of food fell off more than the decline in seed–yield ratios. The barley harvest, by contrast, turned out successfully and greatly eased the subsistence problem. Oats, however, were deficient both in volume and in quality.[145] Other accounts of harvest outcomes in the Paris region confirm this report.[146]

In the provinces to the west of Paris, where the harvest outcomes of 1740 were more successful, the sequence of poor and mediocre yields had created a chronic shortage of grain. Some measure of the succession of low yields can be gained from Michel Morineau's discovery of

143. Ibid., 312.

144. M. du Hamel, "Observations botanico-météorologiques pour l'année 1740," *Histoire de l'Académie royale des sciences* (Paris, 1744), 150–51, 164–68.

145. Ibid.

146. See *Mercure de France*, December 1740, 2,951–52; Desbordes, *Chronique*, 26; Narbonne, *Journal*, 483; Marcel Lachiver, *Histoire de Meulan et de sa région par les textes* (Meulan, 1965), 214–15.

seed–yield ratios on a series of sharecropping farms in Maine. The figures that follow represent average multiples of the seeds sown on eight farms: 1738, 5.2; 1739, 6.3; 1740, 6.4; 1741, 6.5; 1742, 8.2.[147] In fact, seven of the eight farms experienced a decline in seed–yield ratios in 1740. Not until 1742 were grain yields satisfactory.[148] The neighboring province of Anjou also suffered poor or mediocre winter grain yields each year from 1738 to 1741.[149] In Brittany, where the winter grain yields had been no better than mediocre from 1736 to 1739, crop volumes were small in 1740.[150] Normandy likewise experienced deficient harvest yields in 1740, which had been the rule in 1738 and 1739.[151]

The provinces to the north and east of the Paris region, on the other hand, enjoyed more favorable crop volumes in 1740. But the record of tithes suggests that the winter grain harvest was poor in some districts of the Nord,[152] whereas this does not seem to have been the case in upper Alsace.[153] In neighboring Lorraine, however, the "poor harvest of wheat and grains in 1740" was the occasion of "dearth and dearness." Because the damage to the winter grains was considered irreparable, the Parlement at Metz ordered the planting of a second crop on June 22, 1740.[154] Harvest outcomes were also poor in Burgundy, where a severe dearth developed in 1740.[155] Harvest failures were likewise common in the Centre province of the Auvergne.[156] Although the three southern provinces of Languedoc, Provence, and the Dauphiné escaped poor harvest outcomes in 1740,[157] several districts in Languedoc reported deficient harvests in both 1739 and 1740.[158]

147. Michel Morineau, *Les Faux-semblants d'un démarrage économique: Agriculture et démographie en France au XVIIIe siècle* (Paris, 1970), 48.

148. Ibid., 49.

149. Lebrun, *Anjou,* 138–39.

150. J. Delumeau, "Démographie d'un port français sous l'ancien régime: Saint-Malo, 1651–1750," *XVIIe Siècle* 86–87 (1970), 15–16.

151. Mohamed El Kordi, *Bayeux aux XVIIe et XVIIIe siècles* (Paris, 1970), 194.

152. Hugues Neveux, "La Production céréalière dans une région frontalière: Le Cambrésis du XVe au XVIIIe siècle," in J. Goy and E. Le Roy Ladurie, eds., *La Fluctuations du produit de la dîme* (Paris, 1972), 58–66.

153. Béatrice Veyrassat-Herren, "Dîmes alsaciennes," in Goy and Le Roy Ladurie, *Produit de la dîme* 98–101.

154. Jacques Baltus, *Annales de Baltus (1724–1756),* ed. Abbé E. Paulus (Metz, 1904), 103–104.

155. P. de Saint-Jacob, *Les Paysans de la Bourgogne du nord au dernier siècle de l'ancien régime* (Dijon, 1960), 295.

156. Olwen H. Hufton, *The Poor of Eighteenth-Century France, 1750–1789* (Oxford, 1974), 177.

157. Kaplan, *Bread,* II, 458.

158. A. Molinier, *Une Paroisse du bas Languedoc: Sérignan (1650–1792)* (Montpellier, 1968), 34; Jacques Godechot and S. Moncassin, "Démographie et subsistances en Languedoc du XVIIIe siècle au dèbut du XIXe siècle," *Bulletin d'Histoire Economique et Sociale de la Révolution Française* (1964), 45–46.

The grape harvests of 1740 were extremely poor in most wine-producing regions of France. The year 1740 saw the latest grape harvest dates since 1675. In the northern half of France, the date of the *vendanges* averaged seventeen days later than the mean harvest dates from 1599 to 1791, while in the southern half of the country the vintages averaged thirteen days later than the mean, with a national average of a fifteen-day delay.[159] The vintages had been early each year from 1736 to 1739.[160] The quality of the grapes for winemaking was also poor in 1740.[161]

The harvests of 1741 brought improved cereal yields in France. But the recovery in seed–yield ratios was less pronounced than in the British Isles, and grain prices remained elevated through 1741. The extended drought of 1741 apparently reduced crop volumes in the Paris region.[162] The seed–yield ratios, moreover, were not "good" throughout the region administered by the Parlement de Paris.[163] In Anjou and Maine, the harvest yields of 1741 have been described as mediocre.[164] Elsewhere in France, the harvest outcomes were satisfactory rather than abundant, even if the crops of 1741 represented a decided improvement over 1740.[165] Cereal prices did not return to "normal" until after the favorable harvests of 1742.[166]

In summary, the grain harvests in the northern half of France were deficient in 1738, mediocre in 1739, deficient in 1740, and then somewhat mediocre again in 1741 before turning out favorably in 1742. As a consequence, a scarcity of cereals developed in 1739, worsened in 1740, and persisted into 1741 before grain prices fell to normal levels after the harvests of 1742. The dearth was therefore more prolonged in France than in the British Isles. The trend of mortality in France, as in Scotland and Ireland but not in England, paralleled the rise and fall of cereal prices.

In the Low Countries, poor harvest outcomes were also the rule in

159. E. Le Roy Ladurie, *Times of Feast, Times of Famine*, trans. Barbara Bray (Garden City, 1971), 368–70.
160. Micheline Baulant, E. Le Roy Ladurie, and Michel Demonet, "Une Synthèse provisoire: Les Vendanges du XVe au XIXe siècle," *Annales: Economies, Sociétés, Civilisations* 73 (July–August 1978), 765.
161. Molinier, *Sérignan*, 34; Réaumur, "Observations," 211; Hamel, "Observations," 167; Narbonne, *Journal*, 477; Desbordes, *Chronique*, 26; Baltus, *Annales*, 105; Saint-Jacob, *Bourgogne*, 295.
162. Desbordes, *Chronique*, 26–27.
163. Bricourt et al., "Crise," 324.
164. Lebrun, *Anjou*, 138–39; Morineau, *Faux-semblants*, 48.
165. El Kordi, *Bayeux*, 194; Neveux, "Production céréalière," 63–66; Veyrassat-Herren, "Dîmes alsaciennes," 98–101; E. Le Roy Ladurie, *Les Paysans de Languedoc*, 2 vols. (Paris, 1966), II, 824.
166. Labrousse, *Prix*, 9; Labrousse, *Esquisse*, 183; Bricourt et al., "Crise," 324.

1740, but the rye crop escaped with only slight damage.[167] Although severe crop failures were anticipated, a constant snow cover afforded some protection to the winter grains in the southern Netherlands, and the harvests did not turn out badly all along the line.[168] The wheat and spelt yields, however, were significantly reduced.[169] The combination of snow, frost, rain, and thaw proved particularly damaging to wheat.[170] The fact that the harvest could be begun only at the end of August and was not completed until October put upward pressure on cereal prices.[171] In some districts the grain harvest could not even be begun until October.[172] In Liège, according to Etienne Hélin, the wheat crop "was reduced almost to nothing."[173]

The Low Countries also suffered heavy losses among the cattle herds in 1740, mostly from starvation due to the lack of spring pasture and fodder.[174] Jan de Vries found a fall in the Dutch output of milk, butter, and cheese during the years 1740–1741.[175] In the vicinity of Louvain, the weather-induced decline in the size of animal herds was compounded by fatal infectious diseases.[176]

Harvest outcomes in the southern Netherlands were deficient again in 1741.[177] Although the cereal harvests took place on schedule in August, crop volumes proved "quite mediocre."[178] Grain prices in the Low Countries remained high throughout 1741 and failed to decline to normal levels in 1742.[179]

To sum up, a dearth of cereals dominated in the Low Countries from

167. Emile Vanderlinden, "Chronique des événements météorologiques en Belgique jusqu'en 1834," *Mémoires de l'Académie royale de Belgique*, Classe des Sciences, 2d ser., 6 (1924), 188; T. Bernier, "Notice sur l'origine et la tenue des anciens registres d'état civil dans la province de Hainaut," *Mémoires de la Société des sciences, des arts, et des lettres du Hainaut*, 4th ser., 9 (1887), 567; Louis Torfs, *Fastes des calamités publiques survenues dans les Pays-Bas*, 2 vols. (Paris, 1859–62), II, 86.

168. Houtte, *Leuven*, 245; Claude Bruneel, *La Mortalité dans les campagnes: Le Duché de Brabant aux XVIIe et XVIIIe siècles* (Louvain, 1977), 278; H. Houtte, "Législation annonaire," 103; Torfs, *Fastes*, II, 86.

169. Houtte, *Leuven*, 212; Daelemans, "Tithe Revenues," 29–30, 36–41; Gutmann, *War and Rural Life*, 92.

170. Bernier, "Hainaut," 567.

171. Vanderlinden, "Chronique," 188; Bruneel, *Mortalité*, 278.

172. Houtte, *Leuven*, 245.

173. Etienne Hélin, "La Disette et le recensement de 1740," *Annuaire d'Histoire Liégeoise* 6 (1959), 445.

174. Schenck, *Winter*, 31.

175. For a discussion of these relationships in Holland, see Jan de Vries, "Measuring the Impact of Climate on History: The Search for Appropriate Methodologies," *Journal of Interdisciplinary History* 10 (Spring 1980), 604–10.

176. Houtte, *Leuven*, 246; Torfs, *Fastes*, II, 84–85; H. Houtte, "Législation annonaire," 103.

177. Houtte, *Leuven*, 210–16; Daelemens, "Tithe Revenues," 29–30, 36–41.

178. Vanderlinden, "Chronique," 187–89.

179. Houtte, *Leuven*, 39–73, 212, 246.

1739 to 1741, particularly in the southern Netherlands. The subsistence crisis was brought about by yield deficiencies each year form 1739 to 1741, most pronounced in 1740. Wheat and spelt yields, however, fell off more markedly than rye yields. Grain prices did not return to normal levels in 1741, and the dearth was prolonged into 1742, particularly in Brabant and Liège.[180] But mortality did not climb with food prices in the Low Countries during 1740, contrary to the demographic trends elsewhere in northwestern Europe. In 1741, however, the number of deaths rose more than 50 percent. The marginal rise in mortality in 1740 and the abrupt rise in 1741 suggest that the subsistence crisis may not adequately account for the mortality peak in the Low Countries.

The cereal harvests in the German lands also were compromised by frost, drought, and untimely precipitation during the crop year 1739–1740. The rye harvests, however, turned out noticeably less satisfactorily than in the Netherlands, particularly in the Prussian domains. On September 2, 1740, Frederick the Great prohibited the export of cereals from the eastern provinces and instructed that all rye offered for sale in the markets of East Prussia should be bought up for the royal magazine.[181] The rye harvests failed in the province of Pomerania, necessitating the importation of a large quantity of grain.[182] The shortage of food, however, became most acute in the western province of Minden-Ravensberg, "where in places such a famine dominated that dead dogs were dug up and eaten." The Rhenish territories of Prussia likewise suffered harvest shortfalls and food scarcities.[183]

In Germany, as elsewhere, the winter grains sustained the greatest losses from the weather conditions of 1740. Both the wheat and rye yields were deficient in Prussia. Reportedly the farmers of Brandenburg harvested only three or four times the wheat and rye seeds sown, with essentially the same outcome in the provinces of West and East Prussia. In Silesia, a province of the Habsburg monarchy until Prussia's invasion in 1740, the winter grains turned out poorly and also yielded low-quality flour. Crop yields, however, did not fall off significantly in every district of Germany. The barley harvests, as elsewhere, turned out satisfactorily.[184]

180. Vanderlinden, "Chronique," 187; Hélin, "Crises à Liège," 492.

181. Acta Borussica, *Denkmäler der preussischen Staatsverwaltung im 18. Jahrhundert*: *Getreidehandelspolitik*, vol. III: W. Naudé and A. Skalweit, *Die Getreidehandelspolitik und Kriegsmagazinverwaltung: Preussens, 1740–1756* (Berlin, 1910), 104.

182. Ibid., 202, 237, 242.

183. Ibid., 244.

184. Johann Christoph Becmann, *Historische Beschreibung der Chur und Mark Brandenburg*, 2 vols. (Berlin, 1751–53), I, 555–56; Bock, *Ost- und Westpreussen*, 782–85; Johann Christian Kundmann, *Die Heimsuchungen Gottes in Zorn und Gnade über das Herzogthum Schlesien in Müntzen* (Leipzig, 1742), 268–72.

Cereal prices nonetheless rose to very elevated levels, and a genuine dearth unfolded in 1740.[185]

According to contemporary German writers, cattle and sheep perished at an alarming rate in 1740. The grim level of mortality among livestock was not confined to the Prussian provinces; great numbers of farm animals also died in Mecklenburg, Hanover, and the Rhineland.[186] The evidence, however, does not indicate a noticeable lowering of arable productivity from the reduced number of draft animals. The cereal yields of 1741 were favorable in Germany. The Prussian grain harvests of 1741 were categorized as "very good almost everywhere."[187] Cereal prices, however, remained at elevated levels during the entire year.[188]

In summary, the cereal harvests in Germany were mediocre in 1739 and poor in 1740. As was the case in northwestern Europe, the winter grains suffered more than the spring grains in 1740. But rye as well as wheat yields fell off in Germany. Although the evidence indicates that animal mortality was strikingly high in Germany, it is not possible to trace the adverse effects on arable productivity. Then in 1741 cereal yields improved noticeably in all regions of the country. The price of food nonetheless remained elevated for the balance of the year. The mortality figures of table 1 show that the number of deaths rose a moderate 14 percent in 1740, stabilized in 1741, and then dropped sharply in 1742 to the lowest level since 1735. While the trend of mortality in Germany is consistent with the demographic effects of high food prices, the low amplitude of the rise in death rates compared with the general experience in northwestern Europe requires explanation, which I will offer in the final chapter.

Systematic measures of grain yields in Austria and the Habsburg monarchy are extremely scarce. To the extent that cereal prices are a reliable guide to harvest outcomes, they suggest that yields were very poor in 1740.[189] The impressionistic evidence indicates that harvest shortfalls in Austria, Bohemia, Silesia, and Hungary paralleled those in

185. Abel, *Massenarmut*, 181.

186. Becmann, *Chur und Brandenburg*, I, 544, 548–49, 556; Bock, *Ost- und Westpreussen*, I, 798–800; Schenck, *Winter*, 42, 54–58; V. Sonderland, *Die Geschichte von Barmen im Wupperthale* (Elberfeld, 1821), 80; Abel, *Massenarmut* 181; Hanover, Edict issued by George II, dated May 7, 1740, broadside in Boston University, Mugar Library, Rare Book Department, call no. 3198–#122; Kundmann, *Schlesien*, 264–65.

187. Naudé and Skalweit, *Getreidehandelspolitik*, 243–45; Hubatsch, *Frederick the Great*, 58.

188. Naudé and Skalweit, *Getreidehandelspolitik*, 590–93, 607–609, 615–17, 624–27, 633–39; Ebeling and Irsigler, *Getreideumsatz*, 256–57, 267; Elsas, *Preise*, I, 588, 672; II, A, 467–68; II, B, 105, 122.

189. Pribram, *Preise*, 371, 381, 386–87, 391, 396, 405–406, 409–10, 434, 441–42, 531–34.

Germany.[190] The single record of rye seed–yield ratios in Slovakia shows a drastic decline from 5.7 in 1739 to 2.8 in 1740.[191] The Habsburg lands also suffered great animal losses in the winter and spring seasons of 1740, but the state of the evidence does not permit an estimate of its effect on the food supply.[192] The course of cereal prices suggests that harvest yields improved in the crop year 1740–1741.

Swiss cereal harvests, measured by the systematic evidence made available by Pfister, were not significantly deficient in 1740. Harvest outcomes were more favorable in the western state of Bern, however, than in the northeastern canton of Zürich, where rye fell below average.[193] The favorable grain yields in the western Swiss plateau can be traced to the less extreme weather conditions that predominated there. The below-normal temperatures of the spring and late summer, however, delayed the 1740 harvests in all regions of Switzerland.[194] In the eastern alpine cantons, the cereal harvests took place much later than average; not all the rye and oat crops were safely gathered and stored in October, when the first snow fell.[195] The shortage of food in Appenzell was grave enough to result in the consumption of carrion horses, and a few persons apparently starved to death in 1741.[196] Harvest yields were also deficient in the alpine cantons of Glarus and Uri but not to the same degree as in Appenzell.[197] Pfister has suggested that the food shortage in the alpine cantons may have resulted more from the decline in dairy production than from large cereal deficiencies.[198] The long winter of 1740 in Switzerland, as elsewhere, created a shortage of fodder. The combination of the delayed opening of the pastures in the alpine cantons and the delayed oat harvests resulted in a decline in the production of dairy products.[199]

190. Kundmann, *Schlesien,* 265–75; Schenck, *Winter,* 32–47; *London Advertiser,* May 7, 1740.

191. Abel, *Massenarmut,* 181.

192. Bock, *Ost- und Westpreussen,* I, 800; Schenck, *Winter,* 32; Abel, *Massenarmut,* 181; *London Advertiser,* May 7, 1740; Arcadius Kahan, "Natural Calamities and Their Effect upon the Food Supply in Russia," *Jahrbücher für Geschichte Osteuropas* n.s. 16 (September 1968), 372.

193. Pfister, personal communication.

194. Pfister, "Little Ice Age," 670–71.

195. G. Walser, *Appenzeller-Chronik,* pt. 3 *(1732–1772)* ed. G. Nuesch (Trogen, 1830), 166–67; Christoph Trümpi, *Neuere Glarner Chronik* (Winterthur, 1774), 560–61; Pfister, CLIMHIST data bank, 238–42.

196. Walser, *Appenzeller-Chronik,* 167–72.

197. Trümpi, *Neuere Glarner Chronik,* 562–72; Jürg Bielmann, *Die Lebensverhältnisse im Urnerland während des 18, und zu Beginn des 19. Jahrhunderts* (Basel, 1972), 79.

198. Pfister, personal communication, August 9, 1979.

199. Pfister, CLIMHIST data bank, 239, 242; Pfister, personal communication, April 17, 1980.

The crop year 1740–1741, contrary to the experience in northwestern Europe, did not bring improved Swiss cereal harvests. Pfister's production index for Zürich fell off sharply from 98 in 1740 to 78 in 1741.[200] The cantons of Luzern and Uri endured another harvest shortfall in 1741.[201] In Appenzell and Glarus, however, the improved grain harvest volumes in 1741 put an end to the subsistence crisis in that region.[202]

To sum up, the evidence shows two patterns of harvest outcomes in Switzerland in 1740. The western half of the country, in particular the plateau, witnessed satisfactory grain yields, whereas the alpine regions, particularly the eastern cantons, suffered harvest shortfalls. The shortage of food that developed in several alpine cantons also derived from the decline in dairy production. The cereal yields of 1741 exhibited, on balance, no improvement over the harvest outcomes of 1740. Crop volumes did not improve noticeably until 1742.[203] Table 1 shows that the number of deaths in Switzerland rose 27 percent in 1740, declined in 1741, and then climbed to a peak in 1742. The shape of the Swiss mortality peak indicates a more complex demographic pattern than the straightforward effects of high food prices.

In Italy, where the weather conditions of 1740 were less detrimental to cereal yields, the harvest shortfalls were correspondently less significant.[204] Although food prices rose in Lombardy, the inflation was traceable mainly to military and political considerations.[205] The cold seasons of 1740–1741 nonetheless reduced grape harvests and damaged olive trees.[206] Italian mortality levels climbed 16 percent in 1740, but the higher death rates can be explained in part as a return to more normal mortality following the unusually low level of 1739. Mortality in Italy remained moderately elevated through the year 1743, however, and high food prices may have influenced the higher death rates.

On the Scandinavian peninsula, by contrast, a series of subsistence crises punctuated the early 1740s. The cold and dry growing seasons of 1740 proved detrimental to cereal yields. The harvest shortfalls of 1740 were compounded in some districts by the inability to sow winter grains

200. Pfister, personal communication.

201. Hans-Rudolf Burri, *Die Bevölkerung Luzerns im 18. und frühen 19. Jahrhundert* (Luzern, 1975) 78; Bielmann, *Urnerland*, 79.

202. Walser, *Appenzeller-Chronik*, 167–72; Trümpi, *Neuere Glarner Chronik*, 562–72.

203. Pfister, personal communication, August 9, 1979; Pfister, CLIMHIST data bank, 242; Walser, *Appenzeller-Chronik*, 167–69; Trümpi, *Neuere Glarner Chronik*, 562; Anne-Marie Piuz, "Climat, récoltes, et vie des hommes à Genève, XVIe–XVIIIe siècles," *Annales: Economies, Sociétés, Civilisations* 29 (May–June 1974) 615.

204. Corradi, *Annali*, IV, 1,400–1,402.

205. Maddalena, *Prezzi*, I, 98–128, 378–84.

206. Ibid., 101, 114, 384, 405.

during the autumn of 1739, owing to the early winter and a shortage of seed grain.[207] Grain yields also turned out deficiently in Denmark.[208] Famine conditions developed in Finland, where the extreme weather conditions caused harvest failures in every region except the southwestern coastal counties.[209] In Sweden proper, the majority of counties suffered serious harvest shortfalls, from the combination of low temperature levels, untimely precipitation, and caterpillar infestations. Estimated harvest yields are available at the county level in Sweden. In a study of Swedish grain price movements, Lennart Jörberg found that although reputed yields did not always correspond to price trends in a "logical" way, still a clear negative correlation obtained between yields and price movements in the years in which the harvest outcome was termed a "failure" and when the harvest was considered to be "good" or "abundant."[210]

The Swedish harvest outcomes of 1740 diverged from the common European experience in that the spring grains also were badly damaged—in several counties ruined—by the inclement autumn weather. As a consequence, a shortage of food developed even in counties where the rye harvests turned out satisfactorily, as in Uppsala, Stockholm, and Östergötland. A mid-September snowstorm and cold wave struck the barley and oat crops while they were still standing in the fields. The subsistence problem became acute in the southeastern counties of Jönköping, Kronoberg, Kalmar, Gotland, and Blekinge, where both the winter and spring crops were deficient. The poor rye harvests resulted in part from the inability to sow all the arable fields the previous autumn. The southwestern counties of Kristianstad, Malmöhus, Halland, Göteborg and Bohus, Älvsborg, Skaraborg, and Värmland likewise suffered poor winter and spring cereal harvests. The northern Swedish county of Västerbotten and the contiguous Finnish county of Österbotten endured their second consecutive harvest failure and the onset of famine conditions.[211]

Grain harvest outcomes in Norway differed somewhat from those of Sweden-Finland. The severe winter of 1740 was followed by a milder spring season. The moderating trend brought extensive flooding, however, which hindered the planting of spring grains. The spring floods and

207. Imhof, Bevölkerungsentwicklung in den nordischen Ländern, 725–28.
208. Friis and Glamann, Prices, 144.
209. Jutikkala, Bevölkerung Finnlands, 39; Imhof, Bevölkerungsentwicklung in den nordischen Ländern, 728, 732–33.
210. For an extended discussion of the relationships between harvest volumes and price movements in Sweden, see Lennart Jörberg, A History of Prices in Sweden, 1732–1914, 2 vols. (Lund, 1972), II, 56–73.
211. Imhof, Bevölkerungsentwicklung in den nordischen Ländern, 728–32.

low summer temperatures combined to reduce cereal yields.[212] But because the Norwegian population relied less on grain for subsistence and because the harvest shortfalls had been less severe in 1739, the pressure on food supplies was not so acute as in Sweden-Finland.[213]

The Scandinavian agricultural outcomes also differed from the more common European experience in that the weather-related loss of cattle proved considerable enough to reduce the supply of food, chiefly by limiting the arable land that could be cultivated. From 1740 onward, the deficient hay and oat harvests led to an acute shortage of fodder. The size of the herds was further reduced by disease and by the need to slaughter animals that could not be stall-fed. Not only was a smaller area of land plowed and planted in the early 1740s; the fields suffered from a lack of fertilizer. The supply of food declined in addition as the volume of dairy products fell off.[214]

This cumulative effect on the supply of food can be traced in the southern county of Kristianstad. The severe winter of 1740 brought about the death of some 2,097 head of cattle and 871 horses, chiefly from starvation. Because of a shortage of draft animals, a fraction of winter grain fields could not be sown in the autumn of 1740. A somewhat different sequence occurred in the central county of Gävleborg. The long winter season of 1740 delayed the opening of spring pastures until June. Because of the lack of pasture, the production of butter, whose market sale was critical for the welfare of the peasants, fell off considerably. To compound the hardships, the scant hay harvests of 1740 and the early onset of winter weather forced the peasants to dispose of more animals.[215]

Another long winter season in 1740–1741 aggravated the Scandinavian food scarcity. The cereal stocks had melted away following the deficient harvests of 1739 and 1740. In Sweden-Finland, the harvest outcomes of 1741 turned out mediocre to poor, in large part because of the shortage of draft animals and of seed grain. Several counties, including Uppsala and Blekinge, now suffered a third consecutive poor harvest. The capacity to plant and reap cereals was further reduced by the Russian war, which drained agricultural workers off into the army. As a consequence of that series of events, a grave shortage of food developed in the

212. Utterström, "Population Problems," 127; Imhof, *Bevölkerungsentwicklung in den nordischen Ländern*, 734.
213. Michael Drake, *Population and Society in Norway, 1735–1865* (Cambridge, 1969), 70–72.
214. Utterström, "Population Problems," 121; Imhof, *Bevölkerungsentwicklung in den nordischen Ländern*, 736–37.
215. Imhof, *Bevölkerungsentwicklung in den nordischen Ländern*, 816–18.

Swedish counties of Skaraborg, Värmland, Öreboro, and Kopparberg.[216]

The harvest outcomes in Norway were universally poor in 1741, much more deficient than in 1740. The cold spring and summer months of 1741 retarded the growth and then lowered the yields of the spring grains. A scarcity of seed grain after two unsuccessful crop years also contributed to the smaller volumes. The cumulative cereal deficit brought about an acute shortage of food in 1741.[217] In the Danish half of the kingdom, by contrast, the grain harvests turned out satisfactorily in 1741.[218]

To summarize Scandinavian harvest outcomes, the cereal yields of 1740 were deficient throughout the region, but more so in Sweden-Finland than in Norway-Denmark. The harvest shortfalls followed the mediocre yields of 1739. The barley and oat crops as well as the winter grains were deficient in 1740, in contrast to the common European outcome. Food scarcities developed in Sweden-Finland during 1740 and to a lesser degree in Norway-Denmark. In Sweden-Finland, all the cereal harvests of 1741 again were poor but represented an improvement over those of 1740. In Norway, however, the grain yields were extremely low in 1741, particularly the volume of spring grains. A grave shortage of food afflicted Norway during 1741, more so than in Sweden-Finland. In Denmark, the improved cereal harvests of 1741 erased the threat of a prolonged subsistence crisis.

Table 1 shows that the number of deaths rose in each Scandinavian country during 1740. Finland experienced a mortality crisis; mortality climbed 16 percent in Sweden but somewhat less in Norway and Denmark. Scandinavian mortality trends varied in 1741. The number of deaths declined in both Sweden and Finland, whereas Norway suffered a mortality crisis. The Danish mortality level rose marginally in 1741. Table 1 also discloses that mortality remained elevated on the Scandinavian peninsula beyond 1741, whereas elsewhere in Europe the mortality peak centered on the years 1740–1741. It seems doubtful, therefore, that the Scandinavian mortality fluctuations can be fully explained by the food scarcities and high cereal prices that dominated the two-year period 1740–1741. A brief survey of the European harvest outcomes during the years 1742–1744, however, will explain in part the different demographic trends.

216. Ibid., 734–37.
217. Ibid., 737; Drake, *Norway,* 71; Utterström, "Population Problems," 127.
218. Friis and Glamann, *Prices,* 144, 154.

1742–1744

European cereal harvests were generally successful during the years 1742–1744, with some exceptions in the Scandinavian peninsula. European weather patterns following the cold and long winter of 1742 became more favorable for high crop yields. In England, wheat yields were abundant in 1742 in spite of the prolonged drought from January to June. Hoskins has classified the national wheat crop of 1742 as "good," that of 1743 as "abundant," and that of 1744 as "good."[219] In Scotland, the harvest outcomes were good in 1742, abundant in 1743, and adequate in 1744.[220] In Ireland, the cereal and potato crops of 1742 and 1743 proved more than adequate to meet all subsistence needs. According to Rutty, provisions in the winter of 1742 "were as plentiful as they had been scarce for the two last years," and 1743 was "remarkable" for "fertility and plenty in large crops of corn of all sorts."[221] Although cereal crops were deficient in Ireland again in 1744, the combination of high potato yields and large grain imports from England prevented a new dearth.[222]

Table 1 indicates that the death rate in England remained elevated during 1742 and then declined steeply in 1743 and 1744. In Scotland, mortality fell noticeably in 1742 and then in 1743 and 1744 fell to the lowest level since 1738. In Ireland, mortality returned to "normal" in 1742, fell further in 1743, and in 1744 declined to the lowest level of the ten-year period. The curve of mortality in the British Isles followed the downward movement of food prices from 1742 to 1744.

The harvest outcomes in France, the Low Countries, and Germany paralleled the trends in the British Isles during the years 1742–1744. In France, however, grain harvest volumes were not so abundant as in England, as was indicated by the elevated cereal prices of 1742.[223] In the Low Countries, grain yields improved each year from 1742 to 1744.[224]

219. Hoskins, "Harvest Fluctuations," 23–31; Tooke and Newmarch, *Prices*, 43; Huxham, *Observations*, II, 126; Marshall, *Stout of Lancaster*, 230–34; Short, *New Observations*, 345–46; Stratton, *Agricultural Records*, 75; Jones, *Seasons*, 138; Ashton, *Economic Fluctuations*, 20.
220. Flinn et al., *Scottish Population History*, 494–95; Hamilton, *Economic History*, 397–98.
221. Rutty, *Chronological History*, 98, 107.
222. Cullen, *Economic History*, 68–69.
223. Labrousse, *Prix*, 9; Labrousse, *Esquisse*, 183; Bricourt et al., "Crise," 324; Desbordes, *Chronique*, 26–27; Lebrun, *Anjou*, 138–39; Morineau, *Faux-semblants*, 48; El Kordi, *Bayeux*, 194; Le Roy Ladurie, *Languedoc*, II, 824; Neveux, "Production céréalière," 63–66; Veyrassat-Herren, "Dîmes alsaciennes," 98–101.
224. Houtte, *Leuven*, 210–16; Daelemans, "Tithe Revenues," 36–41; Gutmann, *War and Rural Life*, 87.

Cereal prices remained abnormally high in the southern Netherlands into 1742, but then they fell to unusually low levels in 1743 and 1744.[225] Prussian cereal harvests were "very good almost everywhere" in 1742 and 1743.[226] Grain prices also declined noticeably in Prussia during 1742 and 1743. In several southwestern German locations, however, the price of food remained elevated during 1742–1743.[227] Although German grain harvests were successful from 1742 to 1744, they failed, on balance, to match the abundant yields reported in England.[228] The movement of cereal prices in Austria indicates that harvest outcomes were similar to those in Germany.[229]

Swiss cereal yields also improved significantly in 1742. Pfister's grain volume index for the state of Bern rose from 112 in 1741 to 124 in 1742, the highest value since 1737; while the index for Zürich rose to 103 in 1742, the highest value of the ten-year period 1735–1744.[230] Although Swiss cereal yields were less favorable in 1743 and 1744, the price of grain declined, indicating that food was not scarce.[231] Italian cereal harvests were satisfactory during the years 1742 to 1744, but the elevated food prices in Lombardy indicate that harvest outcomes were mediocre in northern Italy.[232]

Contrary to the mortality trends in northwestern Europe, neither Swiss nor Italian death rates declined in 1742. Rather, the number of deaths recorded in Switzerland climbed 23 percent to reach a peak for the period under study, while mortality in Italy rose a more moderate 5 percent. As table 1 shows, the mortality levels in Switzerland and Italy did not fall significantly until 1744. Swiss and Italian death rates did not decline in consonance with the reduction of cereal prices during the years 1742–1744, and thus the mortality peak there will require a more comprehensive explanation.

The level of mortality in the Scandinavian peninsula also rose to a new peak in 1742, but the elevated death rates were paralleled by poor

225. Houtte, *Leuven*, 39–73, 212, 246; H. Houtte, "Législation annonaire," 103–104.

226. Naudé and Skalweit, *Getreidehandelspolitik*, 243–45; Hubatsch, *Frederick the Great*, 58.

227. Elsas, *Preise*, I, 588, 672; II, A, 467–68; II, B, 105, 122; Naudé and Skalweit, *Getreidehandelspolitik*, 590–93; Ebeling and Irsigler, *Getreideumsatz*, 256–57, 267.

228. Naudé and Skalweit, *Getreidehandelspolitik*, 243–45, 590–93; Elsas, *Preise*, I, 588, 672; II, A, 467–68; II, B, 105, 122.

229. Pribram, *Preise*, 371, 381, 386–87, 391, 396, 405–406, 409–10, 434, 441–42, 531–34.

230. Pfister, personal communication.

231. Ibid.; Willy Pfister, "Getreide- und Weinzehnten 1565–1798 und Getreidepreise 1565–1770 in bernischen Aargau," *Argovia* 52 (1940), 258–63; Bucher, *Entlebuch*, 234; Trümpi, *Neuere Glarner Chronik*, 572–74; Walser, *Appenzeller-Chronik*, 177–81.

232. Corradi, *Annali*, 1,398–99; Maddelena, *Prezzi*, I, 379–83.

harvests and food scarcities. The deficient crop volumes of 1742 derived both from the inability to plow arable fields and from detrimental winter weather.[233] The progressive reduction in the size of the animal herds made it increasingly difficult to sow the grain fields. Another cold spring season in 1742 delayed the opening of pastures, further prejudicing the survival of cattle. Farmers in the central Swedish county of Kopparberg complained that the undunged arable fields had become so infertile that the land brought forth neither grain nor grass. Such claims were probably exaggerated, but similar accounts could be multiplied.

The shortage of draft animals became acute in Norway, where the most severe Scandinavian mortality crisis unfolded in 1742. Crop yields In Norway, and in several Swedish counties located along the Norwegian border, were sharply lowered in 1742 by a cold, rainy spell in August and September. The reduced harvest volumes maintained food prices at levels beyond the reach of the poor, and famine conditions afflicted the counties on both sides of the border between Norway and Sweden.[234] The working population of the Swedish county of Värmland was reduced to the hazardous makeshift diets that were common in preindustrial famines. More than 12 percent of the county's population died during 1742. The combination of unfavorable weather conditions in 1742 and idle arable fields also depressed harvest volumes in the northern counties of Sweden and Finland. In the southern Finnish counties, the flight of the rural population before the advancing Russian army and the needs of the foraging Swedish army diminished the available supply of food.[235]

It should be stressed that Norwegian harvest volumes were lower in 1742 than in either 1741 or 1740, which was not the case in Sweden. An almost total harvest failure from north to south proved the rule in Norway. If the accounts can be believed, no grain at all was gathered in some districts. Numerous families were forced to abandon their farms in order to seek work elsewhere or simply to beg. The southern diocese of Akershus, where the population relied most heavily on cereals, was the hardest hit. The national death rate rose to 52.2 per 1,000 in 1742, whereas the rate climbed to 67.3 per 1,00 in Akershus.[236]

Scandinavian weather conditions ameliorated in 1743, and harvest outcomes exhibited a parallel improvement. Although a scarcity of food continued to dominate in some southern Finnish and Swedish counties,

233. Imhof, *Bevölkerungsentwicklung in den nordischen Ländern*, 738–39.
234. Ibid., 738–39, 817–18; Jörberg, *Prices*, I, 632–61.
235. Imhof, *Bevölkerungsentwicklung in den nordischen Ländern*, 739–40; Jutikkala, *Bevölkerung Finnlands*, 40–41.
236. Imhof, *Bevölkerungsentwicklung in den nordischen Ländern*, 740–45; Drake, *Norway*, 65–66, 71–72.

the national subsistence crisis ended in 1743. The Swedish death rate, however, peaked in 1743. As will be shown, the crisis mortality did not derive exclusively from elevated food prices. In 1744, the cereal harvests turned out successfully in all regions of Scandinavia, which put an end to the critical food scarcities of the earlier 1740s.[237]

To sum up, Scandinavian grain harvest yields, contrary to the agricultural experience in northwestern Europe, were deficient in 1742 and mediocre in Sweden-Finland in 1743. A shortage of draft animals, poor weather conditions, and the war between Sweden-Finland and Russia all contributed to the scarcity of food. The Scandinavian death rate peaked in 1742, correlating with the poor crop yields of that year. The elevated Swedish mortality of 1743 reflected the influence of high food prices and the demographic hazards created by wartime conditions.

In conclusion, the evidence shows that European harvest outcomes were on balance favorable during the years 1735–1738, deficient during the years 1739–1740, and mostly favorable from 1741 to 1744. At the same time, Scandinavian grain harvests were mostly unfavorable each year from 1739 to 1743. The level of European mortality moved more or less inversely with the trend of cereal yields during the period from 1735 to 1744. This correspondence, however, exhibited exceptions and lags in Scandinavia, England, and elsewhere. As has been noted, it is the process of reconciling the exceptions and explaining the lags that will throw the maximum light on the issue of the relationship between food shortage and incidence of epidemic disease.

Before focusing on this central question, however, it is necessary to establish the regional amplitude of the rise in food prices. It is also essential to determine the degree to which all the major cereals advanced symmetrically in price during the subsistence crisis. A more balanced cereal culture, in particular the extensive cultivation of spring grains, should have dampened the price pressure on barley and oats in the event of harvest failures and should thus have enabled the working population to shift their demand to these cheaper cereals. There is evidence to suggest that a symmetrical cereal price structure and severe subsistence crises went hand in hand, and accordingly that a shortage of food exercised a greater influence on the death rate when all cereals rose sharply in price.

237. Imhof, *Bevölkerungsentwicklung in den nordischen Ländern,* 745–46; Jörberg, *Prices,* I, 154; Utterström, "Population Problems," 126–31.

5. *Western European Grain Prices, 1735–1744*

The consecutive grain harvest shortfalls of 1739 and 1740 touched off a western European subsistence crisis. A third consecutive year of deficient crop yields in 1741 intensified the shortage of food in some regions, particularly in Scandinavia. The increase of grain prices resulted not only from weather-related crop losses but also from the practice of withholding cereals from the markets in anticipation of still higher prices. Because of the price inelasticity of demand for cereals, the market prices rose proportionately more than the decline in the output of grain. Because no reasonably priced alternative food was available, cereal prices could triple and still remain cheaper than meat and dairy products on a per calorie basis.[1] A the same time, the decline in the volume of cereals harvested during 1739–1740 was not so great as to create national famines. The failure of specific crops, however, produced severe hunger in several provinces and counties of western Europe.

The information needed to measure the relative severity of a food shortage—that is, the actual decline in per capita food supplies—cannot be retrieved from the evidence. In its absence, the annual market prices of grain serve as an index of the fluctuations in crop volumes. But it must be remembered that the price of cereals also reflected the anticipated harvest outcomes in the autumn and the market effects of speculative trading practices.

Table 10 displays the course of European grain prices during the ten-year period from 1735 to 1744. The index numbers represent the annual price movements of the national bread grains. In the thirteen locations indexed, the average price of grain rose 60 percent between 1738 and 1740. Several countries registered steeper price increases. For

1. For evidence of this price-calorie relationship in preindustrial Germany, see Wilhelm Abel, *Massenarmut and Hungerkrisen im vorindustriellen Europa* (Hamburg, 1974), 319–20.

example, the price of grain increased 115 percent in Scotland, 106 percent in Denmark, and 84 percent in the Low Countries during this two-year period. But the amplitude of the price increases remained moderate compared to the fourfold rise of grain prices in France during the 1690s.[2] Nonetheless, the price data show that a subsistence crisis afflicted western Europe in 1740 and that a serious shortage of food had developed in parts of the British Isles and Low Countries.

A comparison of the price indexes of table 10 and the mortality indexes of table 1 discloses that grain prices and the number of deaths rose and fell in tandem during the period 1735–1744, with the changes in prices tending to lead the changes in mortality. The moderate advance of European grain prices during 1736 and 1737 preceded or coincided with the minor mortality peak registered in most countries during the same two years. The correspondence between the two variables is particularly noticeable in the German lands and in Scandinavia. In 1738, both grain prices and the number of deaths fell off considerably in western Europe.

The second advance of European grain prices took place during the last half of 1739 and proved sharper and longer lasting than the earlier upswing. Elevated food prices persisted into 1742 and were paralleled by the prolonged mortality peak of 1740–1742. The decline in grain prices that set in during 1742, however, was not matched by a fall in the number of deaths. Dissimilar regional trends accounted in part for this divergent movement of the two variables. In northwestern Europe, as the index numbers indicate, both grain prices and mortality levels declined, on balance, in 1742. In Scandinavia and west-central Europe, the price of grain remained somewhat elevated and the number of deaths climbed in 1742. During the years 1743–1744, the price of grain and the number of deaths fell sharply in all regions of Europe, with the price decline tending to precede the decline in deaths.

It should be recognized that whether a shortage of food influences the death rate through the physiological interaction of nutrition and infection or as the consequence of social upheaval, the demographic impact would be subject to a time lag of several months or longer. This time lag and the assumed close connection between fluctuations in crop volumes and vital rates inspired the practice of compiling demographic statistics by harvest or crop years rather than by calendar years. In the case of demographic statistics compiled by calendar years, whatever influence fluctuating crop volumes exercised on the level of mortality would be

2. Andrew B. Appleby,"Grain Prices and Subsistence Crises in England and France, 1590–1740," *Journal of Economic History* 39 (December 1979), 870–73.

Table 10. Indexes of annual grain prices in Europe, 1735–1744 (1735–1744 = 100)

Location	1735	1736	1737	1738	1739	1740	1741	1742	1743	1744
England	114	106	94	94	128	156	94	74	67	72
Scotland[a]	103	101	95	79	102	170	96	80	72	103
Ireland (Dublin)	n.a.	92	101	92	96	150	153	93	59	64
France	79	91	92	104	114	122	144	105	75	75
Low Countries[b]	91	78	79	94	115	173	135	86	72	75
Germany[c]	74	97	105	87	93	153	130	92	91	83
Austria[d]	56	72	97	99	93	122	140	135	110	79
Switzerland (Aargau)	78	87	109	67	80	120	109	117	113	117
Italy (Milan)	125	101	74	81	100	108	105	112	106	88
Sweden	97	105	83	72	93	119	128	107	109	98
Finland	69	85	82	76	94	109	155	n.a.	145	84
Norway	82	83	97	88	86	127	141	115	97	84
Denmark	84	111	96	72	83	148	139	102	87	77
Unweighted averages	88	93	93	85	98	137	128	102	93	85

NOTE: The index numbers represent wheat prices for England and France; meal prices for Scotland; combined wheat and rye prices for Scotland; combined rye and barley prices for Sweden and Norway; rye prices for the Low Countries, Germany, Austria, Switzerland, Finland, and Denmark; and mixed grain prices for Italy.

[a]Index numbers computed from "fiars prices" at the markets of Fife, Midlothian, Perth, Roxburgh, and Lanark.

[b]Index numbers computed from rye prices at the markets of Brussels, Ghent, Louvain, and Amsterdam.

[c]Index numbers computed from rye prices at the markets of Berlin, Magdeburg, Minden, Munich, and Leipzig.

[d]Index numbers computed from rye prices at the markets of Vienna and Wels in Upper Austria.

Reprinted from John D. Post, "Climate Variability and the European Mortality Wave of the Early 1740s," *The Journal of Interdisciplinary History*, XV (1984), 15, table 4, with permission of the editors of *The Journal of Interdisciplinary History* and The MIT Press, Cambridge, Massachusetts. Copyright © 1984 by the Massachusetts Institute of Technology and the editors of *The Journal of Interdisciplinary History*.

SOURCES: W. G. Hoskins, "Harvest Fluctuations and English Economic History, 1620–1759," *Agricultural History Review* 16, pt 1 (1968), 31; Michael Flinn et al., *Scottish Population History* (Cambridge, 1977), 489–98; Michael Drake, "The Irish Demographic Crisis of 1740–41," *Historical Studies* 6 (1968), 118; C. E. Labrousse, *Esquisse du mouvement des prix et des revenus en France au XVIIIe siècle* (Paris, 1932), 103, 183; Labrousse et al., *Le Prix du froment en France au temps de la monnaie stable, 1726–1913* (Paris, 1970), 9; Charles Verlinden et al., eds., *Dokumenten voor de geschiedenis van prijzen en lonen in Vlaanderen en Brabant (XVe–XVIIIe eeuw)* (Bruges, 1959–73), 88–90, 486–500; G. van Houtte, *Leuven in 1740, ein krisisjaar: Ekonomische, sociale, en demografische aspekten* (Brussels, 1964), 41; Nicolaas W. Posthumus, *Inquiry into the History of Prices in Holland*, 2 vols. (Leiden, 1946–64), II, 415; Acta Borussica, *Denkmäler der preussischen Staatsverwaltung im 18. Jahrhundert: Getreidehandelspolitik*, vol. II: W. Naudé, *Die Getreidehandelspolitik und Kriegsmagazinverwaltung, Brandenburg-Preussens bis 1740* (Berlin, 1901), 538, 548, 572; ibid., vol. III: W. Naudé and A. Skalweit, *Die Getreidehandelspolitik und Kriegsmagazinverwaltung, Preussens, 1740–1756* (Berlin, 1910), 607–609, 624–27; M. J. Elsas, *Umriss einer Geschichte der Preise und Löhne in Deutschland vom ausgehenden Mittelalter bis zum Beginn des 19. Jahrhunderts*, 2 vols. (Leiden, 1936–49), I, 588, 675; B, 126; Alfred Francis Pribram, *Materialen zur Geschichte der Preise und Löhne in Österreich* (Vienna, 1938), 391, 531; Willy Pfister, "Getreide- und Weinzehnten, 1565–1798, und Getreidepreise, 1565–1770, im bernischen Aargau," *Argovia* 52 (1940), 258–63; Aldo De Maddalena, *Prezzi e mercedi a Milano dal 1701 al 1860*, 2 vols. (Milan, 1974), I, 379; Lennart Jörberg, *A History of Prices in Sweden, 1732–1914*, 2 vols. (Lund, 1972), I, 632; Arthur E. Imhof, *Aspekte der Bevölkerungsentwicklung in den nordischen Ländern, 1720–1750* (Bern, 1976), 762–66; Astrid, Friis and Kristof Glamann, *A History of Prices and Wages in Denmark, 1660–1800*, vol. I: *Copenhagen* (London, 1958), 154.

reflected more in the subsequent year than in the year in which the harvests took place.

The record of annual grain prices is not a complete indicator of the relative degree of stress caused by a shortage of food. The majority of consumers purchased food at weekly or daily markets and were required to pay the prices demanded at the time. Annual average prices can mask important short-term fluctuations in the cost of food. Monthly grain prices at nine regional locations are displayed in table 11; the indexes reveal the greater volatility of food costs measured from month to month. The price data are limited to the twenty-four-month period encompassing the years 1740–1741, the period in which the highest price peaks are found.

As the index numbers indicate, the price of cereals began to climb at the end of 1739, following the poor harvests of that year. In the Low Countries, and to a lesser degree in Germany and France, the price of grain was already noticeably elevated as early as January 1740. It can be seen that despite the enduring frosts and worsening drought of 1740 the price of food climbed only moderately during the first four months of the year. When the unfavorable atmospheric conditions persisted into May and June, however, the market price of grain soared in anticipation of drastically reduced harvest volumes in the autumn.

The price of grain continued to rise during the midsummer months of 1740. The pressure of demand was supported not only by the expected harvest failures but also by the knowledge of the poor grain yields of the previous year. This latter circumstance can most readily be seen in the high index numbers for the southern Netherlands (Brussels), where large harvest shortfalls had been the rule the previous year. Grain prices dipped in the late-summer months of 1740 as the weather improved. In the autumn months, however, the combination of the perceived shortage of food and the practice of withholding the harvested cereals from the markets drove prices upward again. The autumn advance in grain prices signaled the advent of a subsistence crisis, as the price movement was contrary to the normal decline that set in at the end of a crop year.

The market price of grain peaked during the winter months of 1740–1741. Prices began to drift downward in the early spring months, when the pressure of demand was eased by the public policies that brought imported cereals into domestic consumption. Public pressure exerted against grain dealers and producers to bring their hoarded stocks to market also contributed to the decline in prices. In spite of the public countermeasures, grain prices climbed again in the late spring and early summer of 1741, when the supply of food reached its lowest ebb in the

Table 11. Indexes of monthly grain prices in Europe, 1740 and 1741 (1735–1744 = 100)

Location	Jan.	Feb.	Mar.	Apr.	May	June	July	Aug.	Sept.	Oct.	Nov.	Dec.
1740												
England (London)	88	88	94	94	94	175	175	175	88	94	110	110
Ireland (Dublin)	83	89	98	104	113	159	163	180	147	138	148	167
France (Paris region)	101	102	110	97	102	102	118	127	144	144	144	178
Low Countries (Brussels)	143	146	154	159	178	241	222	211	205	200	203	211
Low Countries (Amsterdam)	114	125	142	144	165	170	163	150	142	150	163	173
Germany (Berlin)	88	92	96	117	138	150	163	154	163	171	175	171
Germany (Munich)	102	102	98	104	107	141	135	127	141	147	175	158
Austria (Vienna)	97	113	104	106	127	127	127	128	127	137	142	133
Norway (Oslo)	n.a.	79	79	100	100	107	129	121	129	150	157	n.a.
Unweighted averages	102	104	108	114	125	152	155	153	143	148	157	163
1741												
England (London)	120	120	146	146	136	139	88	94	88	88	88	88
Ireland (Dublin)	164	161	158	181	173	173	138	98	84	91	89	98
France (Paris region)	169	178	169	169	169	169	169	118	118	118	114	114
Low Countries (Brussels)	192	176	127	114	105	111	122	111	108	105	100	89
Low Countries (Amsterdam)	191	173	142	142	142	138	132	132	132	132	122	121
Germany (Berlin)	163	142	138	142	133	121	125	104	96	88	79	79
Germany (Munich)	147	158	147	141	138	180	203	175	180	169	175	161
Austria (Vienna)	122	118	127	125	130	130	118	124	124	127	128	126
Norway (Oslo)	157	157	n.a.	157	129	175	164	136	121	150	150	150
Unweighted averages	158	154	144	146	139	148	140	121	117	119	116	114

NOTE: The index numbers represent wheat prices for London and Dublin; rye prices for Brussels, Amsterdam, Berlin, Munich, and Vienna; barley prices for the Paris region and Oslo.

SOURCES: *Gentleman's Magazine* 10 (1740), 11 (1741); *Faulkner's Dublin Journal*, 1740, 1741; Jacques Dupâquier, Michael Lachiver, and J. Meuvret, *Mercuriales du pays de France et du Vexin français, 1640–1792* (Paris, 1968), 68–69; Charles Verlinden et al, eds., *Dokumenten voor de geschiedenis van prijzen en lonen in Vlaanderen en Brabant (XVe–XVIIIe eeuw)* (Bruges, 1959–73), 496–500; Nicolaas W. Posthumus, *Inquiry into the History of Prices in Holland,* 2 vols. (Leiden, 1946–64), II, 415; Acta Borussica, *Denkmäler der preussischen Staatsverwaltung im 18. Jahrhundert: Getreidehandelspolitik,* vol. III: W. Naude and A. Skalweit, *Die Getreidehandelspolitik und Kriegsmagazinverwaltung, Preussens, 1740–1756* (Berlin, 1910), 624–27; M. J. Elsas, *Umriss einer Geschichte der Preise und Lohne in Deutschland vom ausgehenden Mittelater bis zum Beginn des 19. Jahrhunderts,* 2 vols. (Leiden, 1936–49), I, 675; Alfred Francis Pribram, *Materialen zur Geschichte der Preise und Lohne in Österreich* (Vienna, 1983), 391; Arthur E. Imhof, *Aspekte der Bevölkerungsentwicklung in den nordischen Ländern, 1720–1750* (Bern, 1976), 767.

crop cycle. Finally, the new cereal supplies that appeared in the markets following the harvests of 1741 initiated the new downward movement in prices.

By contrast, the price of grain rose rather than fell in southern Germany during the summer months of 1741. The advance of cereal prices in Bavaria and Austria owed more to the demands of the military campaigns of the War of the Austrian Succession than to deficient harvests. The price of grain also climbed in Norway during the late-autumn months of 1741, as a consequence of the harvest failures of that year. Elsewhere in western Europe, the harvest outcomes proved satisfactory in 1741 and the price of cereals declined. In France and the Low Countries, however, the price of grain remained elevated into 1742.

Monthly grain prices also fail to convey the complete record of the severity of the food shortages of the early 1740s. The price indexes reflect mainly national and restricted regional averages, whereas grain prices could vary considerably in local markets. In southern Norway, for example, low-income consumers had to cope with elevated cereal prices from March 1740 until as late as 1744, when prices finally returned to more normal levels. At the Kristiansand market, the rye price index (1735–1744 = 100) still stood at 143 in October 1743.[3] Norwegian consumers were forced to bridge a more daunting "famine gap" than British consumers. In southern England, low-income consumers faced elevated food prices for about a year, from June 1740 to June 1741. Ideally, the correlation of food prices and death rates should take place at the county level.

The question of the influence of food prices on death rates must also take account of the differential price movements of winter and spring grains. The dissimilar demographic outcomes of the subsistence crisis of 1740–1742 in western Europe prompts consideration of Andrew B. Appleby's proposition that the development of crop diversification was the essential key to the reduction of mortality peaks caused by harvest failures. According to the hypothesis, the cultivation of diversified cereals, but especially a better mixture of winter and spring grains, produced a series of improvements.[4]

First of all, a balanced cereal culture minimized the weather-related damage to total grain output because atmospheric conditions were less likely to be unfavorable the entire year and also because in the event of a severe winter season (as in 1740) the fields could be replanted with barley

3. Arthur E. Imhof, *Aspekte der Bevölkerungsentwicklung in den nordischen Ländern, 1720–1750* (Bern, 1976), 767.
4. Appleby, "Grain Prices," 870–85.

and oats in the spring. The first striking historical illustration of the benefits attached to balanced grain culture occurred in northern France in 1709, when the winter grains were virtually destroyed by the intense cold but widespread famine was nevertheless averted. Because the spring grains had yet to be planted, their yields were unaffected by the low winter temperatures. The winter grain losses were offset in part by the practice of resowing the fields with barley and oats during the spring months. This same practice, as has been seen, was adopted in some regions of western Europe in the spring of 1740.

Appleby found that in the absence of balanced cereal culture the price of all grains tended to advance symmetrically in the event of harvest shortfalls. Not only the more expensive wheat and rye but also the cheaper barley and oats rose sharply in price during subsistence crises. As a consequence, the cost of food for those who customarily subsisted on the cheaper spring grains increased in proportion to the cost of food for the higher income groups. He concluded that a symmetrical cereal price structure and severe subsistence crises "went hand in hand," and accordingly that food shortage had a significant influence on the death rate when all cereals became costly. By contrast, the rise in mortality was constrained when one or more of the spring grains remained relatively cheap.

Appleby proposed that the precocious disappearance of famine from England was traceable to the lack of price correlation between wheat and spring grains that was evident in all regions but northern England as early as the subsistence crises of the 1690s. But it was decidedly the fact of balanced cereal culture rather than the extended cultivation of spring grains that eliminated famines in the seventeenth century. Barley and oats alone could not shield the poor from famine, particularly in northern England, where these spring grains still constituted almost the only cereals grown.[5]

Thus it would seem that the question of the influence of food shortage on death rates also requires a focused examination of the price movements of winter and spring grains. It will otherwise not be possible to gauge the economic hardship and nutritional stress endured by the laboring poor, which made up that segment of the population most likely to succumb during subsistence crises. Also, as has been maintained, it is the process of accounting for the regional departures from national price and mortality trends that promises the most likely opportunity to understand the connection between food shortage and the incidence of epidem-

5. Ibid., 884–85.

ic disease. These procedures necessitate a reexamination of the national price and mortality indexes within a regional framework.

The British Isles

In Britain, the statistical correspondence between the movement of grain prices and mortality during the ten-year period 1735–1744 suggests that price advances initiated rises in the death rate. As tables 10 and 1 show, the elevated grain prices of 1735–1736 preceded the climbing mortality of 1736–1737. Conversely, the trend to lower grain prices in 1737–1738 preceded the decline in the number of deaths during 1738. The time lag can be explained by the fact that the physiological processes that regulate the case-fatality rates of infectious diseases do not respond immediately to changes in nutritional status. A similar explanation could account for the marginal increase of British mortality in 1739, despite the fact that the price of grain rose a substantial 38 percent in England and 29 percent in Scotland.

The dissimilar mortality trends that developed in England and Scotland in the early 1740s demand a more comprehensive explanation. In both countries, the price of grain reached a ten-year peak in 1740. In England, the number of deaths moved upward in 1740 and increased still further in 1741, in correspondence with the previous relationship of prices and mortality. However, the number of deaths continued to rise in England during 1742, in spite of the noticeable decline of food prices during 1741. In Scotland the number of deaths reached a peak in 1740 and then by contrast declined progressively during 1741 and 1742. Several circumstances will account for the difference in mortality patterns. The grain harvest shortfalls of 1739 proved more severe in Scotland than in England.[6] Moreover, the greater scale of public grain purchases in Scotland during 1740 put added pressure on prices. Food prices as well as mortality climbed more steeply in Scotland than in England during 1740. Finally, the British mortality peak of 1740–1742 was not in all likelihood shaped exclusively by diseases that are influenced by nutritional status.

England and Scotland both escaped a national mortality crisis in the early 1740s, contrary to the demographic outcome in Ireland. The relative market price of food alone, however, could not explain the severe crisis mortality suffered in Ireland. As tables 10 and 11 indicate,

6. Michael Flinn et al., *Scottish Population History* (Cambridge, 1977), 216.

the price of grain did not climb appreciably higher in Ireland than in Britain. Can the presence or absence of balanced cereal culture account for the varying mortality effects of the subsistence crisis in the British Isles during 1740–1741?

In England, the lack of price correlation between wheat and the spring grains had become the general market pattern by the beginning of the eighteenth century. When the price of wheat climbed in the wake of poor harvests, consumers who were priced off the wheat market could substitute barley, while those who customarily subsisted on barley were protected by its more stable price behavior. This degree of consumer protection was apparent in 1740. Thomas Short no doubt exaggerated when he wrote that barley was "all the Nation had to depend on," as a consequence of the deficient wheat harvests. But he also noted that the practice of resowing wheat fields with barley was common.[7] The Marsham journal in East Anglia likewise noted "that many farmers in divers parts of the kingdom, despairing of a crop, plowed their lands for barley" in the spring of 1740. Widespread hunger was avoided in England, however, not only because of the availability of lower-priced barley but also because the developed internal trade in cereals guaranteed the flow of food to deficit areas. As the author of the Marsham journal wrote in 1740, the county of Norfolk became "the granary of England," exporting both wheat and barley to "the West and the North."[8]

In the case of Scotland, it remains more difficult to gauge the role of balanced cereal culture in averting crisis mortality in the early 1740s. Although wheat was cultivated to some extent in the northeastern region, the subsistence of the population depended almost entirely on the spring crops of oats, barley, and beans. Was it possible for the Scottish working population to shift demand to cheaper sources of food during the subsistence crisis of 1740–1741? The limited available evidence indicates that a symmetrical price structure still predominated in Scotland. At a market for which data exist, the price index of oats (1735–1744 = 100) rose to 158 in 1740, while the price of barley increased to 162 and that of wheat to 167. Moreover, the price index of "pease" soared to 232, and they sold for the same price per boll as wheat, suggesting that consumers had considerable difficulty in shifting demand to lower-priced

---

7. Thomas Short, *A General Chronological History of the Air, Weather, Seasons, Meteors, etc.* (London, 1749), 256, 278.

8. T. Southwell, "Account of the Severe Winter of 1739–40 and Its Effects in the County of Norfolk in the Year Following," *Norfolk and Norwich Naturalists Society, Transactions* 2 (1875), 128–29.

foods.[9] Nonetheless, despite an increase of 70 percent in the national price of grains in 1740, Scotland escaped crisis mortality, at least in the more developed lowland and border regions. The Scottish success in dampening the rise in the number of deaths during the subsistence crisis of 1740–1741 appears to owe little to a balanced cereal culture.

In Ireland, the lack of knowledge about prevailing crop mixtures and the paucity of comparative price data render it difficult to determine the demographic impact of relative food prices. Price series of wheat are available for the Dublin market, and they have been used to compute the price indexes of tables 10 and 11. A comparison of the price indexes with the mortality indexes of table 1 discloses that the elevated mortality in 1738, 1740, and 1741 followed rising food prices in 1737, 1739, and 1740. In addition, the abrupt fall of wheat prices during July 1741 was followed by the declining mortality of 1742.

Wheat, however, did not serve as the bread grain of the working population of Ireland. Also, it was the southwestern province of Munster, not the Dublin region, that suffered severe crisis mortality during the food shortage of 1740–1741. In Munster, as I have noted, the potato had become a critical component of subsistence for the laboring poor. Price series of potatoes are not available for the 1740s. Michael Drake has suggested that the absence of price data stems from the fact that potatoes were not marketed in any quantity. Some measure of the price pressures created by the loss of the potato crop can be deduced from surviving fragmentary price data. In the Loch Erne district, for example, a barrel of potates sold for 32 shillings in 1740, whereas on the eve of the food shortage the customary price ranged from 8 to 10 shillings.[10]

Oats and barley made up the principal bread grains in Ireland. Neither price series nor the yields of the spring grains are available for the 1740s. The fragmentary evidence suggests, however, that the price of food advanced more sharply in southwestern Ireland than the price of wheat in Dublin. Drake found that the food shortage became more critical in the countryside than in Dublin during the first half of 1740.[11] The loss in the potato crop in Munster placed upward pressure on the price of all cereals, because those who subsisted on potatocs were forced

9. Henry Hamilton, *An Economic History of Scotland in the Eighteenth Century* (London, 1963), 397–98. The data represent the "Prices of Grain by the Haddington Fiars." The "fiars" prices of grain were fixed for each county annually in February and March. The sheriff computed a general average price for each grain, which then served as a standard for determining ministers' stipends and a rate of conversion for payments in kind.

10. Michael Drake, "The Irish Demographic Crisis of 1740–41," *Historical Studies* 6 (1968), 110.

11. Ibid., 106–107.

to shift demand to oatmeal and other provisions. The price of oats, both in Dublin and in the rural districts, rose more steeply than the price of wheat. At Dublin, the average price of a barrel of wheat increased from 25 shillings at the end of September 1740 to 35 shillings at the end of the year, an increase of 40 percent. The price of a barrel of oats at Dublin rose concurrently from 7 to 12 shillings, an increase of 71 percent. The price of oats peaked at 15 shillings a barrel in May 1741, when the price of wheat fell below 35 shillings.[12] As a consequence, consumers in Ireland who relied on oatmeal and potatoes—that is, the laboring poor—were devastated by the advance of food prices, while the more affluent who relied on wheat were relatively less affected.

The evidence thus indicates that crisis mortality and a symmetrical cereal price structure went hand in hand in Ireland but not in Scotland. The evidence also shows that the more pronounced increase of mortality in Ireland than in Britain was not matched by a proportionately higher increase in the price of food. The more severe mortality peak in Ireland no doubt derived in large measure from the destruction of the stored potato crop during the winter of 1739–1740.

Neither Ireland nor Britain constitutes the most appropriate mid-eighteenth-century economy in which to examine the hypothesis of famine abatement through the development of a balanced cereal culture. England had long since adopted diversified cereal crops. Scotland's less accommodating climatic regime made extensive wheat cultivation problematical. In Ireland, the decisive contribution of the potato to the subsistence of the laboring poor in Munster, together with the lack of food price data, makes it difficult to measure the influence of relative cereal prices on mortality. In France and other continental locations, by contrast, the knowledge of the harvest outcomes and the price movement of almost all cereals make it possible to examine the hypothesis in more detail.

France

The price indexes of table 10 and the mortality indexes of table 1 show that in France an increase in grain prices was followed by an increase in the number of deaths during the years 1739–1742. The regional differences in the movement of the two variables also indicate that elevated food prices influenced the level of mortality. In northern

---

12. Ibid., 112–13. Two Dublin barrels of grain were the equivalent of one British quarter measure.

and urban France, the progressive rise of cereal prices that took place from 1738 until 1741 preceded and then paralleled the mortality peak of 1740–1742. Climbing cereal prices at all French markets preceded the peak mortality of 1741 that dominated in all regions of France. The downward trend of grain prices that occurred in southern France alone in 1741 preceded a decline in the number of deaths in that region during 1742.[13] But the correspondence between food prices and death rates failed to hold in 1743, when the number of deaths increased sharply in rural France despite the decline in grain prices during 1742–1743. The rural mortality peak of 1743 probably resulted from epidemic diseases unrelated to nutritional status.

The proposition that severe subsistence crises and a symmetrical cereal price structure went hand in hand can be examined more closely in France because of the availability of price series for wheat, rye, barley, oats, and buckwheat. The movement of barley prices in the Paris region during 1740–1741 formed the basis for Appleby's conclusion that balanced cereal culture was still lacking in France. It should be cautioned, however, that consumers in Paris itself were reluctant to use barley, even when dearth prices for wheat and rye prevailed. He found that famine was nevertheless averted in France despite the symmetrical rise in barley prices and despite the fact that in money terms the price of cereals climbed as high during 1740–1741 as in the famines of the 1690s.[14] Contemporary French writers claimed that famine conditions were forestalled by the relatively successful barley crops of 1740.[15]

Was the market behavior of the Paris region representative of the price movements of spring grains elsewhere in northern France? Was it possible for the working population outside of the Ile-de-France to shift demand from wheat and rye to lower-priced cereals during the subsistence crisis of 1740–1741? To present evidence on the questions, index

13. For regional grain price series, see Micheline Baulant, "Le prix des grains à Paris de 1431 à 1788," *Annales: Economies, Sociétés, Civilisations* 23 (May–June 1968), 540; Pierre Goubert, *Beauvais et le Beauvaisis de 1600 à 1730*, 2 vols. (Paris, 1960), I, 405; Mohamed El Kordi, *Bayeux aux XVIIe et XVIIIe siècles* (Paris, 1970) 286–309; Michel Morineau, *Les Faux-semblants d'un démarrage économique: Agriculture et démographie en France au XVIIIe siècle* (Paris, 1970), 367–70; R. Beaudry, "Alimentation et population rurale en Périgord au XVIIIe siècle," *Annales de Démographie Historique* (1976) 56–57; E. Le Roy Ladurie, *Les Paysans de Languedoc*, 2 vols. (Paris, 1966), II, 822. For regional mortality trends, see Yves Blayo, "Mouvement naturel de la population française de 1740 à 1829," *Population* 30, special no. (November 1975), 52–56.

14. Appleby, "Grain Prices." 870–86.

15. M. du Hamel, "Observations botanico-météorologiques pour l'année 1740," *Histoire de l'Académie royale des sciences* (Paris, 1744), 150–51. 164–68; *Mercure de France*, December 1740, 2,951–52; Marcel Lachiver, *Histoire de Meulan et sa région par les textes* (Meulan, 1965), 214–15.

numbers (1735–1744) have been computed for the annual price movements of buckwheat, oats, and barley at the northwestern markets of
Laval in Maine and Bayeux in Normandy (see table 12). It should be
noted, however, that because Laval (located inland) and Bayeux (near
the Channel coast) had different grain-supply networks, the price comparisons can reveal only approximate tendencies.

Table 12. Indexes for the annual price movements of buckwheat, oats, and barley on selected
French markets, 1735–1744 (1735–1744 = 100)

Year	Buckwheat[a]	Oats[a]	Barley[b]	Oats[b]	Wheat and rye[c]
1735	68	76	79	82	79
1736	85	82	76	75	91
1737	102	82	65	83	92
1738	108	100	113	96	104
1739	102	106	156	101	114
1740	108	100	113	91	122
1741	176	167	174	179	144
1742	114	139	90	105	105
1743	68	73	68	97	75
1744	68	73	66	92	75

NOTE: For purposes of comparison, column 5 reproduces the national price of wheat and rye
found in table 9.
[a]Laval.
[b]Bayeu.
[c]France.
SOURCES: Michel Morineau, *Les Faux-semblants d'un démarrage économique: Agriculture et
démographie en France au XVIIIe siècle* (Paris, 1970), 370; Mohamed El Kordi, *Bayeux aux
XVIIe et XVIIIe siècles* (Paris, 1970), 286–309.

The index numbers show that the price of all spring grains advanced
more sharply than the price of wheat and rye during 1741, despite the
poorer yields of the winter grains in 1740. Also evident is the steep rise
in barley prices at the Bayeux market in 1739, following the harvest
shortfalls of 1738 in northwestern France. The index numbers disclose
that the tendency of spring and winter grain prices to increase symmetrically
during food shortages was still the rule in northern France.

Although barley remained cheaper than rye in money terms, the
differential was not large. At the Beauvais market, for example, the price
of rye averaged 104.6 sols per *mine* during the crop year 1740–1741,
while the price of barley averaged 90.2 sols, or 13.8 percent less, for the
same measure.[16] At the Pontoise market near Paris, the price of barley
rose from six livres per *setier* at Easter 1735 to 22 livres at the end of
1740, an almost fourfold increase. By comparison, the price of rye at the

16. Goubert, *Beauvais*, I, 405.

Pointoise market peaked at 27 livres per setier in the autumn of 1740.[17] Although the evidence presented for France is not sufficient to demonstrate conclusively the existence of a symmetrical grain price structure in the 1740s, it indicates nonetheless that the more favorable demographic outcome in northern France than in the food shortages of the 1690s cannot be adequately explained by the ability of the poor working population to shift demand from winter grains to cheaper spring grains.

The price of both winter and spring cereals climbed steeply in northern France from 1739 to 1741. But a national mortality crisis failed to develop in the early 1740s, as it had in the subsistence crises of the 1690s. The evidence indicates that a symmetrical cereal price structure and famine conditions no longer went hand in hand in France. The fact that not all grain harvests fell significantly short explains in part the more moderate rise in mortality during 1740–1742. The principal explanation of the good fortune will be found, however, in the relatively successful relief programs initiated by public and parochial authorities to cope with the welfare emergencies.

The Low Countries

The Netherlands recorded the most pronounced advance in grain prices during 1740. In the course of 1740, the price of food climbed more than 120 percent above the levels that had prevailed in 1736 and 1737. In 1741, the Low Countries witnessed the highest mortality peak in the northwestern region of Europe. During 1741, the price of cereals in the Low Countries also remained elevated, as tables 10 and 11 show. As table 11 demonstrates, the price of food began to rise earlier in the southern Netherlands than in the Dutch Republic and also climbed to a higher peak in 1740. The average price of grain at the Brussels market increased 68.5 percent from January to June 1740. The higher grain prices in the Austrian Netherlands reflected a more pressing shortage of food, which was traceable in part to the harvest shortfalls that were experienced in 1739.

Cereal yields in the Netherlands proved smaller still in 1740, but not all crop volumes fell off to an equal degree. Wheat and spelt yields declined more significantly than rye yields, according to observers in the southern Netherlands.[18] Rye prices, however, advanced more sharply

17. Jacques Dupâquier, M. Lachiver, and J. Meuvret, *Mercuriales du pays de France et du Vexin français, 1640–1792* (Paris, 1968), 68–79.
18. Emile Vanderlinden, "Chronique des événements météorologiques en Belgique

than wheat prices in all markets of the Low Countries. In the southern Netherlands, the price index of rye (1735–1744 = 100) averaged 173 in 1740 and 135 in 1741,[19] while at the Brussels market the wheat price index averaged 169 in 1740 and 128 in 1741. The money price of rye, however, remained below that of wheat. The price of a setier of rye peaked at 89 *patards* during 1740, while wheat sold for 114 patards.[20]

The price behavior of the spring grains in the southern Netherlands indicates that consumers who were priced off the wheat and rye markets were able to shift demand to cheaper cereals, contrary to the case in northern France. From 1738 to 1744, the price of spring grains remained noticeably more stable than the price of winter grains. This greater price stability can be seen in the index numbers that have been computed (1735–1744 = 100) for the annual price movements of barley, oats, buckwheat, wheat, and rye (table 13). Although it is true that the spring grains also rose sharply in price during 1740, the increases trailed significantly behind those of wheat and rye. Barley prices, for example, advanced 47.2 percent from 1738 to 1740, whereas the price of wheat and rye increased 89.2 percent during the same period.

Table 13. Indexes for the annual price movements of barley, oats, and buckwheat at selected Netherlands markets, 1738–1744 (1735–1744 = 100)

Year	Barley[a]	Oats[b]	Buckwheat[c]	Wheat and rye[d]
1738	97	99	99	93
1739	111	112	111	116
1740	143	134	140	176
1741	106	101	112	127
1742	113	104	112	86
1743	104	101	97	77
1744	96	106	90	86

[a]Average barley prices at the Ghent, Louvain, and Audenarde markets.
[b]Average oat prices at the Ghent, Louvain, and Audenarde markets.
[c]Average buckwheat price at the Louvain market.
[d]Average price of wheat and rye at the Brussels market.
SOURCES: Indexes computed from Charles Verlinden et al., eds., *Dokumenten voor de geschiedenis van prijzen en lonen in Vlaanderen en Brabant (XVe–XVIIIe eeuw)* (Bruges, 1959–73), 84–87, 496–500; G. van Houtte, *Leuven in 1740, ein krisisjaar: Ekonomische, sociale, en demografische aspekten* (Brussels, 1964), 41.

jusqu'en 1834," *Mémoires de l'Académie royale de Belgique,* Classe des Sciences, 2d ser. 6 (1924), 88; T. Bernier, "Notice sur l'origine et la tenue des anciens registres d'état civil dans la province de Hainaut," *Mémoires de la Société des sciences, des arts et des lettres du Hainaut,* 4th ser. 9 (1887), 567; Louis Torfs, *Fastes des calamités publiques survenues dans les Bays-Bas,* 2 vols. (Paris, 1859–62), II, 86.

19. Charles Verlinden et al., eds., *Dokumenten voor de geschiedenis van prijzen en lonen in Vlaanderen en Brabant (XVe–XVIIIe eeuw)* (Bruges, 1959–73), 496–500.

20. G. van Houtte, *Leuven in 1740, ein krisisjaar: Ekonomische, sociale, en demografische aspekten* (Brussels, 1964), 41.

The absence of symmetrical grain price increases during the food shortage of the early 1740s indicates that balanced cereal cultivation was established in the Netherlands. The money price of the spring grains also remained significantly below the price of rye, contrary to the price relationships observed in France. At the Louvain market, for example, the price of barley averaged 29.25 stiver per measure in 1740, the price of oats averaged 22.50 stiver, and the price of buckwheat averaged 20.50 stiver, whereas the price of rye averaged 43.75 stiver per measure, or nearly twice the price of the spring grains.[21] Similar price relationships obtained at the Audenarde market in Flanders.[22] As a consequence, consumers who were priced off the rye market in 1740 could substitute barley, while those priced off the barley market could turn to the still cheaper oats and buckwheat.

Despite the ability of the working population of the Low Countries to shift demand to the cheaper spring cereals during the subsistence crisis of 1740–1741, the number of deaths jumped 50 percent during 1741. Although it is true that the mortality indexes for the Low Countries are based on a small percentage of the presumed number of burials, the documentary evidence leaves no doubt that the southern Netherlands suffered a severe mortality crisis in 1741. The unfavorable demographic outcome in the Netherlands indicates that if balanced cereal culture put an end to famine in preindustrial Europe, the diversification of food crops did not always prevent crisis mortality from developing in the wake of a food shortage. The fact that France escaped crisis mortality despite a symmetrical grain price structure reinforces this conclusion and suggests that crop diversification was not the controlling variable in determining the national levels of mortality during the subsistence crisis of 1740–1741.

The German States

The symmetrical movement of cereal prices and the relatively low mortality peak in Prussia during the early 1740s also supports this finding. The prices of wheat, rye, and barley all advanced steeply in Germany during 1740. The rye price indexes of table 10 were computed from the average prices at five markets in three German states. In 1741, however, two distinct price trends developed in Germany, as table 11 shows. In southern Germany, the price of cereals began to rise again

21. Houtte, Leuven, 41.
22. Verlinden, *Prijzen,* 84–87.

during the summer of 1741, in contrast to the reverse trend both in northern Germany and in northwestern Europe. The advancing cereal prices in Bavaria and Austria, as noted, derived primarily from the military activities in that region during 1741 and 1742.[23] In order to eliminate this complicating variable from the examination of the relative price movements of winter and spring grains, the discussion will concentrate on the markets of the extensive Prussian state, with the average German price of rye serving as a basis for comparison.

The annual grain price movements at Berlin, Magdeburg, and Minden provide a representative record of the behavior of food prices in the Prussian state, which stretched across northern Germany from Lithuania in the east to the Rhineland in the west. Index numbers (1735–1744 = 100) have been computed for the average prices of the four principal German cereals at the three Prussian markets (table 14). Column 5 reproduces the national average price of rye found in table 10.

Table 14. Indexes for the average prices of the four principal German cereals at three Prussian markets, 1735–1744 (1735–1744 = 100)

Year	Wheat	Rye	Barley	Oats	Rye[a]
1735	79	83	83	86	74
1736	86	104	99	100	97
1737	82	106	99	114	105
1738	73	83	81	90	87
1739	86	92	95	97	93
1740	174	172	172	124	153
1741	149	120	108	124	130
1742	96	78	85	83	92
1743	87	82	90	88	91
1744	84	87	95	99	83

NOTE: Oat prices are not available for the Minden market.

[a]For purposes of comparison, the national average price of rye in Germany has been included.

SOURCES: Acta Borussica, *Denkmäler der preussischen Staatsverwaltung im 18. Jahrhundert*: *Getreidehandelspolitik*, vol. II: W. Naudé, *Die Getreidehandelspolitik und Kriegsmagazinverwaltung, Brandenburg-Preussens bis 1740* (Berlin 1901), 538, 548, 572; ibid., vol. III: W. Naudé and A. Skalweit, *Die Getreidehandelspolitik und Kriegsmagazinverwaltung, Preussens, 1740–1756* (Berlin, 1910), 607–9, 624–27.

The figures indicate that a symmetrical cereal price structure still predominated in Prussia. Rye made up the principal German bread grain, but barley was also cultivated and could be substituted to some degree in the event of dearth. As can be seen, the price of rye and barley increased proportionately during the subsistence crisis of 1740 and also during the

23. M. J. Elsas, *Umriss einer Geschichte der Preise und Löhne in Deutschland vom ausgehenden Mittelalter bis zum Beginn des 19. Jahrhunderts*, 2 vols. (Leiden, 1936–49), I, 675; Alfred Francis Pribram, *Materialen zur Geschichte der Preise und Löhne in Österreich* (Vienna, 1938), 391, 531.

earlier price advance of 1736. The price of oats, which were consumed more widely in the eastern than in the western Prussian provinces, increased less sharply than rye and barley in 1740. The price of wheat remained stable during the dearth of 1736–1737, which was centered in East Prussia, but advanced more than rye and barley during the subsistence crisis of 1740–1741. On balance, the movement of grain prices in Prussia suggests that a balanced cereal culture was not established in the 1740s.

The Prussian grain price indexes tend to conceal the fact that the price advances of 1736–1737 and 1740–1741 were dominated by two different geographical patterns. During the years 1736–1737, the price of rye and barley increased more steeply in the eastern than in the western provinces. At the Berlin market, for example, the rye price index (1735–1744 = 100) rose to 113 in 1736 and 125 in 1737, whereas the global Prussian index peaked at 106.[24] In the northeastern town of Stettin, the increase in cereal prices was even more pronounced. The price of rye advanced 43 percent from 1735 to 1737, and the price of barley advanced 56 percent during the same period.[25] As I have noted, the German mortality peak of 1736–1737 derived from a regional mortality crisis in east-Elbian Prussia. During the years 1740–1741, the price of rye and barley increased more sharply in the western than in the eastern provinces. At the Minden market, for example, the rye price index soared to 218 in 1740, while the price of barley climbed even higher, to 240,[26] or 39.5 percent above the global Prussian average.

The increase of Prussian cereal prices in 1740, however, was not paralleled by a proportionate increase in the number of deaths during 1740–1741, as the mortality indexes of table 1 disclose. In spite of the deficient rye harvests of 1740 and the lack of a balanced cereal culture, the level of mortality rose no more than moderately in Prussia and in the German states. As in Scotland and France during the food shortage of the early 1740s, a symmetrical grain price structure and crisis mortality failed to go hand in hand. In these three countries, as will be seen, public welfare and relief programs were successful in blunting the demographic effects of the food shortage, particularly in the Prussian state.

24. Acta Borussica, *Denkmäler der preussischen Staatsverwaltung im 18. Jahrhundert: Getreidehandelspolitik,* Vol. II: W. Naudé, *Die Getreidehandelspolitik und Kriegsmagazinverwaltung, Brandenburg-Preussens bis 1740* (Berlin, 1901), 538, 548, 572; ibid., Vol III: W. Naudé and A. Skalweit, *Die Getreidehandelspolitik und Kriegsmagazinverwaltung, Preussens 1740–1756* (Berlin, 1910) 607–9, 624–27.

25. Naudé, *Getreidehandelspolitik,* 614.

26. Ibid., 538; Naudé and Skalweit, *Getreidehandelspolitik,* 602.

Scandinavia

Sweden boasts the most complete record of cereal prices and of the number of deaths at the county level for the ten-year period under study and thus makes it possible to focus on the relationship between food shortage and death rates in more detail. Rye and barley made up the principal Swedish and Scandinavian bread grains. Modest amounts of wheat were also consumed in Sweden, while oats were cultivated for both food and fodder everywhere in the Scandinavian peninsula. Hay, however, was the major source of fodder for livestock. The absence of a balanced cereal culture in Sweden is apparent from the index numbers (1735–1744 = 100) computed for the annual price movements from 1738 to 1744, shown in table 15.

Table 15. Indexes for the annual price movements of wheat, rye, barley, oats, and hay in Sweden, 1738–1744 (1735–1744 = 100)

Year	Wheat	Rye	Barley	Oats	Hay
1738	67	70	74	76	88
1739	86	92	92	93	94
1740	107	117	117	114	128
1741	139	127	125	124	139
1742	111	109	100	100	111
1743	112	108	108	107	100
1744	105	98	96	93	111

NOTE: County price series are not available for all grains during the period under study but are virtually complete for rye, barley, and oats, less so for wheat and hay. National rye averages, for example, are based on 28 or 29 out of a total of 30 regional prices, while national wheat averages are based on from 11 to 13 regional price series.

SOURCE: Lennart Jörberg, *A History of Prices in Sweden, 1732–1914,* 2 vols. (Lund, 1972), I, 632, 637, 642.

The index numbers show that the cereal price structure in Sweden was essentially symmetrical. The prices of all grains rose and fell together at similar rates of change from 1738 to 1744. The prospects of achieving a fully diversified and balanced cereal culture in the Scandinavian peninsula were limited by the severe winters, late springs, and early autumn frosts. Rye was extensively cultivated as a winter grain, while barley had become the indispensable spring crop. Both plants resist damage from abnormally low seasonal temperatures. In the early 1740s, the fact that the yields of both rye and barley proved deficient compromised the Swedish supply of food.

From 1739 to 1741, the price of rye in Sweden increased 38.0 percent, while the price of barley advanced 35.8 percent. In 1741, the money price of rye averaged 0.81 kronor per hectoliter, while the price of barley averaged 0.66 kronor.[27] The magnitude of the grain price increases in Sweden was more moderate than the advance of grain prices in northwestern Europe during 1740–1741. The price of food in Sweden did not return to customary levels until 1744, however, in contrast to the downward movement of prices in northwestern Europe at the end of 1741.

The mortality indexes of table 1 disclose that the Swedish *national* death rate likewise did not advance to the peaks registered in the majority of the northwestern European countries during 1740–1741. In the first half of the eighteenth century, however, national averages could conceal wide swings of mortality at the county level. The annual fluctuations of county death rates and grain prices supply less equivocal evidence bearing on the question of the influence of food shortage on mortality. Complicating variables are less likely to cloud the issue at the county than at the national level.

In spite of the harvest shortfalls and elevated food prices of the early 1740s, Sweden escaped a national mortality crisis until 1743. But a severe regional mortality crisis developed in four contiguous southwestern counties during 1741. The counties of Värmland, Göteborg and Bohus, Älvsborg, and Skaraborg endured a prolonged period of crisis mortality from 1741 to 1743. The price and demographic evidence indicates that the four southwestern counties experienced significantly higher grain prices and death rates than the national averages during the years 1741–1742. As table 16 shows, the figures exhibit a tendency for a year of increasing cereal prices to precede an increase in the annual death rate, though the relationship failed to hold in every instance. In the year 1741, the more pronounced price advance in the southwestern counties than the national average was matched by crisis mortality in each of the four counties, whereas the national death rate declined. In 1742, the succeeding year, the four southwestern counties suffered a more severe mortality crisis. In 1743, death rates remained more elevated in the southwestern counties than the national average. In 1744, the price of food and the number of deaths fell off both in the southwestern counties and at the national level.

The movement of food prices and death rates in the four southwestern Swedish counties suggests that fluctuations in grain prices triggered changes in mortality. The documentary evidence shows that the crisis

27. Lennart Jörberg, *A History of Prices in Sweden, 1732–1914*, 2 vols. (Lund, 1972), I, 72–74.

Table 16. Indexes for the average price of all cereals (1735–1744 = 100) and annual crude death rates per 1,000, selected Swedish counties and all Sweden, 1739–1744.

Year	Värmland		Göteborg and Bohus		Älvsborg		Skaraborg		All Sweden	
	(1)	(2)	(1)	(2)	(1)	(2)	(1)	(2)	(1)	(2)
1739	85	36.6	84	34.2	88	25.4	87	31.1	93	30.6
1740	103	40.4	119	41.9	121	30.1	117	36.1	119	35.5
1741	145	54.2	146	49.1	n.a.	40.3	141	48.7	128	32.2
1742	115	121.6	108	75.7	n.a.	42.4	119	44.5	107	39.0
1743	105	69.3	105	44.6	117	52.1	114	64.7	109	43.7
1744	85	26.6	111	31.3	95	27.0	89	39.1	98	25.3

NOTE: 1 = cereals price; 2 = crude death rate per 1,000.
SOURCES: Lennart Jörberg, *A History of Prices in Sweden 1732–1914*, 2 vols. (Lund, 1972), I, 133–35, 149–51, 165–67; Arthur E. Imhof, *Aspekte der Bevölkerungsentwicklung in den nordischen Ländern, 1720–1750* (Bern, 1976), 70–74.

mortality in the southwestern counties coincided with a shortage of food.[28] The magnitude of the advance in grain prices during the early 1740s, however, does not indicate that hunger was a major cause of death.

The movement of cereal prices and death rates in the Swedish counties where prices remained more stable also points to the influence of food prices on the level of mortality. The price of cereals advanced least in the contiguous southeastern counties of Kronoberg and Kalmar. In Kronoberg, the grain price index (1735–1744 = 100) fluctuated narrowly between 111 and 116 during the period from 1740 to 1744. The death rate in Kronoberg likewise moved narrowly between 28.1 and 31.6 per 1,000 during the same period. Both grain prices and death rates remained significantly below the national averages. In Kalmar, the grain price index fluctuated between 110 and 116 during the period 1740–1744. Although the death rate fluctuated more than in Kronoberg, ranging between 25.5 and 35.7 per 1,000 during the period, the increase in mortality was less than the national average. At the same time, however, the island county of Gotland, off the coast of Kalmar, experienced a year of crisis mortality in 1742, when the death rate more than doubled, even though food prices remained as stable as in the neighboring southeastern counties.[29]

It is apparent that hunger was not the proximate cause of the crisis mortality in the Swedish counties. The documentary evidence indicates that the elevated Swedish death rate originated primarily in a higher incidence of several epidemic diseases. The evidence also suggests that

28. Imhof, *Bevölkerungsentwicklung in den nordischen Ländern*, 728–40.
29. Ibid., 70–74; Jörberg, *Prices*, I, 133–35.

the epidemics did not derive exclusively from the consequences of food shortage. The three northern counties of Gävleborg, Västernorrland, and Västerbotten all suffered crisis mortality in 1743. After the Russian war erupted in 1741, the three counties became the scene of constant troop movements. However, the northern region of Sweden also experienced weather-related crop losses in the early 1740s. The combination of frosts, heavy summer rains, and unsown fields resulted in large harvest shortfalls during the years 1742–1743.[30] Although no method is available to estimate the relative impact of food shortage, climatic stress, and military activities on the death rate, it seems certain that all three variables promoted the spread of infectious diseases.

To sum up, the price and mortality data drawn from the Swedish counties disclose a tendency for increases in grain prices to be followed by increases in the death rate. But this statistical relationship did not invariably hold true. At the other extreme, for example, the southern coastal county of Blekinge suffered three consecutive poor harvests from 1739 to 1741, whereas the death rate never exceeded 28.4 per 1,000. Conversely, the county of Stockholm registered a death rate of 74.2 per 1,000 in 1743, when the price of cereals had returned to customary levels. The cases of Blekinge and Stockholm, however, did not reflect the typical movement of grain prices and death rates in the Swedish counties during the early 1740s. In the majority of Swedish counties, the price of food and the number of deaths rose and fell in parallel. Finally, it should also be noted that after two years of falling cereal prices not one Swedish county recorded crisis mortality during the period 1744–1745.[31]

Elsewhere in Scandinavia, the movement of cereal prices and death rates also indicates that food prices influenced the level of mortality. In the Finnish counties, the price of grain advanced 43.4 percent between 1738 and 1740. The Finnish population passed through an acute mortality crisis in 1740, when the death rate soared to 52.0 per 1,000, an increase of 63.0 percent over the previous year. As we have noted, the rye harvests were deficient in Finland in 1739 and then failed in 1740 except in the southeastern coastal area. In the huge county of Österbotten, which covered the entire northern half of Finland, the rye crops failed both in 1739 and 1740, creating famine conditions in 1749.[32] Death rates jumped in all Finnish counties during 1740, except the

30. Imhof, *Bevölkerungsentwicklung in den nordischen Ländern*, 737; Jörberg, *Prices*, 133–35, 149–51, 165–67.

31. Imhof, *Bevölkerungsentwicklung in den nordischen Ländern*, 70–74.

32. Eino Jutikkala, *Die Bevölkerung Finnlands in den Jahren 1721–1749*, 38–41; Imhof, *Bevölkerungsentwicklung in den nordischen Ländern*, 728–32, 762–63.

island of Åland. The death rates rose more steeply in the central county of Tavastland (63.8 per 1,000) and in the western coastal county of Satakunta (57.0 per 1,000) than in famine-struck Österbotten (51.1 per 1,000). Despite a further advance in food prices in 1741, the number of deaths fell significantly in all counties except Österbotten, which experienced a second year of crisis mortality with an elevated death rate of 42.1 per 1,000.[33] The evidence suggests that the Finnish mortality crisis of 1740 was not triggered exclusively by a shortage of food. The extreme weather conditions of 1739–1740 and the buildup of Swedish military forces in Finland during 1740 also fostered the epidemic diseases that broke out during the subsistence crisis.

The Finnish mortality crisis of 1742 seems to have been spawned mainly by the Russian war. Military hostilities centered in Finland during 1742. Those counties where marching armies and battlefield maneuvers created havoc recorded the highest death rates in 1742. But the year 1742 was also marked by a shortage of food. The average price of cereals stood 33 to 60 percent above the level that had prevailed in 1740.[34] The harvest shortfalls of 1742 resulted in part from wartime dislocations. The influence of food prices on mortality in Finland during the early 1740s is thus obscured by the concurrent demographic impact of the Russian war.[35] In Norway, by contrast, where the European wars were not a demographic factor, the movement of cereal prices and death rates points to the conclusion that food shortage touched off the prolonged crisis mortality.

The price indexes of table 10 and the mortality indexes of table 1 show that a progressive advance in cereal prices during 1740–1741 was followed by a severe mortality crisis in Norway during 1741–1742. The regional differences in the statistical correspondence between grain prices and death rates, shown in table 17, give some clue as to the major factors responsible for the increase in the number of deaths. As can be seen, none of the Norwegian dioceses experienced crisis mortality in 1740, despite the fact that grain prices climbed sharply in all regions. The national mortality crisis of 1741 was the result of elevated death rates in three of the four dioceses. The increase of mortality in 1741 represented a departure from the downward trend of death rates elsewhere in the Scandinavian peninsula that year. It is the regional variations of mortality within Norway, however, that require explanation.

In the central diocese of Akershus, where Olso is located, the price of

33. Imhof, *Bevölkerungsentwicklung in den nordischen Ländern*, 175.
34. Jutikkala, *Bevölkerung Finnlands*, 39–41.
35. Imhof, *Bevölkerungsentwicklung in den nordischen Ländern*, 175, 762–63.

Table 17. Indexes for the average price of all cereals (1735–1744 = 100) and annual crude death rates per 1,000, Norwegian dioceses and all Norway, 1739–1744

Year	Akershus		Kristiansand		Bergen		Trondheim		All Norway	
	(1)	(2)	(1)	(2)	(1)	(2)	(1)	(2)	(1)	(2)
1739	101	26.2	79	21.3	94	26.5	73	15.2	86	22.8
1740	129	29.9	143	25.2	113	26.8	126	15.4	127	25.1
1741	122	42.4	153	66.0	114	45.0	174	19.1	141	40.8
1742	114	67.3	123	44.4	79	35.4	164	43.2	115	52.2
1743	99	34.2	112	24.9	85	26.9	112	21.7	97	28.4
1744	93	23.2	103	21.6	76	24.8	92	15.8	84	21.4

NOTE: 1 = cereals price; 2 = crude death rate per 1,000. Index numbers for the dioceses represent the average price of rye, barley, and oats. Prices are not available for the *diocese* of Kristiansand; prices for the *town* of Kristiansand have been substituted.

SOURCE: Arthur E. Imhof, *Aspekte der Bevölkerungsentwicklung in den nordischen Ländern, 1720–1750* (Bern, 1976), 178, 766–67.

grain advanced significantly but not to famine levels during 1740. In 1741, the death rate increased to the crisis level, in line with the national mortality trend. However, the far more severe mortality crisis that developed in Akershus during 1742, when the death rate jumped to 67.3 per 1,000, followed a year in which the price of cereals declined. Although it is true that the crisis mortality in Akershus coincided with three consecutive years of elevated food prices, the magnitude of the increase of the death rate was disproportionately greater than the increase in grain prices, as was the case in Ireland. Two circumstances explain in part the severe mortality crisis in Akershus. The price of barley, the cheaper spring grain, advanced more steeply than the price of rye. The barley price index (1735–1744 = 100) climbed to 171 in 1740 and stood at 133 in 1741, whereas the rye price index peaked at 113 during the period 1740–1742.[36] Also, the population of Akershus relied more on cereals for subsistence than was the case elsewhere in Norway.[37]

Even so, the evidence does not suggest that the crisis mortality in Akershus originated in widespread famine. Rather the pronounced increase in the number of deaths during 1741–1742 resulted from a rise in the incidence of a series of infectious diseases. The evidence also shows that the mortality crisis in Akershus coincided with the extreme crisis mortality suffered in the contiguous Swedish county of Värmland. In both locations, the same epidemic diseases became rife. Both Akershus and Värmland also endured an extended period of food shortage. But the extreme mortality peaks registered in the Norwegian dioceses and

36. Ibid., 766–67.
37. Michael Drake, *Population and Society in Norway, 1735–1865* (Cambridge, 1969), 63–66, 70–72.

several Swedish counties suggest that nutritional deficiencies were not primarily responsible for the mortality crises that developed in a limited number of European regions during 1740–1742.

In the southwestern coastal diocese of Kristiansand, the correspondence between changes in grain prices and death rates was more straightforward. The price of grain advanced a precipitous 81 percent during 1740 and climbed higher still in 1741. The proportional increase of all cereal prices in southwestern Norway suggests that consumers had limited opportunity to shift demand to cheaper grains during the subsistence crisis of the early 1740s. At the end of 1740, the Kristiansand price index of rye stood at 183, while the barley index reached 214. In June 1741, the rye price index averaged 151, while the barley index averaged 157. At the end of 1741, the rye price index stood at 183, with the barley index slightly lower at 171.[38] In the year 1741, the Kristiansand death rate rose 61.8 percent above the national average and peaked at 66.0 per 1,000. In Norway, a grain price structure that was essentially symmetrical and crisis mortality went hand in hand in the 1740s.

The movement of grain prices and death rates in the northern diocese of Trondheim, however, does not support a conclusion that the crisis mortality in Kristiansand can be explained by the greater magnitude of the increase in food prices. Trondheim recorded the most elevated food prices in Norway during the three-year period 1740–1742. But the death rate increased only marginally in Trondheim until 1742. While it is true that Trondheim shared the national mortality crisis of 1742, the number of deaths fell by half during 1743, despite the fact that the barley price index (1735–1744 = 100) averaged 171 in 1742 and 121 in 1743.[39]

Altogether the annual trends of national and regional cereal prices and death rates in Norway during the early 1740s indicate that the mortality crises of 1741–1742 were touched off by a prolonged shortage of food. The lack of a balanced cereal culture and the fact that the lower-priced barley advanced in price at least as steeply as rye intensified the subsistence crisis. As in Sweden, however, the Norwegian crisis mortality resulted primarily from a higher incidence of epidemic disease rather than from great numbers of deaths from hunger and starvation. Unlike the case in Sweden, the epidemic diseases that became rife in Norway were not associated with wartime troop concentrations and military activities.

In Denmark, the price of cereals advanced even more steeply than in the Scandinavian peninsula during the year 1740. The price of food in

38. Imhof, *Bevölkerungsentwicklung in den nordischen Ländern*, 767.
39. Ibid., 766–67.

Denmark also remained nearly as elevated during 1741. It might be anticipated that the soaring grain prices in Denmark would be followed by crisis mortality, as in the Norwegian half of the kingdom. In fact, as the mortality indexes of table 1 show, Denmark not only escaped a national mortality crisis but registered no more than a moderate increase in the number of deaths during the period 1740–1742. The dissimilar demographic outcomes suggest that the Danish population was insulated against elevated food prices to a greater degree than Norwegian consumers and that the impact of the food shortage on Norwegian death rates cannot be accounted for by the correspondence in the movement of grain prices and mortality.

If Denmark escaped a national mortality crisis, the population of the island diocese of Seeland was less fortunate. In 1740, the Seeland death rate climbed to 40.1 per 1,000. The diocese of Seeland also experienced the greatest increase in the price of cereals between 1738 and 1740. The price of rye advanced 133 percent, whereas the national average increased 106 percent. Moreover, the price of winter grain in Seeland advanced more sharply than the price of rye in the famine-struck Norwegian diocese of Akershus.[40]

In Copenhagen, the island diocese's metropolis, the advance of food prices proved more moderate. Between the municipal bread assizes of April 15, 1739 and November 21, 1740, when the controlled price of bread reached its peak, the price of "coarse" rye bread advanced 72 percent. The average price of Seeland rye, by contrast, advanced a much steeper 159 percent between March 1739 and August 1740, according to the "Brokers Statements of Grain Prices in Copenhagen."[41] Thus consumers in Copenhagen were protected to some degree from the full impact of the food shortage. Copenhagen also registered a lower death rate (36.6 per 1,000) than the diocesan average in 1740. The ability of Danish public officials to moderate the price impact of the food shortage for poor consumers explains in part the more stable death rates in Denmark than in Norway. As will be shown, however, the mortality crises in the Norwegian dioceses resulted primarily from the inability of the Danish administration to compensate for the per capita food deficit that developed after the series of harvest shortfalls.

In summary, a series of poor grain harvests in Scandinavia touched off severe subsistence crises during the period from 1740 to 1742. The development of famine-like conditions in several regions of the Scandinavian

40. Ibid., 176–77, 764–65.
41. Astrid Friis and Kristof Glamann, *A History of Prices and Wages in Denmark, 1660–1800,* vol. I: *Copenhagen* (London, 1958), 151–56.

peninsula resulted in part from the absence of balanced cereal cultivation, which was reflected in the symmetrical rise of winter and spring grain prices. The corresponding increase of Scandinavian death rates suggests that the crisis mortality derived from the shortage of food. At the same time, the relationship between the movement of food prices and death rates was not always straightforward and positive. As a consequence, it is clear that variables other than elevated food prices influenced mortality. The evidence indicates that an elevated incidence of epidemic diseases was the proximate cause of the increase in the number of deaths. In the Swedish and Finnish counties, the relative severity of the weather patterns and wartime conditions added to the mortality toll, chiefly by fostering the diffusion of infectious disease. Everywhere in Scandinavia, but especially in the kingdom of Denmark-Norway, the effectiveness of public adminstrations in coping with the shortage of food determined the demographic outcome to a critical degree.

Everywhere in western Europe, the regions that escaped famine conditions and crisis mortality during the food shortages of the early 1740s owed this more favorable outcome to imported grain supplies, adequate public welfare, and the effectiveness of public administration. The relative extent and duration of the food shortage and the presence or absence of diversified grain culture also influenced mortality peaks during the subsistence crisis. But the ability to counter the potential fatal consequences of climatic stress, hunger, and social disorder determined whether or not national mortality crises developed. It is true, however, that the success or failure of welfare and relief programs depended in part on the relative severity of the shortage of food, a measure that was not always fully reflected in the movement of cereal prices.

The chapter that follows surveys the relative success or failure of the national welfare and relief programs that were adopted during the subsistence crises of the early 1740s. It will be argued that the ability to adapt to the economic and social consequences of climatic stress and elevated food prices had a more decisive influence on the level of mortality than the actual extent of the food shortage.

6. *Welfare and Relief Programs*

The regions of Europe that escaped famine conditions and crisis mortality during the food shortages of the early 1740s owed their more favorable demogrphic outcome mainly to the effectiveness of public administration. Emergency stores of grain, adequate welfare programs, and willingness to import supplementary supplies of food prevented mass destitution and widespread hunger. The relative success or failure of the welfare and relief measures depended also on the relative severity of the shortage of food, which was not always fully reflected in the movement of cereal prices. An absolute shortage of food, that is to say a per capita supply too small to meet the minimum caloric needs of the population, was the case only in a limited number of provinces and counties, located principally in Scandinavia and Ireland.

Viewed from the perspective of the twentieth century, the primary task of public officials was to compensate for the inability of the destitute, unemployed, and poor to cope with the high market prices of cereals that predominated from 1740 to 1742. In France, the Austrian Netherlands, and most locations where old regime administrations held sway, however, government authorities were more likely to view their task as that of maintaining the proper operation of the grain trade or correcting its malfunctioning. But in any event, public officials pursued similar courses of action almost everywhere. Cereal supplies were purchased abroad and at home on public account, either to put downward pressure on domestic market prices or to ease the hunger of the destitute. Public authorities sold grain wholesale to millers and bakers at prices slightly below the market to subsidize the price of bread in urban locations. In some cases, grain was sold retail to consumers or was even distributed free to the helpless. To put additional downward pressure on prices, public officials coerced speculators and forestallers into bringing their hoarded stocks to market.

Public authorities also created employment opportunities to enhance the purchasing power of the poor. The most common schemes involved textile manufacturing, road repair, and other construction projects. Municipal and parish officials expanded the scale of welfare services and eased the rising cost of living by distributing food, fuel, and money. Charitable campaigns initiated by municipalities, churches, and voluntary associations collected these same items as a method to reduce the level of want. The relative availability and scope of the public and voluntary remedial measures proved critical in determining whether national and provincial subsistence crises evolved into mortality crises during the early 1740s.

The old regime administrations of preindustrial Europe concentrated their efforts on the problem of the distribution of food rather than on questions of supply and demand. This priority was dictated by the fact that the maintenance of public order was inextricably tied up with the distribution of food. In France in particular, public officials tended to view subsistence crises as problems of distribution rather than production, on the assumption that France was a land of abundant food and that most dearths were artificial to a degree. As a consequence, the French "police" believed that they could deal with subsistence problems effectively by administrative methods, with little need to intervene in supply. In the eighteenth century, the word "police" referred mainly to the obligations of ensuring the supply of food in years of abundance and remedying welfare misfortunes in years of dearth. A well-policed state also minimized aberrations in the grain trade and kept under control the conflicts that flared up in cereal markets during times of shortage.[1]

By the middle of the eighteenth century, the nation-states and city-states of western Europe had worked out relatively effective methods of safeguarding the poor from hunger. But the same capacity and concern were not always in place in the more remote territories of the dynastic states united under the British, Danish, Swedish, and Habsburg crowns. The western European states, at the same time, adopted different administrative strategies to carry out this elementary welfare service. England

---

1. This discussion relies on Steven L. Kaplan, "Lean Years, Fat Years: The 'Community' Granary System and the Search for Abundance in Eighteenth-Century Paris," *French Historical Studies* 10 (1977), 197–98; and Charles Tilly, "Food Supply and Public Order in Modern Europe," in Tilly, ed., *The Formation of National States in Western Europe* (Princeton, 1975), 396, 440–41.

created the most developed system to eliminate destitution and hunger. The Tudor system of poor relief, in place as early as 1601, was designed to provide welfare payments as well as work. The English poor law system was administered by the parish, which was required to raise and maintain funds for the purposes of creating employment and relieving the destitute.[2] Scotland, however, lacked a fully operational compulsory public poor law as late as 1740, while in Ireland welfare resources remained almost entirely voluntary.

In the continental states, the capacity to protect the working population from food shortage and to cope with the welfare needs created by harvest failures varied from government to government. In times of dearth, the availability or absence of emergency grain stores and public granaries determined in part the degree of hardship and hunger. By the mid-eighteenth century, writers on the responsibilities of "policed societies" presumed that any well-policed nation anticipated times of scarcity and that "for the purpose of repairing them they have thought to store the grain that they could not consume in places devised to conserve them for long periods." Measured by this standard, as Steven Kaplan has demonstrated, France could not qualify as a policed nation in 1740. Although public granaries and "Chambers of Abundance" had been established in Lyons, Besançon, Marseilles, Strasbourg, and the principal towns of Lorraine, the bulk of the French population was still exposed to famine. In Paris itself, despite the international reputation it had gained for the perfection of its police organization, the grain stores remained in the hands of commerce and no public granaries existed.[3]

In Prussia, by contrast, Frederick William I instituted a statewide system of public granaries for the purposes of stabilizing cereal prices and preventing dearth.[4] In the German city-states, and in Geneva, the Dutch towns, and the principal urban locations of Denmark and Sweden, the storage of emergency grain supplies in public granaries was also a common practice.

Despite the lack of an effective system of public granaries, both France and Scotland escaped national famines and extensive mortality crises in the 1740s, in contrast to the demographic catastrophes they endured during the food shortages of the 1690s. Neither France nor Scotland had adopted a compulsory poor law. In France, Scotland, and other western European locations, however, the decision to import supplementary grain supplies in conjunction with an increase in the scale

2. Ernest Barker, *The Development of Public Services in Western Europe, 1660–1930* (London, 1944), 70–71.

3. Kaplan, "Lean Years," 197–99; the passage quoted appears on p. 197.

4. Barker, *Development of Public Services,* 70–71.

of public, church, and voluntary relief programs accounts in large measure for the success in avoiding famine conditions and high death rates in the wake of the harvest shortfalls of 1739–1741. Public officials in France and Scotland proved better able to cope with the welfare emergencies, which in the 1690s had resulted in pronounced social dislocations.

Crisis mortality was averted in the majority of western European states during 1740–1742 also because of the improved ability to transport grain by maritime routes. Few regions of western Europe remained entirely dependent on their own cereal output. Nonetheless, extended crisis mortality still occurred in Ireland despite its maritime location, and in Norway, in spite of its accessibility by sea and the existence of emergency grain stores in the Danish half of the kingdom. Famine and crisis mortality developed in Ireland and Norway fundamentally because public administrations either neglected or failed to carry out the elementary welfare service of safeguarding the destitute from hunger and starvation.

The institution of effective public welfare programs depends not only on the surplus resources made available by economic growth but also on the commitment of the propertied classes to the wisdom of the concept of state responsibility for remedial measures, for whatever reasons. No doubt the motivation for the increased willingness to accept public welfare obligations during the course of the eighteenth century derived in part from the fear of popular disturbances as well as from "enlightened" ideas as to what constitutes public administration. The European subsistence crises that followed the Napoleonic wars called forth a pronounced increase in the scale of public welfare and private charity, but they also set on foot the last great wave of European food riots.[5]

In the subsistence crises of the early 1740s, as in the harvest shortfalls of 1815–1816, the success or failure of public welfare and relief measures more than any other variable influenced the relative severity of the national mortality peaks. Though during 1740 the entire region of western Europe faced a welfare emergency engendered by thermal stress, the shortage of food, and high cereal prices, not all countries shared in the crisis mortality. Accordingly, it is necessary to survey the national remedial programs in order to assess their influence on the ultimate demographic outcomes. Because the structure and the course of the national welfare crises traced a limited number of similar patterns, it becomes possible to examine the national programs in comparable groups rather than individually.

5. John D. Post, *The Last Great Subsistence Crisis in the Western World* (Baltimore, 1977), 53–69.

Scotland, France, and the Low Countries

In Scotland, France, and the Low Countries the two compelling administrative challenges were to lower the market price of cereals and to provide relief for the elevated number of unemployed and destitute. Famine conditions did not become widespread as in Ireland and Scandinavia. Public authorities in Scotland and France averted national mortality crises by supplying markets with cereals, by assisting the needy, and by creating public employment opportunities. The level of mortality nevertheless increased noticeably in both countries during 1740–1741. Neither country possessed a comprehensive public welfare system. In both countries, the rural population received proportionately much less public assistance. The scale of social disorder and itinerant vagrancy climbed significantly during 1740–1741. Regional mortality crises also occurred in both countries. The southern Netherlands, however, passed through a severe national mortality crisis in 1741. The central administrations of the Austrian Netherlands and the principality of Liège pursued the same welfare and relief measures as in Scotland and France, but less systematically, on a less concentrated scale, and with less success.

Scotland had long since established poor relief by statute. The Scottish poor laws were administered by the magistrates and town councils in urban locations and by the landowners and kirk sessions in rural areas. Although the effectiveness of the poor law had improved since the subsistence crises of the 1690s, the provisions for relief of the needy were still inadequate in 1740. No person who was physically capable of earning a livelihood was entitled to receive public relief. Those eligible for such relief were orphans, deserted children under the age of fourteen, persons over seventy, and those who were severely disabled, and then only as a last resort. Before a parish was liable to provide relief, the applicant had to demonstrate three years of continuous residence.

Under the Scottish poor laws, the welfare funds derived from voluntary contributions and legal assessments. Half of the amounts realized in church collections were allocated to the support of the poor. If the aggregate contributions proved insufficient, the parish was obligated to impose a legal assessment. The landowners paid half of the assessed amount, while the other inhabitants of the parish were required to pay the balance. Welfare emergencies such as the one in 1740 meant a struggle to balance income and expenditures. Scottish officials, unlike their English counterparts, had no method to compel the congregation to contribute. It was necessary to wait until the congregation was ready to accept an assessment.

The long and frigid winter, the increase in unemployment, and the dearth of 1740 produced a significant rise in the number of "occasional" paupers as opposed to "regular" paupers. In such instances, the standard practice had become to assist the unemployed from special collections or voluntary subscriptions, not from the poor-law fund. In the 1740s, the kirk sessions in most lowland parishes intervened in the emergency created by unemployment and high cereal prices, in conjunction with the local landowners. As for able-bodied beggars and vagrants, the Act of 1649 ordered them to be apprehended and put to work.[6]

Relief programs therefore still had to be organized in part through voluntary provisions. Welfare funds in the cities and towns were raised by subscription. The subsistence crisis of 1740–1741 reanimated the movement to establish "charity workhouses" for the poor to ensure that paupers were adequately maintained. There is no evidence that they became common, however. On balance, the majority of the towns and lowland parishes furnished the minimum amount of welfare assistance to the resident unemployed in the early 1740s. The roads of Scotland were not flooded with itinerant vagrants, as they had been during the 1690s. But the appearance of "starving highlanders" in search of work and relief in the lowland districts indicates that the poor law did not function adequately in the Highlands, where neither poorhouses nor legal assessments for welfare were the rule.[7] The evidence suggests that the improved functioning of the Scottish poor law and substantial voluntary relief measures ensured that the high food prices and joblessness of 1740–1741 did not result in widespread crisis mortality. However, the combined welfare measures did not prevent a noticeable increase in the incidence of vagrancy and begging, which explains in part the mortality peak of 1740–1741.[8]

The number of vagrants and beggars rose more sharply in Scotland than in England during 1740. In addition to the shortcomings of the Scottish poor law, the poor harvest outcomes of 1739 created a more

6. R. A. Cage, *The Scottish Poor Law* (Edinburgh, 1981), 1–18; Michael Flinn et al., *Scottish Population History* (Cambridge, 1977), 247; Henry Hamilton, *An Economic History of Scotland in the Eighteenth Century* (London, 1963), 388–90; L. M. Cullen and T. C. Smout, eds., *Comparative Aspects of Scottish and Irish Economic and Social History, 1600–1900* (Edinburgh, 1977), 25–26; Rosalind Mitchison, "The Making of the Old Scottish Poor Law," *Past and Present* 63 (May 1974), 58–93.

7. Flinn et al., *Scottish Population History*, 247.

8. For accounts of vagrants and beggars, see *Caledonian Mercury*, February 25, 1740; January 8, January 27, and August 25, 1741; *Scots Magazine*, December 1740; W. Kennedy, *Annals of Aberdeen* (Edinburgh, 1818), 292.

pressing shortage of food. Municipal officials began to import supplies of grain early in 1740 as a precaution.The subsistence crisis and the unemployment problem were aggravated by the press for seamen that followed the outbreak of war with Spain, which dried up coastal shipping and the transportation of cereals and coal. The urban populations of the towns along the Clyde and the Forth relied on maritime grain shipments for food and on maritime coal shipments for home heating fuel.[9] In the Scottish towns, the price of meal and the price of coal climbed sharply during the winter of 1740. As a consequence, municipal officials found an enormous increase in the number of welfare applicants. The Edinburgh press reported that ''an incredible Number of Poor came to receive Tickets from the Magistrates'' in the middle of January, ''to entitle them to Shares of Meal and Coal.''[10] The voluntary societies and the municipal ''Corporations'' also came to the assistance of the city's paupers.[11]

The welfare crisis in Scotland was triggered by the steep increases in the price of oatmeal during 1740. In the first half of the eighteenth century, it was common for widespread distress to develop when the price of oatmeal reached 12 pence a peck. Severe hardship set in when the price climbed to 15 pence a peck. The elevated unemployment rate had already caused considerable distress before the price of oatmeal reached these benchmark levels in 1740. The town councils and kirk sessions purchased meal for sale below the market price to assist those in employment. The disabled poor and the jobless were relieved by distributions of food and money, by the establishment of workhouses, and by special loans.[12]

The price of oatmeal reached 15 pence a peck in June 1740.[13] In Edinburgh, the magistrates had already purchased ''a vast Quantity of Meal in the Country,'' which was now sold at cost, ''in order to reduce the present exorbitant Price in the Meal-Market.''[14] The price of meal remained at that high level throughout the summer of 1740. The combination of the stortage of food and the anticipated harvest failures in the autumn prompted merchants and producers to withhold grain stocks from the market.[15] In August, the Edinburgh press claimed that ''no less than 80,000 Bolls of Grain have been imported into Leith within these

9. Flinn et al., *Scottish Population History,* 217.
10. *Caledonian Mercury,* January 22, 1740.
11. Ibid., January 14, January 24, and January 28, 1740.
12. Flinn et al., *Scottish Population History,* 217–18.
13. Hamilton, *Economic History,* 375.
14. *Caledonian Mercury,* April 28, 1740.
15. Ibid., June 9 and June 30, 1740.

few Months past and hoarded up in Granaries in expectation of the present High Prices being kept up.'' The same account reported that an anonymous letter had been sent to one of the merchants with large stocks threatening ''Vengence'' if he did not sell out at a moderate price to the ''Poor.''[16]

Despite the fact that the public officials and merchants of Edinburgh imported a considerable quantity of cereals, the market price of oatmeal did not fall in response to the additions in supply. From February 2 to the beginning of September 1740, a total of 39,231 quarters of grain had been brought into the port of Leith.[17] The failure of the price of meal to decline touched off a wave of food riots that began in Edinburgh during August, spread throughout the eastern counties in the autumn, and erupted in the northern counties during the winter and spring months of 1741.[18]

The food riots in Edinburgh occasioned serious public disorder. According to the magistrates, the shortage of food and the extensive joblessness ''brought a great Number of Poor unhappy People in Edinburgh and the Neighborhood into a real Distress; and who feeling their own Wants, without being sensible of the Cause from whence they proceded, have unluckily, taken those to be the Authors of their Misery, who have contributed most towards their Support.''[19] Because of looting and crowd violence, the Edinburgh magistrates found it necessary to guarantee grain importers against losses from food riots.[20] Although it is not possible to determine to what extent this action eased the grain shortages in the Edinburgh market, according to the press the scarcity and high price of cereals persisted not so much from genuine shortages ''as from the Apprehension of the Dealers in Victuals that the Mob may deprive them of such Quantities as they shall import.''[21]

The popular disturbances in Edinburgh were fueled by a large number of beggars. The magistrates, in an attempt to free the city from welfare expenditures on ''those poor who have no title to its charity,'' ordered badges issued to identify ''legal'' beggars. This measure was also justified as a method ''to provide for the maintenance of those who are the proper objects of its care.'' Persons found begging within Edinburgh

16. Ibid., August 22, 1740. The measure ''boll'' varied from cereal to cereal and also from region to region. At Edinburgh, one and one-half bolls of oatmeal equalled the Winchester quarter measure of eight bushels.

17. Ibid., October 6, 1740.

18. Flinn et al., *Scottish Population History,* 218; *Caledonian Mercury,* October 16 and October 27, 1740.

19. *Caledonian Mercury,* October 27, 1740.

20. *Scots Magazine,* December 1740, 577.

21. *London Daily Post,* January 3, 1741.

without a badge were to be committed to the house of correction for forty-eight hours, fed on bread and water, and kept at "hard labour."[22] More than 260 badges were issued. It is not known how many un-authorized beggars elected to endure the penalty rather than to go hungry.

The well-to-do citizens of Edinburgh pledged to fund the maintenance of the destitute by paying a voluntary sum on a weekly or monthly basis. This voluntary welfare program eventually supported 500 beggars and their families. The recipients of the assistance, however, were required to carry out assigned work tasks. If they refused, they also were confined in the Edinburgh house of correction. The *Scots Magazine* described the social scene that gave rise to the systematic support of beggars. "By the great dearth of provisions, so many poor people in the city were reduced to beggary, and at the same time such numbers flock'd in from the country that the clamours and importunities of these miserable objects made it very disagreeable to walk the streets."[23] The ordinance regulating begging apparently put an end to food riots in Edinburgh, for oatmeal still sold at a price of 15 pence a peck as late as January 1741, long after calm had been restored.[24] The degree to which overcrowded penal institutions contributed to the fever epidemics in Edinburgh during 1740–741 is not known.

Elsewhere in Scotland, by contrast, the scale of public disorder intensi-fied during the winter of 1740–1741. Beginning in November 1740 and continuing into May 1741, a wave of food riots erupted at Musselburgh in Midlothian, at Prestonpans in East Lothian, at Hamilton in Lanark, at Montrose in Angus, at Findhorn, Cullen, Nairn, Banff, and Inverness in the northeast region, and at Cromarty, Dingwell, and Tain in the Highland county of Ross.[25] Aberdeen, however, the principal town in the northeast region, escaped the grain riots. The magistrates of the town and the landowners of the county had agreed to purchase 4,000 bolls of meal, which were retailed to the inhabitants of Aberdeen and the countryside at 10 pence a peck. The ability and foresight to import barley from Holland proved instrumental in averting severe hardship and popular disturbances in Aberdeen county. At the same time, the town of Aberdeen could not meet all the demands made on its welfare resources.

22. *Scots Magazine,* December 1740, 577; *Caledonian Mercury,* December 30, 1740.
23. *Scots Magazine,* January 1741, 45–46.
24. Ibid., March 1741, 142, June 1741, 279, October 1741, 475.
25. Flinn et al., *Scottish Population History,* 218; for press accounts of the riots, see *Caledonian Mercury,* November 13, 1740; February 17, March 17, and March 30, 1741; *Scots Magazine,* October 1740, 482–83; *London Daily Post,* February 3, March 31, April 7, April 23, April 28, and April 30, 1741; *London Advertiser,* April 21, 1741.

The destitute of the northeastern Highlands, where the shortage of food "approached almost famine," came to Aberdeen in great numbers "to supplicate, even at any price, a small supply of corn and meal for the sustenance of their families."[26] The welfare programs of Aberdeen and Edinburgh, as was invariably the case in preindustrial towns, attracted an influx of begging vagrants from the rural districts, where parish poor relief proved more problematical and voluntary charity was less available.

The press accounts suggest that the shortage of food and the level of distress became equally trying in the western counties,[27] but the evidence is thin. Not only the poor but reportedly also "creditable Families" found themselves in a "starving Condition."[28] Gangs of vagrants seem to have been common in the western counties.[29] The food shortage in the western lowlands originated in part from the press for seamen, which restricted all coastal shipping and fishing.[30] The food shortage at Greenoch was not relieved until the beginning of 1741, when fifty tons of oatmeal arrived by sea.[31] Charitable collections to raise funds for the needy took place at Greenoch, Glasgow, and other western towns.[32]

Altogether the welfare and relief measures carried out by municipal officials, kirk sessions, and landowners in Scotland proved successful in averting a repetition of the mortality crises that paralleled the food shortages of the 1690's. But the Scottish poor law did not prevent a sharp rise in the death rate in 1740. Neither the structure nor the resources of the welfare system were adequate to meet the elementary needs of the increased number of paupers, beggars, and vagrants. The public and private response to the welfare crisis nevertheless represented a distinct improvement over past experience. The enhanced welfare and relief measures may have been inspired in part by the pressure of food riots, but in the longer view they can be seen as a forward step in the evolution toward a rationalized poor-law system in Scotland. According to Sir John Clerk of Penicuik, the "Magistrates of all the Towns in Scotland did all they cou'd for the support of their poor, and the County Gentlemen contributed very great sums for their relief, particularly in the shire of Edinburgh." He also noted, however, that "we were far from receiving thanks from the Country people whose lives we had supported, that they were either insensible or ungrateful." Clerk lamented the fact

26. Kennedy, *Annals of Aberdeen*, 290–94.
27. *London Daily Post*, December 19, 1740.
28. Ibid., January 3, 1741.
29. *Caledonian Mercury*, February 25, 1740, and January 27, 1741.
30. *London Daily Post*, June 30, 1741.
31. Ibid., January 31, 1741.
32. Flinn et al., *Scottish Population History*, 218.

that the destitute "asserted that all was done for our own private advantage, not believing it possible that we had bought Victual for them at 3d or 4th dearer than we sold it to them, and yet this method of providing for them cost the Gentlemen of this shire above £2,000 ster."[33]

According to the overly optimistic historian of Edinburgh, the cereal imports procured by the magistrates and landowners guaranteed that the "People lived in Plenty in the midst of Famine."[34] As the demographic records show, however, many poor persons in Edinburgh did not survive the subsistence crisis. The unwillingness or inability to assist the destitute vagrants from the countryside no doubt resulted in some deaths that were avoidable. The Edinburgh press complained that "the whole begging power of the Kingdom" seemed of late to have "centered in this City."[35] According to the *Caledonian Mercury*, the city's funds had been exhausted "in supporting above 700 extraordinary begging poor."[36] The welfare and relief resources of Scottish towns were of course limited in the 1740s. In the absence of a compulsory national poor-law system, Edinburgh and the majority of Scottish towns, on balance, seem to have dealt with the welfare emergency about as well as could be expected. The lack of adequate poor relief in the rural districts not only unbalanced the structure of the welfare system but also resulted in migratory flows that were dysfunctional inasmuch as they spread infection.

France, unlike Scotland, lacked a formal set of poor laws. The French welfare system centered on the resources of the general hospitals, supplemented by the charity of the churches and the voluntary activities of the local *bureaux de charité*.[37] A variety of civilian hospitals with beds were found in eighteenth-century France, but they can be placed in three categories: hospitals, *hôtels-Dieu*, and *hôpitaux généraux*. Hospitals, the largest category, provided the entire range of welfare services for the parish in which they were located and usually for that parish only. In addition to taking in the sick, elderly, and abandoned children, the parish hospitals distributed food and clothing in the home. But even these small hospitals were found mostly in towns, whereas more than 80 percent of the population lived in the villages and countryside before the

---

33. M. Gray, ed., *Memoirs of the Life of Sir John Clerk of Penicuik* (Edinburgh, 1892), 159.
34. W. Maitland, *The History of Edinburgh* (Edinburgh, 1753), 124.
35. *Caledonian Mercury*, January 8, 1741.
36. Ibid., August 25, 1741.
37. Shelby T. McCloy, *Government Assistance in Eighteenth-Century France* (Durham, 1946), 284–99, 454–60; Muriel Joerger, "The Structure of the Hospital System in France in the Ancien Régime," in Robert Forster and Orest Ranum, eds., *Medicine and Society in France*, trans. Elborg Forster (Baltimore, 1980), 104–36; Colin Jones, *Charity and "Bienfaisance": The Treatment of the Poor in the Montpellier Region, 1740–1815* (Cambridge, 1982).

middle of the eighteenth century. The hôtels-Dieu, as they were designated, normally admitted only the sick, though on occasion they also assumed responsibility for other charitable services. The hôtel-Dieu was almost exclusively an urban insitution.

The general hospitals were founded in the seventeenth century to confine beggars. In the eighteenth century, however, they took in the same categories of inmates found in the smaller hospitals; they also took in those cast into poverty by a temporary crisis or illness. In addition, those individuals perceived to be deviant, such as the insane and prostitutes, were now confined in the general hospitals. The general hospitals were intended to be regional institutions, designed in part to reduce the pressure of the destitute on the large towns and cities. They were established mainly in urban centers with more than 5,000 inhabitants but were also found in a few smaller localities.[38]

In the first half of the eighteenth century, French charity and welfare assistance derived from the combined activities of the royal government, the provincial and municipal governments, the church, voluntary societies, and individual charitable endowments. No systematic data are available, however, with which to assess the scale or the relative contribution of these interlocking sources of welfare assistance. The church furnished food, fuel, and clothing to the destitute. Bishops and parish clergy participated in, and often dominated, the local bureaux de charité, which existed in almost every parish. These charitable committees were normally headed by the curé, the others members being drawn from the leading political and judicial figures in the locality. The resources of the charitable committees came from legacies, gifts, alms, and, in some cities, a poor tax on the propertied citizens. The bureaux provided food, clothing, medicines, baby linen, and other assistance in kind, rarely in money. The committees perceived their function to be service to the "deserving poor" in their homes. Arguments in favor of expanding the bureaux stressed the fact that home relief permitted the head of a household to continue to work while making it unnecessary for him or his family to resort to begging or vagrancy. Vagabonds and beggars were incarcerated in the general hospitals.[39]

The traditional methods of assisting the needy in eighteenth-century France, however, proved inadequate to cope with the welfare requirements created by the unemployment and destitution that were spawned by the subsistence crises of 1740–1741. Public officials, at the same time, drawing on the experience of previous food shortages, had learned

38. This discussion relies on Joerger, "Structure of the Hospital System," 106–112.
39. McCloy, *Government Assistance,* 448–56; Jones, *Charity,* 131–32.

more effective methods of limiting the rise in the level of distress and thus also in the scale of social disorder. The food shortages of 1709–1710 had demonstrated that the timely importation of grain from abroad was the most useful form of relief. The importation of cereals was almost entirely the work of the officials of the royal government, that is, the controller general of finance and the intendants of provinces. Relief measures undertaken by the central government conflicted with the accepted theory in eighteenth-century France that welfare and charity should be localized, that each parish, town, and province was expected to take care of its relief needs.

But during the famine of 1709–1710 the practice became established that the royal government should lend assistance as a last resort. In the search for cereal supplies, the controller general and the intendants corresponded with French diplomatic representatives in other countries and also sent out purchasing agents to virtually all regions of Europe, North Africa, and the Near East. Even grain wholesalers and bakers were authorized to make purchases abroad if possible. The search for food abroad in 1709 was complicated by the hostilities of the War of the Spanish Succession. As a consequence, the French agents had more success in purchasing grain in the Mediterranean area than in the Low Countries and the German states. Considerable quantities of wheat and other grains were procured in the Barbary States but also in Italy, the Aegean islands, Egypt, and the Levant.

The municipalities also attempted to purchase grain through agents, with money borrowed or raised by voluntary subscriptions. Cities and towns set up large cauldrons of soup made from rice, beans, and other vegetables, which were served free to the needy. Local authorities forced bakers to sell bread to the poor at prices below those in the market, while subsidizing the losses. In the cities of Paris, Bordeaux, Rouen, Amiens, and Orléans the formation of "charitable workshops" to provide employment was discussed. On April 19, 1709, the Parlement de Paris issued a decree ordering the creation of such workshops. On August 6, a royal declaration also called for their establishment. A fund of 30,000 livres raised from voluntary, municipal, church, and parlement sources was to finance the workshops. But it is not clear to what extent they actually came into operation.[40]

Confronted with a similar crisis in 1740, the royal, provincial, and municipal governments adopted the same extraordinary measures that had proved efficacious in 1709. However, the scope and the scale of

40. McCloy, *Government Assistance,* 8–17.

welfare and relief programs were expanded in 1740. Governments made an enhanced effort to create employment through the repair and construction of roads and the setting up of workshops devoted to the spinning and weaving of textiles. But again it was primarily the ability to procure large quantities of grain abroad that made it possible to avert famine conditions and thus to inhibit the rise in mortality. Supplementary grain supplies were imported from the Mediterranean region, the Baltic region, Holland, England, and North America.[41] Although the principal concern was to provision Paris, cereals were also distributed to districts where food shortage and unemployment threatened calamity and riot, thus keeping hunger and disorder at bay. Rice and soup were given to the destitute free of charge. The imported grain supplies in conjunction with the extraordinary welfare and relief measures instituted in France, as was the case in Scotland, were successful in fending off a national mortality crisis during 1740–1741.

A welfare emergency began to unfold in France early in 1739, as the consequence of the harvest shortfalls of 1738. The poor grain harvests led to subsistence crises of varying degrees in the western provinces of Orléanais, Touraine, Anjou, Maine, Poitou, Berry, and the Marche. Famine conditions did not develop in any province during 1739, though they were predicted. Agricultural day laborers and urban wage earners nonetheless faced diminished employment opportunities at a time when the price of food was rising. Rural workers abandoned country districts for the towns, where they hoped to find work. The regional subsistence crisis occasioned not only an increase in the number of vagrants and beggars but also a series of grain market disturbances. According to M. d'Argenson, a former intendant of Hainaut and future secretary of state for foreign affairs, the shortage of food became so pressing in Touraine that the poor were reduced to eating roots, herbs, and grass, a diet that was increasing mortality.[42]

The officials of the royal government responded to the regional subsistence crisis by procuring cereal supplies abroad and elsewhere in France and also by stepping up relief measures. In Poitou, for example, the intendant set up a public granary, purchased grain abroad, had such grain sold at reduced prices in the principal markets, and instituted

41. See the account of grain procurement in Steven L. Kaplan, "The Famine Plot Persuasion in Eighteenth-Century France," *Transactions of the American Philosophical Society* 72 (1982), pt. 3, pp. 31–44.

42. René-Louis d'Argenson, *Journal du marquis d'Argenson*, ed. E.-J.-B. Rathery, 9 vols. (Paris, 1859–67), II, 159–65; Michel Bricourt, Marcel Lachiver, and Denis Queruel, "La Crise de subsistance des années 1740 dans le ressort du Parlement de Paris," *Annales de Démographie Historique* (1974), 285–92.

outlets to sell flour to the inhabitants at a price below the market. The public grain purchases charged to the account of Poitou amounted to 77,160 livres during 1738–1739. The intendant established *ateliers de charité* to carry out work on the roads and highways; workers were paid at the rate of 10 sous per day. He put beggars to work on the piers of Poitiers, for which they received 30 sous per day plus food and lodging. The intendant also spurred on the municipal governments to duplicate the welfare and relief efforts of the royal government. Intendants in other western provinces pursued similar programs, but it is not clear to what extent.[43]

Municipal officials in the western region of food shortage maintained strict control over the marketing of cereals in the towns for fear that the grain riots inspired by high food prices would get out of hand. The cereals purchased by the royal and municipal authorities were sold both to bakers and at retail, at slightly reduced prices, to dampen the rise in market prices as well as to prevent food shortages. In the western provinces, the propertied inhabitants of the towns subscribed to voluntary collections to assist those unable to pay for cereals at the reduced prices. At Laval in Maine, for example, a voluntary subscription raised funds to provide relief for the large number of 12,000 paupers counted in the town. The needy in the rural districts, by contrast, found relief more difficult to obtain. The parish priests in the countryside complained of their helplessness to assist the many destitute and also the "mercilessness of the rich."[44]

According to Narbonne, the superintendent of police at Versailles, a "veritable famine" existed in Maine, Poitou, and the Perche during 1739. The decision to ship wheat from the Paris region to the hard-pressed western provinces contributed to the rise of bread prices in the capital.[45] In Anjou, the intendant and municipal officials succeeded in provisioning markets with cereals purchased in the neighboring province of Brittany, where harvest outcomes had been more favorable in 1738.[46] Nevertheless, the municipal officials and the clergy urged the government to adopt emergency legislation to provision the poor, as the Parlement de Paris had done in the subsistence crisis of 1709–1710. The procureur general, responding for the Parlement, proposed only limited

43. P. Boissonnade, *Essai sur l'organisation du travail en Poitou, depuis le XIe siècle jusqu' à la Révolution,* 2 vols. (Paris, 1900), II, 464–65, n. 48.

44. Quoted in Bricourt et al., "Crise," 293.

45. Pierre de Narbonne, *Journal des règnes de Louis XIV et Louis XV de l'année 1701 à l'année 1744 par P. Narbonne, premier commissaire de police de la ville de Versailles,* ed. J.-A. Le Roi (Versailles, 1866), 478.

46. François Lebrun, *Les Hommes et la mort en Anjou aux 17e et 18e siècles* (Paris, 1971), 138.

relief measures in 1739, owing in large part to the concern of avoiding panic. In addition to the cereals purchased abroad to put downward pressure on market prices, the controller general authorized the intendants and municipalities to purchase their own grain supplies, funded either by loans from the royal government or by local borrowings.

Although the supplementary grain purchases warded off famine conditions in the western provinces, a severe dearth nevertheless developed. The destitute in the countryside often had to turn to makeshift diets. Numerous rural workers deserted the land when employment fell through, and the influx of country people created a welfare problem in the towns. It was reported that bands of vagrants roamed from farm to farm demanding food under the threat of force or arson. Farmers were assaulted and cereal stocks seized in the markets of the western towns. Municipal officials visited private granaries to compel market sales of hoarded stocks as a way of minimizing the shortage of food and of reducing the social turbulence.[47]

The royal government was obliged to intervene more directly in the late spring of 1739, when the shortage of food reached its most intense stage. The controller general authorized additional cereal purchases abroad, and also in provinces with surplus stocks, to ensure the provisioning of Paris and Normandy. To ease the food shortage in the Loire region, the royal government purchased rice in the Mediterranean ports and surplus wheat in Languedoc. Small amounts of money were also distributed to the destitute through the network of churches. In addition, the controller general authorized public works projects to build and repair roads, as described in Poitou, as a means to combat unemployment. The procureur general, however, still refused to ask the Parlement to resort to extraordinary relief measures, in part because of the regional nature of the crisis. In spite of the delays and hesitations, the public and private relief programs of 1739 seem to have met, on balance, minimum needs.[48]

Additional evidence that the shortage of food did not reach crisis proportions in the Paris region during 1739 can be found in the records of the Paris "abundance organization." As we have learned from the research of Steven Kaplan, the Paris abundance organization consisted, in theory at least, of every "community" in the capital (religious, hospital, public assistance, and educational), each of which was supposed to hold a stock of grain equal to three years of its own consump-

47. Bricourt et al., "Crise," 294–98; d'Argenson, *Journal*, II, 159–65.
48. Bricourt et al., "Crise," 298–304; d'Argenson, *Journal*, II, 166; Kaplan, "Famine Plot," 40–41.

tion needs. In the case of a shortage of food, the stocks were to be at the disposal of the public authorities. In the inventory of January 1738, the stock of grain held by the 128 communities enrolled in the program amounted to 9,243 muids (the muid equals 660 liters, or about 4.3 bushels), with an estimated annual consumption of 5,522 muids, thus considerably less than the ideal three years' needs. The total annual Parisian grain consumption needs approximated 90,000 muids. No global tabulation on the amount of grain in stock is available again until 1744, when the total reserve rose to 11,065 muids. Because not all the grain was immediately available, and because Parisian authorities could not expect the communities to divest themselves of their own subsistence, Kaplan concluded that in times of crisis the major contribution to the provisioning of the capital would be the fact that the communities would not compete for available cereal supplies.

The police had issued a call for "community" contribution during 1738, when the shortage of food developed after the poor harvests of that year. In the months from September to December 1738, the communities sent some 422 muids to provision the Paris markets. No information concerning the role of the community abundance organization is available for the next eighteen months, the period in which the scarcity of food became more pronounced. According to the administration of the hôtel-Dieu, however, the police adopted an indulgent policy during the course of 1739. This decision suggests that the shortage of food did not become a critical situation in Paris. Community reserves were allowed to drift downward in 1739 until prices became more favorable for the purchase of replacement stocks. The harvests in the Paris region, however, turned out deficient in 1739, and the price of cereals continued to climb. The Parisian police, in cooperation with the central government, focused their provisioning efforts on grain supplies from abroad and from distant provinces.[49]

The harvest outcomes in the western provinces, by contrast, proved more favorable in 1739 than in 1738, and as a consequence the dearth eased temporarily. But French grain stocks at the beginning of 1740 remained low. The market price of cereals accordingly failed to decline. The prolonged winter of 1740, moreover, brought about a fuel emergency in Paris and other northern urban locations, as it did in the British Isles. The provost of the merchants of Paris, the head of the municipal government, ordered fifty "cart loads" of wood to be distributed to each of the city's fifty-two parishes, in order to ensure that the homes of the

49. Kaplan, "Lean Years," 200–222.

poor would be heated.[50] Barbier, a lawyer who practiced before the Parlement, wrote in his journal that the winter cold, the high food prices, and the joblessness brought hardship to the entire Parisian population, except for the wood merchants, who emptied out their timber yards and made a great deal of money.[51] Also at Metz in Lorraine, the shortage and high price of firewood continued to be a public concern in the winters of 1740 and 1741.[52] In the rural Auvergne, the unavailability of firewood caused great suffering in some districts during the winter of 1740.[53] Epidemics of fatal respiratory disease became rife in France during the late winter and spring months of 1740, in all probability aggravated by widespread hypothermia.

Notwithstanding the fact that the severe winter season of 1740 increased the rate of unemployment, French public officials did not initiate extraordinary relief projects. One exception was the king's scheme to enlist the poor and beggars to break up the ice that still clogged the streets of Versailles in March. Altogether some 500 workers were employed for four days to cart away the ice. The total cost of the operation ran to 2,000 livres. The controller general's refusal to reimburse the municipal officials not only put an end to such extraordinary expenditures but also indicated that the central administration did not regard the needs as pressing.[54] Winter seasons, of course, brought higher welfare demands in preindustrial Europe even in the absence of extreme winters.

But when the price of food continued to climb rather than to decline in the summer of 1740, the central government and the municipal officials were forced to undertake special welfare programs. A renewed outbreak of market disturbances sharpened the urgency of public assistance. Crowds interfered with cereal shipments intended for Paris; public disorder multiplied; and consumers began to seize grain supplies by force. The dramatic food riot that took place in the flour market of Versailles in the autumn of 1740 conveyed the message that relief measures should be stepped up. A group of women, frustrated by the increasing difficulty of buying flour in small quantities at reasonable prices, tried to prevent the carting of supplies to the Paris bakers. The

50. *London Daily Post,* February 1, 1740.

51. E.-J.-F. Barbier, *Journal historique et anecdotique du règne de Louis XV,* 4 vols. (Paris, 1847–56), II, 256.

52. Jacques Baltus, *Annales de Baltus (1724–1756),* ed. Abbé E. Paulus (Metz, 1904), 95–96.

53. A. Poitrineau, *La Vie rurale en Basse Auvergne au XVIIIe siècle (1726–1789),* 2 vols. (Paris, 1965), I, 111–12.

54. Narbonne, *Journal,* 438–39.

police found themselves confronted by 4,000 violent protestors. The crowd stoned millers, dealers, and the Swiss guards called out to restore order. Military patrols became necessary to protect shipments of flour from Versailles to Paris.[55]

In September 1740, the central administration concluded that the evolving subsistence crisis demanded extraordinary measures. The Paris intendant was convinced that the shortage of food derived primarily from the fact that farmers and grain dealers were withholding supplies from the market. He handed down an ordinance that required people holding grain from the previous harvests to market one-sixth of the excess over their own subsistence needs over the next six weeks. The grain that was harvested in 1740 had to be threshed and marketed weekly. Violations of the new grain regulations called for a fine of 300 livres for each offense.[56] Simultaneously, the Parlement de Paris enacted decrees that prohibited the baking of white bread, the brewing of beer, and the use of grain in starchmaking and tanning. Each offense called for a penalty of 1,000 livres. Similar measures had been adopted in 1709 and in 1725. The prohibition of beer brewing raised widespread protest. Not only was it a common beverage, but water could be dangerous to drink in some locations because of the risk of enteric disease.[57]

The royal administration moved to expedite the purchase of additional cereals abroad. The provisioning of Paris was an overriding concern. Cardinal Fleury, the king's chief minister, counted on the controller general, Orry, and the Parisian Assembly of Police to devise a policy to solve the threatening shortage of food. The controller general relied upon little-known men rather than upon the leading victualing specialists to carry out the purchases. The principal supplier of foreign grain in Orry's program was Isaac Thellusson, Geneva's ambassador to France and also a leading Parisian banker. Thellusson proved able to effect cereal purchases in Amsterdam, England, Ireland, America, Hamburg, Königsberg, Danzig, Riga, Archangel, Sicily, Genoa, and Livorno despite the shortage of food throughout western Europe. The central administration also obtained wheat from Albania and the Barbary States and purchased large quantities of rice on public account from Piedmont and the Levant. Thellusson's striking success was owed in part to his personal reputation in the commercial centers of Europe and to his intimate knowledge of the grain trade. He also seems to have anticipated the grain embargoes

---

55. Bricourt et al., "Crise," 309–10, 314; Narbonne, *Journal,* 459–69.
56. Narbonne, *Journal,* 470–73.
57. Bricourt et al., "Crise," 315–16; Narbonne, *Journal,* 473–75; *London Advertiser,* September 18, 1740; Barbier, *Journal,* II, 262–63.

adopted by other European states as well as the critical changes in supply and price.[58]

Between October 1740 and June 1741, Thellusson procured at least and probably more than 27,075 muids of wheat, 4,252 muids of rye, and 1,383 muids of barley. In addition to this stock of grain bought for the king, he furnished the Paris general hospital with grain and acquired large supplies of rice for the royal government, the municipality, and the public insitituions that provided welfare and assistance. Although the precise amount expended by the controller general in the campaign to purchase foreign grain is not known, Kaplan believes that the figure was as high as 80 million livres. Orry was left with a large stock of unsold grain on his hands in the latter part of 1741, perhaps to the value of 13 million livres.[59] In spite of the massive cereal imports, however, the price of grain remained elevated throughout 1741 as the food supplies were slow to arrive. After the requisitions of September 1740, the Parisian "community" magazines were unable to provide any further grain supplies to the procureur general and the police to assist in their efforts to put downward pressure on market prices.[60]

The large-scale foreign grain purchases failed to reduce market prices and to eliminate the distress in the Paris region for several reasons. To begin with, the slow arrival of the foreign grains in the designated markets was traceable to contrary sailing winds as well as to the reluctance of the French provinces to permit food shipments out of districts suffering from dearth.[61] Even after the cereals arrived in government storage locations, however, the controller general's policies curtailed their potential impact on market prices. Orry kept the prices on the royal government's grain almost as high as the prevailing market prices to prevent the king from suffering a significant loss. He not only reprimanded local officials who gave in to consumer pressure and lowered prices but also cut off their supplies. Orry was not motivated exclusively by economy, however, despite the government's budget deficit. He did not believe that stable price conditions would be restored if the king's grain overwhelmed the market forces. The controller general also feared that market prices would soar again once the king's grain was known to be depleted. Orry hoped that the market price of grain would fall in

58. The discussion of French grain purchases relies mainly on the account of Kaplan, "Famine Plot," 31–41; see also Bricourt et al., "Crise," 316–17; d'Argenson, *Journal*, III, 170; Narbonne, *Journal*, 483–85; Barbier, *Journal*, II, 236, 267.

59. Kaplan, "Famine Plot," 42–44.

60. Kaplan, "Lean Years," 222–23.

61. Bricourt et al., "Crise," 316–17; d'Argenson, *Journal*, III, 170; Narbonne, *Journal*, 483–84; Barbier, *Journal*, II, 267.

response to small pressures exerted by the government's stocks. The Paris police also believed that it would be a mistake to sell the king's grain at a price significantly below the market. The fear was that such a move would prompt individual dealers to cut off their supply, that the bakers would buy up all the available grain, and that prices would then rise again, all to the profit of grain merchants. As Kaplan has demonstrated, such policies led to a new episode of the "famine plot persuasion" in France.[62]

As a consequence of the controller general's decisions and the transportation difficulties, the price of cereals at Paris and elsewhere in northern France remained painfully elevated. The French Guards had to patrol the grain markets of Paris to keep order and to enforce the regulations. As a means of putting downward pressure on the price of cereals, a royal declaration issued on October 26, 1740, exempted grain, flour, and legumes from all import taxes until December 31, 1741. The same declaration established a moratorium on rents payable in cereals within the jurisdiction of the Parlement de Paris. The contractual right to payment in kind could still be demanded, but the amounts due were to be computed in terms of the grain prices that prevailed in January 1740. The church and the hospitals, however, were exempted from the moratorium.[63]

The welfare and charitable resources of the districts outside Paris were inadequate to cope with the mounting needs of the working population.[64] The Parlement de Paris, in an attempt to ensure the subsistence of the rural poor, decreed on December 30, 1740, as it had in 1709, that a roll of the destitute be drawn up in each parish. The parishes also were to draw up tax lists to charge all individuals, societies, and religious communities able to contribute to the support of their paupers. In brief, the *arrêt* prescribed that all property owners in a parish contribute one sol per livre of two-thirds of their income to assist the indigent. The lists were to be completed between February 1 and August 1, 1741. A companion decree was aimed at suppressing the public disorder occasioned by the growing number of beggars and vagrants found in urban locations. Itinerant vagrants were bound to return to the parishes in which they were born or face imprisonment and ultimately a sentence in the galleys. The decree also prohibited the giving of alms to the able-bodied.[65]

62. Kaplan, "Famine Plot," 31–35.
63. Bricourt et al., "Crise," 319; *London Daily Post,* September 29, 1740; *London Advertiser,* October 26, 1740.
64. Narbonne, *Journal,* 484; Barbier, *Journal,* II, 267–80; Bricourt et al., "Crise," 317.
65. Camille Bloch, *L'Assistance et l'état en France à la veille de la Révolution* (1908; reprint, Geneva, 1974), 54.

Neither the proposed levy on the more affluent nor the attempt to repress vagrancy could be carried out effectively or uniformly within the framework of the social organization of the 1740s. A skeptical Barbier asked how the poor could leave Paris in order to travel thirty or forty leagues without money, and although they might be native to a village, "where will they stay if there are no homes?"[66] In March 1741, Barbier noted that the provinces were in a miserable state.[67] The combination of dearth and high unemployment rates led to endemic public disturbances and to an increase in the number of crimes. Armed bands roamed through the countryside at night; demanding alms with threats of violence.[68]

Some towns and provinces met the welfare emergency more successfuly than others. At Versailles, for example, the parish clergy and the propertied inhabitants reduced the level of distress by carrying out the Parlement's prescribed relief measures in 1741. At the end of 1740 the number of paupers had become so considerable that the streets were clogged with beggars. The parish charitable resources became so depleted that rice replaced bread in the food distribution to the destitute. A committee made up of a priest and two prominent citizens visited each dwelling in the parish "to inscribe on a roll the names of the persons able to contribute to the poor and the sums they pledged to give each month." On a companion list, the names and occupation of the needy were also compiled, together with information as to the number of adults and children, and the length of time the family had lived in Versailles. The parish of Nôtre Dame discovered some 500 pauper families numbering 1,500 persons. The relief plan entitled each person to one pound of bread daily, at a total monthly expense of 9,000 livres, toward which the king agreed to contribute 200 livres. A similar relief program was carried out in the other parish of Versailles.[69] The ability of the wealthy and well-organized town of Versailles to meet its mounting welfare needs was not always matched in French towns generally.

At Angers in Anjou, widespread distress was still the rule as late as July 1742. The municipal government had already borrowed 50,000 livres from the crown to purchase cereal supplies. Although the intendant and the municipal administration made extraordinary grain purchases to supply the markets of both the town and nearby villages, conditions of dearth still predominated in mid-1742. Looting and interference with food shipments continued to trouble public order, and a military presence

66. Barbier, *Journal*, II, 283–84; Bricourt et al., "Crise," 320.
67. Barbier, *Journal*, II, 289.
68. Bricourt et al., "Crise," 320; Iain A. Cameron, *Crime and Repression in the Auvergne and the Guyenne, 1720–1790* (Cambridge, 1981), 233–35.
69. Narbonne, *Journal*, 488–89.

remained necessary to safeguard the municipal cereal stocks.[70] At Metz, however, the municipal government and the local parlement managed the welfare needs as successfully as Versailles.[71] In Normandy also, the Parlement de Rouen decreed an assessment to provide for the subsistence of the destitute within its jurisdiction.[72]

If some of the provinces and towns of northern France proved able to provide a modicum of relief to their needy, the same degree of assistance was not available in the less-developed provinces, such as the Auvergne, in central France. Not even the large towns of the Auvergne could cope with the welfare emergency that originated in the harvest shortfalls. Because the records of the attempted rescue operations have been retrieved, it is possible to detail the successes and deficiencies of the welfare systems and relief programs in the Auvergne.

As a consequence of repeated deficit cereal harvests that began in 1737, many parishes in the Auvergne were severely tested during 1740–1741. The curé of Bort sketched a tragic picture in 1740. Because of the lack of food, infanticide by neglect had become common. The destitute searched for fern roots as a food of last resort and ate them ''like swine.'' The level of distress endured by the paupers of Bort was not an isolated case. In 1740, the bishop of Clermont wrote to Cardinal Fleury:

> The people of our country live in frightful misery, without beds, without furniture, the majority half of the year lack bread made of barley and oats, which makes up their only nourishment.... To this general poverty have been added these last three years hailstorms and crop deficiencies that have overwhelmed the population. The last winter particularly was so frightful that if we have escaped the famine and wave of deaths that seemed inevitable, it has been owing only to an abundance and promptness of charity that people of all ranks have brought forth to prevent all the misfortunes. The entire countryside was deserted and our towns could hardly manage to contain the numberless multitude of beggars who came to look for bread. The bourgeoisie, the magistracy, and the clergy all came to our aid. You yourself, Monseigneur, have brought about the benevolence of the king to advance us 60,000 livres. It is owing only to the favor of this assistance that half of our arable fields, which were going to remain fallow because of the scarcity and high price of grain, have been planted.[73]

70. Lebrun, *Anjou,* 131, 138–39.
71. Baltus, *Annales,* 103–104.
72. Bloch, *L'Assistance,* 54.
73. Quoted in Joseph Coiffier, *L'Assistance publique dans la généralité de Riom (au XVIIIe siècle)* (Clermont-Ferrand, 1905), 10–12.

The bishop also made a request for additional aid, which Cardinal Fleury instructed the controller general to provide for the Auvergne. The controller general ordered the receiver general of the generality of Riom to study the situation with great care.

The receiver general found that harvests had failed in the Auvergne in 1740 and that famine threatened. He ordered a reduction in taxes and a delay in collecting the payments. He also authorized work on the roads in order to employ the jobless. Finally, he requested funds from the controller general to purchase grain and cattle to be lent to distressed cultivators. The welfare of the population nonetheless went from bad to worse during 1741.

In the large town of Thiers, some 5,000 persons out of a population of 10,000 were counted as either unemployed or ill; 1,500 had to be fed at the public expense of some 200 livres daily. The intendant turned over a lump sum of 500 livres to Thiers early in 1741, which was of course no more than a token. Cardinal Fleury contributed an additional 1,000 livres in response to an urgent appeal from the town's general hospital. A violent epidemic of fever broke out in Thiers during the warm season of 1741. Work stopped and the town's economy fell into decay. The tax officials could no longer collect the state revenue. The hospital could not contain the hundreds who solicited admission. A total of 478 families were left with no other resource than public welfare. During the month of August, some seven or eight persons died of fever each day, or, according to popular rumor, fifteen to twenty.[74]

An earlier attempt to levy a municipal tax on the propertied inhabitants to support the hundreds of beggars in Thiers produced negligible results. On October 30, 1740, the intendant had enjoined the police officials to compile a list of the inhabitants of the town in a position to give alms. Each name on the list was to be taxed a sum proportionate to his resources. The assessment, payable monthly, was to defray the cost of distributing bread to 800 paupers each Saturday, a total of 5,600 pounds of bread weekly. This welfare system established by force was badly received, however, and proved of short duration. A new ordinance threatened those who refused to the pay the poor tax with garnishment.

The December 30, 1740, decree of the Parlement de Paris, which prescribed the organization of similar welfare assistance throughout the

---

74. Paul Bondois, "Un Essai de culture exotique sous l'ancien régime: La 'Peste du riz' de Thiers (1741)," *Revue d'Historique Economique et Sociale* 16 (1928), 613–30; Olwen Hufton, *The Poor of Eighteenth-Century France, 1750–1789* (Oxford, 1974), 177–79; Coiffier, *L'Assistance,* 13–14.

provinces within its jurisdiction, was publicized in each district of the Auvergne. The arrêt of the Parlement stipulated in addition that the donors on the list were obligated to pay their assessment fifteen days in advance, and those who defaulted were liable for a double assessment when the next payment fell due. It is doubtful, however, that these arrêts were widely honored in the Auvergne. Research has turned up donors' lists only in the towns of Thiers and Monton.[75]

Although the welfare crisis that evolved in Thiers during 1740–1741 was perhaps greater than in the other towns of the Auvergne, the relief funds allocated by the royal administration to the towns were clearly inadequate to meet the extraordinary financial needs. The expenses of Thiers and the towns were multiplied by the rural vagrants who sought food, shelter, and assistance within the urban walls. The Auvergne towns requested funds from the central government to clear their streets of literally thousands of beggars. The entire province received less than 17,000 livres during 1741.[76] The subdelegate at Blesle asked the intendant for assistance, writing that the "inhabitants have nothing to put in their mouths." His next request for assistance noted that he was obligated to give soup to 900 paupers. At La Chaise-Dieu, the lacework industry fell through, resulting in a considerable increase in the number of paupers at a time when municipal resources were exhausted. Because of the elevated cereal prices, famine conditions were anticipated at Riom and Montaigut. A wave of panic led to the prohibition of grain shipments out of the province.[77]

The central government, at the same time, did not limit its relief efforts to the royal doles extended to the Auvergne and the other *pays d'élection*. First, some taxes were abated. In such years as 1740, the intendant reported the fact that grain harvests failed and obtained an abatement for the towns and villages that were hardest hit. The amount of the abatements was set each year by the state council, which consulted the intendant charged with allocating the relief.

During 1740–1741, the practice of assisting the unemployed and able-bodied destitute through public works projects became more common. The decree of the Parlement de Paris on December 30, 1740, as well as several royal declarations called for the opening of public works to provide jobs for the poor. The controller general allocated 108,000 livres to the Auvergne in 1740 to carry out this purpose. In provinces experiencing severe distress, as in the Auvergne, the intendant autho-

75. Coiffier, *L'Assistance*, 208-11.
76. Bondois, "Essai de culture exotique," 613–30; Hufton, *Poor*, 177-79.
77. Coiffier, *L'Assistance*, 15–16.

rized employment in the form of *chantiers de charité,* which admitted women, old men, and children under six. Although the Parlement prescribed that the product of such work should repay the price of the hemp and other materials furnished, those so employed received essentially a dole disguised as wages. The public works projects to build and maintain roads, called *ateliers de charité,* were left to the initiative of the intendant and the subdelegates. The "charitable workshops" were in most cases established in proximity to the principal towns, near bridges and along highways. Camps that were designed to provide food for people put to work on such tasks also were located near large towns. The locations along highways were chosen to reduce the welfare pressures that built up in the towns. The flow of vagrants from the rural districts to the towns reflected the negligible welfare resources available in the villages. The corvée, the principle of unpaid roadwork, was temporarily abandoned during the subsistence crisis. The public works expenditures and programs of the royal government, however, could not solve the welfare problem created by the increase in the number of vagrants, beggars, and destitute who inundated the towns of the Auvergne and other less developed provinces during the subsistence crises of the early 1740s. The control of mendicity in the countryside was left primarily to the *bureaux de charité* located in the villages.[78]

Resident municipal paupers did not find themselves devoid of relief, even when the attempts to establish obligatory poor taxes, as in the majority of the Auvergne towns, proved unsuccessful. Christian charitable foundations, funded by gifts and legacies, were common in the towns and villages of all French provinces. The goods, furniture, and real property donated to the poor were administered mainly by the bureaux de charité. These charitable committees tried to assist the poor in their homes. Royal declarations repeatedly prescribed the establishment of relief at home. Public assistance at home, however, does not seem to have been common practice in the Auvergne during the crisis of 1740–1741, except at Thiers.[79] The traditional welfare system of the towns, as stated, focused principally on the general hospitals. The accommodations available in the hospitals, at the same time, proved quite inadequate to cope with the scale of mendicity engendered by a severe subsistence crisis. During 1740–1741, the royal government made sup-

78. Poitrineau, *Auvergne,* I, 93–99, 580–81, 699; d'Argenson, *Journal,* III, 97; Bricourt et al., "Crise," 300–301; Coiffier, *L'Assistance,* 245–50; McCloy, *Government Assistance,* 284–300.

79. Coiffier, *L'Assistance,* 208–11, 227–28; McCloy, *Government Assistance,* 454–56; Jones, *Charity,* 131–32.

plementary donations for the purpose of enlarging the employment opportunities provided by the textile workshops that were attached to the general hospitals.

The welfare resources of the general hospitals were often reserved exclusively for municipal citizens. To the degree that rural vagrants were barred from seeking assistance at urban hospitals, the special donations of the royal government proved of less value. As a consequence of the inherent inability of the hospital system to meet the expanded welfare needs of 1740–1742, a significant fraction of the vagrants and beggars from the countryside did not find assistance in the towns, whose resources continued to be overtaxed.[80] Even if the majority of beggars somehow managed to ward off starvation, the limited success in preventing a large-scale increase in itinerant vagrancy in France during the years 1739–1742 contributed to the elevated mortality of those years.

Yet, despite the lack of a rationalized system of poor relief, the combined welfare and relief programs of the royal government, the parlements, the municipal authorities, the hospitals, the bureaux de charité, the church, and the voluntary associations were successful, on balance, in fending off famine and in preempting a national mortaltiy crisis, unlike the demographic outcome of the food shortages of the 1690s. The procurement of large supplies of grain from abroad put downward pressure on market prices. The sale of grain by the royal administration and the municipalities at discount prices eased the cost of living of the working population and put additional pressure on cereal prices. The distribution of rice and legumes to the destitute free of charge averted the threat of widespread hunger. The creation of jobs through public works projects and charitable workshops provided income for the needy. The stepped-up activities of the general hospitals and the allocation of funds in modest amounts from the royal government to municipalities gave additional assistance to the urban indigent. The relief programs carried out by the bureaux de charité in both the towns and the villages helped families to survive the subsistence crisis.The compulsory poor relief levies adopted by the parlements and some large municipalities, even if not comprehensively carried out, made a contribution to the easing of the welfare crisis.

At the same time, the rise in the scale of vagrancy and mendicity and the endemic public disturbances were symptomatic of the inadequacies

80. McCloy, *Government Assistance,* 298–300, 455–56; Jones, *Charity,* 3–4, 100–103, 131–32; Coiffier, *L'Assistance,* 207; Joerger, "Structure of the Hospital System," 108–119; Poitrineau, *Auvergne,* I, 93–99, 580–81, 699; d'Argenson, *Journal,* III, 97; Bricourt et al., "Crise," 300–301.

of the welfare programs. The relief measures failed to prevent the extended mortality peak of 1740–1742. The underdeveloped northwestern province of Brittany, moreover, suffered crisis mortality reminiscent of the outcome of the food shortages of the 1690s. The elevated Breton death rate orginated in major epidemics of dysentery and typhus fever, not hunger and starvation. Did the unfavorabe demographic outcome in Brittany result in part from the relative absence of welfare resources and remedial measures? It should be noticed that Brittany was outside the jurisdiction of the Parlement de Paris and was thus not obligated to comply with the measures it decreed to assist the destitute. Furthermore, Brittany, unlike the Auvergne and the majority of northern French provinces, was a *pays d'état*, not a *pays d'élection*. Brittany, therefore, with its own assembly and partial control over taxation and expenditures, had to provide its own welfare and relief resources. Even as late as the crisis of 1770, Brittany still had not adopted the practice of setting up public workshops to combat unemployment.[81] While it is true that the scale of royal assistance to the pays d'élections during the subsistence crisis of 1740–1741 was far from massive, it is still possible that the grain and money allocated to these provinces was instrumental in averting crisis mortality.

The southern Netherlands, like the French province of Brittany, suffered a severe mortality crisis in 1741, also as the consequence of widespread epidemics of dysentery and "fever." The provincial administrations of the Austrian Netherlands, and also the principality of Liège, carried out relief programs similar to those documented in France during the food shortage of the early 1740s but with noticeaby less success. The more tragic demographic outcome in the southern Netherlands was the result of several factors. The most critical, however, were the relative lack of welfare resources and the relative absence of effective relief programs.

In the 1730s, the public administrations of the Austrian Netherlands debated the methods that should be adopted to control vagrancy and to assist resident paupers. Public opinion in the first half of the eighteenth century favored the Dutch model of workhouses and houses of correction, that is to say, the confinement of vagrants, beggars, and the destitute, a policy that was also gaining currency in England. The French model, which focused assistance on the general hospitals, was not adopted until the second half of the eighteenth century. Workhouses

---

81. McCloy, *Government Assistance*, 287–88; Pierre Goubert, *The Ancien Régime: French Society, 1600–1750*, trans. Steve Cox (New York, 1974), 134.

nonetheless remained isolated institutions in the Austrian Netherlands. A workhouse was first estabished at Mons in 1717. After the disturbances that troubled Brussels in 1719, the provincial government determined to construct a new workhouse in the capital. In 1734, two *Maisons des Pauvres* were established in Brussels, one for each sex, with a planned accommodation of 200 indigents capable of work. No other workhouses were in operation in the southern Netherlands at the end of the 1730s. In 1738, the first and only general hospital in the Austrian Netherlands was established at Ruremonde.

In 1734, the central administration of the Austrian Netherlands "reinstituted" the welfare laws; the same policies were to be reinstituted again in 1765. The fundamental rule governing the matter of public assistance in the Austrian Netherlands was that each town, parish, or village must be capable of maintaining its poor residents who were unable to work, funded by the income furnished by local boards of charity. These welfare *ordonnances* were directed principally at the problem of pauperism in the villages and countryside, for numerous other public, religious, and voluntary institutions of assistance could be found in the towns. In the case of available resources insufficient to the needs of the boards of charity, the law required the magistrates, parish clergy, and wardens of the poor to search for the least burdensome means to remedy the deficit. If the boards of charity judged it necessary, they could institute a poor tax to fall on the domiciled inhabitants, but only after the central government authorized the measure. The poor-tax provision, however, did not apply to the towns, whose municipal governments were permitted to impose such a tax if it was deemed absolutely indispensable.

Beggars unable to work on account of age or infirmity were permitted to ask for alms in the place of their birth or their legal domicile. If they attempted to beg in other locations, they faced imprisonment. Able-bodied persons were prohibited from begging. Vagrants and idlers—that is, all who, not being in service or at work or following a trade, had no means of subsistence—were ranked together with able-bodied beggars. The welfare policies of the mid-eighteenth century of course did not envisage the condition of involuntary unemployment as a result of the lack of jobs. The jobless, in fact, were also included among the indigent authorized to beg or admitted to public assistance, the letter of the law notwithstanding. During times of subsistence crisis, however, the welfare policies of the Austrian Netherlands became essentially a dead letter, in spite of the formal laws.

The relief of paupers by the boards of charity proved deficient even in years without food shortages and high unemployment rates. Boards of charity did not exist in a number of rural communes; neither did other public welfare institutions. Moreover, in villages where boards of charity were established, their resources were almost always inadequate to the needs of normal years. The combination of the large number of paupers, who multiplied during subsistence crises, and the relative lack of private charity simply overburdened the responsibilities of the poor boards. Although hospices for the old and infirm were numerous in the southern Netherlands, even in the villages, they were mostly very small establishments that sheltered only a few pensioners. The twenty-one hospices counted in Brussels as late as 1753 lodged only a total of 192 persons.[82]

The national mortality crisis that erupted in the southern Netherlands was traceable to the succession of low grain harvest yields from 1739 to 1741 as well as to the inadequate welfare resources and programs. The price of cereals in the Low Countries, as tables 10 and 11 show, more than doubled during the last half of 1740. The shortage of food in the Austrian Netherlands had already become acute in the autumn of 1739, prompting a series of decrees prohibiting the export of grain.[83] The provincial councils of the Austrian Netherlands aggravated the regional shortage at the same time by forbidding the shipment of cereals to neighboring provinces.[84] The scale of vagrancy, begging, riot, and looting reached greater proportions than in France and Scotland as a result of both more elevated food prices and a more serious welfare crisis.

Food riots broke out in Brussels as early as January 1740. The looting of shops and grain market disturbances occurred with greater frequency in the spring of 1740, when the wave of social disorder spread from Brabant to the Flemish towns.[85] The central government enacted harsher penalties for looting in response to the multiplying public disturbances. In May, a new ordinance made food rioters "liable for the death penalty if they have gone into a shop or house or if they have carried off anything." Moreover, any person faced with a demand for food accompanied by force or threats was permitted to defend himself, "even to kill

82. The discussion of the welfare laws, resources, and institutions of the Austrian Netherlands relies on Paul Bonenfant, *Le Problème du paupérisme en Belgique à la fin de l'ancien régime* (Brussels, 1934), 92–96, 102–103, 110–14, 134–52, 176, 201–206.

83. H. van Houtte, "La Législation annonaire des Pays-Bas à la fin de l'Ancien Régime et la disette de 1789 en France," *Vierteljahrschrift für Sozial- und Wirtschaftsgeschichte* 10 (1912), 102.

84. Etienne Hélin, "La Disette et le recensement de 1740," *Annuaire d'Histoire Liégeoise* 6 (1959), 443; H. Houtte, "Législation annonaire," 102.

85. A. Henne and A. Wauters, *Histoire de la ville de Bruxelles,* 2 vols. (Brussels, 1845), I, 254–55; *Mercure de France,* May 1740, 1,012–13; *London Daily Post,* May 3, 1740.

the aggressors.''[86] Also in May 1740, the central government of the Austrian Netherlands ordered a general inspection of all granaries, in order to inventory the cereal resources and to discourage hoarding. Peasant producers were directed to sell their harvested grain and were forbidden to stockpile cereals beyond family needs.[87] The government also removed all taxes on imported cereals.[88]

The population of the ecclesiastical principality of Liège similarly passed through a severe subsistence crisis. Food riots broke out as early as June 1739, when a crowd looted bakeries in the parish of Outre-Meuse. At the beginning of 1740, the Liège government adopted a series of measures intended to ease the shortage of food. All foreign beggars were expelled in the first week of January. On January 12, the government began to make special distributions of food to the needy. A particularly elevated unemployment rate intensified the subsistence crisis in Liège. The economy of the entire southern Netherlands suffered from a prevailing customs' war between Liège and the Austrian Netherlands.

In Liège, as elsewhere in the southern Netherlands, the number of public disturbances multiplied during the spring of 1740. Riots, thefts, and looting became more frequent. Military patrols had to be put in place both in the city and in the countryside. The majority of landowners and ecclesiastical canons continued to keep their grain in storage, and public officials charged them with allowing the poor ''to die of hunger.'' To organize the distrbution of bread along the line of rationing, the government ordered the taking of a general census on May 21.[89]

The food shortage and public disorder in the Austrian Netherlands prompted public officials to keep a close watch on all granaries in the hope of minimizing the hoarding of cereal stocks.[90] After the harvests fell short again in 1740, however, the government concluded that additional cereal supplies were essential to avoid famine conditions and also to put an end to the food riots.[91] Because the Austrian provinces had adopted mutual grain embargoes, the supplementary cereals had to be procured either in the Dutch provinces or overseas.

The established grain markets of Holland proved the most convenient

86. Hélin, "Disette," 443; H. Houtte, "Législation annonaire," 102–103.

87. G. van Houtte, *Leuven in 1740, ein krisisjaar: Ekonomische, sociale, en demografische aspekten* (Brussels, 1964), 245; Hélin, "Disette," 443.

88. H. Houtte, "Législation annonaire," 102; G. Houtte, *Leuven,* 245.

89. Etienne Hélin, "Le Déroulement de trois crises à Liège au XVIIe siècle," in Paul Harsin and Etienne Hélin, eds., *Problèmes de mortalité* (Liège, 1965), 490–92; Hélin, "Disette," 444–50.

90. Claude Bruneel, *La Mortalité dans les campagnes: Le Duché de Brabant aux XVIIe et XVIIIe siècles* (Louvain, 1977), 277.

91. G. Houtte, *Leuven,* 246.

source of supply.[92] Cereals could still be purchased in the Dutch markets, even though the population of the northern provinces also endured a severe subsistence crisis. The Dutch towns likewise were troubled by high food prices, market disturbances, and a growing number of paupers. The propertied citizens of Amsterdam and The Hague also found it necessary to contribute to the unemployed and destitute.[93] The Dutch grain markets nonetheless filled the orders of the governments of the southern Netherlands. The municipal accounts of Liège show that the expenditure of 222,000 florins for imported cereals from September 1740 to September 1741 led to public borrowings of 168,000 florins.[94]

The sale of imported grain at reduced prices and the distribution of food to the needy in the southern Netherlands did not eliminate widespread distress or prevent an increase in the scale of itinerant vagrancy. At Liège, the parish clergy who carried out the daily distribution of bread found themselves threatened and assaulted by overanxious beneficiaries.[95] At Louvain, the municipal government set up similar special welfare assistance programs for the deserving destitute. The number of applicants, however, swelled beyond the resources of the town, and officials attemped to reduce expenditures by forcing out many of the destitute. The town waged a campaign to get rid of beggars, idlers, the unemployed, loiterers, vagabonds, and strangers, who were perceived as "useless mouths" and accused of responsibility for the looting, robbery, and thefts committed in attempts to obtain food.[96] The majority of such rootless persons fell outside the welfare policies and programs of the Austrian Netherlands. In the countryside of Brabant, the impoverished population pleaded for a moratorium on taxes and rents.[97] The rural population of the Austrian Netherlands sought assistance in the towns mostly in vain. The destitute, both in the countryside and the towns, became the victims, and in part the vectors, of the murderous epidemics that swept the region in 1741.

The welfare and relief programs undertaken by the city of Liège also failed to ward off crisis mortality during 1741. According to Etienne Hélin, the relief measures failed in large part because the clerical organizations—that is, the chapters, monasteries, convents and abbeys—resisted sharing their cereal supplies with the poor. A government

92. Ibid.; Bruneel, *Mortalité*, 277.
93. Heinrich C. F. Schenck, *Die Wunder Gottes im Winter* (Arnstadt, 1741), 45–48.
94. Hélin, "Disette," 450–51; Hélin, "Crises à Liège," 492.
95. Hélin, "Disette," 456–57; Hélin, "Crises à Liège," 492–93.
96. G. Houtte, *Leuven*, 246.
97. Bruneel, *Mortalité*, 278; G. Houtte, *Leuven*, 246.

investigation concluded that "the clergy of Liège have hardly applied themselves to the terrible suffering of the poor people in this time of extreme dearth of food."[98] A more effective welfare system in the southern Netherlands would have reduced the number of vagrants and beggars and in so doing would have inhibited the spread of epidemic diseases, as was the case in the more successful welfare and relief programs pursued in France and Scotland. The crisis mortality in the Low Countries coincided with a prolonged period of climatic stress, food shortage, and elevated unemployment rates. The Dutch provinces also registered significantly higher mortality during 1740–1741. The severe winters, poor summers, and high food prices produced intense suffering among the working population of both the northern and southern Netherlands.[99] Although there is no method available to assess the relative percentages of the excess deaths of the early 1740s that originated in extreme weather events, undernutrition or malnutrition, and infections diffused by changes in behavior and community spacing, it seems certain that more effective welfare and relief programs would have cut down the mortality peaks in the Low Countries, France, and Scotland.

Ireland

The more acute shortage of food and the greater paucity of welfare resources in Ireland resulted in a mortality crisis as appalling as the outcome of the European famines of the 1690s. The urban locations of Ireland, as throughout western Europe, confronted a welfare emergency beginning with the severe winter season of 1739–1740. The increase in the price of coal as well as the increase in the price of food produced great hardship for the laboring population of Dublin, who were "not able to work this cold Season."[100] The great frost curtailed urban and industrial employment in Ireland and in so doing brought immediate distress to the working poor, even though the price of cereals did not climb so steeply as in France and the Low Countries.

Because of the absence of a formal poor law in Ireland, the welfare needs of the population depended on voluntary charitable collections. The clergy, churches, and notables of Dublin and other towns contributed to the alleviation of distress during the winter of 1740. Dean Jonathan Swift, for example gave £10 to assist the poor of Dublin, and the

98. Hélin, "Disette," 458–59; Hélin,"Crises à Liège," 492–93.
99. C. R. Boxer, *The Dutch Seaborne Empire, 1600–1800* (London, 1965), 284.
100. *London Advertiser,* January 15, 1739/40.

Lord Lieutenant of Ireland contributed £150. Accounts of charitable collections and contributions filled the press during the winter of 1740. It is not possible, however, to estimate the total sums involved.[101] The Irish privy council ordered the first general food embargo in the history of Ireland to begin in February and to continue during "this rigorous Season."[102] The measure was intended to dampen the rise in the market price of cereals rather than to ease an anticipated shortage of food. Ireland at this time was self-sufficient in oats, its main cereal, and produced a surplus of barley.[103]

Because of the absence of public programs to create jobs and income, the Dublin press suggested methods of easing the problem of large-scale unemployment. One example will convey the nature of the schemes. "There being great Numbers of poor people starving for Want of employment, we recommend it to them to save and pick Linnen Rags, for which they will get a good price."[104] Such makeshift projects could not of course compensate for the lack of public works projects and charitable workshops such as those initiated in France. With the passing of the winter season, however, the level of hardship declined temporarily in Ireland.

In the course of 1740, the growing shortage of food created renewed distress and revived the need for extraordinary welfare and relief assistance. The pronounced rise in the price of food during the late spring produced mounting hardship among the laboring poor in Ireland. Charitable subscription lists were opened in Dublin, Cork, Limerick, Waterford, Clonnel, Wexford, and other urban locations, but notwithstanding the outpouring of private generosity, the distress deepened. The scarcity of provisions was not helped by the lifting of the food embargo in April. Bread riots broke out in Dublin on May 31 and persisted for three consecutive days.[105]

A series of public relief programs was put in place during the summer of 1740, aimed at preventing hunger among the needy. In Dublin, a total of 180,000 pounds of oatmeal were sold to the poor during one week in July alone, at a price of a penny a pound.[106] The magistrates of

101. Michael Drake, "The Irish Demographic Crisis of 1740–41," *Historical Studies* 6 (1968), 105–106; *Faulkner's Dublin Journal*, January 19–22, January 22–26, and February 5–9, 1740.

102. *London Advertiser*, February 2, 1739/40.

103. L. M. Cullen, *An Economic History of Ireland since 1660* (London, 1972), 68.

104. *Faulkner's Dublin Journal*, March 24–28, 1740.

105. Drake, "Irish Demographic Crisis," 113–14; *Faulkner's Dublin Journal*, May 31–June 3, 1740; *London Advertiser*, April 24, 1740; Charles Creighton, *A History of Epidemics in Britain*, 2 vols. (Cambridge, 1891–94), II, 240; Cullen, *Economic History*, 56–57.

106. *Faulkner's Dublin Journal*, July 19–22, 1740.

Drogheda and other towns purchased oatmeal to be sold to poor inhabitants at a price below a penny a pound.[107] These municipal relief measures offered oatmeal at about one-third of the retail selling price. Public officials also took steps to bring down the price of cereals. The lord mayor of Dublin, for example, prohibited meal and grain factors from buying cereals, so that all available stocks would be brought directly to the markets. He also persuaded the corporation of bakers not to pay more than 70 shillings a quarter for wheat. Such measures contributed to the stabilzation of grain prices in Dublin in 1741, but the price of food had already advanced to famine levels.[108]

In the absence of a parish or public welfare system, the sale of food at discount prices alone could not avert widespread hunger among the unemployed and destitute of Ireland. Extraordinary relief programs became absolutely essential, and they were instituted in urban locations. Soup kitchens were set up to feed the needy of Dublin, Waterford, Drogheda, Newry, Powerscourt, Clonnel, Cashel, and all towns large and small. In the famine-struck province of Munster, the towns of Cork, Clonnel, and Cashel fed thousands of men, women, and children daily during the spring of 1741.[109] At Dublin, "upwards of 8,000 poor objects" were fed daily at the municipal house.[110] The towns and counties also initiated private relief programs to supply food to the needy.[111]

The number of food riots in Ireland remained far below those in Scotland, France, and the Low Countries. A series of minor disturbances, however, occurred during the spring of 1741. In Dublin, a group of young men forced bakers to sell their meal "at a very low price."[112] At Carick, a crowd tried to prevent a cargo of oats from being shipped to Waterford. A similar grain riot broke out at Sligo in western Ireland.[113] In sum, though, the popular disturbances that took place in Ireland during the subsistence crisis of 1740–1741 were far fewer than the number that occurred in Britain, France, and the Low Countries.

The public and voluntary welfare and relief measures in Ireland

107. *London Advertiser,* June 24, 1740.

108. Drake, "Irish Demographic Crisis," 114–15; *Faulkner's Dublin Journal,* December 13–16 and December 20–23, 1740.

109. *Pue's Occurrences,* March 24–28, 1741; *Faulkner's Dublin Journal,* May 5–8, May 9–12, and May 19–23, 1741; Drake, "Irish Demographic Crisis," 115; Charles Smith, *The Antient and Present State of the County and City of Cork,* 2 vols. (Dublin, 1750), II, 229–30.

110. *Pue's Occurrences,* March 10–14, 1741.

111. *London Daily Post,* January 27, 1741; *Pue's Occurrences,* March 24–28, 1741.

112. *Pue's Occurrences,* March 10–14, 1741.

113. *Faulkner's Dublin Journal,* April 21–24, 1741; *London Daily Post,* May 2, 1741; *Pue's Occurrences,* April 21–25, 1741.

proved less successful in averting famine conditions than was the case in Scotland and France, for several reasons. In addition to the absence of a legal poor law, Ireland did not possess either the agricultural or commercial development that can provide insulation against famine. The majority of the relief programs were centered in urban locations. Rural paupers, therefore, were forced to abandon their villages and homes in the search for food and employment. As a consequence, a massive wave of itinerant vagrancy engulfed the country during 1740–1741 and soon overwhelmed the limited welfare resources of the towns.[114]

In southwestern Ireland, where true famine conditions developed, the many thousands of beggars and vagrants created a welfare crisis that became unmanageable. The streets of Cork were inundated with beggars as early as June 1740.[115] The beggars in Edinburgh were counted in hundreds, not thousands. The historian of Cork summed up the unhappy outcome of the welfare and relief efforts: "notwithstanding all ranks of people distinguished themselves by a liberal and universal charity on this melancholy occasion, great numbers of the poor perished."[116] Many of the destitute of Munster and elsewhere in Ireland perished from hunger and prolonged undernutrition, but the majority died from typhus fever and dysentery, infections that vagrants and beggars helped to spread.

According to Bishop Berkeley, who gave assistance to the needy of Cloyne, the poor perished because of the numerous absentee landowners in the countryside of Munster. Unlike the practice in England, few private employment projects were undertaken in rural Ireland.[117]

The per capita deficiency of food in southwestern Ireland could have been alleviated by imported cereals. Although grain imports were officially encouraged, they failed to arrive in time or in sufficient quantities to avert crisis mortality. Press notices of the arrival of grain ships from America and elsewhere did not appear until May and June 1741.[118]

The national mortality crisis, however, was rooted more in the inadequate welfare and relief measures than in an absolute per capita shortage of food. The national epidemics were inescapably tied to the wave of itinerant vagrants and beggars who crowded into the towns. The Irish demographic catastrophe would be repeated in the 1840s, again largely as the result of inadequate welfare resources and programs.

114. Drake, "Irish Demographic Crisis," 124.
115. *London Daily Post,* August 2, 1740.
116. Smith, *Cork,* II, 229.
117. A. A. Luce and T. E. Jessop, eds., *The Works of George Berkeley, Bishop of Cloyne,* 9 vols. (London, 1956), VIII, 251.
118. For press accounts of foreign grain imports, see *Pue's Occurrences,* May 16–19, May 19–23, and June 13–16, 1741.

Although a legal poor law was finally instituted in Ireland by 1840, the welfare and relief system was concentrated on regional workhouses, which proved far too limited in capacity to assist the hundreds of thousands of needy persons. As was the case in 1740–1741, the destitute facilitated the spread of lethal epidemics of fever and dysentery as a consequence of the mass vagrancy prompted by the inability to obtain elementary assistance.

Scandinavia

The severe crisis mortality in Norway also was rooted in the combination of inadequate welfare and relief programs and an elevated incidence of vagrancy. Cereal imports, at the same time, were absolutely essential to offset the pronounced per capita food deficiencies that prevailed in Norway during 1741–1742. Even in years of favorable harvests, Norwegian grain consumption was greater than production. The mounting cereal deficits of the early 1740s had to be met with a larger quantity of imports to prevent famine conditions. According to the figures of the Norwegian land register of 1723, the annual per capita grain production approximated three hectoliters in the inland southwestern region, two and one-half in the western region, and two hectoliters per capita in the northern coastal districts. Annual per capita cereal consumption amounted to about four hectoliters, or slightly more than ten bushels. As a consequence, grain imports were needed to cover the considerable gap between production and consumption during years of average harvest volumes.

Denmark possessed a legal monopoly of the grain trade in the southern Norwegian dioceses of Akershus and Kristiansand. The coastal communities of western and northern Norway, however, were free to obtain grain from outside the kingdom. These coastal districts had developed a foreign trade in which fish was exchanged for cereals, which were supplied by sea. Although a few small agricultural districts near Oslo produced grain surpluses, and coastal Kristiansand could legally obtain grain anywhere in Europe, the population of South Norway depended on Danish exports to cover its cereal deficit. Despite the fact that Norway and Denmark were part of the same kingdom, the ability of Norway to procure adequate and timely food imports became more problematical with the universal western European harvest shortfalls of 1740.[119]

119. Ståle Dyrvik et al., *The Demographic Crises in Norway in the Seventeenth and Eighteenth Centuries* (Bergen, 1976), 6.

The Norwegian population had long been aware that weather-related grain harvest shortfalls posed the threat of famine. The practice of storing food to meet extended emergencies was well developed by 1740. The population commonly put aside salted herring, sour milk, cheese, butter, flatbread, dried fish, and meat as a precaution against harvest failures. In years when spring arrived late and summer proved short, however, and when anomalous weather also reduced cereal yields and diminished the possibilities of exploiting the mountain pastures—the precise climatic conditions that predominated from 1740 to 1742—an acute shortage of food became inevitable.[120]

The Norwegian public authorities had to procure larger than normal grain imports to fend off famine and crisis mortality. From a practical and legal standpoint, the bulk of the imports could orginate only in Denmark, across the Skagerak. The ruling house of Oldenburg had closed southern Norway to foreign grain in 1735, as part of a program to promote economic complementarity in the dual kindgom. During the five-year period from 1736 to 1740, southern Norway imported an annual average of 97.1 thousand barrels of grain, of which 95.9 thousand originated either in Denmark or in the Oldenburg German duchies. The dioceses of Bergen and Trondheim imported 75 percent of their grain from England and the Baltic ports during the same period.[121]

The Danish royal government, prompted by the shortage of food, adopted a program aimed at securing the provisioning of the Norwegian dioceses and putting downward pressure on market prices throughout the kingdom. In September 1740, the export of grain was prohibited from Denmark-Norway, and a month later the embargo was extended to the duchies of Schleswig and Holstein. The Danish government opened its grain magazines to provision the markets of southern Norway. The Danish records indicate that substantial quantities of grain were shipped from Denmark to Norway. The city of Oslo, located in Akershus, was sent 69,443 barrels of grain in 1741, 89,426 barrels in 1742, and 58,708 barrels in 1743, or a total of more than 217,000 barrels during the subsistence crisis. The diocese of Akershus, including Oslo, was sent 270,000 barrels in the famine year of 1742, or almost three times the normal imports of all southern Norway during the years of the late 1730s. The Danish government shipped 18,263 barrels of grain to the diocese of Trondheim in 1740, 32,000 barrels in 1741, and 150,000 barrels in

120. Michael Drake, *Population and Society in Norway, 1735–1865* (Cambridge, 1969), 66–67, 71.
121. J. O. Lindsay, *The Old Regime, 1713–63* (Cambridge, 1957), 344; Arthur E. Imhof, *Aspekte der Bevölkerungsentwicklung in den nordischen Ländern, 1720–1750* (Bern, 1976), 740–41.

1742. The diocese of Bergen imported a total of 86,481 barrels of grain in 1743.

The massive cereal shipments from Denmark to Norway notwithstanding, famine conditions developed in many Norwegian parishes. The failure of the rescue operations can be traced to the lengthy period of time that elapsed between decisions to ship cereals from Denmark and their availablity to destitute Norwegian consumers. In addition, the largest food shipments took place during 1742–1743 rather than during 1740–1741, and in many locations arrived too late to prevent acute nutritional stress. As an indication of the tardy resolution of the food shortage in Norway, the Danish government approved an emergency grain shipment to Akershus as late as March 11, 1743. Foreign ships anchored in Norwegian waters were still selling grain directly to purchasers in 1743. Also in 1743, the diocesan magistrate in Olso reported to Copenhagen that "many hundreds of men" from far and near had migrated to the city to seek food and bread, but that neither was available in Oslo. As a consequence of the food shortage in Oslo, the number of thefts in the city had multiplied. The Danish government lifted the prohibition against importing foreign grain into southern Norway, but not until July 1741.

The assistance provided by the bishops of the Danish church was likewise tardy. Collections taken up for the purpose of helping needy Norwegians pay for the government's grain yielded the sum of 14,000 reichstaler. On the late date of October 12, 1742, it was decided to turn over half of the sum to the diocese of Akershus, which was both the most populous diocese and also suffered from the greatest need. The diocese of Trondheim was given a quarter of the fund, while the dioceses of Bergen and Kristiansand were alloted one-eighth each.

In spite of the public, parochial, and private assistance measures, famine was not averted in Norway. From August 1742 onward, reports of death attributed to starvation began to increase. The welfare and relief programs fell short of providing timely and adequate aid for the desperate families in the Norwegian parishes. The pastors of the Norwegian parishes were instructed to draw up a list of the needy, for the purpose of an equitable distribution of the funds collected by the Danish church officials. The surviving reports made by the pastors indicate that numerous families had been reduced to absolute wretchedness by the end of 1742. The report submitted by the pastor of Jevnaker in Opplands Fylke in January 1743, for example, counted 229 families or individuals as destitute. He was allotted a total of 68 reichstaler from the church collections, which he distributed among the 28 neediest families or individuals. No family, regardless of the number of children, received more than five taler; some individuals received one. At this time, a *sack* of grain in the diocese of Akerhus sold for between two and three taler.[122]

As a consequence of the failure to meet the welfare needs of the Norwegian population, a series of mortality crises ravaged the dioceses of Norway. As in Ireland, the majority of excess deaths resulted from epidemics of dysentery and typhus fever, but some deaths were traceable to prolonged undernutrition. Also as in Ireland, the number of itinerant vagrants and beggars increased as the subsistence crisis deepened. The paupers who deserted their rural homes to migrate to Oslo and other towns, or simply to beg from door to door, facilitated the diffusion of the epidemic diseases that produced mortality crises in the Scandinavian peninsula each year from 1740 to 1743. By contrast, the Danish dioceses registered only a moderate increase in death rates during the years 1740–1742.

In Sweden-Finland also, a similar combination of climatic shocks, repeated harvest failures, high food prices, and diminished employment opportunities created welfare needs that proved too great for the resources available and the underdeveloped infrastructure. In some regions, the military activities of the Russian war intensified the distress and suffering. As in Norway and Ireland, the public officials in a number of Swedish counties faced a welfare emergency that originated not only in high food prices and unemployment rates but also in a shortage of food. Neither the stage of economic development nor the advance in social organization in Sweden-Finland had reached the point where authorities could cope with extraordinary welfare demands that persisted for three consecutive years.

The extreme weather events and harvest shortfalls produced a particularly steep increase in the level of joblessness in Sweden. More than 80 percent of the population earned a livelihood in agricultural pursuits, which meant that the overwhelming majority or workers and their families were directly dependent on the outcome of the grain harvests for income and subsistence. Agricultural day laborers and farm servants, who composed 20 to 30 percent of the population, made up by far the largest share of the lowest income groups. As a consequence, the fall-off in agricultural output during the run of poor cereal harvests from 1739 to 1743 translated directly into rural unemployment and hardship.

Employment opportunities shrank in parallel with the decline in cereal

122. Imhof, *Aspekte der Bevölkerungsentwicklung,* 742–45.

volumes. Farm positions became progressively more difficult to find, and as a result, young single persons were forced to migrate to find jobs. Though Stockhom and the other large towns were able to provide welfare assistance to the resident needy, the available resources were not adequate to the meet the needs generated by the influx of poor vagrants, particularly in the midst of an extended subsistence crisis. The harvest shortfalls of the early 1740s drive up the number of mendicants in Sweden, as throughout most of western Europe. The prolonged shortage of food and crisis mortality that prevailed in the southwestern counties of Värmland, Älvsborg, and Skaraborg reflected the deficiencies of the welfare system in Sweden.[123]

As was the case in Denmark-Norway, royal grain magazines existed in Sweden-Finland. In the Swedish public granaries, however, the volume of cereals stored in the 1740s was quite inadequate to offset the large harvest shortfalls, as the following figures indicate. The crown magazines sold or lent an aggregate total of 1,800 barrels of grain in 1739, 14,900 barrels in 1740, 26,800 barrels in 1741, 28,700 barrels in 1742, and 11,400 barrels in 1743. Private granaries, though a common topic of discussion, practically did not exist in the early 1740s. Several Swedish counties, located for the most part in the central region, produced grain surpluses, but cereals could be transported only short distances overland. The degree of commercial development in Sweden precluded the possibility of famine relief to inland southwestern counties by means of either internal grain shipments or imported cereals.[124]

Sweden normally imported a fraction of its cereal needs, first of all rye, then malt, barley, and wheat. By 1740, considerable quantities of grain were regularly imported from abroad, principally from the Baltic ports of Swedish Pomerania, Russia, Prussia, and Poland but also from England and Denmark. In 1740, 43 percent of all Swedish grain imports originated from western Pomerania, while approximately a combined 50 percent came from Russian (25 percent), Polish (15 percent), and Prussian (10 percent) ports. The harvest shortfalls of the early 1740s dictated a significant increase in foreign grain to compensate for the lower domestic output. But the proliferations of food embargoes in anticipation of harvest failures in 1740 made grain progressively more difficult to procure in international markets. The records show that the volume of Swedish cereal imports in fact fell off sharply in 1740, declining from 336,000 barrels in 1739 to 229,000 in 1740, or a decline

123. Ibid., 713, 981–83, 1,080–82; Eino Jutikkala, *Die Bevölkerung Finnlands in den Jahren 1721–1749* (Helsinki, 1945), 39–41; Gustaf Utterström, "Some Population Problems in Pre-industrial Sweden," *Scandinavian Economic History Review* 2 (1954), 130–31.
    124. Imhof, *Aspekte der Bevölkerungsentwicklung*, 895–97, 1,078.

of 31.8 percent. While the volume of imported grain recovered to 345,000 barrels in 1741, not until 1742, when 523,000 barrels were imported, was it possible to purchase the quantities of cereals needed to compensate for the series of deficient harvest yields.[125]

The public welfare and relief efforts undertaken in Sweden-Finland also failed to create employment for the jobless and destitute. The rural day laborers who were thrown out of work migrated to the towns or other districts in search of employment and assistance, occasioning vagrancy on a scale that public authorities were powerless to manage. As will be shown, the wave of vagrancy contributed to the diffusion of the epidemic diseases that produced crisis mortality in the Scandinavian peninsula. Contemporary writers were convinced of a direct cause-and-effect relationship. Unlike the case in Norway, however, in Sweden-Finland the crisis mortality of 1742 and 1743 also originated in the infections spread by marching armies, not only by paupers who deserted their rural districts.

England

England escaped the crisis mortality that beset Scandinavia and Ireland, owing to the existence of an obligatory poor law and the absence of widespread itinerant vagrancy. The Elizabethan, or Old, Poor Law required each parish to provide work for the unemployed and to relieve the "lame, impotent, old, blind, and such other among them being poor and not able to work." The poor law recognized three main conditions that rendered persons unable to work: sickness, old age, and absence of a husband in a household including children. The poor law similarly provided for the maintenance of orphan, neglected, and pauper children. It was also the duty of parish officers to relieve the able-bodied destitute who were temporarily unemployed or underemployed.[126]

The relief measures taken by parish officers under the Old Poor Law varied from place to place and from time to time. A great variety in practices and administration existed from county to county and from parish to parish. On balance, however, pension payments (so-called outdoor relief) remained the characteristic form of welfare assistance under the Old Poor Law. The pension system not only constituted the

125. Ibid., 892–95, 1,078; Wilhelm Naudé, *Die Getreidehandelspolitik der europäischen Staaten vom 13. bis zum 18. Jahrhundert* (Berlin, 1896), 402–406; Edmund Cieślak, "Aspects of Baltic Sea-borne Trade in the Eighteenth Century: The Trade Relations between Sweden, Poland, Russia, and Prussia," *Journal of European Economic History* 12 (1983), 257–62.

126. Dorothy Marshall, *The English Poor in the Eighteenth Century* (London, 1926), 2–6; G. W. Oxley, *Poor Relief in England and Wales* (Newton Abbot, 1974), 57–59.

least expensive method of giving relief (the amounts involved often were very small) but also offered the advantage of flexibility in that payments could be increased or reduced in accordance with changes in the cost of living or in family circumstances. The parish poor also received food, fuel, housing, and clothing when such assistance was deemed appropriate and expedient.[127]

The workhouse movement, however, was well under way in England by the 1740s. Beginning in 1696 with Bristol, the towns petitioned Parliament for permission to build municipal workhouses to confine paupers. The Workhouse, or General, Act of 1722–1723 permitted groups of parishes to build workhouses and in addition to apply a "test" that required any person asking for relief to enter these institutions in order to receive assistance. By 1740, the majority of English municipalities that were the size of market towns or larger contained workhouses. In the smaller urban locations and in rural districts the traditional small parish poorhouse remained the rule. The system of outdoor relief nevertheless remained the least expensive method of providing parish welfare in the eighteenth century. Because of this fact, the population found in the workhouses was made up chiefly of the elderly, the sick, women, and children, with practically no able-bodied men. The workhouses functioned as a rule with outdoor relief as the basis of the welfare system. Parishes preferred to assist able-bodied men by providing income through public works projects. Parish officers also adopted the practice of supplementing low wages with small cash doles.[128]

Not all destitute persons in England could claim relief under the provisions of the Old Poor Law, but parish officers often elected to make welfare disbursements to the "casual poor." The casual poor were made up mainly of persons outside the Acts of Settlement of 1662; not qualifying as the settled poor of the parish, according to the act, they had no legal claim to relief. In the urban parishes, particularly in London, destitute persons often drifted into a parish and subsequently fell into some misfortune. Technically such persons had no right to parochial relief, but in most cases it was simpler and less expensive to provide assistance than to discover their legal settlement and then attempt to send them back. Because able-bodied workers were not entitled to relief under

127. Oxley, *Poor Relief,* 57–64, Marshall, *English Poor,* 100–115.
128. E. M. Hampson, *The Treatment of Poverty in Cambridgeshire* (Cambridge, 1934), 74–75, 264–69; J. D. Marshall, *The Old Poor Law, 1795–1834* (London, 1968), 14–15; Oxley, *Poor Relief,* 81–108; Dorothy Marshall, "The Old Poor Law, 1662–1795," *Economic History Review* 8 (1937), 301–303; Marshall, *English Poor,* 125–45; Philip Anderson, "The Leeds Workhouse under the Old Poor Law: 1726–1834," *Publications of the Thoresby Society* 56 (1980, pt. 2), 75–78, 87–95.

the poor law, persons falling into this category were almost forced to violate the settlement laws if they could not find employment at home. Migrants who failed to find employment and a settlement became vagrants and often turned to begging or to crime.[129] In years of economic crisis, such as 1740–1741, however, migrants did not always find parish authorities willing to make discretionary payments.

Persons who were not native-born Englishmen likewise had no claim on the parish authorities. Not even Scottish or Irish emigrants had a legal right to relief in an English parish. But in London, at least, more prosperous fellow countrymen provided assistance to the destitute of a few fortunate nationalities. The Scottish Corporation of London had been chartered in 1665 for the relief of "poor Natives of North-Britain who are not entitled to any parochial Relief in England."[130] French Protestants resident in London founded La Maison de Charité de Spittlefields in the winter of 1689–1690 to assist needy Huguenot silk weavers. The wealthy members of the Huguenot community founded the French Hospital in London. The treasurer of the hospital devoted a personal legacy to institute an external relief program in November 1739, to assist those awaiting admission and also the elderly married couples ineligible for admission under the hospital's bylaws. La Maison de Charité had been founded to help Huguenot weavers faced with the competition of Irish weavers who were willing to work for lower wages.[131]

Irish migrant workers in England apparently found neither assistance nor sympathy. The Bristol municipal authorities, for example, rounded up Irish vagrants and shipped them back to Ireland at public expense. Reportedly this area of England attracted an "influx of paupers from Ireland." By virtue of the vagrancy act passed in the spring of 1740, the court of quarter sessions that met in August of that year fixed the rates to be paid to masters of ships for the reconveyance of vagrants to their native land. The payment fixed for each adult was six shillings, six-pence, including food, with children to be transported at half price. Inasmuch as the voyage to Ireland could last from a week to almost a month, the shipowners could not have made a significant profit.[132] The fate of destitute Irish vagrants returned to their famine-struck homeland during 1740–1741 is unknown.

The income for the administration of the poor law derived from the

129. Marshall, *English Poor*, 61, 161–76.
130. David Owen, *English Philanthropy, 1660–1960* (Cambridge, Mass., 1964), 67.
131. Charles F. A. Marmoy, "The Case Book of 'La Maison de Charité de Spittlefields,' 1739–41," *Proceedings of the Huguenot Society of London* 55 (quarto ser., 1981), iv–v.
132. J. Latimer, ed., *The Annals of Bristol in the Eighteenth Century* (Bristol, 1893), 227–28.

parish poor rate, which was assessed and levied twice yearly. The money was collected by the overseers of the poor; the amount due was based on an assessment procedure similar to the method of determining land and real property taxes. The precise rate "in the pound" was established by the parish vestry. Poor rates fluctuated from year to year, governed by current needs, and they also varied significantly from parish to parish in the same year. Unfortunately, neither systematic nor complete records of parish poor rate expenditures are available for the first half of the eighteenth century. Welfare crises such as that of 1740–1741, however, plainly drove poor rates up to record levels.[133]

To some degree, the pressures on poor rates in years of economic crisis were eased by the emergency voluntary relief collections inspired by severe winters and food shortages. In the event of a dramatic rise in the level of distress in eighteenth-century England, it became common practice for a group of notables to sponsor a charitable subscription list and to succeed in raising considerable sums of money.[134]

Notwithstanding the insulation provided by the established poor law system, the outpouring of voluntary charity, and the advanced level of economic development, England registered a mortality peak as pronounced as those of Scotland and France. The welfare demands mounted in England before the advent of sharply higher cereal prices. The prolonged arctic winter of 1739–1740, the related jump in fuel prices, and the concomitant rise in unemployment rates all combined to bring about a substantial increase in the number of persons unable to meet the cost of basic necessities. The welfare needs of the urban population became pressing during the first half of 1740. The jobless rate climbed not only because of the weather-related decline in economic activity but also because of the trade restrictions occasioned by the war with Spain, which had been declared in October 1739. Both the winter cold spells and a press for seamen made ship masters reluctant to put to sea and consequently curtailed the coastal shipping that brought food and coal to London and other British seaports.[135]

The hardship engendered by environmental stress and unemployment in the winter of 1740 taxed the normal operation of the parish poor relief system. Because of the perceived great increase in the number of paupers, the churches, municipal officials, and voluntary organizations

133. Marshall, *English Poor,* 11–13, 76–81; Anderson, "Leeds Workhouse," 87; W. E. Tate, *The Parish Chest,* 3d ed. (Cambridge, 1969), 7; Oxley, *Poor Relief,* 12, 24–25, 51–52.
134. Owen, *English Philanthropy,* 65–66.
135. T. S. Ashton, *Economic Fluctuations in England, 1700–1800* (London, 1959), 34–35; Flinn et al., *Scottish Population History,* 217; *London Daily Post,* January 9, January 17, and January 29, 1740; *London Advertiser,* January 25 and January 26, 1739/40.

deemed it prudent to raise emergency welfare funds. Appeals were directed to the sympathy and social responsibility of well-to-do persons, and their benevolence was reported in detail in the press.[136] Charitable urban merchants supplied coal "to the poor" at customary prices.[137] The increase in the price of coal during the winter months of 1740 became a more pressing problem for the urban poor than the increase in the price of bread. At London, the price of a chaldron of coal advanced from 25 shillings in January 1739 to 70 shillings in January 1740. The price of coal averaged 50 shillings in February 1740.[138] Similar increases were the rule in other British cities and towns. At York, for example, the price of a chaldron of coal climbed from 13 to 34 shillings during January 1740.[139]

Municipal and parish officials organized community collections of money and basic necessities to supplement the resources of the poor law. The first press account of the London collections appeared on January 12: "Considerable Collections have been made in the Parishes of St. Faith's and St. Gregory's near St. Paul's, for the poor House-keepers of those Parishes, which were distributed immediately among such as were recommended as proper Objects; every Body, whose Circumstances would admit, contributed chearfully; and we hope to hear of the like influences of Charity in other Parishes."[140] The press adopted the practice of recounting the individual contributions made by notable figures. George II gave £150 to his own parish for coals and £100 to each of the other parishes within the liberty of Westminster. Sir Robert Walpole donated the generous sum of £1,000 "to be distributed among the poor House-keepers in the several Parishes of the City and Liberty of Westminister."[141] Municipal officials in all English cities and towns instituted similar charitable campaigns.[142] Endless notices of parish collections appeared in the British press throughout the winter of 1740.[143]

The extraordinary charitable collections came to an end with the winter season. Not all welfare needs, however, were met by the outpouring of private generosity. A fraction of the destitute fell outside a welfare

136. *London Advertiser,* January 9 and January 10, 1739/40.
137. Ibid., January 15, 1739/40.
138. *Gentleman's Magazine* 9 (1739), 10 (1740).
139. *London Advertiser,* January 18, 1739/40.
140. Ibid., January 12, 1739/40.
141. Ibid., January 23, 1739/40; *London Daily Post,* January 23, 1740.
142. For examples, see *London Advertiser,* January 18 and January 22, 1739/40; *London Daily Post,* January 24 and January 29, 1740.
143. See *London Daily Post,* January 16, January 18, and January 23, 1740, and virtually every number during February 1740.

system based on settlement in a parish. The recipients for the most part were the poor "House-keepers" with an established residence in the parish. Some members of the floating population became casualties of the winter cold. Beggars, the elderly, and vagrants "having no legal Settlements" made up the victims of exposure hypothermia reported in the press.[144]

The level of distress and the welfare demands declined temporarily in England with the passing of the severe winter season of 1740 and the resumption of many trades. But the rapid increase in the price of food during the course of 1740 created renewed hardship for the poor and with it the need for stepped-up relief measures. The suffering of the working population was most pronounced in the western counties, owing to the continuing high rate of unemployment in the protoindustrial towns and villages. Because of the fall-off in demand, numerous clothiers in southwestern England were forced to close down operations. In the county of Somerset alone, more than 10,000 textile workers were thrown onto parish poor relief. In Devonshire, Gloucestershire, and Wiltshire thousands of unemployed clothing workers reportedly lacked bread. Neither the employment opportunities nor the cost of subsistence improved in the western counties during the course of 1740. Textile manufacturers complained of a deep slump, and the production of leather and paper also declined during 1740.[145] In Lancashire, according to William Stout, the sale of woolen, linen, and iron manufactures fell off sharply, while the wages of spinners declined, "so that poor labouring people are much straitened to live."[146]

The parish poor law and the developed social organization of England made it possible to deliver welfare benefits that offset in part the hardships produced by the elevated unemployment that predominated in the western counties. For example, at Tiverton, an industrial town in Devonshire that suffered from widespread joblessness in 1740, "a large woolen manufacture was set up in the hospital for the full employment of the poor there." A voluntary public subscription raised £1,020 to cover the initial expenses. From a business standpoint, the manufactory sustained a large loss, so that the operation was closed down in 1741, when the jobless problem eased somewhat.[147] At Chipping-Campden, in

144. For examples, see *London Daily Post,* January 8 and January 30, 1740; *London Advertiser,* January 8, January 28, and February 15, 1739/40.

145. Ashton, *Economic Fluctuations,* 35–36, 44, 146–47; R. W. Wearmouth, *Methodism and the Common People of the Eighteenth Century* (London, 1945), 55.

146. J. D. Marshall, ed., *Autobiography of William Stout of Lancaster, 1665–1752* (Manchester, 1967), 231.

147. M. Dunsford, *Historical Memoirs of Tiverton* (Exeter, 1790), 228; Marshall, *English Poor,* 146.

Gloucestershire, the public authorities reported that they "employ all their Labourers that are out of work in repairing their Highways, and give them 8d. per Day."[148] Accounts such as these can be multiplied. In all probability, however, the public statements were unduly optimistic. The needy in the western counties were still in dire straits in the late spring of 1741.[149] The prolonged welfare demands in the western counties drove up poor rates significantly. In Somerset and in other western parishes, the poor rate climbed to the extraordinary level of "6 and 7s. in the pound" by the end of 1740. In addition, cereals remained "very scarce and dear," with still "little or no pasture."[150]

The scarcity of cereals and the high price of food during 1740 led to a wave of public demonstrations. European governments in the eighteenth century, motivated in part by the fear of riots, invariably prohibited the exportation of food products during dearths. In England, the export of grain and other foods was not prohibited until November 1740. Unlike the embargo adopted by the Irish privy council, however, the English order was to remain in force until December 25, 1741.[151] In the meantime, the working population protested against the failure of the government to control the grain trade. Crowds turned to time-honored food riots, popular demonstrations, looting, and interference with cereal shipments. The urban population of preindustrial Europe commonly resorted to violence and rioting when harvest shortfalls resulted in food shortages, undue speculation, hoarding, or panic buying, a set of circumstances that threatened hunger. In Britain, waves of popular distrubances coincided with elevated cereal prices in 1709–1710, 1727–1728, 1740–1741 and would continue until the great demonstration of 1816–1819.[152]

Food riots became endemic in England during the spring of 1740, coincident with the steep rise in the market price of wheat. The majority of the popular demonstrations took place in the eastern counties. The riots were concentrated near ports from which grain was being shipped out of the country and also in the major grain-growing regions. The export of grain rather than fear of shortage of food inspired most of the

148. *London Advertiser,* November 27, 1740.
149. For such accounts, see *London Daily Post,* February 18, March 25, and April 16, 1741.
150. *London Advertiser,* November 18, 1740.
151. Donald G. Barnes, *A History of the English Corn Laws from 1660 to 1846* (London, 1930), 16; *London Advertiser,* December 2, 1740. An embargo was placed "on all Ships in the Ports of Great Britain, laden, or to be laden, with Corn, Grain, Starch, Rice, Beef, Pork, or any Provisions or Victuals, to be exported to Foreign Parts." The order was to remain in force until December 25, 1741.
152. For a discussion of grain riots and the details of the European popular disturbances during the years 1816–1819, see Post, *Last Great Subsistence Crisis,* 68–86.

collective actions. Consequently, the largest number of demonstrations were mounted at mills, granaries, storehouses, and on the highways rather than grain markets, as was the case in France and the Austrian Netherlands. The popular hostility to grain exports originated mainly in the perceived failure of public authorities to regulate the grain trade in accordance with the urgency of the prevailing dearth.[153]

The wave of riots in eastern England began when the inhabitants of villages near Wakefield assembled at the end of April to prevent the shipment of food into the neighboring county of Lancashire, where the shortage of grain was more acute, and where grain therefore commanded higher prices. The crowd, numbering about a thousand, came "by Beat of Drum" and carried away "all the Corn and Meal they found." The rioters could not be dispersed until a detachment of soldiers was dispatched from York to Wakefield. The crowd damaged several grain mills and assaulted local officials in the process of looting cereal supplies.[154] In line with the prevailing local rather than national sense of identification, protesters attempted to prevent the shipment of grain to nearby domestic destinations. At Derby, likewise, a crowd stopped two wagons loaded with flour destined for Leeds. The flour was distributed among the demonstrators, who considered the food to be "contraband property."[155]

Attempts to ship grain by sea touched off more violent riots. At the port of Stockton, in the northern county of Durham, some 3,000 "idle and disorderly persons" demonstrated over a three-day period to prevent the export of grain. They could not be dispersed short of a military assault.[156] At Dover, the export of wheat occasioned a food riot by women, who seized sacks of grain brought to the port to be shipped out, "and afterwards pelted the Teams and their Drivers with Stones for three Miles out of Town."[157] In June, the export of grain from Newcastle, where food was in short supply, led to a violent riot by colliers and keelmen. The demonstrators destroyed the town hall and the homes of merchants who were believed to be exporting grain abroad. The magistrates attempted to end the disturbances "by settling the Prices," but the demonstrators carried out their plan to prevent a grain ship from sailing

153. Andrew Charlesworth, ed., *An Atlas of Rural Protest in Britain, 1548–1900* (London, 1982), 83–85.
154. *London Advertiser,* May 10, 1740; for an account of this Yorkshire grain riot, see Wearmouth, *Common People,* 19.
155. Michael Thomas, "The Rioting Crowd in Derbyshire in the Eighteenth Century," *Derbyshire Archaeological Journal* 95 (1975), 37–39.
156. *London Daily Post,* June 21, 1740; Wearmouth, *Common People,* 19–20.
157. *London Daily Post,* May 24, 1740.

and also looted the granaries. Finally, three companies of infantry were called on to put an end to the week-long rioting. The authorites arrested forty demonstrators in the ensuing violence.[158] At Norwich, in East Anglia, a crowd seized a boat, sold its contents, and then paraded through the town extorting money and provisions. The military was called out and killed eight rioters in dispersing the demonstration. All the while the press remained outspokenly critical of the failure of the government to embargo cereal exports, pointing out that "charity should begin at home."[159]

In the western counties, in spite of the fact that food prices and unemployment rates were higher, popular disturbances were less common than in the eastern and northern regions, perhaps because of the fewer attempts to export grain. At Bristol, however, the army was required to pacify a demonstration demanding wheat at lower than market prices.[160] Food riots did erupt in the industrial area of northeastern Wales, where harvests were especially poor and grain exports were attempted. In the Vale of Clwyd, the press accounts maintained that "familys were starving for want of Bread." When the public learned that grain was being shipped from the port of Rhuddlan, a crowd of about a thousand demonstrators marched from the countryside into the port, asserting that they would rather be "Hanged than Starved." The arrival of a military detachment and the promise that no more grain would be exported until the subsistence crisis passed put an end to looting and property damage.[161]

The English food riots ended in fact with the new cereal harvests and the grain embargo enacted in November 1740. Although the British government delayed in prohibiting the export of cereals, the balance of the grain trade during the years 1740–1741 indicates that exports were nonetheless drastically curtailed. The number of quarters of wheat and flour exported from Britain declined from 588,284 in 1738 to 54,391 in 1740 and then to 45,417 quarters in 1741. In 1742, when the domestic food shortage had subsided, the volume of wheat exports rose to 295,698 quarters. Wheat and flour imports, which had been virtually nonexistent in the 1730s, increased to a modest 5,469 quarters in 1740 and 7,540 in 1741.[162] While it is true that the quantity of grain imported during the subsistence crisis was small, the foreign cereals put

158. Ibid., July 2 and July 3, 1740.
159. *London Daily Post,* May 5, 1740; *London Advertiser,* July 14 and July 22, 1740.
160. *London Advertiser,* September 23, 1740; *London Daily Post,* September 30, 1740.
161. K. L. Gruffydd, "The Vale of Clwyd Corn Riots of 1740," *Flintshire Historical Society Publications* 27 (1975–76), 36–39.
162. Barnes, *History of English Corn Laws,* 299.

downward pressure on market prices in a few locations of chronic food shortage—at Bristol, for example.[163]

The English parish poor law and the voluntary collections met most, if not all, welfare needs during the emergency created by severe weather, unemployment, and dearth. According to William Ellis, a farmer in Buckinghamshire, the arctic winter of 1740 "occasioned the Death of many poor People who wanted Heat and Victuals; notwithstanding it was observed that there were never greater Acts of Charity displayed than in this season."[164] Although thousands of Englishmen went cold and hungry for months on end, few died of starvation. The majority of the excess deaths in 1740 derived from the inroads of hypothermia and an elevated incidence of respiratory infections. The English working population suffered from unemployment and high cereal prices rather than from a true shortage of food, to say nothing of famine conditions. The availability of barley and oats at much lower prices than wheat guaranteed basic subsistence to all but a small number of unfortunates. The inability to afford the white wheaten loaf was nevertheless perceived as genuine deprivation.[165] For the unemployed and the destitute, basic subsistence was provided by public welfare and private charity. The scale of welfare resources and the rationalized social organization in England proved adequate to ward off the mortaity crises that occurred in Ireland and Scandinavia.

The English welfare and relief measures kept to a minimum but did not prevent an increase in the incidence of itinerant vagrancy and mendicancy. Although the rise in food prices and joblessness did not trigger the mass vagrancy experienced in Ireland and in districts of France and the southern Netherlands, the distress led to an increase in the number of thefts and crimes against property. A sharp rise in the number of arrests for theft augmented the number of persons in jails awaiting trial.[166] The demonstrators who were arrested in the popular disturbances also swelled the jail population. London alone seems to have witnessed a pronounced increase in the number of beggars and vagrants.[167] The fact that mass vagrancy did not occur on a national

163. *London Daily Post,* February 24, 1741.
164. Quoted in Charlesworth, *Atlas of Rural Protest,* 83.
165. *London Advertiser,* August 22, 1740.
166. J. M. Beattie, "The Pattern of Crime in England 1660–1800," *Past and Present* 62 (February 1974), 73–78; Beattie, "Crime and Courts in Surrey, 1736–1753," in J. S. Cockburn, ed., *Crime in England, 1550–1800* (Princeton, 1977), 155–86; Douglas Hay, "War, Dearth, and Theft in the Eighteenth Century: The Record of the English Courts," *Past and Present* 95 (May 1982), 125–26, 132–34.
167. *London Daily Post,* January 29, 1740; *London Advertiser,* February 15, 1739/40; Wearmouth, *Common People,* 55–57.

scale explains in part why England escaped a national mortality crisis. Death rates nonetheless rose noticeably during the years 1740–1742, in spite of the relative success of the welfare and relief programs. As will be shown, the welfare policies adopted contributed to a degree to the mortality peak.

Prussia and Germany

The Prussian administration was more successful than its British counterpart in preventing significant increases in unemployment, vagrancy and public disorder. The ability to avoid widespread destitution and social upheaval in spite of harvest shortfalls and wartime campaigns accounts in large part for the more moderate rise in German mortality during 1740–1741. The Prussian government, in advance of the public policies of other European states, had established an extensive network of royal granaries for the express purposes of maintaining stable food prices, protecting the population from famine, and provisioning the army. It may be argued that in the first half of the eighteenth century the Prussian state, whatever the motivations, showed more concern for the welfare of peasants than did the governments of the other major European countries.[168]

Prussia's grain policy was formulated by Frederick William I on the basis of strict mercantilistic principles, which prohibited the importation of grain and promoted its export. A shortage of food, of course, calls for a public policy that is exactly the reverse of such mercantilistic guidelines. However, the Prussian policy presupposed that an adequate supply of cereals would be at hand in the royal granaries (i.e., *Magazines*) to dampen price increases and to prevent dearth. True to mercantilistic convictions, Frederick William refused to embargo the export of grain during the food shortage that developed in the early months of 1740. Not until immediately before his death, in May, did the king assent to limited grain embargoes in Cleves and Magdeburg, the locations in the Prussian state where the subsistence crisis had become acute. Because of the distress occasioned by the severe winter weather conditions and the prevailing high food prices, the king also authorized the public sale of cereals from the royal magazines located in Berlin, Cleves, Minden,

168. For this view, see Betty Behrens, "Government and Society," in *The Cambridge Economic History of Europe*, vol. V: *The Economic Organization of Early Modern Europe* (Cambridge, 1977), 609–13. Also see Reinhold A. Dorwart, *The Prussian Welfare State before 1740* (Cambridge, Mass., 1971).

Pomerania, the Kurmark, and the Neumark. In addition to the sale of grain to local officials and to bakers in urban locations, the Prussian state advanced cereals and seed grain to needy peasants.[169]

As a consequence of the public sales and the reluctance to import grain supplies, however, the granaries were nearly empty at the time of Frederick William's death. An inventory returned on May 16, 1740, showed a count of 12,928 *Wispel* (a large grain measure equivalent to about 1,000 kilograms), excluding the food requirements of the army. During most of the 1730s, the royal magazines contained 40,000 to 50,000 Wispel of grain. Although Frederick William insisted on the prohibition of grain imports during the spring of 1740, he ordered the transshipment of surplus rye stocks from East Prussia to Pomerania and Cleves, the two hardest-hit provinces. The state also instituted maximum prices for producers and traders in those two provinces. As a precautionary measure, Frederick William authorized the purchase on public account of all cereals available in the East Prussian market of Königsberg in order to replenish the granaries located in that province.[170]

Because of the increased welfare needs created by the Prussian subsistence crisis of 1740, the new king, Frederick II, authorized the free importation of grain from abroad in the first week of his accession. Through merchant intermediaries, the Prussian state purchased grain in Poland, Livonia, and Russia before embargoes closed off virtually all foreign markets. Because of the embargoes, the greatest percentage of public grain purchases made during 1740, however, originated in the eastern province of Prussia and Lithuania, whence they were shipped to the markets of central and western Prussia. East Prussia not only disposed of surplus grain supplies; the provincial government also made purchases in Polish markets. After the invasion of Silesia and the resulting war with Austria, the Prussian government stepped up its attempts to procure grain abroad.[171]

In pursuing policies to protect the working population from dearth, Frederick the Great and the Prussian administration were not motivated exclusively by welfare concerns. The interest of the state dictated that distress and public disorder be minimized, if not avoided altogether. The

169. For a discussion of the grain policies of Frederick William I and Frederick the Great, see Walther Hubatsch, *Frederick the Great of Prussia: Absolutism and Administration,* trans. Patrick Doren (London, 1975), 58–61.

170. Acta Borussica, *Denkmäler der preussischen Staatsverwaltung im 18. Jahrhundert: Getreidehandelspolitik,* vol. II: W. Naudé, *Die Getreidehandelspolitik und Kriegsmagazinverwaltung, Brandenburg-Preussens bis 1740* (Berlin, 1901), 251–52, 276–78, 323; ibid., vol. III: W. Naudé and A. Skalweit, *Die Getreidehandelspolitik und Kriegsmagazinverwaltung: Preussens, 1740–1756* (Berlin, 1910), 61, 85–86; *London Daily Post,* June 7, 1740.

171. Naudé and Skalweit, *Getreidehandelspolitik,* vol. III, 61–62.

Prussian government understood that effective relief programs reduced the potentially large economic and demographic losses. The public granaries were intended to guard not only against hunger but also against the second- and third-order effects of weather-related food shortages. One single famine year could weaken the population for years by leaving arable fields uncultivated and by promoting the spread of contagious diseases.

Frederick accordingly instituted a comprehensive rescue operation. Cabinet orders and rescripts attacked the intensifying level of hardship in the summer of 1740. The provincial government of Pomerania, where famine conditions threatened to develop, for example, was instructed to assist the peasants in need, to see that seed grain remained available, and to ensure that the arable fields were cultivated. The Prussian central administration transferred cereal stocks to Pomerania from granaries located elsewhere in the kingdom. The Stettin government distributed 150 Wispel of rye to the needy Pomeranian population during the first week of June and an additional 322 Wispel in mid-June. In line with the standard Prussian policy, the government sold rye and flour to peasants at prices that were significantly below those paid in the markets.[172] The shortage of food in the western province of Minden-Ravensberg and in the Rhineland also necessitated the transshipment of emergency grain supplies from East Prussia. The central administration authorized the provincial government at Cleves to purchase 3,000 Wispel of rye from the northeastern province of East Prussia.[173]

The Prussian government also instituted policies aimed at alleviating the distress of the urban poor as well as the peasants by putting downward pressure on the rising price of cereals. A general edict in November 1740 called upon all nobles and lessees of crown land to sell their grain stocks in the markets within two weeks. Otherwise all cereals beyond those needed for home consumption would be confiscated at a price set by the crown. The manufacture of spirits from grain was prohibited in Cleves and Pomerania. When the rye harvest volumes proved deficient again in 1740, the king prohibited the exportation of grain from the eastern provinces as well. To prevent practices that would drive up prices further, the Prussian central administration bought up all rye offered for sale in the markets of East Prussia.[174]

172. Ibid., 237–44; Johann Christoph Becmann, *Historische Beschreibung der Chur und Mark Brandenburg*, ed. B. L. Bekmann, 2 vols. (Berlin, 1751–53), I, 556–57; Friedrich Samuel Bock, *Versuch einer wirtschaftlichen Naturgeschichte von dem Königreich Ost- und Westpreussen*, 5 vols. (Dessau, 1782–85), I, 801–802; *London Daily Post*, August 4, 1740.
173. Naudé and Skalweit, *Getreidehandelspolitik*, vol. III, 244–45.
174. Ibid., 86, 90–91, 102–104, 196–201.

The provisioning of the Prussian urban population was facilitated by long-standing policies. Magistrates and town councils for decades had been careful to accumulate grain stocks as a precaution against food shortages. Urban bakers were required to maintain several months' supply of flour at all times. The Prussian market police regulated every facet of the urban grain trade. Frederick the Great's policy was to keep the price of rye, the staple bread grain of the working population, as low as possible and to be relatively unconcerned about the price of wheat. Frederick William, on the day of his death, ordered the Berlin magazine to sell 400 Wispel of rye to the city's bakers so that the price of bread could be reduced to the level that had prevailed six months earlier. Frederick the Great made public grain stocks available at cost to the poorhouses, hospitals, and orphanages of Berlin. On October 29, 1740, the city of Berlin received rare permission to import bread from the surrounding countryside. A second exceptional measure, permitting the baking of barley bread in Berlin during 1740, indicated a serious shortage of food.[175]

The sale of grain from the public granaries and the transfer of cereals from East Prussia to other provinces eased the subsistence crisis in Prussia. During 1740–1741, according to the records, a total of 14,250 Wispel of grain were shipped on public account from East Prussia to Pomerania, Minden-Ravensberg, and the Rhenish provinces. Adding in the grain shipped out of East Prussia by merchants before the prohibition of exports, a total of 20,000 Wispel were transferred to the central and western provinces. The market price of cereals, however, remained elevated in Prussia until the more favorable grain harvests of 1741.

After the Prussian army invaded Silesia at the end of 1740, Frederick gave military needs priority over the grain stored in the royal magazines. This decision curtailed to some degree the distribution of food to towns and needy peasants. Notwithstanding the continuing high cereal prices, the scale of the Prussian central government's relief program diminished during 1741. The provincial governments and the landlords were expected to provide more assistance on their own. When the government of Pomerania asked for additional grain supplies, Frederick enjoined the nobility to take better care of its subjects. The newly conquered province of Silesia was an exception to the policy of cutbacks in public assistance. The Silesian peasants, for example, were given seed grain by the Prussian army in 1741.[176]

175. Naudé, *Getreidehandelspolitik*, vol. II, 323; Naudé and Skalweit, *Getreidehandelspolitik*, vol. III, 281–99.
176. Naudé and Skalweit, *Getreidehandelspolitik*, vol. III, 62–63, 196–201, 244–45.

Altogether, the grain stocks available in the public granaries, the grain policies of Frederick the Great, the social control exercised by the Prussian state, and the landlord and peasant relationship of "hereditary subjection" that predominated in the eastern provinces had the effect of minimizing the rise in unemployment, work migrations, vagrancy, and begging. Although Prussia was less developed and "modernized" than England, the relative success in carrying out traditional preindustrial relief measures as a means of buffering the shortage of food proved more effective in constraining the rise in mortality. In particular, the Prussian state's welfare and relief policies and programs kept down the potential increase in such dysfunctional social behavior as crowding into towns, workhouses, or even jails.

Other German governments, especially those of the "city-states," likewise achieved some measure of success in coping with the welfare emergency created by the shortage of food. But not all German states faced serious subsistence crises. Mecklenburg and Saxony, for example, continued to export grain to Prussia until climbing domestic food prices dictated otherwise. In Hanover, the dearth prompted the elector to issue an edict that encouraged the sale of grain to the needy at discount prices. The edict also attempted to discourage grain sales abroad if demand held up in domestic markets.[177] The tenor of the document does not suggest, however, a serious shortage of food in Hanover. The states located in the northwestern coastal region of Germany for the most part did not experience pronounced food shortages, in some measure because of the ability to import cereals by sea. The city of Bremen, for example, kept its public granaries relatively filled, and also made cereal purchases in the Baltic ports to put downward pressure on market prices.[178]

By contrast, the interior cities and states of western Germany, owing to the greater difficulties in obtaining imported cereals by sea, could not prevent a dearth and a welfare crisis from developing during the years 1740–1741. Attempts to import cereals ran into the embargoes adopted by neighboring states. The city-state of Aachen suffered a grave subsistence crisis, in part the consequence of the refusal by the duchy of Jülich to allow grain to be transshipped through its territories. The price of food in Aachen reached famine levels, and the number of burials climbed correspondingly. Only when the city was permitted to resume the importation of cereals from abroad did the crisis ease. The south-

177. Hanover, Edict issued by George II, dated May 7, 1740 (broadside in Boston University, Mugar Library, Rare Book Department, call no. 3198-#122).

178. Wilhelm Abel, *Massenarmut und Hungerkrisen im vorindustriellen Europa* (Hamburg, 1974), 181–82.

western city-state of Nuremberg confronted a similar subsistence problem when neighboring states embargoed grain exports. The sharp rise in
unemployment rates in Nuremberg and other German cities and towns
worsened the crisis. The demand for manufactured products and craftmen's
services fell off as a consequence of the draining of discretionary
purchasing power by elevated food prices. In Nuremberg, Aachen, and
Leipzig, the prices of cloth and textile products weakened as the prices
of cereals strengthened.[179]

On balance, however, the German cities passed through the welfare
emergency with some success. The municipal records of Cologne make
it possible to follow step-by-step the response of public officials to the
subsistence crisis. The city of Cologne was the capital of the larger
ecclesiastical state of Cologne. In July 1739, the city council decided to
supply bakers with low-priced grain from the municipal granary in order
to prevent the price of the cheap mixed-grain loaf of *Malterbrot* from
rising too steeply. Although the grain embargo instituted by Jülich at
the end of 1739 reduced Cologne's supply of food, the municipal grain
stocks remained adequate to keep bread prices relatively stable until
April 1740. Bread prices began to climb noticeably in May. As a
consequence, the city council prohibited the export of cereals, flour, and
bread. As a precautionary measure, municipal officials inventoried all
bakeries and private granaries to assess the aggregate food supply.

Cologne's policy of selling public grain to the city's bakers did not
solve the subsistence needs of paupers and the helpless. On May 18, the
city council agreed to distribute 1,000 loaves of bread daily at a price
below that set at the bakeshops. Municipal officials also drew up a list of
the city's poor who were deemed to be entitled to purchase bread at the
subsidized price. Some two thousand families were found to qualify. As
a pure welfare measure, the city donated 38,364 loaves of bread to the
municipal poorhouse. An inventory of the public grain stocks taken on
August 5, 1740, returned a count of 19,826 *Malter* (a grain measure
equal to 108 kilograms) of rye, which was not significantly less than the
23,669 Malter counted on August 29, 1739.

Because of the poor grain harvest outlook for 1740, however, the
granary authority decided to procure additional cereal supplies from the
rural districts of the state and to import grain from Holland and the
Baltic ports. During the course of 1740 and 1741, the city of Cologne
imported a total of 46,501 Malter of rye. The supply of grain improved
to the point where in July 1740 the city council concluded that it was no
longer necessary to continue the direct sale of bread to the poor at

179. Ibid., 182–87.

discount prices. Instead, the city sold rye to the bakers at a price low enough to permit the seven-pound loaf of Malterbrot to be sold at 12 Albus, a figure that was double the price that prevailed from 1734 to 1737.

The city council was forced to reinstitute the practice of direct sales of bread to the needy in November, when the price of grain jumped again. The city government distributed tokens to those certified to buy low-priced public bread. Each adult was permitted to purchase one seven-pound loaf weekly, a daily ration of one pound of bread, which amounted to approximately 2,500 calories. Children were entitled to half rations. The price of the welfare loaf of Malterbrot was fixed at 10.67 Albus, whereas the market price of the same loaf was set at 13 Albus. The sale of municipal bread at discount prices remained in force until the spring of 1741, when the price of rye began to decline. But the system of bread tokens had to be restored in the autumn of 1741, when the price of Malterbrot rose above 10 Albus.

The rural poor in the state of Cologne, unlike those in Prussia and England but like those elsewhere in Europe, remained outside the established system of welfare and relief to a detrimental degree. Beggars and vagrants from the rural districts drifted into Cologne during the subsistence crisis. At the same time that the municipal government instituted the practice of bread tokens, it also initiated a program to drive out nonresident beggars.[180] In Nuremberg as well, the city council rejected the welfare claims of the rural destitute, and meted out harsh penalties to beggars who transgressed the municipal ordinances.[181]

Considered as a whole, the public administrations in Germany nevertheless proved relatively successful in preventing widespread hunger and in meeting the increased welfare needs. The food resources found in public granaries warded off famine conditions. Welfare and relief programs distributed food to the destitute and, in Prussia, seed grain to peasants. Grain purchases made abroad on public account fended off severe food shortages and put downward pressure on the market price of cereals. But as elsewhere in western Europe, the relief measures carried out in the German states could not prevent a significant increase in mortality during the subsistence crises of 1740–1741.

All the same, the amplitude of the German mortality peak of 1740–1742 remained moderate compared with the demographic outcomes elsewhere in western Europe. The more favorable outcome in Germany

180. Dietrich Ebeling and Franz Irsigler, eds., *Getreideumsatz, Getreide- und Brotpreise in Köln, 1368–1797*, pt. 2: *Brotgewichte und Brotpreise: Wochen-, Monats, und Jahrentabelle Graphiken* (Cologne, 1977), xxxiii–xli.
181. Abel, *Massenarmut*, 187; Schenck, *Winter*, 44.

derived in large measure from the modest rise in Prussian death rates. The ability of the Prussian welfare system to constrain the increase in the number of beggars and vagrants had the beneficial effect of closing off some of the pathways and restricting some of the networks that could generalize contagious diseases in preindustrial Europe.

To sum up, the regions of Europe that avoided crisis mortality in the early 1740s owed their more favorable demographic outcome to the effectiveness of public welfare and relief programs, the availability of surplus resources, and the improvement of social organization. The success or failure of the relief measures depended also on the relative stage of economic development and on the relative severity of the food shortage. The public administrations of the Scandinavian peninsula faced a more daunting welfare problem than their counterparts in Britain and France.

In Britain, France, the Dutch Republic, Germany, and Denmark, the primary welfare task was to compensate for the inablity of the jobless and needy to cope with the elevated market price of cereals during 1740–1741. Each of these countries and regions succeeded, though to varying degrees, and in so doing averted national mortality crises. The parish poor law in England and lowland Scotland and the network of public granaries in Prussia and Denmark prevented the shortage of food from progressing to widespread hunger and starvation. The Dutch Republic had become, of course, almost the granary of western Europe.

In France and the southern Netherlands, where welfare assistance still depended to a critical degree on medieval institutions, church-directed charity, and public relief measures governed by the perceived gravity of the emergency, not all rural districts and locations distant from political capitals obtained the scale of assistance that the needs dictated. Although the governments of France and the Austrian Netherlands achieved a measure of success, the welfare and relief efforts failed to prevent a sharp increase in the number of beggars, vagrants, and popular disturbances.

The kingdom of Sweden-Finland proved unable to avert national mortality crises. The somber demographic outcome of the extreme weather events and the shortage of food was traceable to the combined problems engendered by a relatively underdeveloped economy, the obstacles to inland transportation of cereals, the demands of foreign war, and the difficulty in procuring sufficient grain abroad to ease the dearth.

In Norway and Ireland, where the severe shortages of food and inadequate welfare resources and measures led to famine conditions, mortality crises developed that recalled the great European famines of the 1690s. Norway in particular, and southwestern Ireland, needed additional grain to make up for per capita food deficiencies. Both lands lacked political control over grain policies and an effective system of public welfare. Norway and Ireland, consequently, were at the mercy of timely and appropriate administrative decisions that would be made elsewhere. The needed food supplies became available neither in time nor in sufficient quantity to avoid hunger and crisis mortality in Norway and Ireland. Backwardness in economic and social organization and in public administration meant that Norway and Ireland would also remain at the mercy of climatic variability and harvest outcomes beyond the 1740s.

The mortality wave of the early 1740s resulted primarily from an elevated incidence of epidemic disease. The rising epidemic mortality coincided with an extended period of climatic variability and a series of grain harvest shortfalls. It is thus likely that climatic stress, prolonged undernutrition, and the subsistence crises all contributed to the spread of contagion. In order to discover the critical epidemiological links, it is necessary to examine the specific infections that became rife during 1740–1742. The mortality peak also originated in an increase in the number of deaths traceable to hypothermia and hunger. Before I examine the functional relationships between food shortage and the diseases that became epidemic in 1740, I shall attempt in the next chapter to assess the relative demographic impact of the extreme weather conditions and prolonged hunger that paralleled the epidemics.

7. Mortality from Hypothermia and Hunger

The European mortality peak of 1740–1742 was touched off by a combination of climatic variability, food shortages, social disarray, and, in some regions, warfare. Death rates climbed mainly from a higher incidence of epidemic diseases. It is a truism that in western Europe food shortages have occasioned more deaths from infectious disease than from hunger.

In the early months of 1740, however, the rising death rates resulted more from abnormally low atmospheric temperatures than from the shortage of food and elevated cereal prices. As tables 6 and 7 show, the mean atmospheric temperatures in western Europe remained considerably below normal from October 1739 through the end of May 1740, with arctic-like weather conditions predominating in January and February. The extended period of low atmospheric temperatures brought about an increase in mortality that was largely unrelated to higher food prices. The number of burials rose during the first half of 1740 in part as a consequence of meteorological stress, which enhanced the risks of fatal hypothermia and respiratory disease.

Thermal Stress

On the basis of present-day knowledge of the life-threatening effects of hypothermia, it seems certain that the abnormally low European temperatures recorded in the winter and spring of 1740 led to a noticeable increase in the number of deaths. *Exposure* hypothermia, however, does not seem to have claimed a great many lives. The evidence suggests that in western Europe altogether perhaps several hundred persons working at outdoor occupations, such as seamen and post riders, fell victim to the spells of arctic weather. The number of deaths traceable to *accident* hypothermia, by contrast, became pronounced during the first five months of 1740. Modern medical findings disclose that the elderly and young infants make up the principal victims of accident hypothermia.[1]

The term "accident hypothermia" refers to the unintentional decline of deep body temperature, measured rectally, to a reading below 95°F. If body temperature falls below this approximate threshold, it will continue to decline and death will result in the absence of corrective action. It is difficult for systemic hypothermia to occur in a normal conscious person. As the body temperature drops toward 95°F, several physiological responses are triggered to halt the decline.

The initial responses to a decline in body temperature are a rise in blood pressure; an acceleration of the pulse rate; the activation of the shivering reflex which generates heat through muscle contraction; increased oxygen and energy consumption; peripheral vasoconstriction of blood vessels so that warm blood flows mainly in the deeper, more critical parts of the body; and an increase in systemic vascular resistance. Cardiac work is increased. But when the core body temperature drops below the approximate 95°F threshold, shivering stops. Blood pressure, heart rate, and cardiac output start to fall in a linear and progressive manner. As temperature falls further, the heart becomes progressively slower and ultimately arrests. The temperature at which cardiac function ceases is variable, but cardiac standstill is probably the terminal event in all victims of accidental hypothermia.

The victims of accident hypothermia are for the most part people who are unable to defend normal body temperature in an environment that has become colder than normal. It is the combination of decreased production of body heat, increased loss of body heat, and impaired body thermoregulation that gives rise to the risk of accident hypothermia. Although the shivering reflex will increase heat production severalfold when the environmental temperature drops, this response is either impaired or absent in the elderly and does not develop in infants until they are several months old. The clinical evidence indicates that a specific portion, but not all, of the elderly population is particularly susceptible to hypothermia. The process of hypothermia is accelerated by both fatigue and inactivity, which have the effect of decreasing heat

1. For discussion of the body heat balance in humans, see S. W. Tromp, *Medical Biometeorology* (Amsterdam, 1963), 208–18; K. E. Cooper and A. V. Ferguson, "Thermoregulation and Hypothermia in the Elderly," in Robert S. Pozos and Lorentz E. Wittmers, Jr., eds., *The Nature and Treatment of Hypothermia* (Minneapolis, 1983), 35–45; Richard S. K. Young, M.D., and Keith H. Marks, "Hypothermia and the Pediatric Patient," in ibid., 20–34.

output. It should be especially noted that exposure to low temperatures increases heat loss, while hunger and malnutrition reduce heat output.[2]

These physiological relationships are pertinent to the environmental and economic circumstances that predominated during the first half of 1740, when the abnormally cold winter and spring temperatures produced climbing unemployment rates and fuel prices. Medical authorities today are convinced that accident hypothermia is a significant cause of death in regions that experience low winter temperatures, particularly in places where home heating is inadequate. Although the number of deaths from hypothermia is not systematically known, surveys completed in Britain during the 1960s–1970s indicate that the annual number of victims may reach 20,000. According to a survey carried out in England, some 11 percent of all elderly persons registered temperatures of 95°F or below.[3] In twentieth-century England, the common victims of hypothermia have been those suffering from chronic malnutrition and those unable to move. The majority of such deaths have occurred in dwellings where indoor temperatures were maintained below 45°F and in cases where clothing was often inadequate.[4] The incidence of hypothermia in the elderly today seems to be higher in Britain than in the other countries of the northern Western world. It may be a reflection of the prevailing old housing stock in Britain, which lacks effective central heating. In North America and Scandinavia, where central heating is the rule, death rates do not climb so noticeably as in Britain during the cold months. To prevent hypothermia among the elderly, an indoor temperature range between 65° and 70°F is commonly recommended.[5]

It has been shown, by contrast, that during the cold spells of the winter of 1740, indoor temperature readings fell below the freezing point for extended periods of time, even in the most elite dwellings in England. We can only speculate on the indoor temperatures that predominated in the homes and hovels of the European poor, where fuel

---

2. Cooper and Ferguson, "Thermoregulation and Hypothermia," 37–41; Bruce C. Paton, M.D., "Cardiac Function during Accidental Hypothermia," in Pozos and Wittmers, *Nature and Treatment of Hypothermia*, 134–35; Martin C. Moore-Ede, "Hypothermia: A Timing Disorder of Circadian Thermoregulatory Rhythms?" in ibid., 69–71, 78; Richard W. Besdine, M.D., "Accidental Hypothermia: The Body's Energy Crisis," *Geriatrics* 34 (December 1979), 51–53; *Massachusetts General Hospital News* 39 (December 1980), 1–4; E. T. Renbourn, M.D., *Materials and Clothing in Health and Disease* (London, 1972), 221–23; Lawrence K. Altman, M.D., "Unnoticed Loss of Body Heat Can Kill," *New York Times, Science Times,* December 25, 1979, 13, 15; Judith Gedrose, R.N., "Prevention and Treatment of Hypothermia and Frostbite," *Nursing* 10 (February 1980), 34–36.

3. Altman, "Body Heat," 15; Besdine, "Accidental Hypothermia, 51–52.

4. Renbourn, *Materials and Clothing*, 222; K. J. Collins, "Urban Hypothermia in the United Kingdom," in Pozos and Wittmers, *Nature and Treatment of Hypothermia*, 235–36; Cooper and Ferguson, "Thermoregulation and Hypothermia," 43.

5. Gedrose, "Prevention," 36.

was commonly lacking or insufficient. The known risk factors of accident hypothermia suggest that the number of deaths among the elderly and young infants must have risen noticeably during the winter and spring months of 1740.

The surviving evidence is too impressionistic to permit accurate quantitative measurement, but the scale of deaths from hypothermia proved numerous enough to command notice. During the winter months of 1740, the English press carried almost daily reports of elderly persons found dead at home who were believed to have died "with the Extremity of Cold."[6] According to the Edinburgh press, "Great Numbers" of the poor perished in January from the "Severity of the Season."[7] Thomas Short claimed that "Multitudes of poor people were lost," both in dwellings and in fields, as a result of the "Severity of the Cold."[8] The British evidence is ambiguous because death from hypothermia was often called "starving."[9] In the southern Netherlands, large numbers of the infants of the poor froze to death in their cradles.[10] Similar accounts circulated in Holland, Germany, and Scandinavia.[11] Despite such evidence, the number of deaths from hypothermia in 1740 does not appear to have reached the level of major demographic importance.

The process and effects of hypothermia, however, can lead to a number of fatal complications.[12] Pneumonia is common enough in cases of accident hypothermia for physicians to anticipate the finding.[13] But hypothermia alone will not account for the increase in the number of deaths that has been found to correlate with temperature changes. The evidence discloses a close statistical relationship between sharp temperature changes and movements in death rates from pneumonia, bronchitis, heart attacks, and strokes.[14]

The examination of daily deaths in England and the Netherlands has shown a correlation between temperature changes and changes in the number of deaths from pneumonia, bronchitis, and arteriosclerotic heart

6. See, for example, *London Advertiser,* January 21, 1739/40.

7. *Caledonian Mercury,* February 11, 1740; *London Advertiser,* February 14, 1739/40.

8. Thomas Short, *A General Chronological History of the Air, Weather, Seasons, Meteors, etc.* (London, 1749), 255.

9. See, for example, *Caledonian Mercury,* January 14, 1740; *Scots Magazine,* January 1740, 42. It will be recalled that the Buckinghamshire farmer William Ellis wrote that the winter cold of 1740 "occasioned the Death of many poor People who wanted Heat and Victuals"; see Charlesworth, *Atlas of Rural Protest,* 83.

10. G. van Houtte, *Leuven in 1740* (Brussels, 1964), 245.

11. See Heinrich C. F. Schenck, *Die Wunder Gottes im Winter* (Arnstadt, 1741), 19.

12. Tromp, *Medical Biometeorology,* 249–51, 505–10.

13. Altman, "Body Heat," 15; Besdine, "Accidental Hypothermia," 53.

14. G. M. Bull and Joan Morton, "Environment, Temperature, and Death Rates," *Age and Ageing* 7 (1978), 210–24; Tromp, *Medical Biometeorology,* 249–51, 498–510.

disease in the absence of clinical hypothermia. Recorded monthly deaths in the United Kingdom show a close association between death rates and external temperatures, particularly in deaths resulting from myocardial infarction, stroke, and pneumonia, and the association is strongest among the elderly. Pertinent for the investigation of the European mortality wave of the early 1740s is the finding that deaths from pneumonia, bronchitis, and heart disease increased significantly as the minimum atmospheric temperature fell below −10°C (14°F). Short-term temperature changes (those lasting one or two days) apparently have little effect on death rates. Medium-term drops in temperature (from seven to ten days) and longer-term cold spells (three weeks or more), however, were associated with "very significant changes in death rates." Death rates climbed in correspondence with the duration of the low atmospheric temperature readings. The investigation also found a more pronounced relationship between temperature and death rates among people over sixty years old than among younger individuals.[15]

Although the proximal link in the chain of a causal relationship between temperature change and deaths from a series of diseases is not known with certainty, it has been established that in a cool environment any serious illness in an elderly person with autonomic nervous system dysfunction can produce accident hypothermia. It has been shown that in such individuals there is a progressive reduction in the ability to sense and to control temperature as age increases. Moreover, the elderly are slower to detect temperature differences and consequently slower to shiver; also they are less successful in conserving body heat. Finally, it is clear that thermal stress could affect the general resistance of the human body to infectious disease.[16]

In light of the foregoing medical findings, it would be anticipated that the abnormally low atmospheric temperatures that predominated in western Europe during the first five months of 1740 would correlate with an increase in the number of deaths from respiratory infections and arteriosclerotic heart disease. Although deaths from heart attacks and strokes are difficult to document in the eighteenth century, a significant increase in the number of deaths among the elderly and in the incidence of respiratory diseases inevitably left a few traces. The evidence does in fact show that deaths among the elderly and the cases of fatal respiratory infection climbed during the winter and spring months of 1740. In all

15. Bull and Morton, "Environment," 210, 222; K. J. Collins, "Urban Hypothermia," 236; Paton, "Cardiac Function," 135.
16. Tromp, *Medical Biometeorology,* 516; Besdine, "Accidental Hypothermia," 59; Cooper and Ferguson, "Thermoregulation and Hypothermia," 35–43.

probability, the increase in the European death rate originated in the health consequences of the long period of close indoor confinement with extremely low ambient temperature. The atmospheric temperatures, as the meteorological records show, remained considerably below normal throughout western Europe from January until June 1740.[17]

If thermal stress contributed to the European mortality peak, the number of deaths recorded in the cold months of 1740 should be disproportionately higher than the deaths that occurred during years of milder winter and spring seasons. The London Bills of Mortality provide one of the few available records of monthly burials in which the approximate ages of the deceased are included, and thus offer an opportunity to examine the hypothesis. The comparison of the number of burials registered during the first five months of 1740 with those during the same periods of 1739 and 1741, years when the mean temperatures of these months were more normal, reveals a pronounced increase in the number of deaths in 1740, followed by a marked decrease in 1741, as table 18 indicates. The total number of burials registered in the first five months of 1740 not only increased 53.1 percent over the number of burials during the same period of the previous year but also represented a 54.1 percent increase over the average burials during 1735–1739, which were years marked by mild winter seasons. Moreover, the 16,647 burials recorded during the first five months of 1740 accounted for 54.0 percent of the annual deaths, whereas the same percentages for 1739 and 1741 were 42.8 and 38.4, respectively.

Table 18. Burials counted in London, January–May 1739–1741

Month	1739	1740	Percentage change	1741	Percentage change
January	2,127	2,724	+28.1	2,580	−5.3
February	2,032	3,886	+91.2	2,054	−47.1
March	2,620	2,732	+4.3	2,419	−11.5
April	2,090	3,314	+49.6	2,510	−24.3
May	2,007	3,991	+98.9	2,877	−27.9
Total	10,876	16,647	+53.1	12,440	−25.3

SOURCE: Demographic statistics taken from the London bills of mortality and appearing in the monthly numbers of *Gentleman's Magazine* 9–11 (1739–1741).

The fluctuations in the number of burials during the first five months of the years 1739–1741 suggest that climatic variability and thermal stress were responsible in part for the elevated death rates of 1740. A

17. See the evidence presented in Chapter 3.

more conclusive finding would call for comparative data on the annual number of deaths from hypothermia, respiratory diseases, and heart attacks, together with age-specific mortality. Such refined vital statistics are of course lacking. However, the age groupings found in the London bills and the stated causes of death make it possible to examine the hypothesis somewhat further.

The stated causes of death found in the London bills were derived essentially from clinical symptoms. The accuracy of such declarations is decidedly deficient compared with the precision obtained by the modern practice of determining the cause of death by laboratory tests and post-mortem examination grounded on the theory of disease etiology. Several infectious diseases, such as smallpox and measles, were identified with some accuracy in the eighteenth century. By contrast, a variety of fatal contagious diseases were grouped together under the imprecise rubric "fever." The classification "aged" presumably referred to those elderly people who died with no apparent clinical indications of disease.

It is known that children accounted for approximately half of London's deaths in the eighteenth century, with those under two years of age constituting the largest category. It is also known that a substantial fraction of the deaths of young infants, particularly those who died in the first few months of life, were not recorded in the burial figures of London or elsewhere in western Europe. If young infants were the most common victims of hypothermia, the annual fluctuations of such deaths would not be adequately reflected in mortality series distributed by age group. These statistical shortcomings aside, table 19 shows the total number of burials counted during the first five months of 1739, 1740, and 1741, distributed in accordance with the overlapping age categories adopted in the bills of mortality.

As can be seen, the figures in table 19 show an increase in the number

Table 19. Burials counted in London, January–May 1739–1741, by age group

Age group	1739	1740	Percentage change	1741	Percentage change
Under 2	4,001	5,553	+38.8	4,098	−26.2
2–5	965	1,481	+53.5	899	−39.3
5–10	307	556	+81.1	443	−20.3
10–20	371	498	+34.2	430	−13.7
20–40	1,764	2,607	+47.8	2,402	−7.9
40–60	1,971	2,999	+52.2	2,455	−18.1
Over 60	1,497	2,953	+97.3	1,713	−42.0
Total	10,876	16,647	+53.1	12,440	−25.3

Source: Demographic statistics taken from the London bills of mortality and appearing in the monthly numbers of *Gentleman's Magazine* 9–11 (1739–1741).

of deaths among all age groups in 1740, followed by a significant decline in all groups in 1741. As a consequence, it is not possible to draw definitive conclusions from these data. The figures also show, however, that the age group "over 60," which is most susceptible to death from sharp temperature change and thermal stress, exhibited the most pronounced increase in death rates during the winter and spring of 1740 (97.3 percent) and likewise the steepest decline in the number of burials during 1741 (42.0 percent).

The statistical fluctuations of seasonal and age-specific mortality found in the London bills of mortality strongly suggest that climatic variability and thermal stress were in large part responsible for the increase in the number of burials during the winter and spring of 1740. Apart from London, neither comprehensive nor systematic vital statistics are at hand for examination. In England itself no more than fragmentary monthly burial figures are available. At Plymouth, in the southwest, however, the annual mortality trends corresponded to those found in London during the years 1739–1741. During the first five months of the year, the number of burials recorded in three Plymouth parishes increased 65.3 percent in 1740 and then decreased 40.2 percent in 1741. Moreover, the evidence indicates an unusually high number of deaths from pneumonia during the winter of 1740.[18] At the extreme micro level of investigation, eleven pensioners at Morden College in Charlton, Kent, nearly one half of their number, died in the months "which succeeded the hard frost in 1739–40."[19]

The estimated national monthly mortality totals in England during the years 1739–1741 parallel the trends found in the London bills but exhibit less pronounced fluctuations. Although the Cambridge Group's estimated monthly burials are based on a sample that does not include any London parishes and also is not precisely representative of the national distribution of the English population around 1740, this comprehensive time series indicates that the elevated mortality of the first five months of 1740 was a national phenomenon. Table 20 shows the estimated number of monthly burials in England during the first five months of 1739, 1740, and 1741, together with the annual percentage changes.

Compared with the average number of deaths in the first five months of the year during the quinquennium 1735–1739, the level of mortality in 1740 rose a somewhat higher 15.4 percent. It should be noted that the

18. N. C. Oswald, "Epidemics in Devon, 1538–1837," *Devonshire Association* 109 (1977), 102–103.

19. Mary Schove Dobson, "A Chronology of Disease and Mortality in Southeast England, 1601–1800" in chap. 7, "Patterns of Disease," of her D. Phil. diss. (University of Oxford, 1982).

Table 20. Estimated number of monthly burials in England, January–May 1739–1741 (in thousands), with annual percentage changes

Month	1739	1740	Percentage change	1741	Percentage change
January	15.3	16.7	+9.2	12.4	−4.3
February	13.0	15.0	+15.4	14.5	−0.5
March	17.4	15.8	−9.2	16.9	+1.1
April	15.2	18.0	+18.4	16.8	−1.2
May	13.1	18.0	+37.4	18.1	+0.1
Total	74.0	83.5	+12.8	78.6	−5.9

NOTE: Monmouth has been excluded from the totals.
SOURCE: E. A. Wrigley and R. S. Schofield, *The Population History of England, 1541–1871* (Cambridge, Mass., 1981), 508.

decline in the number of deaths during the first five months of 1741 took place despite the more elevated food prices than prevailed in the comparable months of 1740 and despite the fact that "fever" epidemics had become rife in England. With the recurrence of another severe winter in 1742 and the epidemic diseases that blanketed England at the same time, however, the number of deaths during the first five months of 1742 surpassed the total in 1740.

Together the estimated number of national monthly burials and the London bills of mortality show that mortality in England rose significantly during the extended period of abnormally low atmospheric temperatures in 1740. The London bills, moreover, point to hypothermia as a cause of the higher death rate. The surviving medical evidence also sheds some light on the reasons for the increase in burials during the winter and spring of 1740. According to John Huxham's entry for February 1740, "Pleurisies, Peripneumonies, Quinsies, and Rheumatisms were very rife everywhere." In April he wrote that, "the same Constitution of the Air remaining, the reigning Disorders were still the same, and now indeed were much more severe. Great Numbers died both in Town and Country." This entry also comments on "a most terrible kind of Pleurisy, which suffocated Numbers." The term "pleurisy" can refer to the complications of a variety of respiratory infections, and it is thus not possible to identify disease entities. The entry for May 1740 noted that the first week had been "amazingly cold, for this time of Year," and added that "Pulmonary Fevers were yet very rife."[20]

The medical evidence points to an increase in the morbidity rate and mortality from acute respiratory infections during the first half of 1740,

20. John Huxham, *Observations on the Air, and Epidemic Diseases from the Beginning of the Year 1738, to the End of the Year 1748*, trans. from the Latin by John Corham Huxham, 2 vols. (London, 1759–67), II, 54–60.

even if cases of pneumonia, bronchitis, pleurisy, and influenza cannot be distinguished from Huxham's clinical descriptions. Pneumonia, as already noted, is a common complication of accident hypothermia. The incidence of bronchitis in western Europe has been found to correlate with low atmospheric temperatures, fog, and smoke. The case-fatality rates of most respiratory diseases have been observed to increase noticeably with falling temperature, fog, and smoke.[21] The risks of bronchitis and other respiratory diseases must have been heightened in the eighteenth century by the circumstance that the majority of cottages were sealed tight during cold nights and also lacked chimneys for the efficient escape of smoke. Moreover, the crowded living conditions of the European working population in both urban and rural locations could only have enhanced the spread of acute respiratory diseases during prolonged cold seasons.

In Scotland also, the evidence bearing on the influence of low atmospheric temperatures on mortality in 1740 is sparse. However, the Edinburgh bills of mortality, like the London bills, suggest that hypothermia was in part responsible for the increase in the number of burials during the winter and spring of 1740. During the winter months, the number of deaths among those sixty years of age exceeded 20 percent (compared to 17.7 percent in London) of all recorded burials. During the winter seasons of 1739, 1741, and 1742, such deaths among the elderly made up less than 20 percent of all burials.[22] The 149 burials recorded in January 1740, the *Caledonian Mercury* observed, constituted "the greatest Mortality (in a Month) that has happened this Century."[23] The record was quickly shattered in February, however, when 160 burials were counted in Edinburgh. While the surge in the number of deaths during the winter months of 1740 indicates that thermal stress was responsible for the excess mortality, more direct evidence is lacking.

The Dublin bills of mortality likewise provide the only systematic evidence of the demographic impact of low atmospheric temperatures in Ireland. As in England, however, the surviving medical accounts furnish additional knowledge about the causes of the elevated mortality of the first half of 1740. John Rutty wrote that the winter months of 1740 proved a "fatal season to many, not only the old, infirm, and asthmatic,

21. Tromp, *Medical Biometeorology,* 501–502, 571–72.

22. Michael Flinn et al., *Scottish Population History from the Seventeenth Century to the 1930s* (London, 1977), 220–21; W. Maitland, *The History of Edinburgh* (Edinburgh, 1753), 218–19. Unfortunately the Edinburgh bills do not always include the same parishes. In some years they are limited to burials in the parishes located within the city of Edinburgh, whereas in other years the figures include the city and the west kirk together.

23. *Caledonian Mercury,* February 11, 1740.

but to children also." According to Dr. Rutty, the increase in the death rate resulted from "inflammatory disorders," which became "more violent" during January and February, "the time of the great frost, which was very prolific in coughs, attended with sore throats, pleurisies, and peripneumonies, which were very frequent both in the town and country." Corresponding with Huxham's account in southwestern England, the medical evidence for Ireland indicates a marked rise in the incidence of fatal respiratory infections during the extended cold season of 1740. The Dublin bills of mortality climbed to 130–140 burials a week during the winter months, nearly three times the average number.[24]

Evidence regarding the causes of seasonal fluctuations in mortality is even sparser for the continental countries than for the British Isles, but some pertinent information is available. In France, the number of deaths recorded at the Paris Hospital (hôtel-Dieu) rose significantly during the first five months of 1740. The hospital population was made up mainly of the sick poor, that is, the truly indigent and helpless, the majority of whom were elderly.[25] Deaths at the Paris Hospital jumped from 5,837 in 1739 to 7,894 in 1740, an increase of 35.2 percent.[26] A large percentage of the increase in mortality occurred in the spring of 1740, as the consequence of severe respiratory epidemics.[27] The increase in the number of deaths among the general Parisian population in 1740 amounted to 13.9 percent.[28]

The parish registers of nearby Meulan also recorded high mortality during the cold season of 1740. Eighty burials took place during the first quarter of the year, and an additional fifty-six deaths occurred during the second quarter. The Meulan parishes averaged forty-four burials per quarter during the entire eighteenth century. According to the notations made by the parish clergy, the mortality wave during the cold season of 1740 resulted from the low atmospheric temperatures, not from hunger. "The severity and length of the winter, which has lasted more than six months, caused inflammation of the lungs everywhere, from which a number of persons died in Mureaux."[29] According to the chronicle of

24. John Rutty, M.D., *A Chronological History of the Weather and Seasons, and of the Prevailing Diseases in Dublin* (London, 1770), 78–80.

25. Jean Meuvret, "Les Crises de subsistance et la démographie de la France d'ancien régime," *Population* 1 (1946), 649–50.

26. M. Messance, *Recherches sur la population des généralitiés d'Auvergne, de Lyon, de Rouen, et de quelques provinces et villes du royaume* (Paris, 1766), 315–26.

27. *London Daily Post*, May 9, 1740.

28. E. Charlot and J. Dupâquier, "Mouvement annuel de la population de la ville de Paris de 1670 à 1821," *Annales de Démographie Historique* (1967), 511.

29. Marcel Lachiver, *Histoire de Meulan et sa région par les textes* (Meulan, 1965), 196, 214–15.

Varreddes, also in the Paris region, the long and deep frost "caused illnesses as much in this country as the great number elsewhere, from which a great many people died."[30]

The investigation of the French subsistence crisis of 1740 by Bricourt, Lachiver, and Queruel found that the number of burials in northern France multiplied from February to May 1740. All writers insisted that the deaths of adults and the elderly rather than of children were responsible for the increased mortality. The parish records of the Paris region and the provinces west of Paris exhibited mortality peaks from February to May 1740. The available clinical descriptions of the predominant respiratory illness suggests epidemic influenza and pneumonia. "It began with a constant pain in the side, grew worse with inflammation of the lungs and chest pains. A relapse was always fatal. In some houses everybody died." Everywhere in northern France the clinical evidence referred to inflammation of the lungs and also made it clear that the victims were adults, not children. The respiratory epidemics ended in June, when the long cold season had finally run its course.[31]

The symptoms of pleuritis, as I have noted, are a complication of several pulmonary diseases, and thus it is almost impossible to identify respiratory disease entities from eighteenth-century clinical descriptions. It should be noted, however, that almost all acute respiratory diseases can prove fatal when they are attended with hypothermia. Conversely, acute respiratory infections can induce accident hypothermia in low ambient temperature.[32]

The dean of the Faculty of Medicine at Angers in the northwestern province of Anjou drew up a clinical description of the epidemic of acute respiratory disease responsible for the increase in mortality during the first half of 1740. The epidemic broke out at the end of January and "always attacked the chest and sometimes had the signs of true peripneumonia, and other times those of a pleurisy that progressed into peripneumonia." According to the dean's account, the disease was contagious and almost completely spared children, striking adults and the elderly, who succumbed most often to relapses rather than to the first attack. The principal victims were individuals of the poorest economic

30. Jean-Michel Desbordes, ed., *La Chronique villageoise de Varreddes (Seine-et-Marne): Un document sur la vie rurale des XVIIe et XVIIIe siècles* (Paris, 1969), 25.

31. The quoted passage is in Michel Bricourt, Marcel Lachiver, and Denis Queruel, "La Crise de subsistance des années 1740 dans le ressort du Parlement de Paris," *Annales de Démographie Historique* (1974) 306–307. The description was written by the curé of the parish of Béhard in Maine-et-Loire.

32. Tromp, *Medical Biometeorology*, 516, 571–72; Besdine, "Accidental Hypothermia," 53.

status, who, as a consequence of "poor nourishment and the excessive cold, against which they could not defend themselves," proved to be "particularly exposed to this epidemic malady."[33] The long period of close confinement in crowded, smoky, unhygienic living quarters must have facilitated the diffusion of the infections, irrespective of the exact respiratory diseases involved.

The Anjou parish registers reflect the virulence of the infection. The number of burials registered began to double and then triple, beginning in February. At the Angers hospital, more occupants died during February, March, and April (a total of 447) than during the other nine months of the year combined. In the parish of Challain, where normally two-thirds of burials involved children, adults accounted for more than half the burials during the period from March to May 1740. Within the town of Angers, the burials in the poorest parish increased fourfold above average during the same period, whereas in the most affluent parish the number of burials rose only moderately.[34]

The housing conditions and the household practices of the poor inhabitants of the towns and villages of Europe invariably promoted a high morbidity rate from respiratory infections during prolonged cold seasons. In Angers and in almost all towns, the homes of the poor contained far fewer beds than family members. With several persons sleeping together, the more extended the winter season, the greater the likelihood of communicating respiratory disease. The lower the atmospheric and ambient temperatures, the greater the risk the crowded living conditions would abet the diffusion of respiratory infections. Cottage doors were hermetically closed to protect against cold nights. Parents and children slept together on a straw mattress; if one family member became ill, the others still shared the same bed.[35] As a consequence, the combination of a long, severe winter and the regular household practices of the working poor were calculated to increase the morbidity rates of the reigning infections.

In the German and Scandinavian lands, the evidence bearing on the probable causes of seasonal fluctuations in mortality is mostly impressionistic. The number of deaths in Brandenburg, according to Johann Christoph Becmann, was driven up during the first half of 1740 by fatal cases of pneumonia and other respiratory diseases, but no

33. Quoted in François Lebrun, *Les Hommes et la mort en Anjou aux 17e et 18e siècles* (Paris, 1971), 368–70.

34. Ibid.

35. Ibid., 226–68; for similar housing conditions and household practices in eighteenth-century Scotland, see T. C. Smout, *A History of the Scottish People, 1560–1830* (Glasgow, 1969), 285–87.

figures are given.[36] In the town of Durlach, in Baden, fifty-three deaths were recorded during the first four months of 1740, for a twofold increase above the average number of burials during the milder winters of the three previous years. As elsewhere in western Europe, the mortality peak in Durlach involved mostly adult burials; 59 percent of those who died in 1740 were above the age of sixty.[37] This evidence that hypothermia influenced mortality in Germany during the winter and spring of 1740 is extremely thin; without more data we cannot conclude that it did so.

The causes of death in Scandinavia were not systematically recorded until 1749 and then only in Sweden.[38] Some tentative conclusions can be drawn, however, from the monthly distribution of deaths available for a limited number of Finnish parishes.[39] The Finnish mortality crisis of 1740, according to Eino Jutikkala, originated mainly in an epidemic wave that spread over the entire country.[40] The fragmentary parish burial records disclose, at the same time, an abnormally high number of deaths during the cold season of 1740. In the twelve parishes for which monthly figures are available, a disproportionately large percentage of annual burials took place in January, February, and March. In the first three months of 1740, the number of burials increased 46 percent above the total for the same period of 1739 and also aggregated to 35 percent of annual deaths, whereas the number of burials in the same period of 1739 represented only 23 percent of annual deaths. The number of burials registered in the first three months of 1741 declined to a similar 22 percent of annual deaths, corresponding to the winter mortality trends traced in Britain during the years from 1739 to 1741.[41]

To sum up, the hypothermia, thermal stress, and respiratory diseases fostered by low atmospheric temperatures and abetted by prolonged confinement indoors in low ambient temperature were responsible in large part for the climbing western European mortality in the first half of 1740. Pronounced climatic variability can produce a first-order effect on human health, particularly in preindustrial societies, in which the hous-

---

36. Johann Christoph Becmann, *Historische Beschreibung der Chur und Mark Brandenburg,* ed. B. L. Becmann, 2 vols. (Berlin, 1751–53), I, 546–48.

37. Otto K. Roller, *Die Einwohnerschaft der Stadt Durlach im 18. Jahrhundert* (Karlsruhe, 1907), 64–71.

38. E. Hofsten and H. Lundstrom, *Swedish Population History* (Stockholm, 1976), 43.

39. Arthur E. Imhof, *Aspekte der Bevölkerungsentwicklung in den nordischen Ländern, 1720–1750* (Bern, 1976), 136, 727–28.

40. Eino Jutikkala, *Die Bevölkerung Finnlands in den Jahren 1721–1749* (Helsinki, 1945), 37–38; for a similar conclusion see Imhof, *Bevölkerungsentwicklung in den nordischen Ländern,* 645.

41. Imhof, *Bevölkerungsentwicklung in den nordischen Ländern,* 606–11.

ing conditions and household practices facilitate contagion and make it difficult to defend normal body temperature. Protracted cold seasons, such as that in 1740, lengthen the period of time spent in close indoor personal contact. Because the living quarters of Europe's working population were small and substandard, the probability of spreading infections was maximized during severe winters.

The statistical rise in the number of adult and elderly burials during the first five months of 1740 reflects the influence of prolonged environmental stress. It is now known that sharp temperature changes induce an increase in the number of deaths from cardiovascular disease and from respiratory infections, particularly among the elderly, chronically ill, and badly nourished. Although the evidence is silent on deaths from heart attacks and strokes, respiratory epidemics became rife during the early months of 1740, and an unusually high number of people succumbed to hypothermia. The evidence indicates that environmental stress influenced the rising death rates more decisively than hunger and undernutrition. Widespread hunger and famine developed only in Ireland and Scandinavia, and the demographic impact of prolonged undernutrition registered mainly after the first half of 1740.

Hunger

A pronounced shortage of food developed in regions of Ireland, Norway, Finland, Sweden, and scattered districts elsewhere in western Europe. Crisis mortality followed in the wake of the famine conditions. The critical question becomes the extent to which the mortality peaks were shaped by hunger and starvation as opposed to epidemic diseases fostered by the subsistence crisis. Although references to death from starvation can be found in the food shortages of the early 1740s, medical opinion today is that starvation is rarely an ascertainable cause of death.[42] Historians also have argued that starvation was uncommon in western Europe. As Jean Meuvret put it, death from starvation is an extreme case in European subsistence crises.[43]

42. For clinical evidence supporting this view, see Vernon R. Young and Nevis S. Scrimshaw, "The Physiology of Starvation," *Scientific American* 224 (October 1971), reprinted in *Readings from Scientific American* (San Francisco, 1973), 44–51; George F. Cahill, Jr., M.D., "Starvation in Man," *New England Journal of Medicine* 282 (March 1970), 668–75.

43. Jean Meuvret, "Demographic Crisis in France from the Sixteenth to the Eighteenth Century," trans. Margaret Hilton, in D. V. Glass and D. E. C. Eversley, *Population in History* (London, 1965), 519; also see the discussion in Michael W. Flinn, *The European Demographic System, 1500–1820* (Baltimore, 1981), 50–51.

Yet medical experience during famines, particularly the famine conditions induced during the Second Word War, makes it clear that prolonged undernutrition can lead to death apart from either "starvation" or complicating infectious disease. Deaths of this nature have been ascribed to a condition called "famine disease," the cardinal symptoms of which include emaciation, edema, and diarrhea.[44] The attempt to identify deaths from prolonged undernutrition in historical research is complicated by the circumstance that morbidity during famine exhibits a mixture of the symptoms of starvation and of several infectious diseases with like symptoms, particularly bacillary dysentery. Historical research is further complicated by the fact that severe malnutrition has a strong influence on the mortality of young children.

"Starvation" implies the almost total elimination of food and as a consequence the rapid development of severe undernutrition and emaciation. "Undernutrition" refers to the pathologic state that results from the consumption of an inadequate quantity of food over an extended period of time.[45] It is probable that some cases of death from starvation pure and simple occurred in Europe during the food shortages of the early 1740s. From a demographic standpoint, however, the evidence indicates that only deaths that resulted from prolonged undernutrition—that is, famine disease—proved quantitatively important.

Clinical and laboratory studies have demonstrated that human adults have a remarkable capacity to survive without food for long periods of time and that the body is able to accommodate a prolonged lack of food. The basal metabolic rate slows as the process of starvation goes on, and also the need for calories is reduced by the loss of weight. A starving person, moreover, normally reduces physical activity and, on balance, uses the available energy more efficiently. But the ability to survive depends on such individual variables as surplus body fat and body size and also on such environmental factors as ambient temperature. The paramount human defense against starvation, however, is the ability to conserve the expenditure of protein while at the same time continuing to synthesize the daily requirement of glucose necessary to maintain vital body functions.

The critical loss of protein is controlled by the body's capacity to derive a substitute source of energy from the fatty tissues. But the ability of an adult to survive lack of food for several months is not shared by

44. Per Helweg-Larsen et al., *Famine Disease in German Concentration Camps: Complications and Sequels*, supp. 274, *Acta Medica Scandinavica* (Copenhagen, 1952), 74–77, 124–33.
45. N. S. Scrimshaw, C. E. Taylor, and J. E. Gordon, *Interaction of Nutrition and Infection* (Geneva, 1968), 19.

young children. The growth process stops almost immediately in a starving child because the energy required to build protein is great. A starving child will develop the emaciated condition known as marasmus, which is seen in some underdeveloped societies today.[46]

The impressionistic evidence does not indicate that deaths from starvation became common among either adults or young children during the food shortages of the early 1740s, though the number of deaths traceable to prolonged undernutrition seems to have been demographically significant in Ireland, Norway, and several counties in Sweden and Finland. But as I have cautioned, it is difficult to distinguish deaths caused by prolonged undernutrition from deaths caused by dysentery. The problem is complicated by the fact that bacillary dysentery was the most common fatal disease observed during the mortality peak of 1740–1742.

In the absence of laboratory tests, deaths caused by dysentery cannot always be distinguished from deaths that result from "famine diarrhea." This diagnostic problem became apparent during World War II. Terminal diarrhea was found to be the most common cause of "natural" death among the prisoners confined in German concentration camps. In view of the wretched living conditions in the camps, it might be assumed that the majority of cases of diarrhea were caused by pathogenic microorganisms. But in fact the majority of cases tested proved to derive from prolonged undernutrition, not from infectious disease. The diarrhea was a symptom of starvation, not a complication of disease. It can therefore be concluded that in the northern European countries mentioned above, some deaths were indeed caused by the process of starvation.

In the course of human starvation, a series of pathological changes, such as atrophy and ulceration, attend the loss of weight in the intestines and impair their normal function.[47] Such pathology results in watery stools containing mucus, undigested food, and on occasion blood, as in cases of dysentery, or "bloody flux." The end result of the impaired intestinal function is to upset the body's water and salt balance, a condition that ultimately leads to death. These pathological symptoms are called famine diarrhea. During protracted food shortages the symptoms can become common.[48]

46. The explanation of the human body's capacity to withstand prolonged starvation has been reduced to basic essentials. For a comprehensive physiological explanation, see Cahill, "Starvation," 671–72; Young and Scrimshaw, "Physiology of Starvation," 44–50.

47. Helweg-Larsen et al., *Famine Disease,* 73–77, 124–33.

48. W. R. Aykroyd, "Definition of Different Degrees of Starvation," in G. Blix et al., eds., *Famine: A Symposium Dealing with Nutrition and Relief Operations in Times of Disaster* (Uppsala, 1971), 18; Ancel Keys et al., *The Biology of Human Starvation,* 2 vols. (Minneapolis, 1950), I, 587–91; II, 799; Helweg-Larsen et al., *Famine Disease,* 91, 152.

Despite the methodological obstacles, the relative demographic impact of prolonged undernutrition can be gauged from region to region. Although the evidence does not permit quantitative estimates, the scale of mortality from hunger can be categorized as of consequence, incidental, or insignificant. In the British Isles, for example, mortality from prolonged undernutrition was pronounced in Ireland, varied in significance from region to region in Scotland, and was virtually absent in England.

The development of famine conditions in Ireland centered in the southwestern province of Munster, where potato cultivation had become critical for the subsistence of the laboring population. In the spring of 1741, Rutty wrote that there was "famine among some of the poor" and also that "the dysentery raged." He apparently accepted the mortality estimate of physician Maurice O'Connell, his contemporary, for he concluded that a total of 80,000 persons "died in this kingdom of the fever, dysentery, and famine" during the years 1740–1741.[49] In Rutty's time, as today, however, it remains difficult to distribute the excess number of deaths in terms of the three factors responsible for the mortality crisis.

The press accounts of mortality from hunger, fever, and "flux" did not become numerous until the last months of 1740, which was nearly a year after the loss of the potato crop. As we have seen, the accounts emanated chiefly from the counties of southwestern Ireland. In December, *Faulkner's Dublin Journal* reported that county Cork suffered from an "uncommon mortality amongst the poor people, by fevers and fluxes, owing no doubt, in great measure, to their poor living."[50] Accounts of the same tenor originated in nearby counties.[51] But Drogheda, north of Dublin, also reported "a great Mortality amongst the poor People, who die in great numbers of Fluxes and Fevers" as a consequence of hunger.[52] During the winter of 1740–1741, press accounts from almost all regions of Ireland related the same information: large numbers of poor people were dying of fluxes and fevers "for want of proper food."[53] It seems probable that the protracted shortage of food led to fatal cases of famine diarrhea as well as multiplying the cases of dysentery.

The surviving descriptions of the hunger that stalked the poor in the

49. Rutty, *Chronological History,* 82–91.
50. *Faulkner's Dublin Journal,* December 6–9, 1740.
51. Ibid., December 13–16, 1740; Michael Drake, "The Irish Demographic Crisis of 1740–41," *Histprical Studies* 6 (1968), 116–17.
52. *London Advertiser,* January 24, 1740.
53. *Faulkner's Dublin Journal,* February 17–21 and March 24–28, 1741; Drake, "Demographic Crisis," 116-17.

provinces of Munster and Connaught leave little doubt that deaths from undernutrition added significantly to the crisis mortality in southwestern Ireland. Bishop Berkeley lamented the "great devastations made by bloody fluxes, fevers, and want, which carry off more than a civil war."[54] An operational definition of the term "want" can be found in the well-known letter from "Publicola," addressed to the lord primate from Cashel on May 25, 1741. "Multitudes have perished, and are daily perishing under hedges and ditches, some of fever, some of fluxes and some through downright cruel want in the utmost agonies of despair." The author claimed to have "seen the aged father eating grass like a beast," and the "helpless orphan exposed on the dunghill, and none to take him in for fear of infection."[55] A letter to the London press from county Galway reported that many were "obliged by the extream Scarcity of Provisions of all Kinds to eat Horses and Dogs."[56] The documentary evidence indicates that the shortage of food in southwestern Ireland was grave enough to foster both famine diarrhea and epidemics of dysentery.

Several anonymous writers in Ireland portrayed a grim picture of the ravages of the food shortage. The author of *The Groans of Ireland*, a pamphlet published in Dublin in 1741, wrote of "roads spread with dead and dying bodies; mankind of the colour of the docks and nettles which they fed on."[57] "Triptolemus" recounted that "whole thousands have perished, some of hunger, and others of disorders occasioned by unnatural, unwholesome, and putrid diet."[58] While such accounts could be extended, neither evidence nor method is at hand to estimate the percentage of excess deaths that resulted from prolonged undernutrition uncomplicated by infectious disease. The clear evidence of famine and the references to death from hunger lead to the conclusion that a considerable fraction of the excess deaths during the years 1740–1741 originated in "famine disease." As we shall see, however, the evidence strongly indicates that the majority of the famine deaths in Ireland resulted from widespread epidemics of dysentery and typhus fever.

A shortage of food and elevated cereal prices predominated in Scotland from the winter of 1739–1740 to the spring of 1741. But deaths from want and hunger were confined chiefly to the remote Highland districts

54. George Berkeley, *The Works of George Berkeley, Bishop of Cloyne*, ed. A. A. Luce and T. E. Jessop, 9 vols. (London, 1956), VIII, 255.
55. Quoted in Drake, "Demographic Crisis," 103.
56. *London Daily Post*, April 7, 1741.
57. Quoted in Drake, "Demographic Crisis," 103.
58. Ibid., 104.

and to the counties of the region of the far north.[59] In the lowland counties, the more effective welfare and relief programs reduced the toll of hunger to a small number of unfortunate vagrants.[60]

The shortage of food in some Highland counties bordered on famine conditions. In Sutherland, for example, a minister's diary entry for June 13, 1741, bewailed the fact that "people are at the Starving beyond what has been seen by the oldest alive as they tell!"[61] In the summer of 1741, Highland shearers arrived in Edinburgh in advance of the usual schedule, forced out apparently by hunger and want. Several shearers, moreover, died soon after arrival. In the far north, the scant available evidence indicates widespread hunger during the years 1740–1741.[62] In the united parishes of Birsay and Harray, on the Orkeney Islands, "many died for want."[63] In the Shetland parish of Unst, by contrast, "none are known to have absolutely died for want," despite the "excessive scarcity."[64] Scattered evidence of near famine can be found in other Scottish counties. The parish of Speymouth, in the northeastern county of Moray, appointed a fast in November 1740, "on account of the threatened famine." The number of burials in fact soared during 1741–1742 but more as a consequence of infectious diseases.[65] The Highland parish of Fearn, in the county of Ross, recorded that "no one died for want," but still "many starved."[66] On balance, the evidence indicates that the number of deaths from prolonged undernutrition remained demographically incidental in the Scottish subsistence crisis of 1740–1741 with the possible exception of the Highland counties, for which no burial figures are available.

No county in England suffered from conditions of famine. T. S. Ashton has written of "the great famine of 1740."[67] R. W. Wearmouth's

59. William Kennedy, ed., *Annals of Aberdeen* (Edinburgh, 1818), 294; Flinn et al., *Scottish Population History*, 218–20; M. M. MacKay, "A Highland Minister's Diary," *Cornhill Magazine* 152 (November 1935), 572–73.

60. Flinn et al., *Scottish Population History*, 218–20; Maitland, *Edinburgh*, 124; *Caledonian Mercury*, August 25, 1741; *Scots Magazine*, January 1741, 45; A. Allardyce, ed., *Scotland and Scotsmen in the Eighteenth Century from the MSS of John Ramsay of Ochtertyre*, 2 vols. (Edinburgh, 1888), II, 211–12; Kennedy, *Aberdeen*, 290–94.

61. MacKay, "Minister's Diary," 572. The diary was kept by Murdoch MacDonald, minister of Durness, in Sutherland.

62. Flinn et al., *Scottish Population History*, 219, 486.

63. Sir John Sinclair, *The Statistical Account of Scotland*, 21 vols., (Edinburgh, 1791–98), XIV, 319.

64. Ibid., XII, 199.

65. Ibid., XIV, 378.

66. Ibid., IV, 300.

67. T. S. Ashton, *An Economic History of England: The Eighteenth Century* (London, 1955), 53.

account of the "Common People" contains such statements as "thousands and thousands of families are starving."[68] In neither work, however, are the words "famine" and "starving" meant to convey the subsistence conditions that developed in Highland Scotland, to say nothing of Ireland. Rather the statements refer to the extreme hardship that resulted from the combination of unemployment and elevated food prices that prevailed during the years 1740–1741. The documents that speak of "manufacturers starving by thousands" in the Spitalfields district of London and in southwestern England should be understood as the fear of starving "for want of work."[69]

The level of distress occasioned by unemployment peaked in the industrial towns and villages in the western counties. In Wiltshire and Gloucestershire thousands were said to be "unemploy'd and near starving."[70] William Stout remarked on the depressed state and mass unemployment that predominated in the textile industries. As for the degree of want, he commented that "poor labouring people are much straitened to live."[71] Robert Marsham noted in his journal that in Herefordshire "the poor were almost starved."[72]

It is true, nonetheless, that given the high food prices and scanty welfare benefits, the unemployed English laboring poor must have suffered from intensified nutritional deficiencies. The subsistence problem was especially pronounced in the clothing and textile manufacturing districts of the West. In a country with an obligatory parish welfare system, however, the nutritional status of the unemployed did not deteriorate to the depths observed in Ireland and in the Scottish Highlands. English social reality is more nearly reflected in the contemporary observation that in Somerset more than 10,000 poor "who used to live by the Sweat of their Brows, will become a Burthen to their different Parishes for their *Daily bread*."[73] In a country where wheat bread and animal products were now considered to be regular fare for the majority of the working population, inability to include such decencies in the straitened household budgets of 1740–1741 was understandably per-

68. R. W. Wearmouth, *Methodism and the Common People of the Eighteenth Century* (London, 1945), 55.

69. Quoted in T. S. Ashton, *Economic Fluctuations in England, 1700–1800* (London, 1959), 146–47.

70. Quoted in Wearmouth, *Common People,* 55.

71. J. D. Marshall, ed., *Autobiography of William Stout of Lancaster, 1665–1752* (Manchester, 1967), 231.

72. T. Southwell, "An Account of the Severe Winter of 1739–40 and of Its Effects in the county of Norfolk in the Year Following," *Norfolk and Norwich Naturalist Society, Transactions* 2 (1875), 129.

73. Quoted in Wearmouth, *Common People,* 55.

ceived as genuine deprivation and distress. Complaints were most often couched in such terms as "Many families have no Wheaten Bread at all." Farmers in the neighborhood of Taunton and Ilchester were brought "so low and miserable" as to subsist on grains.[74] Even if deaths from want were isolated events in England during the early 1740s, the high food prices and unemployment rates nevertheless contributed to the mortality peak, as will be demonstrated.

Deaths from hunger and starvation on the continent of Europe seem to have been almost as rare as in England, despite the fact that the majority of countries lacked an obligatory welfare system. In France, the correspondence of the *procureur général* contains only one document that mentions death from starvation, despite the series of harvest shortfalls that occurred in the northwestern provinces from 1738 to 1740. Accounts can be found, however, of the poorest people in the rural districts reduced to eating grass, roots, and cabbages. The stepped-up public relief programs and the importation of cereals from abroad during 1740 headed off famine conditions even if they did not eliminate hunger.[75] While it is true that the chronicle of Varreddes relates a "great famine among all the poor people," no deaths from hunger or starvation are reported.[76] The parish records of Meulan state that deaths from hunger were in fact avoided.[77]

At the same time, François Lebrun concluded that the food shortage and the attendant undernutrition in northwestern France had a noticeable impact on the mortality peak of the early 1740s, the welfare and relief programs notwithstanding. Although it is true that famine was sidestepped, inability to meet the high price of cereals was largely responsible for the increase in the number of burials. For Lebrun, it was fundamentally poverty that killed.[78] The chain of causation from harvest shortfalls to crisis mortality, however, was more complex and more contingent than the impact of elevated cereal prices on the death rate.

In the poor province of the Auvergne also no deaths were reported from starvation. But the fact that the destitute were reduced to eating "fern roots" indicates that hunger was common.[79] It is possible that the epidemics of dysentery that developed in France during 1741 may have

74. Ibid., 54–55.
75. Bricourt et al., "Crise," 291–96, 312–25, 332–33.
76. Desbordes, *Varreddes,* 26.
77. Lachiver, *Meulan,* 196, 214.
78. Lebrun, *Anjou,* 367–68, 386–87.
79. A. Poitrineau, *La Vie rurale en Basse Auvergne au XVIIIe siècle (1726–1789),* 2 vols. (Paris, 1965), 92–93.

concealed cases of famine diarrhea,[80] as in Ireland. In France as in England, however, the number of deaths that resulted from prolonged undernutrition appear to have been demographically insignificant during the subsistence crisis of 1740–1741.

This generalization is also valid for the Low Countries, in spite of the prolonged shortage of food in the southern Netherlands, which suffered the most elevated cereal prices of any continental country.[81] The number of deaths from hunger proved substantially fewer than contemporary observers feared.[82] The crisis mortality of 1741 resulted primarily from murderous epidemics of dysentery.[83] As elsewhere in western Europe, the dysentery epidemics probably concealed cases of famine diarrhea, but the evidence does not permit quantitative estimates.

The evidence available for the German lands likewise does not disclose an appreciable number of deaths from hunger and starvation during the early 1740s. The Prussian documents report the practice of eating carrion animals in Minden, where the shortage of food was acute in 1740, but no deaths from starvation are mentioned.[84] According to Becmann, the shortage of food in Brandenburg forced the poor to resort to "unnatural foods," but again no deaths from hunger are reported.[85] In Germany, as almost everywhere in western Europe, dysentery became epidemic during 1741. The German epidemics, however, were less severe than those in Ireland, northwestern France, and the southern Netherlands.[86]

On the Scandinavian peninsula, as in Ireland, the number of deaths that were traceable to conditions of hunger and undernutrition added

80. Julien Offray de La Mettrie, *Oeuvres de médecine* (Berlin, 1755), 279–81; Jean-Pierre Goubert, *Malades et médecins en Bretagne, 1770–1790* (Paris, 1974), 327–32.

81. Etienne Hélin, "La Disette et le recensement de 1740," *Annuaire d'Histoire Liégeoise* 6 (1959), 443–45; Houtte, *Leuven*, 246; D. Van Assche–Van Cauwenbergh, "Deux Villages du Brabant sous l'ancien régime: Bierges et Overyse: Etude de démographie historique," in *Cinq Etudes de démographie locale (XVIIIe–XIXe siècles)* (Brussels, 1963), 33.

82. Claude Bruneel, *La Mortalité dans les compagnes: Le Duché de Brabant aux XVIIe et XVIIIe siècles* (Louvain, 1977), 278–79.

83. Ibid., 280–82; Louis Torfs, *Fastes des calamités publiques survenues dans les Pays-Bas*, 2 vols., (Paris, 1859–62), I, 102; Hélin, "Disette," 444; Maurice-A. Arnould, "Mortalité et épidemies sous l'Ancien Régime dans le Hainaut et quelques régions limitrophes," in Paul Harsin and Etienne Hélin, eds., *Problèmes de mortalité* (Liège, 1963), 479–80.

84. Acta Borussica, *Denkmäler der preussischen Staatsverwaltung im 18. Jahrhundert: Getreidehandelspolitik*, vol. II: W. Naudé, *Die Getreidehandelspolitik und Kriegsmagazinverwaltung: Brandenburg-Preussens bis 1740* (Berlin, 1901), 323.

85. Becmann, *Chur und Brandenburg*, I, 556–57.

86. Heinrich Haeser, *Lehrbuch der Geschichte der Medizin und der epidemischen Krankheiten*, 3d ed., 3 vols. (Jena, 1875–82), III, 468; W. Jungkunz, "Die Sterblichkeit in Nürnberg, 1714–1850," *Mitteilungen des Vereins für Geschichte der Stadt Nürnberg* 42 (1951), 299, 307–308, 338–40.

measurably to the national mortality peaks of the early 1740s. In Finland, the mortality crisis of 1740 originated both in famine and epidemic disease. Jutikkala found that severe undernutrition contributed markedly to the elevated death rates of 1740. In the county of Österbotten, which encompassed all of northern and central Finland, the shortage of food evolved into a genuine famine. The rural population of the county exhibited "bloated bodies and swollen faces," which were attributed to the "all too scanty food." The protracted shortage of food in Österbotten was responsible in part for the crisis mortality that carried over into 1741.[87] Widespread edema in a population is clear evidence of extreme hunger and undernutrition. Death from hunger became common in Finland again in 1742. The shortage of food and crisis mortality of that year, however, was occasioned more by military operations than by weather-related harvest failures.[88]

In Sweden proper, the mortality rate climbed only moderately in 1740, more from thermal stress than from hunger or epidemic disease. During 1741, however, both a shortage of food and an increasing incidence of dysentery overspread much of Sweden.[89] The most pronounced Swedish crisis mortality developed in the southwestern counties of Älvsborg, Skaraborg, and particularly Värmland, touched off by food shortage and epidemics of dysentery, typhus fever, and malaria. Resident physicians focused on prolonged undernutrition as the underlying cause of the regional mortality crisis.[90] The level of mortality peaked in 1742, when Värmland registered a crude death rate of 121.6 per 1,000, and the rates remained in excess of 40 per 1,000 in Älvsborg and Skaraborg.[91] Although the number of deaths that resulted from undernutrition was considerable in Sweden, the percentage of deaths from hunger was far less significant than in Norway.

The Norwegian mortality crisis of 1741–1742 matched the Irish mortality crisis in severity and duration. In both locations, deaths that derived from the process of starvation made up a significant fraction of the excess mortality. Hunger and diarrheal disease became rife in Norway during 1741, as the poor were reduced to makeshift diets. The worsening shortage of food in 1742 produced extensive famine, with the destitute forced to eat grass, leaves, and tree bark. Famine conditions became most acute in the diocese of Akershus, where the parish registers

87. Jutikkala, *Bevölkerung Finnlands,* 39.
88. Ibid., 40–41.
89. Imhof, *Bevölkerungsentwicklung in den nordischen Ländern,* 171, 637–40.
90. Ibid., 649–53; Gustaf Utterström, "Some Population Problems in Preindustrial Sweden," *Scandinavian Economic History Review* 2 (1954), 128–30.
91. Imhof, *Bevölkerungsentwicklung in den nordischen Ländern,* 172.

contain references to death from starvation pure and simple.[92] The majority of the excess deaths in Norway, however, as in Ireland, resulted from epidemics of dysentery and typhus fever, not from hunger and starvation.

In summary, the food shortages that prevailed in western Europe during the early 1740s led to a noticeable number of deaths from hunger and prolonged undernutrition. But only in Ireland, Norway, and Finland did the scale of mortality from hunger register a measurable impact on national death rates. Moreover, the deaths from hunger and hypothermia combined proved less demographically significant than the mortality that resulted from the elevated incidence of epidemic diseases. It should be noted at the same time that the western European mortality peak of 1740–1742 was touched off by climatic variability as well as the shortage of food. In addition to the risk of death from thermal stress and the weather-related subsistence crises, a series of functional relationships can be found between the climatic variability and the common epidemic diseases of the early 1740s. The last chapter will document the epidemics and specify the relationships between the weather events and the widespread infections.

92. Ibid., 641–42, 657–60; Michael Drake, *Population and Society in Norway, 1735–1865* (Cambridge, 1969), 67.

8. *The Epidemic Diseases of the Early 1740s*

Mass infectious diseases are no longer a major cause of death in the Western world. There is agreement that the combination of improved nutrition and reduced human exposure to disease pathogens have been responsible for the decrease in their prevalence.[1] The unresolved question, however, is whether the high mortality from epidemic disease in preindustrial subsistence crises resulted *primarily* from nutritional deficiencies that weakened the human immune response to invading pathogens or from enhanced contact with pathogenic microorganisms and disease vectors. Although epidemic mortality often marched in lockstep with food shortages, it is not clear to what degree the increase in the number of deaths derived from the accepted synergistic relationship between nutritional deficiency and infection.

The elevated mortality from epidemic disease in subsistence crises originated no doubt in both larger morbidity rates and higher case-fatality rates. The number of persons who contract infectious diseases during food shortages tends to rise for several reasons. The disruption of the normal production and distribution of cereals occasioned by harvest shortfalls leads, as has been shown, to such dysfunctional behavior as crowding together, uncontrolled work migrations, and the necessity to turn to begging. When people abandon homes and villages and congregate in welfare, health, and penal installations, their exposure to pathogens increases, and in the environmental conditions of preindustrial Europe infections spread inevitably. The public installations that are set up or expanded to meet the increased welfare needs inevitably promote a

---

1. See John Rose, ed., *Nutrition and Killer Diseases* (Park Ridge, N.J., 1982), for a series of medical papers showing that dietary factors influence fatal chronic diseases. With the exception of the mycotoxins, however, the "killer diseases" discussed do not include the acute infections, the so-called famine fevers, that have commonly increased in prevalence in the course of European preindustrial subsistence crises.

breakdown in personal cleanliness and often become networks for diffusing infections. Marching and billeted armies also could add to the epidemiological hazards, as they did in some locations during the 1740s.

Not all the epidemics that broke out in the 1740s can be traced to subsistence crises and military operations. Climatic variability alone can have a direct effect on human health by promoting an increase in disease vectors and pathogens. Also, the appropriate weather conditions can bring about widespread outbreaks of mold poisonings such as ergotism and alimentary toxic aleukia.[2] The medical evidence suggests that mold poisonings were a health problem in some districts during the early 1740s but did not become a major cause of death. The incidence of some common infections appears to be independent of changes in either the level of human well-being or the weather. Each infection possesses to varying degrees an autonomous life of its own. As a consequence, the phenomenon of epidemic disease cannot be investigated as an entity but must be disaggregated. The first task therefore becomes the identification of the diseases described in the historical documents.

The evidence discloses that the mortality peak of 1740–1742 originated in a higher incidence of dysentery, "fever," and respiratory diseases. Epidemics of smallpox, influenza, measles, and malaria also broke out in the early 1740s, but they were neither universal nor perennial. The identification of the infections implicated in the epidemics of "continued fever," which together with bacillary dysentery swept over western Europe during the years 1740–1742, is fundamental in accounting for the mortality peak. Because each essential fever possesses an inherent case-fatality and age-specific death rate, as well as some degree of seasonality, it is also imperative to translate the eighteenth-century medical terms into the infections recognized in the modern method of classifying diseases by etiological and anatomical principles.

The translation of eighteenth-century medical concepts into modern terminology is not always possible. Diseases that fell under a single diagnosis in the past, such as "fever" and "typhus," are now differentiated into several entities. It has also been suggested that the character of some diseases has changed over time.[3] In any event, the descriptions of

2. For the pioneering investigation of the role of mycotoxins or mold poisoning in European population history, see Mary K. Matossian, "The Throat Distemper Reappraised," *Bulletin of the History of Medicine* 54 (1980), 529–43; "Mold Poisoning: An Unrecognized English Health Problem," *Medical History* 25 (1981), 73–84; and the forthcoming full-length study "Ergot, Molds, and History."

3. Jean-Pierre Peter, "Disease and the Sick at the End of the Eighteenth Century," in Robert Forster and Orest Ranum, eds., *Biology of Man in History*, trans. Elborg Forster and Patricia M. Ranum (Baltimore, 1975), 95–96.

diseases left by eighteenth-century physicians are often difficult to match with present-day diagnoses. Physicians then classified diseases in accordance with symptoms and syndromes. This diagnostic practice, based on nosological principles, was commonly accurate in the case of smallpox, measles, dysentery (bloody flux), and malaria (intermittent fever). The diagnosis of "fever" or "putrid fever," however, does not identify adequately the infections that became rife in the epidemics of the early 1740s.

The concept of fever as a disease played a critical role in the practice of medicine in the eighteenth century. Although fever was perceived as a disease entity, because of the similarity of symptoms, the fact that fevers exhibit varying clinical courses led to attempts to classify them in accordance with their degree of continuousness. Essential fevers—that is, fevers that are not strictly symptomatic, as in the case of smallpox— were categorized as "periodic" and "continued." Within the group of continued fevers, physicians distinguished two broad types, "inflammatory" and "low nervous." The term "inflammatory" generally referred to cases with acute respiratory, intestinal, or cutaneous symptoms. "Low nervous fevers" were characterized by a more gradual systemic reaction attended by such neurological symptoms as headaches, restlessness, delirium, and coma.

Within the category of low nervous fevers, physicians practicing in the 1740s commonly distinguished "putrid" fevers, a term applied to those cases that had a tendency to the discharge of pungent body fluids or wastes. Later in the eighteenth century, the classification "low nervous fever" tended to be replaced by the term "typhus." Theorists stressed the insidious onset of this low-grade fever, which also exhibited pronounced headaches and the gradual appearance of "typhomania."[4]

The clinical descriptions of the epidemics of low nervous and putrid fevers that predominated in the early 1740s point almost certainly and almost exclusively to the louse-borne infections of typhus and relapsing fever and the enteric infection typhoid fever. But it should be borne in mind that the terms were not in accurate use at the time. Physicians practicing in the eighteenth century also called these same infections

4. The discussion of the medical term "fever" in the eighteenth century is drawn from Dale C. Smith, "Gerhard's Distinction between Typhoid and Typhus and Its Reception in America, 1833–1860," *Bulletin of the History of Medicine* 54 (Fall 1980), 368–69; Guenter B. Risse, "Epidemics and Medicine: The Influence of Disease on Medical Thought and Practice," ibid. 53 (Winter 1979), 510–13; Todd Savitt, *Medicine and Slavery: The Diseases and Health Care of Blacks in Antebellum Virginia* (Urbana, 1979), 138; Lester S. King, *The Medical World of the Eighteenth Century* (Chicago, 1958), chap. 5, "Of Fevers," 123–55; chap. 7, "Nosology," 193–226.

malignant fevers when morbidity and case-fatality rates soared, particularly in the case of typhus fever. In the absence of detailed clinical descriptions, it is not possible to separate typhus from typhoid fever (unless the former is called petechial fever or, with a less degree of certainty, spotted fever).

The Fever Epidemics

No region of western Europe suffered crisis mortality in the early 1740s in the absence of epidemic fever or dysentery or both. Historically the continued fevers and dysentery in Europe have been associated with the intensification of human deprivations that has invariably taken place during economic crises. Typhus epidemics in Europe have broken out chiefly in colder regions where badly nourished, overcrowded populations with poor personal hygiene have fostered the multiplication and dissemination of the louse vector of the disease. Epidemics of louse-borne fever are thus associated with the social phenomena promoted by unemployment, hunger, and war. Epidemics have generally reached a peak during the winter and spring months or whenever the weather encourages close indoor personal contact and at the same time reduces the ability to wash clothing and to bathe. The clothes of typhus victims in preindustrial societies were either passed on in the family or were sold rather than destroyed and consequently constituted a source of further infection, particularly the underclothes.[5]

Because typhus normally exhibits a decidedly higher case-fatality rate than either typhoid or relapsing fever, the predominant infection implicated in the epidemics of 1740–1742 must be identified in order to assess the impact on mortality. Despite some ambiguities, the distinctive symptoms and clinical course of the three fevers make it possible to distinguish the infections with some degree of accuracy. Typhus, as I have noted, was commonly designated "petechial fever." Petechiae are small, pinpoint, nonraised, round, purplish-red spots caused by intradermal or submucous hemorrhages, which turn blue or yellow. But not all cases of typhus exhibit petechiae. In addition, eighteenth-century physicians often confused petechiae with typhus' distinctive rash, which led to

5. Sir William MacArthur, "Medical History of the Famine," in R. Dudley Edwards and T. Desmond Williams, eds., *The Great Famine* (New York, 1957), 305; Abram Benenson, ed., *Control of Communicable Diseases in Man*, 12th ed. (Washington, D.C., 1975), 259; Sir Macfarlane Burnet and David O. White, *Natural History of Infectious Disease*, 4th ed. (Cambridge, 1972), 145–47; James R. Busvine, *Insects, Hygiene, and History* (London, 1972), 52–53.

its designation as "spotted fever."[6] The distinctive symptoms and clinical course of typhus fever nonetheless make it possible to identify this infection in most instances.

The clinical onset of typhus is marked by a severe and unrelieved headache, which in most cases is frontal. Fever accompanies this symptom, and the body temperature slowly rises to approximately 104°F, where it remains the greater part of the acute stage of the disease. Roaring in the ears followed by deafness is frequently an early symptom. The characteristic rash of typhus does not appear before the third day of illness and usually breaks out between the fifth and seventh days. The rash appears first on the upper chest, the upper back, and the upper arms. The rash can cover the entire body but is almost never seen on the face. As the disease progresses, the lesions become dark red or bluish red. In severe cases, the rash may be accompanied by an extensive petechial eruption, involving the hair follicles of the trunk and limbs. As the rash develops, the skin of the face, forehead, and neck assumes a dusky, cyanotic hue, while the face, particularly the eyelids, appears puffy.

There is a close correlation between the extensiveness of the rash and the severity of the infection. In some light-skinned individuals, however, the rash is never seen for certain even when the disease proves fatal. From the time the rash appears until the fever returns to normal, the typhus victim is nearly helpless and cannot eat or drink without assistance; in many cases survival depends on constant nursing care. In the second week of the disease, a state of severe prostration, delirium, and stupor are the rule. Bacterial pneumonia is a common complication of typhus during the second week of the disease. Those victims who do not recover generally die in the second week of illness from an overwhelming infection, with coma and vascular failure, or from such complications as pneumonia.[7]

Typhoid fever is also a systemic infection characterized by continued fever, headache, malaise, and a body rash. The rash of the two diseases is not easily confused when the rash of typhus is distributed over the body. In typhoid fever, rose-colored spots appear on the trunk in the second week of illness. The onset of typhoid is more insidious than that of typhus, and the victim is less prostrated in the first week of illness. Typhoid, moreover, is a more protracted disease, and the symptoms may

6. C. A. Murchison, *A Treatise on the Continued Fevers of Great Britain* (London, 1862), 127–32.

7. This clinical description is drawn from Andrew Yeomans, "The Symptomatology, Clinical Course, and Management of Louse-borne Typhus Fever," in F. R. Moulton, ed., *Rickettsial Diseases of Man* (Washington, D.C., 1948), 126–27; Murchison, *Continued Fevers,* 127–226.

continue for a month or longer, whereas the fever in typhus rarely continues beyond the third week. From a nosological standpoint, typhoid is much more commonly attended with nosebleeds and, characteristically, with intestinal hemorrhages in advanced cases. Death from typhoid fever may occur at any time during the third or fourth week of illness, caused by peritonitis, exhausting diarrhea, or intestinal hemorrhaging.[8]

Relapsing fever, like typhus fever, is a disease transmitted by the human body louse. The two contagions have commonly occurred together as "famine fevers." Although the symptoms of relapsing fever may simulate typhus during the first week of illness, its ultimate clinical course makes it possible to distinguish the two diseases in most cases. In the severe strains of relapsing fever, a general and deep jaundice has been a common complication, hence its designation "yellow fever" in Irish and Scottish epidemics. Hemorrhages from the nose are also common in relapsing fever, whereas they rarely occur in cases of typhus. But the decisive clinical difference is that in relapsing fever the fever itself ends after five days with a sharp crisis attended by profuse sweating and exhaustion. After an interval of about seven days a relapse occurs, and several more may follow before the disease runs its course. Typhus, by contrast, is characterized by a fever that continues for about fourteen days unless death supervenes.[9]

Typhus can also be distinguished from typhoid and relapsing fever by its age-specific morbidity and mortality rates. Typhus is generally a disease of adulthood, though no period of life is exempt from the infection. The age of the victim is the critical factor in the case-fatality rate of typhus, which rises rapidly with increasing age. In hospitalized people under the age of fifteen, for example, the case-fatality rate may be less than 10 percent, whereas in individuals over fifty years of age it can approach 50 percent and in elderly persons can reach 100 percent. Typhoid fever, by contrast, generally exhibits a case-fatality rate between 10 and 15 percent, and the rate is not influenced by age. Children and adolescents have been the most common victims of typhoid fever. The seasonal prevalence of the fever also differs. Epidemics of typhoid have occurred chiefly in the autumn months, particularly after dry summers. As for relapsing fever, in European epidemics age has not been a factor in morbidity, and case-fatality rates have averaged less than 10 percent.[10]

8. Benenson, *Communicable Diseases,* 349–51; Murchison, *Continued Fevers,* 385–531.

9. Sir William MacArthur, "Famines and Fevers in England and Ireland," *Journal of the British Archaeological Association,* 3d ser., 9 (1944), 70–71; MacArthur, "Medical History," 267–68; Murchison, *Continued Fevers,* 22, 170–71.

10. Yeomans, "Louse-borne Typhus Fever," 126–30; Murchison, *Continued Fevers,* 61–62, 127–32, 219, 222, 385–531; Benenson, *Communicable Diseases,* 349–51; Stanhope Bayne-

The etiology of typhus and relapsing fever does not suggest that either malnutrition or undernutrition fosters these infections. Typhus is spread primarily by means of the infected feces of the louse, the pathogenic rickettsiae penetrating the skin during the act of scratching. The pathogens can also enter through the mucous membranes of the respiratory tract from infected dust circulating in the air of unventilated rooms. Relapsing fever is usually contracted by crushing an infective louse over a bite wound or other abrasion of the skin. The louse becomes infective by ingesting pathogenic spirochetes from a human ill with relapsing fever. In both louse-borne typhus and relapsing fever, humans are the reservoirs of infection.[11] Typhoid fever, like bacillary dysentery (shigellosis), is most commonly communicated from person to person by direct or indirect fecal-oral transmission from an infected person, or from an inapparent carrier of infection. The most common mode in infection is found in food and water that have been contaminated by feces or urine. Individuals who fail to cleanse contaminated hands or fingernails are primarily responsible for transmission of typhoid fever and dysentery. Both bacterial infections are worldwide in occurrence, with humans being the only significant reservoir of infection.[12]

The fever epidemics of 1740 became rife first in the British Isles and in Finland. In Britain, the Devon port of Plymouth was struck by an epidemic of fever during the early spring months. In April of that year, the resident physician John Huxham noted that "Acute Disorders were now attended with the Petechiae." By June the fever had become "pestilential" and rampant among sailors. Huxham traced the origins of the epidemic to the men-of-war (the *Panther* and *Canterbury*) that had

---

Jones, "Epidemic Typhus in the Mediterranean Area during World War II," in Moulton, *Rickettsial Diseases*, 9, for similar case-fatality rates in the twentieth century.

11. Andrew Yeomans, "Typhus Fever" (an essay in a medical text whose title I seem to have lost), 447–53; MacArthur, "Medical History," 267–68, 275–76; Benenson, *Communicable Diseases*, 259–60, 354. The spread of epidemic typhus fever depends on the presence of human body lice. Body lice live in the clothing worn next to the skin. The body louse is infected when it feeds on the blood of a person with febrile typhus fever; the pathogenic microorganisms (rickettsiae) circulating in the infected person's blood are drawn into the intestinal tract of the louse. Infected lice do not regurgitate the microorganisms in feeding; rather they excrete rickettsiae in their feces, and transmission takes place when feces or crushed lice are rubbed into the wound made by the bite or into superficial abrasions. The inhalation of dried louse feces as dust, which can remain infective for many months, accounts for other infections. Relapsing fever is caused by a spirochete. After being swallowed by the louse, the spirochetes multiply in the insect's body—not in the intestinal cells like rickettsiae in typhus—and are extruded in large numbers onto the host's skin if the insect is crushed or damaged. The delicate legs and antennae of lice are easily broken off, and the exuding fluid swarms with spirochetes. These microorganisms in turn are readily transferred to others, by fingers, and can cause infection by penetrating the skin or the eye.

12. Benenson, *Communicable Diseases*, 285–88, 349–53; Murchison, *Continued Fevers*, 409–19; Savitt, *Medicine and Slavery*, 58–63; MacArthur, "Medical History," 268–86.

put into Plymouth earlier in the year.[13] It should be noted, however, that by the middle of the eighteenth century numerous endemic centers of typhus, typhoid, and dysentery had long been established in the British Isles. As for Plymouth, epidemics of typhus as well as smallpox had been responsible for the elevated mortality of 1735.[14]

The typhus epidemic at Bristol also was traced to the arrival of a specific ship. Physicians in Bristol, however, had in fact seen "the very same Fever some Time before that Accident"; the fever, "according to the Best Accounts," was "Endemical" in Bristol.[15] Unlike the case of bubonic plague, humans maintain continued fevers during interepidemic phases. But it is true that on occasion epidemics of fever were touched off by international shipping in the eighteenth century.

The fever epidemic that broke out in Plymouth during the first half of 1740 spread throughout the county of Devonshire and by 1742 the infection was reported to be epidemic in all regions of England. The clinical evidence indicates that typhus was the major fever that fueled the epidemics and the high mortality. Huxham recorded the progress of the infection month by month. In May 1740, he noted, a "putrid petechial Fever was very rife, which sent a Number of Sailors, and the lower kind of People to their Graves."[16]

Huxham's *Observations* leave little doubt that the fever was mainly typhus. "There came on ... acute pain in the Head ... , nay the very Balls of the Eyes themselves were greatly pained." After three or four days "there followed a Phrensy, or restless Coma" Between the sixth and eleventh day, "sometimes sooner, sometimes later, Violet-coloured, livid, brown, and even quit black Petechiae, very often made their Appearances ... dark, small, and numberless Spots in the Skin, like Freckles, were always a very bad Omen; but the worst of all was black and blue Marks."[17]

The fever epidemic in Plymouth reached a peak in July 1740 and then gradually declined, but not before it had laid the groundwork for a mortality crisis in Devonshire. According to Huxham, "The common Burials were increased to at least six Times the Number; nor did this

13. John Huxham, *Observations of the Air, and Epidemic Diseases from the beginning of the Year 1738 to the end of the Year 1748*, trans. from the Latin by John Corham Huxham, 2 vols. (London, 1759–67), II, 57–66.
14. N. C. Oswald, "Epidemics in Devon, 1538–1837," *Devonshire Association* 109 (1977), 102–103.
15. John Barker, M.D., *An Inquiry into the Nature, Cause, and Cure of the present Epidemic Fever* (London, 1742), 138.
16. Huxham, *Observations*, II, 57–59.
17. Ibid., 61–66.

disorder prevail only here, but also through the whole Neighbourhood."[18] The evidence suggests that in the late summer months of 1740, in line with the seasonal prevalence of continued fevers, Huxham began to see cases of typhoid fever as well as typhus, especially as some of his fever patients did not die until the twentieth day or even later in the illness.[19] During the winter of 1740–1741, the number of typhus cases flared up again. "The petechial Fever was somewhat more rife." For the balance of 1741, Huxham recorded an epidemic incidence of "putrid fevers," with and without the petechial symptoms, with the former predominating in the spring months and the latter during the late summer months.[20]

By the spring of 1741, the fever epidemics had spread over most of Devonshire. Huxham wrote in May that "slow and nervous" fevers prevailed in southern Devonshire, "more petechial; but the Spots were now much more florid."[21] By August, cases of typhoid fever became more prevalent. "Putrid Fevers of a long Continuance (perhaps *mesenteric*) were very rife amongst the lower Kind of People . . . some were attended with a Phrensy, but those destroyed the Patients much sooner."[22] As late as April 1742, he continued to describe epidemic typhus. "A contagious, putrid Fever, and very pestilential attended with Restlessness, Delirium . . . proved very fatal.—Frequently Petechial, and those very black, broke out in the State of the Fever." Huxham believed that the Devon epidemics originated in prisons and were "disseminated far and near by the County Assizes."[23] During the years 1743 and 1744, the incidence of continued fever in Devonshire remained low.[24]

Epidemics of fever became widespread in almost all English counties by the spring of 1741. In the western county of Worcestershire, the account of the physician John Wall indicates that typhus was the most common infection. His clinical description of a "heavy Pain in the forepart of the Head" and the fact that "about the 7th Day, *Petechiae* or Spots sometimes appear upon the Breast or arms" corresponded to the cardinal symptoms of typhus. Such symptoms as "Haemorrhages from the Nose, Mouth . . . and other Parts" suggest that he was also seeing cases of typhoid and relapsing fever.[25] Wall, like Huxham, connected the

18. Ibid., 77–78.
19. Ibid., 84–85.
20. Ibid., 66, 83–96.
21. Ibid., 96–99.
22. Ibid., 102–103.
23. Ibid., 116–18.
24. Ibid., 121–60.
25. John Wall, "Account of the Epidemic Fever of 1740, 1741, 1742," in *Medical Tracts, collected by Martin Wall, M.D.* (Oxford, 1780), 337–38, 345–52.

epidemic with the proceedings of the criminal justice system. But he also believed that the general elections of 1741 generalized the fever.[26] According to a surgeon resident in Wolverhampton, however, the fever epidemics emanated from unemployment and want.[27]

The physician John Barker, by contrast, traced the fever epidemics to the bad weather conditions and the ensuing crop deficiencies. He pointed out the similarities between the present national epidemic and the great fever epidemic of 1684–1685. In both the present and the past epidemic, the anomalous weather and the resulting food shortage were responsible for promoting the infections. According to Barker and to all other commentators, the fever epidemic began in the west, fostered by high unemployment and severe want.[28]

As for Barker's clinical description of the fever, he designated the infection the "Putrid Petechial Fever of the Year 1741." He noted that the fever "went by the Name of the Gaol-Fever." as it was supposed to have appeared first among the prisoners at Exeter.[29] The clinical course of the disease in Barker's patients again points to typhus. "After the seventh Day, Petechiae, or Spots, sometimes appear upon the Breast, or arms. These commonly are of a Pale-red Colour almost like the Meazles, and sometimes Purple, like so many small Flea-bites. In a very few they have been of a deep violet and in others very broad like Scurvy Spots or Bruises." The prevalence of the fever year round and the fact that some of Barker's patients did not die until the end of the third week of illness indicate that typhoid fever was also present.[30]

The physician Thomas Short, practicing in the Midlands, believed that the fever cases he saw differed from the infection described by Huxham. The evidence indicates that his patients suffered from both typhus and relapsing fever. Short clearly observed the pronounced crisis characteristic of relapsing fever. "After the crisis, they were liable to many Relapses, often more dangerous and fatal than the first Fever." The higher case-fatality rates among his fever patients during the winter of

---

26. Ibid., 337–38.

27. Charles Creighton, *A History of Epidemics in Britain,* 2 vols. (Cambridge, 1891–94), II, 79–80.

28. Barker, *Present Epidemic Fever,* 44–45, 54.

29. Ibid., 37.

30. Ibid., 40–41. For a medical analysis of Barker's clinical descriptions, see B. W. Alexander, "The Epidemic Fever (1741–42)," *Salisbury Medical Bulletin* 11 (1971), 24–29. This article includes a note from Dr. P. J. Wornald: "I think this epidemic was almost certainly one of typhus." Barker's reference to "broad like Scurvy Spots or Bruises" was a common clinical observation during the fever epidemics. In all probability these symptomatic purpura reflected the complications of scurvy. According to Murchison, *Continued Fevers,* 132, 170, when typhus fever was complicated by scurvy during the Crimean War, both purpura and nosebleeds were common.

1741–1742, however, suggests that typhus was a common infection.[31]

A great fever epidemic broke out in London during 1741. An anonymous medical essay indicates that typhus was the predominant infection. "Florid Eruptions" appeared mainly on the breast and arms. In fatal cases, death occurred toward the end of the second week of illness, except in persons "attacked with the strong Delirium," in which cases the patient "generally dies about the 8th day."[32]

The London bills of mortality afford some measure of the demographic impact of the English fever epidemics. The bills contain an omnibus category called "Fevers and Purples," which apparently included the majority of deaths resulting from all essential fevers, periodic and continued, "inflammatory" as well as "nervous." Table 21 shows the annual number of burials registered during the ten-year period 1735–1744, the annual number of "fever" deaths during the same period, and their percentage of total deaths, together with the same information for smallpox deaths.

Table 21. Annual number of burials registered in London and annual number of deaths from "fever" and smallpox, 1735–1744

Year	Total burials (thousands)	Deaths from fever	Percentage of total deaths	Deaths from smallpox	Percentage of total deaths
1735	23.5	2,544	10.8	1,594	6.8
1736	27.6	3,361	12.2	3,014	10.9
1737	27.8	4,580	16.4	2,084	7.5
1738	25.8	3,890	15.1	1,590	6.2
1739	25.4	3,334	13.1	1,690	6.6
1740	30.8	4,003	13.0	2,725	8.8
1741	32.4	7,528	23.2	1,977	6.1
1742	27.4	5,108	18.6	1,429	5.2
1743	25.2	3,837	15.2	2,029	8.1
1744	20.6	2,670	13.0	1,633	7.9
Average	26.7	4,086	15.3	1,977	7.4

NOTE: Information regarding smallpox deaths has been included for purposes of comparison.
SOURCE: Demographic statistics taken from the London bills of mortality and appearing in the monthly numbers of *Gentleman's Magazine* 5–15 (1735–44).

Fever and smallpox were in fact the only major causes of death whose numbers fluctuated substantially during the ten-year period. The figures indicate that the elevated death rate of 1740 derived from an increase in the number of deaths from smallpox as well as from thermal stress. The crisis mortality of 1741, however, stemmed predominantly from the steep increase in fever deaths, which carried over into 1742.

31. Thomas Short, *A General Chronological History of the Air, Weather, Seasons, Meteors, etc.* (London, 1749), 267–78.
32. *Observations on the present epidemic Fever* (London, 1741), 1, 5–8.

Although the evidence does not permit a breakdown of the classification "Fevers and Purples" into the component diseases and fevers, the fluctuations in the age distribution of the London burials yield some measure of the relative prevalence of the more fatal typhus fever. Typhus not only exhibits the highest case-fatality rates among the "continued fevers" but in addition is characterized by a death rate that rises significantly with age. The London fever epidemic raged for a twelve-month period beginning in March 1741 and ending in February 1742. If the fever was predominantly typhus, a noticeable increase in the relative number of deaths among mature adults and the elderly would be anticipated. In fact, people over thirty years of age suffered unusually high mortality in London during 1741. This age category accounted for 44.5 percent of annual recorded deaths, whereas during the ten-year period 1735–1744, the same age category averaged 40.7 percent of annual deaths.[33]

A similar analysis of the Cambridge Group's estimated national monthly deaths is not possible, owing to the absence both of the causes of death and of the age distribution of the burials. But the fluctuations of seasonal mortality disclose that national trends corresponded with the movement of the London bills, reflecting the demographic impact of thermal stress, the fever epidemics, and the epidemic of influenza that struck in the spring of 1743. Table 22 shows the estimated national burials by season, together with seasonal percentages of deaths.

As can be seen, the majority of deaths during the ten-year period occurred during the winter and spring months (the first six months of the year), 54.8 percent of the total. The high mortality of the winter of 1742

Table 22. Estimated number of burials in England, by season, 1735–1744 (in thousands)

Year	Winter No.	Winter %	Spring No.	Spring %	Summer No.	Summer %	Autumn No.	Autumn %	Annual deaths
1735	40.3	27.7	36.7	25.3	31.0	21.4	37.2	25.6	145.3
1736	44.8	29.3	38.5	25.1	34.0	22.2	35.8	23.4	153.1
1737	44.3	26.5	38.7	23.1	35.4	21.1	49.0	29.3	167.4
1738	41.4	27.4	37.7	25.0	33.9	22.5	37.9	25.1	150.9
1739	45.6	29.9	40.1	26.3	32.5	21.3	34.1	22.4	152.3
1740	47.6	27.5	51.3	29.7	34.9	20.2	39.3	22.7	173.0
1741	43.9	22.7	48.6	25.1	44.9	23.2	56.2	29.0	193.6
1742	63.2	31.3	55.6	27.5	40.6	20.1	42.7	21.1	202.2
1743	42.4	26.6	54.2	34.0	31.0	19.4	32.0	20.1	159.6
1744	42.0	30.3	38.3	27.7	27.9	20.1	30.4	22.0	138.5
Average	45.6	27.9	44.0	26.9	34.6	21.1	39.5	24.1	163.6

SOURCE: E. A. Wrigley and R. S. Schofield, *The Population History of England, 1541–1871* (Cambridge, Mass., 1981), 515–16.

33. *Gentleman's Magazine* 5–15 (1735–1744).

stands out. The number of deaths climbed to a level 38.6 percent above the average winter mortality for the period. The elevated death rate of that season derived from the fever epidemics that were still rife in the early months of 1742 and also from the fact that winter was nearly as severe that year as in 1740. The second highest number of winter burials was recorded during the arctic cold weather of 1740, the season before the fever epidemics broke out and became epidemic.

The most noticeable demographic pattern, however, was the high mortality each spring from 1740 to 1743. In 1740 and 1741, more deaths were recorded in the spring than in the first three months of the year. The elevated spring mortality of 1740 can be traced mainly to the extended cold season and high urban unemployment rates of that year, while the spring mortality of 1741 reflected the impact of the dearth and the expanding fever epidemics. The peak spring mortality of 1742 resulted from the combination of the fever epidemics, from the effects of another severe and extended cold season, and in all probability from the residual demographic impact of two years of high food prices and elevated unemployment rates. Although the number of spring burials declined slightly in 1743, the highest percentage of spring deaths during the ten-year period occurred this season, largely as a consequence of the national influenza epidemics.[34] Despite the influenza epidemic, however, the level of mortality in England declined significantly in 1743 with the passing of the fever epidemics, the dearth, and the high unemployment rates and with the return to more normal weather patterns.

Summer mortality remained characteristically low throughout the entire ten-year period 1735–1744, with the exception of 1741, when the number of deaths rose 29.7 percent above the seasonal average. The summer of 1741 was the only one in which dearth, fever epidemics, and elevated unemployment prevailed at the same time. The autumn seasons also exhibited low mortality, except in 1737 and 1741. By the autumn of 1741, fever epidemics were rampant in England, and the working population had passed through an extended period of high unemployment paralleled by elevated food prices. The high autumn death rate of 1737 derived primarily from the wave of smallpox epidemics that swept over western Europe during 1736 and 1737.[35]

The year 1743 in England proved the first since 1739 that was free of extreme weather events, high unemployment rates, food shortages, and epidemics of continued fever. The year 1744 brought a more precipitous falloff in English mortality, in spite of the more active British interven-

34. Ibid., 14 (May 1743), 272. Huxham, *Observations*, II. 147.
35. Huxham, *Observations*, II, 128–31; also see London bills of mortality.

tion in the continental war. Thus it is unlikely that either such fortuitous diseases as influenza and smallpox or wartime conditions exercised a dominant demographic influence on the English mortality peak of 1740–1742. The evidence indicates rather that the mortality wave originated in the combined effects of thermal stress, epidemics of continued fever, joblessness, and high food prices.

The authors of the seminal work *The Population History of England, 1541–1871* suggest that the mortality peak of 1740–1742 derived mainly from epidemic dysentery and not from the fever epidemics. They also found that the climatic variability and the high food prices of 1740–1741 had little influence on the mortality wave. They suggest that perhaps the typhus epidemics were confined to Plymouth and Bristol.[36] The clinical evidence examined here, the demographic trends found in the London bills, and the epidemiological record elsewhere in western Europe all fail to support these conclusions. Although it is true that a higher incidence of dysentery contributed to the English mortality peak as well as to the European mortality peak of 1740–1742, the English medical evidence indicates that epidemic typhoid fever was rife during the summers of 1740–1742. Epidemics of continued fever particularly influenced the English mortality peak, as will be shown.

The fever epidemics are well documented throughout Devonshire, where they brought burial rates comparable to those witnessed during the Civil War.[37] "Spotted Fever" carried off "about one in twelve" in the industrial town of Tiverton.[38] At Exeter, the peak mortality of 1741 was associated with a "great typhus outbreak," which followed a smaller epidemic in 1740.[39] English medical practitioners perceived the fever epidemics as the major public health crisis.[40] Charles Murchison remarked more than a century ago that all the great typhus epidemics that have devastated Great Britain and Ireland have occurred during seasons of food scarcity and want.[41]

In Scotland also, epidemics of continued fever, dysentery, and smallpox drove up the death rate during 1740–1741, but louse-borne fevers were not so widespread as in England. The evidence suggests that typhoid fever and dysentery were the more common fatal infections. The clinical medical record, however, is decidedly thinner for Scotland than

36. Wrigley and Schofield, *Population*, 669–70.
37. Oswald, "Epidemics in Devon," 103–104.
38. M. Dunsford, *Historical Memoirs of Tiverton* (Exeter, 1790), 228.
39. Ransom Pickard, M.D., *The Population and Epidemics of Exeter in Pre-Census Times* (Exeter, 1947), 64–67, 71.
40. Creighton, *Epidemics in Britain*, II, 78–79; Barker, *Present Epidemic Fever,* 44–45, 54, 87.
41. Murchison, *Continued Fevers,* 74–75.

for England. Systematic vital statistics and the causes of death are available for Edinburgh, at least for some of the years under study. To the extent that the causes of death found in Edinburgh bills were typical of urban Scotland, they indicate that the incidence of "fever" increased noticeably from 1740 to 1741.

Table 23. Percentage of deaths reported from principal causes, Edinburgh, 1740 and 1741

Cause	1740	1741
Old age	8.2	9.6
Consumption	22.4	21.6
Dysentery	0.2	2.2
Fever	13.0	18.8
Measles	8.1	6.9
Smallpox	22.1	12.7

SOURCE: *Scots Magazine*, 1741, 144, 432, 476.

Table 23 shows the percentage distribution of the principal causes of death in Edinburgh during 1740 and 1741. As can be seen, the Edinburgh mortality wave resulted from a high incidence of smallpox and measles as well as from fever. While the percentage of deaths attributed to "consumption" was high in Edinburgh, as in London, it should be recognized that the term was not equivalent to pulmonary tuberculosis but included a variety of wasting diseases. The figures also disclose that the percentage of fever deaths increased sharply from 13.0 percent in 1740 to 18.8 percent in 1741.

The number of fatal fever cases climbed as steeply in Edinburgh as in London, also nearly doubling from 1740 to 1741. The clinical evidence refers to "nervous fever" in accounts of the fatal epidemics. The symptoms described in the autumn of 1741 indicate that typhoid fever was the predominant infection, with louse-borne fevers less prevalent. The physician Ebenezer Gilchrist's account of the clinical course of the epidemic fever points to typhoid. Both its protracted course and its symptoms suggest typhoid fever. "The Fever runs out to the 20th, 25th, 30th, and sometimes to the 35th Day." Gilchrist stressed the ominous presence of "frequent Haemorrhages" and "Bloody Stools." He noted that death seldom occurred before the third week of illness. But he also saw fever cases whose symptoms point to typhus. "I meet with some Instances of a Fever" which "comes to an End about the 14th Day . . . the Sick are constantly almost under a Coma or Raving: and they die of an absolute Oppression of the Brain."[42]

42. Dr. Ebenezer Gilchrist, "Of Nervous Fevers," in *Medical Essays and Observations, Published by a Society in Edinburgh*, 5 vols. (Edinburgh, 1733–44), V, pt. 2, 525–27, 539, 572.

The seasonal distribution of fever deaths at Edinburgh suggests that the epidemics of continued fever were made up of typhus and typhoid fever. In 1741, for example, the number of monthly fever deaths peaked at thirty-six in March, a time of the year when typhus predominates and when typhoid normally declines to a low point. In July, the number of fever deaths fell to the lowest figure of the year. Fever deaths climbed to a secondary peak of thirty-four in September and thirty-three in October, months in which typhoid is generally rife, particularly after a period of drought, as in 1741.[43] Gilchrist's medical treatise is dated in the autumn of 1741. Fever deaths began to climb again and reached a maximum during the winter months of 1742, when they accounted for more than 30 percent of all deaths. The Edinburgh mortality wave subsided after the winter of 1742, when the number of deaths from all causes fell off sharply.[44]

Although mortality statistics are not available for the large Scottish region of the Highlands and Hebrides, the sparse literary evidence suggests that crisis mortality prevailed in some districts. The most revealing document of epidemic disease in the Highlands is the diary of the minister of Durness in the northern county of Sutherland. His account relates a high number of deaths from ''fever'' and dysentery, which were thought to have originated in the shortage of food. Two of the clergyman's servants died of fever, and he describes himself as having been critically ill with the same disease. Three of his children also became gravely ill with fever. His account implies, however, that dysentery was the most widespread threat to life.[45]

Altogether the evidence indicates that the Scottish mortality peak originated in epidemics of dysentery and continued fever, both typhoid and typhus, in conjunction with an elevated number of fatal cases of smallpox and measles. But even in the lowland regions the documentary references to infectious disease are sparse. An epidemic of malignant ''nervous fever'' broke out in the border county of Dumfries during the autumn of 1741. Whereas the seasonal prevalence suggests typhoid, the fourteen-day course of the fever points to typhus.[46] Even in light of today's advanced medical knowledge it remains unclear to what degree such infections as smallpox and measles are prejudiced by prolonged undernutrition. In Scotland as elsewhere in western Europe, however,

43. Michael Flinn et al., *Scottish Population History from the Seventeenth Century to the 1930s* (London, 1977), 220–21; Murchison, *Continued Fevers*, 64, 416.

44. Flinn et al., *Scottish Population History*, 220–21.

45. M. M. Mackay, ''A Highland Minister's Diary,'' *Cornhill Magazine* 152 (November 1935), 572–73.

46. Flinn et al., *Scottish Population History*, 220.

the subsistence crisis of 1740–1741 seems to have influenced mortality more decisively by fostering epidemics of continued fever and dysentery than by enhancing the case-fatality rates of common viral infections.

Epidemics of louse-borne fever and dysentery produced crisis mortality in Ireland as early as 1740, by which time destitution and hunger had become widespread. Sir William MacArthur has pointed out that on the heels of every famine in Ireland, whether in 1740, 1800, 1816, or 1845, an epidemic of "fever" broke out with such regularity that it came to be confidently predicted whenever a shortage of food developed. By "fever" was meant not the sporadic cases of infection that were daily possibilities in Ireland but a rising tide of pestilence that eventually engulfed the whole country. Moreover, rampant dysentery either preceded, accompanied, or followed the fever epidemics in regions struck by famine.[47]

John Rutty, who practiced medicine before such a pattern of famine and fever became established in Ireland, detected a historical pattern in which health problems throughout the British Isles were touched off by severe winters and droughty springs. He believed that the malignity of "fever" was influenced by the relative severity of the food shortage.[48] Physicians in Rutty's time were not able to distinguish the less fatal relapsing fever from typhus. MacArthur found, however, that epidemics of relapsing fever have predominated in Ireland during dearths, while typhus has been the common louse-borne infection during famines.[49]

In Ireland as in Britain, the louse-borne fevers had become endemic infections before 1740. Rutty, for example, wrote in the autumn and winter of 1734–1735, "We had the low fever called nervous (and sometimes petechial from the spots that frequently attended)." He added that "it is no new thing with us for this kind of fever to prevail in the winter season." His description of the fever epidemic that broke out in Dublin during the second half of 1739 indicates that the infection was mainly the less fatal relapsing fever. "It terminated sometimes in four, for the most part in five or six days, sometimes in nine, and commonly in a critical sweat; it was far from being mortal. I was assured of 70 of the poorer sort at the same time in this fever . . . who all recovered. The crisis, however, was very imperfect, for they were subject to relapses, even sometimes to the third time."[50]

47. MacArthur, "Medical History," 264–65, 286.

48. John Rutty, M.D., *A Chronological History of the Weather and Seasons, and of the Prevailing Diseases in Dublin* (London, 1770), 93.

49. MacArthur, "Famines and Fevers," 67.

50. Rutty, *Chronological History,* 75–76; Creighton, *Epidemics in Britain,* II, 239.

Rutty's account is a textbook description of the clinical course of relapsing fever as it has occurred in the British Isles. The relative prevalence of typhus and relapsing fever during epidemics can be gauged to a degree by class-specific attack rates and age-specific morbidity rates as well as by their distinctive case-fatality rates. The transmission of relapsing fever invariably requires the crushing of an infected louse to release the pathogenic spirochetes and therefore presupposes louse infestation, unlike typhus, which can be transmitted through infected dust circulating indoors. As a consequence, the fatal cases of relapsing fever have been confined chiefly to the destitute, that is, to such as Rutty's patients "of the poorer sort." Also unlike typhus, relapsing fever attacks persons of all ages, from infants to oldsters, with no distinct age-specific mortality rate among those stricken.[51]

Relapsing fever proved the predominant louse-borne infection in Ireland during 1740, whereas typhus became widely epidemic in the famine conditions of 1741, corresponding to MacArthur's generalization. The first press accounts that anticipated the impending demographic calamity appeared in June 1740. It was said that in the city of Cork "thousands of Poor" were "starving for want of food." The streets were "so crowded with Beggars" that there was "no passing for them."[52] Not until the final months of the year, however, did epidemic disease claim great numbers of lives. Press accounts from county Cork reported elevated mortality among "poor people by Fevers and Fluxes."[53] By the end of February 1741, reports from all regions of Ireland related "numbers of people" dying of "fluxes and fevers." Epidemics of fever and dysentery were rampant throughout the spring and summer months of 1741, particularly in the counties of southwestern Ireland.[54]

Rutty summed up the course of the Dublin fever epidemic. His description of its high case-fatality rate in 1741 and its spread to all social classes indicates that the predominant louse-borne infection was typhus fever. "It was common to this city, to Cork, Bristol, and London, and often eluded the skill of physicians. It raged through the provinces of

51. For the relative incidence of typhus and relapsing fever in Irish famines, and their respective epidemiologies, see MacArthur, "Medical History," 275–84; MacArthur, "Famines and Fevers," 66–71; Creighton, *Epidemics in Britain*, II, 241–45; F. Rogan, M.D., *Observations on the Condition of the Middle and Lower Classes in the North of Ireland As it Tends to Promote the Diffusion of Contagious Fever* (London, 1819), 19–52; F. Barker, M.D., and J. Cheyne, M.D., *An Account of the Rise, Progress and Decline of the Fever Lately Epidemical in Ireland*, 2 vols. (Dublin, 1821); William Harty, M.D., *An Historic Sketch of the Causes, Progress, Extent, and Mortality of the Contagious Fever Epidemic in Ireland during the Years 1817, 1818, and 1819* (Dublin, 1820).

52. *London Daily Post*, August 2, 1740.

53. Ibid., December 18, 1740.

54. *Faulkner's Dublin Journal*, February 17–21, 1741; for previous accounts of the same

Munster, Leinster, and Ulster; but was not fatal to the first, where their poor were worse provided for, from whom the disease spread to the richer sort.''[55] The fever epidemic in Dublin reached its greatest intensity in the summer of 1741. ''The mortality increased with the advancing season; and with us, in Dublin, arrived at its heighth about the end of August . . . the article of fevers in our weekly bills, amounted to 30, above double their late usual number.''[56] In Ireland as elsewhere in western Europe, the epidemics of continued fever in the late summer were made up of both typhoid and typhus fever.

In the province of Munster, where firsthand estimates calculated that 20 percent of the population perished from fever, dysentery, and hunger during 1740–1741, the impressionistic accounts suggest that the morbidity and mortality rates of fever became devastating. At Limerick, a ''Purple Fever'' carried off ''great Numbers,'' and reportedly there was scarcely a family ''without some Sick of that Distemper.''[57] The pastor of the Limerick parish of Cullen, struck by the enormous mortality, carried out an enumeration of his parishioners in August 1741 and found that 38 percent of the parish population had died.[58] According to the computations of David Dickson, the mortality index (1701–1775 = 100) for rural Munster rose from 187 in 1740 to 287 in 1741, and the index for urban Munster climbed from 133 in 1740 to 253 in 1741. At Dublin, by comparison, the mortality index declined from 145 in 1740 to 123 in 1741.[59] Several counties in the western province of Connaught also passed through lethal typhus epidemics. Fever raged so virulently in the town of Galway ''that Physicians say 'tis more like a Plague.''[60] Judges and physicians in Galway refused to face the risk of contracting typhus fever.[61] In the county of Roscommon, the ''Poor'' continued to die ''very fast of Fevers and Fluxes'' in the summer of 1741.[62] Although the greatest mortality from continued fever was centered in southwestern Ireland, the epidemics were a national phenomenon. According to a Dublin press account, ''Never were Malignant Fevers known in this

---

tenor, see ibid., December 6–9 and December 13–16, 1740; January 3–6, 1741; *London Advertiser,* January 24, 1740/41; Michael Drake, ''The Irish Demographic Crisis of 1740–41,'' *Historical Studies* 6 (1968), 116–17.

55. Rutty, *Chronological History,* 83, 86.
56. Ibid., 86–87.
57. *London Daily Post,* July 25, 1741.
58. Ibid., September 1, 1741.
59. David Dickson, ''Famine in Ireland, 1700–1775: A Review,'' paper presented at the Famine in History Symposium, Vevey, Switzerland, July 1981, app. 3. I am indebted to Dr. Dickson, Trinity College, Dublin, for permission to refer to his study.
60. *London Daily Post,* August 1, 1741.
61. *London Advertiser,* September 8, 1741.
62. Ibid., August 11, 1741.

Kingdom, both in Town and Country, to be so epidemical and Mortel to rich and poor, as at present."[63]

The decline of the continued fever and dysentery epidemics in Ireland during the autumn of 1741 suggests that neither typhoid fever nor dysentery was primarily responsible for the extremely high mortality of the summer months. By October 1741, the weekly Dublin bills had fallen below 60 burials, "which is but a very small Number, it having been often known, that 180 have died in a Week in this City."[64] According to Rutty, both the "malignant fever" and the dysentery, "though abated in autumn," did not cease entirely.[65] The winter of 1742, however, "concluded healthy," and reported deaths fell noticeably.[66] Dickson's mortality index for rural Munster fell off sharply to 82 in 1742, while the index for urban Munster declined significantly, from 253 to 110.[67] Rutty, in agreement with other contemporary physicians, connected the end of the crisis mortality to a change in the "atmospheric constitution" and to the fact that "Provisions, this winter, were as plentiful as they had been scarce for the last two years."[68]

Smallpox epidemics added to the mortality crisis in Ireland, as was the case in Britain and elsewhere in Europe. The evidence indicates, however, that its demographic impact was less significant than fever, dysentery, and possibly also hunger. Smallpox deaths were nonetheless particularly elevated at Dublin and Cork during 1740.[69] Smallpox is not an infection that has been connected with nutritional deficiencies and thus may be considered in the nature of a "fortuitous" disease. But it is possible that the large-scale itinerant vagrancy in 1740 enhanced the morbidity rate and therefore also mortality from smallpox. Dickson has suggested that such vagrancy exposed a whole new cohort within isolated communities to smallpox infection.[70] Medical knowledge indicates that nutritional modulation of immunity may be an important determinant of mortality in a variety of infections, particularly in children, but smallpox does not appear to be an outstanding case in which undernutrition prejudices case-fatality rates.[71]

Finland, like Ireland, suffered a severe mortality crisis in 1740, in

63. Ibid., July 28, 1741.
64. Ibid., September 22, 1741.
65. Rutty, *Chronological History,* 91.
66. Ibid., 92.
67. Dickson, "Famine in Ireland," app. 3.
68. Rutty, *Chronological History,* 96–98.
69. Ibid., 80–81; Dickson, "Famine in Ireland," 12–14.
70. Dickson, "Famine in Ireland," 12.
71. R. K. Chandra and P. M. Newberne, *Nutrition, Immunity, and Infection* (New York, 1977), 1–6; C. W. Dixon, *Smallpox* (London, 1962).

large part the consequence of epidemics of fever. The Finnish death rate was driven up by the outbreak of an epidemic disease that proved far more virulent that the earlier epidemics of relapsing fever or malaria. Although the evidence is not conclusive, the infection was probably louse-borne typhus fever. The town of Turku and nearby district of East Tavastland were the major foci of infection. According to the investigation of Eino Jutikkala, the epidemic began as a "camp fever" among the military units garrisoned there and then spread to the civilian population.[72] It should be noted, however, that several diseases had become common in Finland by the end of 1739, among them typhus, relapsing fever, dysentery, and scurvy.[73] The early and severe winter of 1739–1740 and the famine conditions of 1740, moreover, must have intensified louse infestation and in the process increased the risk of louse-borne fevers among the Finnish population. The prolonged low atmospheric temperatures as well as the troop garrisons fostered the spread of louse-borne infections.

The evidence indicates that epidemics of continued fever influenced mortality less decisively on the Continent than in the British Isles and Scandinavia. In Flanders, however, typhus, relapsing, and typhoid fever became rife together in 1740 and developed into a lethal epidemic. According to Heinrich Haeser, typhus fever broke out in the Netherlands in 1740.[74] The evidence speaks of a malignant "purple fever" in the Austrian Netherlands.[75] At the end of 1741, J. B. Scheppere, a physician resident at Ghent, published his reflections "on the subject of a malignant fever which is rife in this country," in which he distinguished the prevailing infection from the less lethal fever epidemic of 1737.[76]

The symptoms described in Scheppere's treatise indicate a mixed epidemic of typhus, typhoid, and relapsing fever. He was particularly concerned to distinguish the present epidemic from the less dangerous epidemic of "putrid malignant fever" that broke out in 1737. His

72. Eino Jutikkala, *Die Bevölkerung Finnlands in den Jahren 1721–1749* (Helsinki, 1945), 38–39.
73. Arthur E. Imhof, *Aspekte der Bevölkerungsentwicklung in den nordischen Ländern, 1720–1750* (Bern, 1976), 645.
74. Heinrich Haeser, *Lehrbuch der Geschichte der Medizin und der epidemischen Krankheiten*, 3d. ed., 3 vols. (Jena, 1875–82), III, 477.
75. Claude Bruneel, *La mortalité dans les campagnes: Le Duché de Brabant aux XVIIe et XVIIIe siècles* (Louvain, 1977), 281; T. Bernier, "Notice sur l'origine et la tenue des anciens registres d'état civil dans la province de Hainaut," *Mémoires de la Société des sciences, des arts, et des lettres du Hainaut*, 4th ser., 9 (1887), 568; D. Van Assche–Van Cauwenbergh, "Deux Villages du Brabant sous l'ancien régime: Bierges et Overyse: Etude de démographic historique," in *Cinq Etudes de démographie locale (XVIIIe–XIXe siècles)* (Brussels, 1963), 33.
76. J. B. Scheppere, *Détail historique et curatif de la fièvre maligne qui règne actuellement en toute la Flandre et ailleurs depuis l'an 1737* (Ghent, 1741), 3–8.

account of the clinical course of the earlier disease indicates relapsing fever. The symptoms of the reigning fever, by contrast "more obstinate, more aggravated, and more ominous, overwhelm the patient almost from the beginning." In the fever of 1737, a dramatic crisis occurred at the end of about six days, with patients subject to one or two relapses. In the present epidemic "small red spots, often mixed with blue spots," appeared on the chest and elsewhere on the skin before the ninth day of illness. "The whole face is puffed up" and "the delirium and the transports of the brain often intensify, up to the point of mania." Patients died by the fourteenth day of illness, when the fever proved fatal. Scheppere's description of the predominant infection points clearly to typhus fever.[77]

The gravity of the fever epidemics in the Austrian Netherlands elicited comment in the London press. "We hear that a violent Fever rages at Bruges, Antwerp, and other Parts of Flanders, and carries off Numbers of People every Day."[78] The clinical evidence of a severe epidemic of louse-borne fever in Flanders is supported statistically by the monthly trend of burials in the district of Veurne-Ambacht. Crisis mortality prevailed for a seven-month period from November 1741 to May 1742, which is the season when typhus is generally prevalent. In the course of this seven-month period, a total of 107 burials were registered in the nine parishes for which records are available. Fewer than 107 annual burials were recorded in the years from 1735 to 1739, by comparison. In three parishes where the burials of children were included, neither 1741 nor 1742 exhibited a significant increase in the number of juvenile deaths.[79] Scheppere also saw cases of typhoid fever. The devastating floods that inundated the towns in the Low Countries and contaminated wells and drinking water must have increased the risks of typhoid epidemics.[80]

The northwestern region of France was the other continental location that was struck by severe epidemics of typhus fever. In Brittany-Anjou the level of mortality climbed 50.8 percent in 1741 and remained elevated until 1744. The number of burials registered in rural Brittany-Anjou rose from 105,300 in 1740 to 158,800 in 1741 and did not fall

77. Ibid., 6–19.

78. *London Advertiser,* December 1, 1741.

79. D. Dalle, *De bevolking van Veurne-Ambacht in de 17e en 18e eeuw* (Brussels, 1963), 371–74, 417.

80. Bernier, "Hainaut," 568; Bruneel, *Mortalité,* 281, 525–26; Myron P. Gutmann, *War and Rural Life in the Early Modern Low Countries* (Princeton, 1980), 154, 158–61; Etienne Hélin, *La Population des paroisses liégeoises aux XVIIe et XVIIe siècles* (Liège, 1959), 172.

below 111,000 until 1744.[81] According to J.-P. Goubert, the epidemics of typhus and dysentery that swept over Brittany during the years 1741–1743 accounted for some 80,000 deaths.[82]

The Breton epidemics, like those of Plymouth and Bristol, were traced to naval vessels. Ships put ashore a number of fever patients at Brest in 1741. Cases of typhus fever, however, had occurred in Brittany during 1740 and in prior years. The same was true of dysentery, which began to influence the level of mortality as early as 1738. Crisis mortality erupted when both typhus and dysentery became rife simultaneously in the latter part of 1741. In the districts where medical data are available, the case-fatality rates of the two infections varied between 15 and 50 percent. It has been pointed out that the Breton demographic crisis of 1741–1743 fell on a society already affected by a long, unfavorable conjunction of bad weather, economic stagnation, and undernutrition.[83]

J.-P. Goubert's medical history of Brittany in the eighteenth century concluded that hygiene and nutrition were of overriding importance in the diffusion of epidemics among the deprived segment of the population and also that these two conditions determined the permanence of endemic disease. Although both typhus and typhoid fever maintained themselves into the nineteenth century, typhus proved a more unequivocal reflection of the material, sanitary, and sociocultural underdevelopment of most Breton rural districts. Goubert found that even though the epidemics seemed to follow laws of their own, the Breton social milieu in which they evolved, in combination with the hazards of climate and crop yields, played an essential role in governing the specific years, such as the early 1740s, when the most dangerous and lethal epidemics erupted. Goubert also found that in the 1740s subsistence was still the "vector" of some epidemic diseases in Brittany. The conditions of rural housing and personal hygiene almost guaranteed that whenever food shortages and cycles of endemic infectious disease coincided, years of crisis mortality would ensue.[84]

The medical evidence for the other regions of northern France is less revealing about the specific diseases responsible for the mortality peak of

81. Yves Blayo, "Mouvement naturel de la population française de 1740 à 1829," *Population* 30, special no. (November 1975), 52–56.

82. Jean-Pierre Goubert, *Malades et médecins en Bretagne, 1770–1790* (Paris, 1974), 329–30.

83. J. Delumeau, "Démographie d'un port français sous l'ancien régime: Saint-Malo, 1651–1750," *XVIIIe Siècle* 86–87 (1970), 15–21; for similar views and conclusions, see Goubert, *Malades*, 330–32, 349, 352.

84. Goubert, *Malades*, 215–22, 343–48, 380–82.

1740–1742. According to La Mettrie's medical writings, epidemics of typhus, typhoid, and dysentery were rife together but were apparently confined chiefly to northwestern France.[85] At Paris and the Norman towns of Caen and Bayeux, the number of burials peaked in 1740 rather than 1741 and derived mainly from respiratory epidemics and the consequences of thermal stress.[86] In Caen, an epidemic of "putrid fever" also erupted in 1740, which seems to have been typhoid fever.[87] Although the evidence of continued fever is thin, typhus epidemics were not confined to northwestern France. Typhus became epidemic in the eastern province of Lorraine during the winter of 1741–1742, when it was "rife in the royal prisons," and "carried off a large number of prisoners." Typhus deaths also occurred in locations that were remote from the prisons.[88]

Somewhat more is known about the causes of the high death rates in the central French province of Auvergne. Unemployment, vagrancy, a welfare crisis, epidemics, and a shortage of food drove up the number of burials in 1740 and 1741. A mortality wave struck the town of Thiers during the last five months of 1741 and carried over into the early winter of 1742. Sixty percent of the annual 1,214 burials fell within the three-month period from August to October 1741. In August, some 5,000 of the town's 12,000 population were reported to be ill from "putrid fevers," and of that number 1,500 had to be fed at public expense because they were also destitute. The evidence suggests that typhoid fever and malaria were the most common infections.[89]

Although France escaped widespread epidemics of continued fever and national crisis mortality, the high death rates of the early 1740s have been attributed to the direct and indirect consequences of inclement weather and grain harvest shortfalls. It has been found that the shortage of grain in the Auvergne created a pathogenic environment that favored infectious diseases, which were generalized by the increase in the number of beggars and vagrants.[90] In Brittany subsistence crises exer-

85. Julien Offray de La Mettrie, *Oeuvres de médecine* (Berlin, 1755), 269, 279–87.

86. Blayo, "Mouvement naturel," 52–56; Jean-Claude Perrot, *Genèse d'une ville moderne: Caen au XVIIIe siècle,* 2 vols. (Paris, 1975), II, 958–62; Mohamed El Kordi, *Bayeux aux XVIIe et XVIIIe siècles* (Paris, 1970), 115, 143–44, 167, 194; Michel Bricourt, Marcel Lachiver, and Denis Queruel, "La Crise de subsistance des années 1740 dans le ressort du Parlement de Paris," *Annales de Démographie Historique* (1974), 305–309.

87. Perrot, *Caen,* II, 928.

88. Jacques Baltus, *Annales de Baltus (1724–1756),* ed. Abbé E. Paulus (Metz, 1904), 108.

89. A. Poitrineau, *La Vie rurale en Basse Auvergne au XVIIIe siècle (1726–1789),* 2 vols. (Paris, 1965), 92–100; Paul Bondois, "Un Essai de culture exotique sous l'ancien régime: La 'Peste du riz' de Thiers (1741)," *Revue d'Histoire Economique et Sociale* 16 (1928), 611–30.

90. Poitrineau, *Auvergne,* I, 93–98.

cised a more decisive influence on rural than on urban death rates, owing to the poorer living conditions.[91] In Anjou eighteenth-century mortality peaks resulted neither from pure famines nor from pure epidemics. Rather, the epidemic illnesses and dearths ravaged those members of the working population who were pushed to the limit of misery.[92]

The German states, the Swiss cantons, and Italy also escaped national epidemics of continued fever and crisis mortality. The towns of southern and western Germany, however, suffered epidemics of typhus and dysentery during the years 1740–1743, diffused in part by the military activities of the War of the Austrian Succession.[93] The war notwithstanding, the Prussian provinces escaped severe epidemics of either kind. Moreover, the German mortality peak remained the lowest in western Europe, and the level of mortality declined after 1740.

Typhus fever contributed to the elevated German death rates of 1740–1741, becoming epidemic in some districts long before the war began. Typhus erupted in central Germany as early as the winter of 1737–1738, at Gosler, in Braunschweig, for example, and at Römhild, on the southern slopes of the Thuringian forest. It intensified at Römhild during the frigid winter of 1739–1740, particularly among the poorer inhabitants. According to Haeser, typhus became prevalent in Germany during 1740, even in regions untouched by war.[94] By the autumn of 1741, typhus was widespread in the central German state of Hesse-Homburg as well as in Thuringia.[95] The typhus epidemic that broke out in Silesia during the spring of 1741, however, derived more from military activities than from cold, wet weather and the shortage of food.[96]

The movement of French and Austrian troops into southwestern Germany, Bohemia, and Silesia during the last half of 1741 and in 1742 was followed by severe epidemics of typhus and dysentery. The most

91. Goubert, *Malades,* 32–33, 189–91, 314, 327–28, 332, 343.

92. François Lebrun, *Les Hommes et la mort en Anjou aux 17e et 18e siècles* (Paris, 1971), 266–70, 279, 386–87.

93. W. Jungkunz, "Die Sterblichkeit in Nürnberg, 1714–1850," *Mitteilungen des Vereins für Geschichte der Stadt Nürnberg* 42 (1951), 299–308, 312, 333–42; François G. Dreyfus, "Prix et population à Trèves et à Mayence au XVIIIe siècle," *Revue d'Histoire Economique et Sociale* 34 (1956), 246; E. François, "La Population de Coblenz au XVIIIe siècle," *Annales de Démographie Historique,* (1975), 305–15, 335–36; Haeser, *Epidemischen Krankheiten,* III, 468–79; Friedrich Prinzing, *Epidemics Resulting from Wars* (Oxford, 1916), 81; Karl Kisskalt, "Epidemiologisch-statistische Untersuchungen über die Sterblichkeit von 1600–1800," *Archiv für Hygiene und Bakteriologie* 137 (1953), 37–41.

94. Haeser, *Epidemischen Krankheiten,* III, 477.

95. J. A. F. Ozanam, *Histoire médicale générale et particulière des maladies épidémiques, contagieuses, et épizootiques,* 2d ed., 5 vols. (Paris, 1817–23), IV, 204–205.

96. Haeser, *Epidemischen Krankheiten,* III, 478.

destructive fever epidemic erupted in Prague, where reportedly 30,000 persons were carried off by typhus, many of them French soldiers. But it should be noted that "typhus and purples raged" in Prague in advance of the arrival of the French and Bavarian armies.[97] Bavaria was overrun by Austrian troops in 1742, while the French army retreated across the Rhine. During this stage of the war, epidemics of continued fever and dysentery broke out in the Bavarian towns both among the civilian population and among the military garrisons. After the battle of Dettingen in 1743, typhus and dysentery became rife in the English camps at Hanau and in the nearby villages. The British sick were transported from Germany to Flanders; more than half of the 3,000 victims died of either typhus or dysentery.[98]

The records of burials in several Bavarian towns testify to the higher death rates provoked by epidemic typhus and dysentery during the war years of 1741–1743. At Passau, near the border shared with Austria and Bohemia, the annual burials increased from 489 in 1740 to 1,014 in 1742 and to 1,195 in 1743 before falling off to 313 in 1744. Because the excess mortality of 1742 and 1743 occurred during the first four months of the year, and because such mortality involved adults rather than children, typhus was in all probability the most destructive infection.[99] A similar mortality pattern unfolded at the southwestern Bavarian town of Landsberg, which was besieged and captured by Austrian troops in 1742. The annual number of burials rose from 120 in 1740 to 142 in 1741 and peaked at 263 in 1742. Among the 263 deaths registered in 1742, "malignant fever" is noted as the cause of death in 142 cases. Because the crisis mortality occurred during the cold season, and because the number of children's deaths declined in 1742, it seems likely that the fever was typhus.[100] The town of Weiden in the Upper Palatinate suffered crisis mortality for four consecutive years, from 1740 to 1743. The death rate doubled, from 28.9 per 1,000 in 1738 to 56.6 per 1,000 in 1740, presumably as a result of dearth and thermal stress, because no epidemics are noted. From October 1742 to June 1743, the death rate peaked, reaching 69 per 1,000 the latter year. The French troops retreating from Prague brought in continued fever, typhus in all probability, which was chiefly responsible for the soaring death rate.[101]

97. Ibid.; Prinzing, *Epidemics,* 81.

98. Kisskalt, "Sterblichkeit," 37–41; Prinzing, *Epidemics,* 80–81; F. Seitz, *Der Typhus, vorzüglich nach seinem Vorkommen in Bayern geschildert* (Erlangen, 1847), 109–11; Haeser, *Epidemischen Krankheiten,* III, 479.

99. Kisskalt, "Sterblichkeit," 37–41.

100. Franz Schmölz and Therese Schmölz, "Die Sterblichkeit in Landsberg am Lech von 1585–1875," *Archiv für Hygiene und Bakteriologie* 136 (1952), 526–36.

101. D. G. Baümler, "Medizinalstatistische Untersuchungen über Weiden (Oberpfalz) von 1551 bis 1800," *Archiv für Hygiene* 120 (1938), 218, 226.

The imperial cities of Nuremberg and Augsburg also recorded crisis mortality in the early 1740s, the consequence of epidemic fever and dysentery. Dysentery was the main cause of the elevated mortality in Nuremberg during 1740 and 1741, while 118 persons died from an epidemic of "hot fever" during 1742–1743. Although it has been suggested that the epidemic was typhoid fever, neither the seasonal incidence (the first half of the year) nor the age-specific mortality (mainly mature adults) is typical of this disease.[102] The towns of western Germany shared the Bavarian morality pattern of peak burials during 1742–1743, owing in part to the passage of troops. Mainz, Koblenz, and Giessen all recorded peak mortality in 1743 as well as in 1740–1741, mostly from epidemic dysentery.[103]

The low amplitude of the German mortality peak, as I have noted, was the result of the moderate increase in Prussian death rates, particularly in the east Elbian region. Almost all Prussian provinces avoided epidemics of continued fevers and dysentery. Mortality rose sharply at Berlin during 1740–1741 and then fell off during 1742–1743, as was the case in London, Edinburgh, Dublin, Paris, and Amsterdam. The death rate increased from 40.9 per 1,000 in 1739 to 56.9 per 1,000 in 1740, or 39.1 percent, primarily as a consequence of low atmospheric temperatures and high food prices.[104] A similar demographic pattern predominated in the other Prussian locations for which annual burials are available. The Prussian mortality peak was most pronounced in the central region, which included Magdeburg and Mansfeld, Halle, and Halberstadt.[105]

In the eastern provinces, where mortality during 1740–1741 remained below the levels reached during 1736–1737, Pomerania alone registered a significant rise in the number of deaths; burials in 1741 increased 8.8 percent above the elevated number of 1740. Pomeranian public officials complained of a shortage of food and of deaths from infections traced to undernutrition, but the nature of the illness was not described.[106]

102. Jungkunz, "Nürnberg," 299–307, 312, 333, 336, 338–42; A. Schreiber, "Die Entwicklung der Augsburger Bevölkerung vom Ende des 14. Jahrhunderts bis zum Beginn des 19. Jahrhundert," *Archiv für Hygiene* 123 (1939–40), 166.

103. Dreyfus, "Trèves et Mayence," 246; François, "Coblenz," 305–15, 335–36; Arthur E. Imhof, "Die nicht-namentliche Auswertung der Kirchenbücher von Giessen und Umgebung," in Imhof, ed., *Historische Demographie als Sozialgeschichte* (Darmstadt, 1975), 120–23, 233–34.

104. Berlin, *Statistisches Jahrbuch der Stadt Berlin* 34 (1915–19), 101.

105. Johann Peter Süssmilch, *Die göttliche Ordnung in den Veränderungen des menschlichen Geschlechts*, 4th ed., 3 vols. (Berlin, 1775), I, 48–49, 85, 92–93, 100–101, 104–5, 110, 118, 121–24.

106. Acta Borussica, *Denkmäler der preussischen Staatsverwaltung im 18. Jahrhundert: Getreidehandelspolitik*, vol. II: W. Naudé, *Die Getreidehandelspolitik und Kriegsmagazinverwaltung: Brandenburg-Preussens bis 1740* (Berlin, 1901), 323; ibid., vol. III: W. Naudé and A. Skalweit, *Die Getreidehandelspolitik und Kriegsmagazinverwaltung: Preussens, 1740–1756* (Berlin, 1910), 245; Süssmilch, *Göttliche Ordnung*, I, 92–93.

The epidemics cited by writers in Prussia during 1740–1741 are difficult to identify, but the accounts do not convey the impression that such "fatal fevers" led to strikingly high death rates.[107] Johann Christian Kundman, writing in Breslau in 1741, remarked that in spite of the severe winter of 1740, epidemic diseases were not common in Silesia. He noted an increase in respiratory illnesses but no significant increase in fever. Smallpox became rife both in the city and in the countryside during the first half of 1740.[108] Friedrich Samuel Bock observed that several diseases increased in prevalence in Prussia during the spring of 1740 and that "many old and weak persons lost their lives."[109] Neither typhus nor typhoid fever became epidemic except in Silesia during 1741–1742.[110]

Nor does the evidence disclose to what extent epidemic disease provoked the relatively higher death rates in central and western Prussia. Both typhus fever and dysentery were widespread in central Germany during the early 1740s. However, harsh winters and fatal respiratory diseases were capable of inducing high death rates apart from famine fevers. In the western location of Minden, the price of cereals climbed to famine levels. The price of rye more than doubled, and the price of barley rose threefold over the average prices of 1738.[111] Burials rose to a level 68 percent above the number recorded in 1738 and remained elevated in 1741. But the evidence fails to mention epidemic diseases.

The relative absence of epidemics of continued fever and dysentery in Prussia and northern Germany in general accounts for the more moderate rise in German death rates during the years 1740–1742. It seems doubtful that the Prussian administration was simply the beneficiary of good fortune. Atmospheric temperatures fell to lower readings than in the British Isles, France, and the Low Countries. Housing standards in Prussia were not superior to those prevailing in Britain and France.[112] The harvest shortfalls in Prussia were as deficient as in many regions of northwestern Europe. Epidemics of continued fever and dysentery broke out in neighboring states but not to the same extent in Prussia.

In the Swiss cantons, epidemics of smallpox and influenza were

107. See, for example, Johann Christoph Becmann, *Historische Beschreibung der Chur und Mark Brandenburg,* ed. B. L. Bekmann, 2 vols. (Berlin, 1751–53), I, 547–48.

108. Johann Christian Kundmann, *Die Heimsuchungen Gottes in Zorn und Gnade über das Herzogthum Schlesien in Müntzen* (Leipzig, 1742), 328.

109. Friedrich Samuel Bock, *Versuch einer wirtschaftlichen Naturgeschichte von dem Königreich Ost- und Westpreussen,* 5 vols. (Dessau, 1782–85), I, 803–804.

110. Ozanam, *Maladies épidemiques,* IV, 207; Prinzing, *Epidemics,* 81.

111. Naudé, *Getreidehandelspolitik,* 323, 538.

112. Jerome Blum, *The End of the Old Order in Rural Europe* (Princeton, 1978), 179–83; François, "Coblenz," 311–15.

mainly responsible for the mortality peak of 1742. Epidemics of continued fever and dysentery smoldered each year from 1740 to 1742 but did not burst forth.[113] The availability of age-specific mortality for Geneva makes it possible to match the demographic fluctuations with epidemics. The mortality peaks of 1737 and 1742 stand out from the records. Severe smallpox epidemics erupted in both years. In 1737, smallpox accounted for 14 percent of all deaths in Geneva, while in the more severe epidemic of 1742 this infection was responsible for 23 percent of all deaths. As would be anticipated, the age category ranging from one to fourteen years exhibited the greatest increase in mortality. In 1740, by contrast, elderly and infant deaths accounted for most of the increase in mortality, as would be anticipated if thermal stress was the cause of the elevated death rate. The winter of 1742 proved equally severe in western Switzerland and brought an increase again in the mortality of infants and the elderly. In 1743, an epidemic of influenza drove up the death rates of mature and elderly adults in Geneva. Neither the demographic evidence nor the mortality trends suggest that typhus fever or dysentery contributed significantly to Geneva's elevated death rates during the years 1740–1743.[114] The town of Basel also registered high mortality during 1742–1743,[115] in all probability as a consequence of the widespread Swiss epidemics of smallpox and influenza.

The eastern Alpine cantons of Appenzell and Glarus, which were hard hit by severe winters, experienced pronounced harvest shortfalls and a dairy crisis during the years 1740–1742, in contrast to the less unfavorable agricultural outcomes in the western cantons. According to the investigations of Christian Pfister, the pasture regions (Hirtenland) of eastern and central Switzerland suffered a sharp decline in dairy production during the years 1740–1742, which contributed to the Swiss mortality peak.[116] The demographic evidence for the Innerrhoden parishes of Appenzell shows a natural decrease of the population each year from 1740 to 1742. Complete figures are available only from 1740, but they

113. E. Olivier, *Médicine et santé dans le pays de Vaud*, 2 vols. (Lausanne, 1962), II, 667–69, 1,144–50, 1,192–99, 1,227; Alfred Perrenoud, *La Population de Genève du seizième au début du dix-neuvième siècle: Etude démographique*, vol. I: *Structures et mouvements* (Paris, 1979), 456, 529; A. Burckhardt, *Demographie und Epidemiologie der Stadt Basel während der letzten drei Jahrhunderts, 1601–1900* (Basel, 1908), 16, 90, 98; Hans-Rudolf Burri, *Die Bevölkerung Luzerns im 18. und frühen 19. Jahrhundert*, (Luzern, 1975), 76–78; M. Schürmann, *Bevölkerung, Wirtschaft, und Gesellschaft in Appenzell-Innerrhoden im 18. und frühen 19. Jahrhundert* (Appenzell, 1974), 304, 319–25; S. Bucher, *Bevölkerung und Wirtschaft des Amtes Entlebuch im 18. Jahrhundert* (Luzern, 1974), 16–40, 86–91.

114. Perrenoud, *Genève*, I, 456, 529.

115. Burckhardt, *Basel*, 16, 90, 98.

116. Christian Pfister, personal communication, July 20, 1981.

indicate a noticeable increase in adult burials.[117] The Appenzell Chronicle relates that a virulent epidemic fever broke out in the autumn of 1739. The clinical description of a severe pain in the head, deep delirium, and death by the seventh day of illness points to typhus fever. During the first half of 1741, "many infections and diseases erupted" in Appenzell.[118] The Glarus Chronicle also records cases of "a dangerous spotted fever breaking out here and there."[119] The central canton of Luzern passed through crisis mortality each year from 1740 to 1743. Although the epidemic diseases have not been identified, the seasonal incidence and age-specific mortality suggest smallpox and dysentery rather than typhus fever.[120]

The mortality peak was less pronounced in Italy than in Switzerland. Italy also escaped widespread subsistence crises during the early 1740s. A recent study of Italian demographic crises found no steep national mortality peaks during the ten-year period from 1735 to 1744.[121] The elevated death rates of 1736, evident in the mortality indexes of table 1, originated chiefly in epidemics of smallpox.[122] In the first half of 1740, several northern Italian locations, including Padova, Venice, and the Tuscan province of Carrara, recorded a noticeable increase in the number of burials.[123] Northern Italy shared the low atmospheric temperatures and widespread respiratory infections of the winter and spring months of 1740 to some degree.

Epidemics of continued fever did break out in Italy during the winter of 1740–1741. Epidemics of "acute putrid fever," either typhoid or typhus fever, erupted after the floods of late 1740 and persisted for four months "until the appearance of true summer heat."[124] Epidemics of

---

117. Schürmann, *Appenzell-Innerrhoden,* 304, 319–25.

118. G. Walser, *Appenzeller-Chronik,* pt. 3 (1732–1772), ed. G. Nuesch (Trogen, 1830), 163–81.

119. Christoph Trümpi, *Neuere Glarner Chronik* (Winterthur, 1774), 557–70.

120. Burri, *Bevölkerung Luzerns,* 76–78, 180–83; Bucher, *Entlebuch,* 16–40, 86–91.

121. L. Del Panta and M. Livi Bacci, "Chronologie, intensité, et diffusion des crises de mortalité en Italie: 1600–1850," *Population* 32, special no. (September 1977), 420–25.

122. U. Tucci, "Innesto del vaiolo e società nel Settecento veneto," *Annales Cisalpines d'Histoire Sociale* 1 (1973), 206; Alfonso Corradi, *Annali delle epidemie occorse in Italia dalle prime memorie fino al 1850,* 8 vols. (Bologna, 1865–94), VIII, 170–71; P. Donazzolo and M. Saibante, "Lo sviluppo demografico di Verona e della sua provincia dalla fine del sec. XV ai nostri giorni," *Metron* 6 (1926), 80–84; Daniele Beltrami, *Storia della popolazione di Venezia dalla fine secolo XVI alla caduta della repubblica* (Padova, 1954), 112–27; Athos Belletini, *La popolazione di Bologna dal secolo XV all'unificazione italiana* (Bologna, 1961), 142.

123. Lorenzo Del Panta, "Cronologia e diffusione delle crisi di mortalità in Toscana della fine del XIV agli initi del XIX secolo," *Ricerche Storiche* 7 (1977), 325–29; Giuseppe Ferrario, *Statistica medica di Milano dal secolo XV fino ai nostri giorni,* 2 vols. (Milan, 1838–50), II, 200; Beltrami, *Venezia,* appendix, table 7.

124. Corradi, *Annali,* IV, 1,400–1,402. 1,396 [sic]. The pagination is incorrect in this edition of the work; p. 1,400 is followed by p. 1,396, etc.

typhus fever broke out in Genoa, Florence, and the duchy of Modena. According to Alfonso Corradi, the "petechial fever" in Genoa began on the galleys and then gradually spread throughout the city, attacking all age groups among the working population. The infection, however, was probably a mixed epidemic of typhus and relapsing fever, with the latter disease predominating. The described symptoms, the low case-fatality rate of 7 percent, and the absence of the typical age specificity of typhus fever support this conclusion.[125]

The death rate in Italy, as in Switzerland, peaked in 1742 and derived mainly from epidemics of influenza. Influenza proved particularly destructive in Rome, where the number of burials increased 46.6 percent between 1741 and 1743.[126] As the English press reported, "a Sort of Plague has broke out there which destroys Abundance of their People, and they call it the *Influenza*. As this Distemper has almost infected every individual, the holy Pontiffe has determined to cause a *Land Quarantine* to be proclaimed to prevent its Progress."[127] Ancona, Bologna, Verona, and Venice were also severely affected by influenza.[128] Altogether the moderate Italian mortality peak of the early 1740s originated more in "fortuitous" epidemics and less in "famine fevers" than was generally the case in western Europe.

In Scandinavia, however, epidemics of typhus fever and dysentery were primarily responsible for the mortality peaks of 1740–1743. The diseases involved in the earlier wave of epidemics that overspread Scandinavia during 1736–1737 have not been definitely identified, but the evidence suggests that smallpox was not the only major contagion. Dysentery and influenza seem to have been as common as smallpox. In any event, all writers have concluded that the wave of epidemics spread to Scandinavia from the Continent in 1736. Norway, it should be noted, escaped the epidemics and a mortality peak.[129] The wave of epidemics essentially disappeared by 1739, when the global Scandinavian death rate fell to 29.1 per 1,000. The death rate climbed to 35 per 1,000 in

125. Ibid., VIII, 171, 250; Haeser, *Epidemischen Krankheiten*, III, 477; G. Pratolongo, *Della febbri che si dicono putride, sequito da due dissertazioni delle febbri che furono epidemische, nelle citta e territorio di Genova l'anno 1741, 1742 e 1743* (Genoa, 1786–88).

126. Süssmilch, *Göttliche Ordnung*, I, tables, p. 15.

127. *Gentleman's Magazine* 13 (1743), 206.

128. Corradi, *Annali*, VIII, 171; Donazzolo and Saibante, "Verona," 82–86; Beltrami, *Venezia*, appendix, table 7.

129. Arthur E. Imhof and B. I. Lindskog, "Les Causes de mortalité en Suède et en Finlande entre 1749 et 1773," *Annales: Economies, Sociétés, Civilisations* 29 (September–October 1974), 916; Gustaf Utterström, "Some Population Problems in Pre-industrial Sweden," *Scandinavian Economic History Review* 2 (1954), 121–26; Jutikkala, *Bevölkerung Finnlands*, 28–35.

1740, but epidemic diseases were widespread only in Finland, where the death rate soared to 52 per 1,000.[130]

A new wave of epidemic diseases became generalized in Scandinavia during 1741 and were far more lethal than the earlier wave of 1736–1737. The combination of thermal stress, food shortage, and the demands of war promoted the spread of infectious diseases. The war between Sweden-Finland and Russia broke out on July 28, 1741, and thus influenced the Scandinavian death rates more in 1742 than in 1741.[131]

The European wars, however, had little or no influence on Norwegian death rates. Mortality in Norway was driven up by an epidemic of typhus fever in the autumn of 1741. Pehr Hamnerin, medical officer for the neighboring Swedish county of Värmland, characterized the fever as "quite as infectious and fatal as the plague itself."[132] The Norwegian death rate reached a peak of 52.2 per 1,000 in 1742, as epidemics of typhus fever, dysentery, smallpox, and also hunger contributed to the mortality wave.[133]

The global Scandinavian death rate also reached a peak in the year 1742, when it climbed to 40.7 per 1,000. The war between Sweden-Finland and Russia was in part responsible for the increase of mortality but more in Finland than in Sweden and hardly at all in Denmark-Norway. The fact that camps and ships were concentrated in Finland led to the diffusion of infectious diseases from military personnel to the civilian population. Although no battles were fought in the Swedish counties, the marshaling and passing of troops, together with naval vessels returning to Swedish ports, disseminated the reigning epidemics of continued fever and dysentery.[134]

At the same time the regional distribution of the increase of mortality in Sweden requires a more complex explanation for the epidemics than merely wartime conditions, as Gustaf Utterström has pointed out. In 1742, the national excess of deaths over births amounted to 9,601 exclusive of Stockholm. The excess mortality in the three contiguous southwestern counties of Värmland, Älvsborg, and Skaraborg alone accounted for 93.6 percent of the national population decrease, even

130. Imhof, *Bevölkerungsentwicklung in den nordischen Ländern*, 623–40; Utterström, "Population Problems," 126–27; Jutikkala, *Bevölkerung Finnlands*, 36–37.

131. Imhof and Lindskog, "Mortalité en Suède," 916; Utterström, "Population Problems," 127–28; Imhof, *Bevölkerungsentwicklung in den nordischen Ländern*, 641–45; Jutikkala, *Bevölkerung Finnlands*, 39.

132. Utterström, "Population Problems," 130–31.

133. Michael Drake, *Population and Society in Norway, 1735–1865* (Cambridge, 1969), 52.

134. Jutikkala, *Bevölkerung Finnlands*, 39–40; Imhof, *Bevölkerungsentwicklung in den nordischen Ländern*, 645–49.

though they contained only 18.5 percent of the Swedish population.[135] The three southwestern counties are located along or near the border of the Norwegian diocese of Akershus and thus distant from the military activities of the Russian war.

The population of southwestern Sweden had become destitute as a consequence of the succession of abnormal seasons, deficient harvests, and the loss of farm animals during the years from 1740 to 1742. According to the medical officer Pehr Hamnerin, a long succession of crop failures had "pauperized" the working population "almost to a man." The mortality crises in the southwestern counties resulted primarily from epidemics of typhus fever and dysentery. The Värmland death rate leaped to a startling 121.6 per 1,000 in 1742; that is, 12 percent of the population died in a single year.[136]

Typhus began to ravage the border between Värmland and Akershus in February 1742. Hamnerin claimed that the "spotted fever" was brought into the poor Swedish district of Finnmark from Norway, where typhus had been epidemic since the end of 1741. Travelers between the two countries were believed to have introduced the infection into Värmland. Within the Finnmark, typhus was spread by beggars who passed from croft to croft. Swedish Finns who made coffins for the dead in the Norwegian crofts also disseminated the spotted fever, as did the Swedes who crossed the border to claim inheritances from relatives in Akershus.[137] This sequence of economic and social events discloses one of the pathways by which typhus fever spread in the wake of preindustrial subsistence crises.

Typhus fever became common in the other counties of southwestern Sweden but not to the same degree as in Värmland.[138] Värmland and the neighboring counties also suffered an epidemic of "hot fever," whose identification remains unclear. The infection broke out in the spring of 1742, intensified during the autumn months, and continued into 1743. The epidemic has been traced to the return of ill seamen to the inland port of Karlsbad. But Hamnerin believed that the infection had been brought to Karlsbad from the western districts of the county by persons coming to buy provisions. Some half of the county's population was thought to be ill with the "hot fever" at the beginning of 1743. Hamnerin's report stressed that the hot fever was far less fatal and virulent than the spotted

135. Utterström, "Population Problems," 128.
136. Quoted in ibid., 129; Imhof, *Bevölkerungsentwicklung in den nordischen Ländern,* 652.
137. Utterström, "Population Problems," 130–31.
138. Ibid., 131.

fever.[139] Copenhagen also suffered an epidemic of "hot fever" at the end of 1741.[140]

The Dysentery Epidemics

Bacillary dysentery was the other major killer responsible for the mortality peak of 1740–1742 and in some regions proved more lethal than typhus, particularly in the southern Netherlands. Dysentery was called the "country disease" in the eighteenth century. As I have already noted, bacillary dysentery (shigellosis), like typhoid fever, is communicated from person to person by direct or indirect fecal-oral transmission. Although susceptibility to dysentery is general, the disease is more severe in children than in adults. However, the elderly, the debilitated, and persons of all ages suffering from nutritional deficiencies also exhibit higher case-fatality rates.

The case-fatality rate of bacillary dysentery can be markedly higher than that of typhoid fever and, as in the case of typhus, may approximate 20 to 30 percent. The dysentery epidemics of 1740–1742 were often attributed to the practice of eating unsuitable foods. It is true that carrion animals, improperly cooked starchy foods, and raw fruits and vegetables can be a source of infection. Moreover, the intestinal upsets that result from eating unwholesome foods predispose a more virulent case of dysentery, and any exhausting disease that accompanies shigellosis can increase its fatality rate.[141] But epidemics of virulent dysentery could erupt in mid-eighteenth-century Europe quite apart from the consumption of unwholesome food.

The mortality crisis that stemmed principally from a murderous epidemic of dysentery in the countryside of the Austrian Netherlands in the last half of 1741 illustrates the epidemiology of the infection. According to Claude Bruneel, the "demographic event" of eighteenth-century Brabant occurred in the autumn of 1741, when crisis mortality evoked the "terrors of yesterday." If the eighteenth-century Brabançons were no longer carried off by famine, they were still preyed upon by dearth. For Bruneel, the dysentery epidemics and elevated death rates were essentially the consequence of prolonged undernutrition.[142] The

139. Ibid., 129. The port of Karlsbad is located on Lake Vänern, which is Sweden's largest lake (87 miles long, 50 miles wide); the lake is drained by the Gota River to the Kattegat.
140. *London Advertiser,* October 21, 1741.
141. Benenson, *Communicable Diseases,* 285–88, 349–53; Murchison, *Continued Fevers,* 409–19; Savitt, *Medicine and Slavery,* 58–63; MacArthur, "Medical History," 268–86.
142. Bruneel, *Mortalité,* 212–16.

epidemics were not limited to Brabant; all provinces of the Austrian Netherlands as well as the principality of Liège were struck in 1741.[143] A notation in the parish register of Villers-Perwin, in Hainaut, states that "dysentery raged universally; there were locations in Flanders and France where an immense number of deaths occurred."[144] The majority of the villages in the province of Hainaut passed through mortality crises caused by epidemic dysentery. The number of burials peaked during September, October, and November, the season when dysentery is normally most rife. At Familleureux, for example, it is necessary to go back to 1693 in the parish registers to find more burials than in 1741. At Uccle, it is necessary to be back to the plague epidemic of 1668.[145]

Dysentery became universally epidemic in the southern Netherlands after the warm and dry summer of 1741. The epidemics died down with the arrival of low atmospheric temperatures in December but did not disappear.[146] At Louvain, where parish burials with age specification are available, the figures indicate that dysentery continued to exact a heavy toll in 1742 and even as late as the summer of 1743.[147] For the most part, however, the lethal dysentery epidemics that visited the Brabant towns and villages were concentrated in the year 1741.[148] In the rural parish registers sampled by Bruneel, the number of burials in 1741 increased threefold above the already elevated mortality of 1740 and then declined in 1742 to the same level as in 1740.[149]

Bruneel found that dysentery was the most common fatal infection of the Brabant countryside in the eighteenth century. The droughtlike summer of 1741 established the preconditions for epidemic dysentery. The majority of the population had to quench its thirst from the muddy water that remained at the bottom of the wells, water trenches, and rivers, no matter how unsafe for drinking. The very poor were also forced to make their daily fare from unwholesome foods when the prices of cereals reached inaccessible heights, as it did in 1740 and 1741. After

143. Louis Torfs, *Fastes des calamités publiques survenues dans les Pays-Bas,* 2 vols. (Paris and Tournai, 1859–62), I, 102; Bernier, "Hainaut," 568; Maurice-A. Arnould, "Mortalité et épidemies sous l'Ancien Régime dans le Hainaut et quelques régions limitrophes," in Paul Harsin and Etienne Hélin, eds., *Problèmes de mortalité* (Liège, 1963), 479–80; Scheppere, *Fièvre maligne,* 3–8; Hélin, *Population,* 172, 177; Gutmann, *War and Rural Life,* 154, 159.

144. Bernier, "Hainaut," 568.

145. Arnould, "Mortalité," 479–80.

146. Bruneel, *Mortalité,* 281–82.

147. G. van Houtte, *Leuven in 1740, ein krisisjaar* (Brussels, 1964), 201–203.

148. Van Assche–Van Cauwenbergh, "Deux Villages," 33; De Brouwer, "De demografische evolutie in de meierij Erembodegem en de heerlijkheld Oordegem gedurende de XVIIe en XVIIIe eeuw," in *Cinq Études,* 86, 98–115.

149. Bruneel, *Mortalité,* 638–41, 644, 649–62, 663–70; some parish registers include the burials of both children and adults, others only adults.

two years of physiological stress, the poor working population of the southern Netherlands was probably less able to resist the shock of severe gastrointestinal disease. The development of dysentery appears to be favored by stress, excess fatigue, and nutritional deficiency.[150] The diffusion of dysentery was abetted by the widespread begging, vagrancy, and rioting that occurred in the southern Netherlands during 1740 and 1741.[151]

Rural housing conditions, sanitary practices, and standards of personal cleanliness also predisposed the population to endemic dysentery in eighteenth-century Europe, particularly in the less-developed regions. Large families lived in small huts, which were shared with animals and were not noted for cleanliness under the best of conditions. The daily life of tenants and subtenants in Highland Scotland, for example, explains in part the dysentery epidemics of 1740–1741.

An English sojourner in Highland Scotland has left a firsthand account of sanitary practices that explains why dysentery could become so explosive during years of distress, such as 1741. "The young children of the ordinary Highlanders are miserable objects indeed, and are mostly overrun with that distemper [diarrhea] which some of the old men are hardly ever freed of from their infancy. I have often seen them come out of their huts early in a cold morning, stark naked, and squat themselves down (if I might decently use the comparison) like dogs on a dunghill."[152]

Exposure to dysentery was heightened by the ubiquitous dunghill located close to the cottage door. Whether children used the area as a latrine or, as was common custom in the countryside, the fecal evacuations of persons healthy and sick were thrown on the dunghill, the putrefying matter passed through the soil and saturated the land with the bacteria that cause dysentery. The mucus that contaminated the soil would sooner or later be brought back inside the house to infect others. The bacteria in waste water could also seep into the drinking water. Moreover, the young children who played in the area surrounding peasant cottages could not avoid ingesting the pathogenic microorganisms by the hand-to-mouth method. Accordingly, by one mode or another, the bacteria became diffused, and dysentery was permanently endemic in much of eighteenth-century rural Europe.[153]

150. Ibid.
151. For the extensive social turbulence in the southern Netherlands during 1740–1741, see Houtte, *Leuven,* 112–46, 246–47; Etienne Hélin, "La Disette et le recensement de 1740," *Annales d'Histoire Liègeoise* 6 (1959), 443–61; Bruneel, *Mortalité,* 276–78.
152. T. Burtt, *Letters from a Gentleman in the North of Scotland,* 2 vols. (London, 1749), II, 180, quoted in T. C. Smout, *A History of the Scottish People, 1560–1830* (Glasgow, 1969), 317.
153. For a discussion of the sanitary and hygiene conditions that facilitated epidemics of

For endemic rural dysentery to evolve into national epidemics in the course of preindustrial subsistence crises depended in part on the scale of vagrancy and migration, which in turn was influenced by the relative availability of welfare resources in rural districts. Because rural housing conditions were on balance less primitive in England than in Scotland, and because vagrancy remained on a smaller scale, epidemic dysentery claimed relatively fewer lives in the course of the English dearth. Although the evidence indicates that the incidence of dysentery climbed significantly in England during 1740–1742, it remained a less critical health problem than elsewhere in the British Isles.[154]

In Scotland, the more pressing food shortage and the less effective poor-law system resulted in a greater exodus from rural districts, particularly from the Highlands. Edinburgh's rising number of deaths from dysentery, a tenfold increase from 1740 to 1741,[155] reflected the influx of Highland shearers and similarly destitute rural persons. Large numbers of Highland shearers came down early to the Edinburgh region in the summer of 1741, many in a starving condition; some died soon after arrival.[156] Numerous poor people were reduced to begging, among whom "numbers flock'd in from the country."[157] Those who were incubating gastrointestinal infections contributed to the dissemination of dysentery. We need not speculate on the standards of personal cleanliness maintained by the majority of beggars and vagrants who drifted in from the rural hinterland or migrated from the Highlands. Quantitative evidence as to the prevalence of dysentery in the Highlands is scarce for the 1740s. The minister of Durness, however, saw dysentery as the most widespread threat to life in 1741. On June 13, he noted that a "pestilential Flux . . . dispatches many off in a few Days!" By August, some forty persons on one side of his parish—nearly 10 percent of the population— had died of dysentery.[158]

In northern France also, rural housing conditions and sanitary practices predisposed the population to dysentery in 1741 and 1742. Dysentery became widespread in Brittany as early as 1738. The exceptional

---

bacillary dysentery and typhoid fever among the rural population of eighteenth-century Europe, see Bruneel, *Mortalité*, 519–24; Olwen H. Hufton, *The Poor of Eighteenth-Century France, 1750–1789* (Oxford, 1974), 48–51.

154. For examples, see Huxham, *Observations*, II, 77, 83, 84, 93, 98, 104; Short, *Chronological History*, 263, 287; *Gentleman's Magazine* 10–12 (1740–42); Wrigley and Schofield, *Population*, 669–70.

155. *Scots Magazine*, 1741, 144, 432, 476.

156. Flinn et al., *Scottish Population History*, 219–20; *Caledonian Mercury*, August 18 and August 24, 1741.

157. *Scots Magazine*, January 1741, 45.

158. Mackay, "Minister's Diary," 572–73.

mortality among children in a severe autumn epidemic in 1740 suggests dysentery.[159] Goubert concluded that the rural housing conditions in Brittany guaranteed endemic dysentery, which then became epidemic during food shortages. La Mettrie wrote that the dysentery infection was especially malignant in 1741 and that this disease "depopulated" the province of Brittany, accounting for more than 30,000 deaths in that one year. He attributed the lower case-fatality rates of the urban population to better living conditions. La Mettrie traced the dysentery epidemics to the succession of severe winters and dry summers.[160]

In Anjou likewise, dysentery was the most serious infection from which the population suffered, particularly in the districts of chronic misery. The development of bacillary dysentery was favored by the peasant farmyards, made dangerous by the dunghill located at the center, by the fact that peasant families commonly had but one bed at their disposal, and by chronic undernutrition, which was worsened by the food shortages and high cereal prices of 1740–1742. All of these conditions combined to intensify the virulence of the infection. In 1742, a summer epidemic in Anjou killed mainly young children and drove death rates nearly as high as in 1740. Although neither medical reports nor clerical notations disclose the nature of the infection, the seasonal incidence, the age-specific mortality, and the prevailing epidemic in neighboring Brittany suggest dysentery.[161]

The dysentery epidemics in Ireland proved as lethal on a national scale as in the Austrian Netherlands. In 1740, dysentery preceded rather than followed the fever epidemics in regions struck by famine.[162] Rutty noticed a rise in the incidence of dysentery as early as October 1739. The more dramatic increase in morbidity, however, did not take place until July 1740 and then began to explode in the autumn months.[163] The first press reference to the "bloody flux" appeared in February 1740, when it was reported that several poor prisoners in a debtor's jail were stricken with dysentery as a consequence of eating rotten potatoes.[164]

The evidence does not permit estimates as to the relative number of deaths from dysentery and fever in the Irish mortality crisis. Bishop Berkeley's letters written in Munster indicate that dysentery more than fever was responsible for the high death rates during the winter of

159. Delumeau, "Saint-Malo," 15–21.
160. Goubert, *Malades,* 215–22, 343–48, 380–82; La Mettrie, *Oeuvres de médecine,* 269, 279–87.
161. Lebrun, *Anjou,* 266–70, 279, 386–87, 509.
162. MacArthur, "Medical History," 264–65, 286.
163. Rutty, *Chronological History,* 77, 81.
164. Drake, "Demographic Crisis," 116; *Faulkner's Dublin Journal,* February 9–12, 1740.

1740–1741. The resident physician Maurice O'Connell came to the same conclusion.[165] Berkeley, writing from Cloyne in February, recounted that "the bloody flux has increased in this neighborhood, and rages most violently in other parts of this and adjacent counties." In May he conveyed an impression of the impending disaster: "The distresses of the sick and poor are endless. The havoc of mankind in the counties of Cork, Limerick, and some adjacent places, hath been incredible." Entire villages became depopulated from disease and flight.[166] Dysentery also became rife in the county of Galway during the winter months.[167]

Bacillary dysentery has always been attendant on famine in Ireland, where the infection has been known since ancient times. In Ireland as well the widespread and fatal dysentery of 1740–1741 was commonly traced to the practice of eating carrion horses and dogs, or nettles and docks, and to starvation, but the infection would not of course have broken out unless the specific pathogenic microorganisms had been present. As I have noted, numerous inapparent cases of bacillary dysentery were always common in eighteenth-century rural Ireland and western Europe.[168]

Because the infection is so easily spread by contaminated fingers, water, and flies as well as by food, and because the infectious nature of dysentery was not understood and thus no precautions were taken, the disease could become epidemic in the absence of such social crises as famine and war. During times of hunger, however, when standards of cleanliness and sanitation deteriorated and the risk of eating contaminated foods expanded, and when thousands deserted their homes and villages in search of subsistence, the possibilities of extending dysentery were multiplied. Moreover, food and water became more easily contaminated under the drought conditions that predominated in 1740 and 1741, and the bacteria that cause dysentery can be carried through the atmosphere in particles of dust.[169]

Both dysentery and the louse-borne fevers were almost certain to be diffused in Ireland by the enormous number of itinerant vagrants searching for food and employment during 1740–1741. The author of *The*

165. George Berkeley, *The Works of George Berkeley, Bishop of Cloyne*, ed. A. A. Luce and T. E. Jessop, 9 vols. (London, 1956), VIII, 248–49; Creighton, *Epidemics in Britain*, II, 241–42.

166. Berkeley, *Works*, VIII, 248–55.

167. *Faulkner's Dublin Journal*, March 24–28 and April 28–May 2, 1741; Drake, "Demographic Crisis," 117.

168. For a discussion of epidemic dysentery in Ireland, see MacArthur, "Medical History," 268–86; for a discussion of endemic dysentery in the rural Low Countries, see Bruneel, *Mortalité*, 519–23.

169. Drake, "Demographic Crisis," 217; Creighton, *Epidemics in Britain*, II, 242.

Groans of Ireland described "roads spread with dead and dying bodies."[170] In a similar vein, Publicola wrote that "multitudes have perished, and are daily perishing under hedges and ditches."[171] Triptolemus painted the same grim picture of the Irish countryside, claiming that the dead in the fields were being eaten by dogs.[172] The hungry and destitute who failed to reach urban destinations also contributed to the spread of infectious disease. Both dysentery and typhus fever were carried from infected districts to locations that had been previously free of the diseases, which were also transmitted from the poor to the remaining population by the hoards of starving cottars in search of food. The destitute migrants hoped to reach towns where relief installations were set up, and when successful they swarmed into the poorer sections. Wherever they went, they served as networks for the dissemination of infectious diseases.[173]

Epidemic dysentery also preceded or accompanied the typhus epidemics in the southwestern German towns, more as a consequence of garrisoned armies than of massive vagrancy. Epidemic dysentery at the same time had been observed in Thuringia as early as 1739 and was reported as "raging epidemically" In Würzburg in 1741.[174] A lethal epidemic of dysentery erupted in the imperial city of Nuremberg in August 1740. This infection accounted for half of the deaths registered from August through October. Epidemics of dysentery, typhus, typhoid, and smallpox were rife in Nuremberg each year from 1740 to 1743, products of the extreme weather events, the subsistence crisis, and the passage of troops in 1741 and 1742.[175]

The elevated German death rates of 1742–1743 in the southwestern urban locations were primarily the result of epidemics provoked by military activities. The imperial city of Augsburg and the town of Weiden, in the Upper Palatinate, registered more deaths in 1742–1743 than in 1740–1741. Troops were billeted in Weiden beginning in 1741. From October 1742 to June 1743, the town's death rates peaked among all age groups.[176] The urban locations of western Germany shared the Bavarian mortality trends. Dysentery became rife throughout the Rhineland in the early 1740s. A severe dysentery epidemic, triggered by the

170. Quoted in Drake, "Demographic Crisis," 103.
171. Ibid.
172. Ibid., 104.
173. Ibid., 116; Dickson, "Famine in Ireland," 12; MacArthur, "Medical History," 272.
174. Johann Philipp Wolff, *Consilium Medicum, welches über die dermahlen hier und dar anfangend und epidemicé grassirende Ruhr-Krankheit gestellet und mit getheilet hat* (Schweinfurth, 1743), 3; Haeser, *Epidemischen Krankheiten*, III, 478.
175. Jungkunz, "Nürnberg," 299–307, 312, 333, 336, 338–42.
176. Baümler, "Weiden," 218, 226; Schreiber, "Augsburger Bevölkerung," 166.

passage of troops, touched off a mortality crisis at Koblenz in 1743.[177]

Dysentery became epidemic in several Swiss towns and districts during the early 1740s. At Basel, in northwestern Switzerland, the mortality peak of 1740 derived from an epidemic of dysentery.[178] During October 1741 the Entlebuch district of Luzern was struck by a mortality wave that was probably caused by dysentery.[179] In Appenzell, which suffered from anomalous weather, dysentery became "dreadfully rife in all locations" after the warm and dry summer of 1741, and "carried off many persons."[180] The Glarus Chronicle also records a severe epidemic of dysentery in 1741, following the subsistence crisis.[181] Except for the dearth-stricken eastern alpine cantons and a few other locations, however, Switzerland was spared widespread epidemics of dysentery and typhus. Italy also escaped a significant food shortage and extensive epidemics of dysentery.[182]

In Scandinavia as in Ireland, the mortality crises originated in epidemics of dysentery and typhus fever. Dysentery had become epidemic in Scandinavia during 1736–1737, and subsequently its incidence was determined by meteorological, social, and military events. Epidemics of dysentery continued to occur in the counties of Sweden and Finland during 1738 but substantially disappeared in 1739.[183] Dysentery became common again in Finland at the end of 1739, and then, as in Ireland, marched in step with epidemic typhus.[184]

The Norwegian mortality crises of 1741 and 1742 were punctuated by epidemics of dysentery as well as of typhus, but it is not possible to estimate their relative demographic significance.[185] In the Danish half of the kingdom, dysentery became epidemic on the island diocese of Seeland and in Copenhagen during the autumn of 1741. In Copenhagen, "Bloody Flux" was the most "fatal Distemper," with "double the Number of People dying to what has been known in the Memory."[186]

177. François, "Coblenz," 305–15, 335–36; Dreyfus, "Trèves et Mayence," 246.

178. Burckhardt, *Basel*, 16, 90, 98.

179. Bucher, *Entlebuch*, 16–40, 86–91.

180. Walser, *Appenzeller-Chronik*, 163–81.

181. Trümpi, *Neuere Glarner Chronik*, 557–70.

182. Corradi, *Annali*, VIII, 170–71; Del Panta and Livi Bacci, "Crises de mortalité," 420–25; Del Panta, "Toscana," 325–29.

183. Imhof, *Bevölkerungsentwicklung in den nordischen Ländern*, 623–36; Utterström, "Population Problems," 121–27; Jutikkala, *Bevölkerung Finnlands*, 28–37; Imhof and Lindskog, "Mortalité en Suede," 916.

184. Jutikkala, *Bevölkerung Finnlands*, 38–39; Imhof, *Bevölkerungsentwicklung in den nordischen Ländern*, 645.

185. Imhof, *Bevölkerungsentwicklung in den nordischen Ländern*, 641; Drake, *Norway*, 52, 71; Utterström, "Population Problems," 130–31.

186. *London Advertiser*, October 21, 1741.

Both Copenhagen and Seeland recorded elevated death rates in 1741, 40.9 and 38.0 per 1,000, respectively.[187] The level of mortality, however, remained below Norway's national death rate. The Finnish mortality crisis of 1742 also derived in part from widespread epidemics of dysentery.[188]

Epidemic dysentery became rampant in Sweden during 1741–1742. The severe crisis mortality in the southwestern counties of Värmland, Älvsborg, and Skaraborg was in part a consequence of widespread dysentery. According to Hamnerin, the long succession of crop failures had forced the population of Värmland to eat foodstuffs unfit for human consumption, which had lowered their resistance to infection and had also depressed their will to live. In explaining the explosion of dysentery, he cited the consumption of unwholesome foods, unripe and spoiled grains, the prolonged hunger, putrid water, and the fact of infectious contact from person to person. Hamnerin cautioned that the epidemics of dysentery could not be expected to abate in southwestern Sweden until the peasantry obtained sound grain in adequate quantities.[189]

During the first half of 1743, epidemics of dysentery, typhus, typhoid, and malaria continued to erupt in Sweden and Finland, with dysentery remaining epidemic the entire year.[190] The persistence of high death rates in Sweden into 1743 is explained mainly by the continuing dissemination of dysentery and louse-borne fevers from military personnel to the civilian population.[191] The preconditions for the epidemics among the population had been put in place, however, by three consecutive years of anomalous weather, food shortage, and high unemployment rates.

Gustav Utterström has written that "without the outbreak of dysentery and the other contagious diseases in 1736 and without the war with Russia in 1741–1743, the mortality curve for Sweden-Finland would almost certainly have had a very different appearance." He added that the rise in the death rate did not result solely from crop failures and the camp fevers spread by the military; waves of epidemics also "passed over Sweden from infected Europe, both from the east and the west."[192]

These conclusions may be essentially valid, but they can be somewhat off the mark when one is attempting to discover the full range of

187. Imhof, *Bevölkerungsentwicklung in den nordischen Ländern*, 176.

188. Jutikkala, *Bevölkerung Finnlands*, 39–40; Imhof, *Bevölkerungsentwicklung in den nordischen Ländern*, 645–49.

189. Utterström, "Population Problems," 129–30; Imhof, *Bevölkerungsentwicklung in den nordischen Ländern*, 652–53.

190. Imhof, *Bevölkerungsentwicklung in den nordischen Ländern*, 657–60; Jutikkala, *Bevölkerung Finnlands*, 41.

191. Utterström, "Population Problems," 121–22, 131.

192. Ibid., 127, 131–32.

pathways and networks that diffused infectious diseases in preindustrial Europe. Although it appears that Sweden incurred high death rates during the years 1740–1743 from infections that were primarily "imported" or spawned by military operations, the comparative European epidemiological and demographic trends do not support this conclusion. Utterström's explanation will not account for either the extended and severe mortality crises in Norway and Ireland or the absence of crisis mortality in Prussia. Both Norway and Ireland were spared the risks of camp fever in the early 1740s and the dysentery epidemics of the late 1730s, whereas Prussia was exposed to the earlier epidemics and also became a theater of war in 1740–1741.

Conclusions

The evidence shows that the western European mortality peak of 1740–1742 coincided with a period of climatic variability. In the course of 1740, the level of mortality climbed in all regions of western Europe. The most pronounced increase in death rates occurred in Finland, the location most exposed to the shocks of the continental climatic regime that set in at the end of 1739. The death rates in the remaining Scandinavian countries, however, did not rise significantly higher in 1740 than those registered in the more environmentally sheltered locations of England and France. Weather-related harvest shortfalls, elevated cereal prices, and a rising incidence of dysentery and louse-borne fevers paralleled the mortality wave of 1740–1742 throughout western Europe. But there was no marked and invariable correspondence between the amplitude of the national mortality peaks and the magnitude of increases in national grain prices.

The evidence indicates that success in buffering the potential economic and social consequences engendered by climatic stress and food shortage influenced the national demographic outcomes more decisively than the relative increase in the price of cereals. At the same time, the fact of a more advanced stage of economic development did not ensure a more moderate rise in mortality. Although the ability of public administrations to dampen the rise of food prices minimized the danger of death from hunger and starvation, this remedial measure by itself did not necessarily eliminate widespread epidemics.

The epidemics of continued fever and dysentery were promoted to some degree by climatic variability distinct from the shortage of food. Two separate functional relationships connect the extreme weather events to the major epidemics that swept over western Europe during the years 1740–1742. The potential impact of climatic variability on human health can be summed up in the following model-like statement.

Pronounced climatic variability produces a first-order effect on the biological processes of plant growth, the survival of animals, and the activity of disease vectors and pathogens. Extreme weather events can also have a more direct impact on human health, particularly in view of the housing conditions and the behavioral practices common in preindustrial societies. In eighteenth-century Europe, severe and protracted cold seasons inevitably lengthened the period of time that the working population spent in close indoor personal contact. Because the living quarters of the majority of Europe's working population were small and poorly ventilated, and the common standards of personal hygiene were marginal, the risks of contracting respiratory and louse-borne diseases were intensified by extended cold seasons. During the warm seasons, on the other hand, extended periods of drought fostered the diffusion of the bacteria that cause dysentery and typhoid fever.

The straightforward biological effect of climate on plants and animals can touch off second-order economic effects, such as an increase or decrease in the supply of cereals, which in preindustrial Europe not only governed the price of food but also largely determined the levels of economic activity and employment. In the event of a significant decline in cereal output, the economic fluctuation frequently triggered a series of third-order social effects. The volume of grain harvested influenced the scale of such social phenomena as vagrancy, mendicancy, migration, popular disturbances, and crime, as well as the nutritional status of the working population.

Climatic variability in the eighteenth century could also lead to a prolonged period of undernutrition and a worsening of the nutritional status of the working poor and large number of paupers. The critical question to be answered is the extent to which the western European epidemics of 1740–1742 originated in the biological effects of undernutrition or malnutrition, as distinct from the role played by climatic stress and social disarray. The conclusion of medical research that nutritional deficiency reduces human resistance to infection is virtually unquestioned. It has been demonstrated that nutritional modulation of immunity can be an important determinant of mortality in a variety of infections, particularly in the case of children.[193] Even though the interaction of

193. Nevin S. Scrimshaw, Carl E. Taylor, and John E. Gordon, *Interactions of Nutrition and Infection* (Geneva, 1968) (see especially the tables on 61–63 and 69–75); David Morley, "Severe Measles," in Neville F. Stanley and R. A. Joske, eds., *Changing Disease Patterns and*

malnutrition and infectious disease is now "well established as synergistic,"[194] the question remains as to the degree to which nutritional deficiency provokes the epidemic diseases observed during such famines and severe food shortages as those of the early 1740s. Clinical evidence indicates that nutritional stress does not influence all common infections equally, and that its influence on several diseases prevalent in famines is seemingly nil. It must be recognized, however, that it is always difficult to determine the causal relationship between nutritional status and infection when, as in preindustrial Europe, human living conditions also involve a pronounced deficiency in housing amenities, in personal hygiene, and in environmental sanitation.[195]

A number of recent medical writers have questioned the finding that undernutrition necessarily leads to increases in the severity or frequency of infections. Ann G. Carmichael has called attention to the fact that the "physiological and microbiological aspects of synergism" have not yet been demonstrated in controlled laboratory studies. Biologists point out, moreover, that the human immune system fails only when nutritional stress is severe. Apparently it is not chronic undernutrition but starvation that "precipitates the fatal interaction between infection and undernutrition, and then only in the final stages of illness."[196] John and Anne Murray, drawing on personal observations made in the African famines of the mid-1970s, have generated doubts that malnutrition inevitably aggravates infection. They encountered examples of "grossly malnourished small children who, though heavily exposed to measles, infectious hepatitis, and poliomyelitis, either failed to develop the disease or had it in a surprisingly mild form." They also encountered clinical instances of increased resistance to infection in some cases of undernutrition, a relationship that, they hypothesized, may result from specific nutritional deficiencies that impede the virulence of microorganisms directly or stimulate human immune function, or perhaps both.[197]

The evidence linking malnutrition and mortality from epidemic disease thus is neither conclusive nor unambiguous. The best evidence that

Human Behavior (New York, 1980), 115–28; R. K. Chandra and P. M. Newberne, *Nutrition, Immunity, and Infection* (New York, 1977), 1–6, 41–42.

194. John Gordon, "Epidemiological Insights on Malnutrition: Some Resurrected, Others Restructured, a Few Retired," *American Journal of Clinical Nutrition* 31 (1978), 2,339.

195. For discussion of the fact that malnutrition and high rates of infectious disease invariably occur together in poor communities, see ibid., 2,343–45; and Sidney L. Kark, *Epidemiology and Community Medicine* (New York, 1974), 249.

196. Ann Carmichael, "Infection, Hidden Hunger, and History," *Journal of Interdisciplinary History* 14 (1983), 250–51.

197. John Murray and Anne Murray, "Suppression of Infection by Famine and Its Activation by Refeeding—A Paradox?" *Perspectives in Biology and Medicine* 20 (1977), 475–78.

272   Food Shortage and Epidemic Disease

supports the view that malnourished individuals are more likely to die from infectious diseases derives from studies of present-day populations in poor, underdeveloped societies. These investigations have been criticized, however, on the grounds that the groups studied were too small to permit statistically significant estimates of the effect of malnutrition. Even in those studies in which the experimental and control groups could be matched, it has been noted that differences remained in social variables that are known to affect mortality. Such criticisms notwithstanding, the results of the studies of underdeveloped societies provide evidence that malnutrition and mortality are linked in twentieth-century populations suffering from chronic malnutrition. The investigations have focused, however, principally on children and not on adults. There may also be the methodological question as to the extent to which findings made in contemporary developing countries can be carried into the European past. It is possible to discover significant environmental, behavioral, and cultural differences between present-day underdeveloped societies and preindustrial European societies, and they may affect any interpretation of the relationship of famine and disease.[198]

The methodological problem in assessing the influence of nutritional deficiency on epidemic mortality under famine conditions is readily apparent. Carl E. Taylor, physician and epidemiologist, doubts that we can ever resolve the question of the apparent synergism between undernutrition and epidemics.[199] General agreement does exist, however, that not all common infections are influenced by nutritional status to the same degree. This accepted medical finding provides a methodological starting point. On the basis of clinical evidence, it has been found that some infections are so virulent that they produce disease regardless of human difference in resistance. Such lethal diseases as plague, influenza, smallpox, and cholera, for example, have produced mortality crises throughout the course of history, without necessarily preying on malnourished populations.[200] The outcomes of other diseases—typhoid fever, malaria, typhus—have been found to be only slightly, if at all, related to nutritional status. By contrast, tuberculosis, diarrheal diseases, measles, pertussis, and some respiratory diseases are numbered among the common infections believed to be definitely influenced by nutritional status.[201]

198. Susan Cotts Watkins and Etienne van de Walle, "Nutrition, Mortality, and Population Size: Malthus' Court of Last of Last Resort," *Journal of Interdisciplinary History* 14 (1983), 218–22, 224–25.
199. Carl E. Taylor, "Synergy among Mass Infections, Famines, and Poverty," in ibid., 484.
200. Carmichael, "Infection," 252, 257.
201. "The Relationship of Nutrition, Disease, and Social Conditions: A Graphical Presentation," *Journal of Interdisciplinary History* 14 (1983), 503–506; Watkins and van de Walle, "Nutrition," 225.

The European mortality peak of 1740–1742, as has been documented, originated in an increase in the morbidity and mortality rates of typhus, typhoid, dysentery, smallpox, influenza, and unidentified respiratory diseases. With the exception of dysentery, these infections are believed to be not at all or only slightly related to nutritional status. The etiology of louse-borne typhus and relapsing fever does not suggest that nutritional deficiency influences their morbidity rates. Although prolonged undernutrition may prejudice case-fatality rates, typhus is so virulent that probably not even good nursing care would influence the outcome of infection.[202] Typhoid fever is also classified among those infections exhibiting no or perhaps minimal interaction with nutrition. In the case of dysentery, by contrast, both morbidity and mortality are believed to be influenced by nutritional deficiency.[203] Smallpox is not an infection in which undernutrition or malnutrition either promotes morbidity or prejudices case-fatality rates.[204] Influenza epidemics, finally, are neither created nor sustained by the existence of individuals or societies suffering from nutritional deprivation.[205]

On the basis of medical findings in regard to the influence of nutritional status on these specific infections, the probable conclusion is that the western European epidemics of 1740–1742 did not originate primarily in the biological effects of undernutrition or malnutrition. Neither does the evidence support the view that the epidemics prevalent in preindustrial subsistence crises were chiefly provoked by nutritional deficiency and impaired immune response. It is true that the widespread epidemics of dysentery can be connected to the prolonged undernutrition of the years 1740–1742 and also that dysentery was responsible for a significant percentage of the excess deaths. But as the evidence shows, even in the case of dysentery there was a lack of a strong rank-order correspondence between the magnitude of the national increases in food prices and mortality from this infection. The evidence indicates that variables in addition to nutritional status contributed to the elevated morbidity rates of bacillary dysentery.

The epidemics of both dysentery and continued fever were promoted by the combination of environmental stress, economic hardship, and dysfunctional social behavior, with the outcome of diarrheal and some respiratory diseases prejudiced by the prolonged period of undernutrition. But the wretchedness and social disarray that resulted from thermal

202. Benenson, *Communicable Diseases,* 259–60, 354; MacArthur, "Medical History," 267–68, 275–76; Dale C. Smith, "The Rise and Fall of Typhomalarial Fever: Origins," *Journal of the History of Medicine and Allied Sciences* 37 (1982), 195.
203. "Relationship of Nutrition, Disease, and Social Conditions," 505–506.
204. Chandra and Newberne, *Nutrition,* 1–6; C. W. Dixon, *Smallpox* (London, 1962).
205. Carmichael, "Infection," 252.

stress, joblessness, and high food prices facilitated rather than triggered the epidemics. Such infections as dysentery, typhus, typhoid, and relapsing fever had previously become endemic among Europe's working population. These smoldering infections could become epidemic under a variety of environmental and social conditions. The economic destitution and social upheaval created by dearth and war occasioned the greatest risks of fostering epidemics in preindustrial Europe. Both sets of conditions allowed the preexisting foci of infection to extend their range and to become widely prevalent. The coexistence of climatic variability, food shortage, and major epidemics in the early 1740s was not a coincidence. Although the progress from extreme weather events and dearth to widespread infectious disease was not automatic, the protracted climatic stress set the stage for epidemics in preindustrial Europe.

The process that made up the chain of causation from severe and prolonged cold seasons to epidemics of typhus fever has been outlined. Extreme winters as well as food shortages tended to foster louse-borne infections. Extended periods of low atmospheric temperatures together with the social upheaval engendered by subsistence crises were capable of transforming endemic typhus into national epidemics. The weather that curtailed the production of cereals from the summer of 1739 to the spring of 1742 also brought about a further breakdown in the already marginal standard of personal hygiene. The long periods during which people remained indoors in crowded conditions intensified the scale of louse infestation. The sequence of drawn-out cold seasons, unemployment, elevated food prices, and such dysfunctional social behavior as itinerant vagrancy facilitated the outbreaks of epidemic louse-borne fever in 1740–1741. The public installations that were set up, or expanded, to meet the welfare needs of the destitute, beggars, and vagrants, such as soup kitchens, temporary shelters, workshops, poorhouses, workhouses, and hospitals, became networks of infection as a consequence of crowding and thus changes in normal community spacing, which was a first-line defense against spreading contagion.

The chain of causation is most apparent in Ireland and Norway, where famine conditions and social turbulence increased the risk of epidemics to an inordinate degree. But continued fevers could become widely diffused even in the absence of a severe shortage of food, as the English epidemics demonstrate. The links between the weather and the English epidemics of 1740–1742 are found in the specific events that intensified louse infestation and in the epidemiological conditions that permitted the endemic foci of infections to expand and to spread.

Huxham's explanation, which traced the fever epidemics to infection among seamen on naval vessels, does not account for the eruption of the contagion in every region of the country. Multiple cases of "ship fever" were a common occurrence in English ports during the eighteenth century, but national epidemics were extremely rare. The English working population did not suffer from a prolonged dearth and subsistence crisis. The extreme winters and high unemployment rates, however, in conjunction with a shortage of fuel and high coal and food prices, translated into real hardship for the majority of townspeople and protoindustrial workers, particularly in London, the large seaports, and the urban settlements in the western counties.

According to the physician John Barker, the fever epidemic began in the west among the poor urban workers. He pointed to the high level of joblessness and considerable hardship that prevailed in England's western counties as the proximate cause of the outbreak and spread of the infection.[206] The majority of English physicians traced the epidemic fevers to jails, prisons, and the proceedings of the criminal justice system. Barker also noted that the fever epidemic became general and "began to be talk'd of in the *West* about the Spring assizes of 1741. It then went by the Name of the Gaol-Fever."[207] Cases of "gaol-fever," however, were also common in eighteenth-century England, but again, national typhus epidemics were rare.

It is nonetheless true that a significant increase in the number of arrests for theft during the years 1740–1742 inflated the jail population and led to further overcrowding.[208] An investigation of crime in Surrey during the years from 1736 to 1753 found that the number of offenders charged with crimes against property peaked in 1740–1741. It was also found that the number of offenders who died in jail awaiting trial peaked between 1739 and 1742, especially during the winter of 1740–1741. A severe outbreak of gaol fever in the Surrey county jail in 1740–1741 carried off large numbers of prisoners.[209] The increase in the number of cases of gaol fever unquestionably added considerable fuel to the typhus epidemics but represented only one of the networks that disseminated the infection.

The growing practice in England of providing workhouse rather than

206. Barker, *Present Epidemic Fever*, 138.
207. Ibid., 37; see also Wall, "Epidemic Fever," 337–52; *Gentleman's Magazine* 11 (December 1741), 655; *Observations on the Present Epidemic Fever*, 1–8.
208. J. M. Beattie, "The Pattern of Crime in England, 1660–1800," *Past and Present* 62 (February 1974), 73–78; Beattie, "Crime and the Courts in Surrey, 1736–1753," in J. S. Cockburn, ed., *Crime in England, 1550–1800* (Princeton, 1977), 155–86; Douglas Hay, "War, Dearth, and Theft in the Eighteenth Century: The Record of the English Courts," *Past and Present* 95 (May 1982), 125–26, 132–34.
209. Beattie,"Crime in England," 88–92.

outdoor relief added to the risk of epidemics, for example. The work-houses gave refuge to people in great distress as a last resort and not always in conformity with the poor law. It has been found that the Leeds workhouse sheltered an increasing number of inmates during the winter season. Not only the harsher weather conditions but also the fact that employment opportunities diminished with the intensity of the cold resulted in crowded workhouses in eighteenth-century England. Al-though the number of inmates in the Leeds workhouse during the winters of 1740–1742 is not exactly known, apparently nearly a quarter of the workhouse population died during January 1741,[210] a month in which epidemic typhus was rife in English towns.

Altogether it is difficult to rank the multiple variables that spawned the English fever epidemics of 1740–1742. Protracted cold seasons, joblessness, high food and fuel prices, crowded jails, welfare installations, riots, wartime naval operations, and the increase in the number of vagrants and beggars all contributed to the elevated incidence and spread of continued fevers. The fever epidemic in London was particularly associated with a buildup of vagrants and beggars. John Wesley noted that the sight of an unusual number of "Clamorous Beggars" in the streets of London became a matter of parliamentary concern in 1741.[211] During the spring of 1741, La Maison de Charité de Spittlefields found it necessary to distribute more than a thousand portions of soup monthly to the destitute Huguenots whom it was set up to serve.[212] The scale of vagrancy in London during the early 1740s inspired Parliament to enact new laws to deal with vagrants in both 1740 and 1744. Eighteenth-century opinion held that vagrancy was one of the most common means by which fever was spread.[213] It seems almost certain that the extremely cold winters and concomitant unemployment created the preconditions for typhus epidemics. Then the series of dysfunctional social phenomena, which were the third-order effects of climatic variability, transformed the endemic foci of infection into regional and national epidemics.

The series of dry spring and summer seasons during 1740–1742 created the preconditions for a higher incidence of dysentery and typhoid fever and thus constituted another functional relationship linking climatic

210. Philip Anderson, "The Leeds Workhouse under the Old Poor Law: 1726–1834," *Publications of the Thoresby Society* 56 (pt. 2, 1980), 88–95.

211. R. W. Wearmouth, *Methodism and the Common People in the Eighteenth Century* (London, 1945), 55; see also Murchison, *Continued Fevers,* 34.

212. Charles F. A. Marmoy, "The Case Book of 'La Maison de Charité de Spittlefields,' 1739–41," *Proceedings of the Huguenot Society of London* 55 (quarto ser., 1981), v.

213. Dorothy Marshall, *The English Poor in the Eighteenth Century* (London, 1926), 227–38.

variability and epidemic disease. The droughtlike weather conditions facilitated the diffusion of the bacteria that cause dysentery and typhoid fever. The cereal harvest shortfalls that touched off the social turbulence were a consequence not only of the detrimental weather but also of the decline in the number of farm animals. The low precipitation levels caused a shortage of grass and fodder, which led to the death or premature slaughter of livestock. In some districts, it proved impossible to sow all the arable fields owing to the decimation of cattle herds. The connection between climatic variability and the dysentery epidemics of the early 1740s can be illustrated by tracing the sequence of atmospheric, economic, and social events in Sweden.

Dysentery became a national health problem in Sweden at least as early as the 1690s, a decade of food shortages and crisis mortality in the Scandinavian peninsula and elsewhere in western Europe. After 1699, there is no evidence of widespread dysentery in Sweden until the second half of the 1730s, notwithstanding the epidemiological risks of the Great Northern War, which dragged on from 1701 to 1721. The origins of the epidemics that erupted in 1736 remain obscure. But whether the dysentery epidemics spread from northern Germany or exploded under the impetus of favorable atmospheric and environmental conditions, the prevalence of the infection had fallen off sharply before 1740.

After 1740 dysentery became epidemic throughout Sweden, almost certainly as a consequence of the meteorological and agricultural conditions and the social and military events of the early 1740s. Severe cold seasons, droughts, harvest shortfalls, food shortages, and the movement of migrants and military personnel promoted higher morbidity rates in counties of endemic infection and also disseminated dysentery to districts and towns that had previously been free of the disease.[214]

The harvest shortfalls meant not only higher food prices but fewer rural employment opportunities as well. In the 1740s, every propertyless person in Sweden, a class made up mostly of young people of both sexes, was obligated to seek a job; jobs were provided for the most part by peasant employers. Poor harvests, however, compelled such young people to migrate or to seek positions in towns. Because of the succession of cereal harvest shortfalls in Sweden from 1739 to 1742, the scale of migration to Stockholm and other towns intensified. The urban living conditions that predominated in preindustrial European towns facilitated the spread of bacillary dysentery even apart from an influx of migrants

---

214. Utterström, "Population Problems," 120–26; Imhof, *Bevölkerungsentwicklung in den nordischen Ländern*, 582–87.

and beggars. To begin with, urban populations lived in crowded and unhygienic quarters. The common practice of depositing human and animal excrement in the streets created an additional health hazard. In the event of dry weather and a large increase in the number of migrants, as in the early 1740s, the explosion of dysentery became a greater risk. As Arthur E. Imhof has written, the years of harvest failure and dearth resulted in the withering of the well-being of the Swedish peasantry and led not only directly to a more fertile soil for the spread of infectious diseases but also to their easier diffusion for the reason that the poorest classes—whose numbers were augmented by dearth—reacted to a series of poor harvest years by migration and mendicancy.[215]

In December 1740, the Swedish public health commission believed that "if the cold and hunger would cease, the illnesses would disappear by themselves."[216] The statement was probably unduly optimistic. Once dysentery and typhus fever had become widespread, the prevailing poor personal and environmental hygiene in preindustrial Europe virtually ensured that the infections would not die down instantaneously. In fact, neither the sequence of cold winters nor the elevated food prices subsided for several more years. The war with Russia then accelerated the spread of dysentery and continued fevers, as military camps, troop movements, and ships lacking in hygiene became an added network of infection. It should be noted, however, that Norway experienced a similar if not higher incidence of typhus fever and dysentery during 1741–1742, without the additional risks created by warfare, as was also the case in Ireland during 1740 and 1741.

The evidence shows in total that climatic shocks could still touch off mortality fluctuations and economic downturns in mid-eighteenth-century Europe, in both environmentally sheltered and more exposed societies. States that boasted rationalized public administrations and some degree of economic development had learned to prevent the famine conditions and crisis mortality that occurred in Finland, Norway, and Ireland, which still remained hostage to demographic crises of the *ancien* kind. At the same time, the number of deaths climbed in all western European countries during 1740–1742, in large part because climatic variability created preconditions for epidemics of dysentery and continued fevers. These infectious diseases became epidemic by following pathways that were not necessarily closed off by the social strategies adopted to buffer the consequences of climatic stress. As I have noted, endemic infections became epidemic in large part through the social disorder and turbulence

215. Imhof, *Bevölkerungsentwicklung in den nordischen Ländern*, 582–98, 1,073–82.
216. Quoted in ibid., 707.

that were third-order effects of climatic variability. These functional relations may explain Ronald Lee's finding that in preindustrial England the level of mortality was increased more decisively by below-normal temperatures from December to May and by high temperatures from June to November than by elevated food prices.[217]

The evidence indicates that the most effective method to minimize the risk of epidemics of louse-borne fever and dysentery was to preempt the dysfunctional social behavior promoted by climatic stress and food shortages. Public policies that put downward pressure on the potential rise in the scale of unemployment, migration, vagrancy, begging, and popular demonstrations tended to reduce the likelihood of epidemics. Such public welfare and relief programs did not necessarily derive from a "modernized" economy, as the relative success of the Prussian administration's policies make clear. The lower mortality peak in Prussia in the years 1740–1742 can be explained as the combined effect of the public granaries, the state's grain policies, the social control exercised by the precocious welfare state, and the landlord-and-peasant relationship of "hereditary subjection" that predominated in the eastern rural districts.

The principal link between climatic variability and epidemic disease in the early 1740s, and probably in preindustrial subsistence crises in general, was accordingly more social than nutritional, in the sense that it owed more to social upheaval than to dangerously lowered human resistance to louse-borne infections, typhoid, and dysentery. It is no doubt true that the case-fatality rates of dysentery and some common respiratory diseases were exacerbated by prolonged undernutrition. In mid-eighteenth-century Europe, however, the changes in patterns of behavior and the dilution of normal components of resistance within a society, such as community spacing and personal hygiene, rather than the nutritional impact of food shortages, were primarily responsible for allowing endemic infections to flare into epidemic diseases.[218]

217. Wrigley and Schofield, *Population*, 368–99.
218. For discussion of the ecological and behavioral changes that provoke epidemics of typhus fever and dysentery, see Frederick B. Bang, "The Role of Disease in the Ecology of Famine," in John R. K. Robson, ed., *Famine: Its Causes, Effects, and Management* (New York, 1981), 61–75.

Bibliography

Sources

Acta Borussica. *Denkmäler der preussischen Staatsverwaltung im 18. Jahrhundert. Getreidehandelspolitik.* Vol. II: W. Naudé, *Die Getreidehandelspolitik und Kriegsmagazinverwaltung: Brandenburg-Preussens bis 1740.* Berlin, 1901.

———. Vol. III: W. Naudé and A. Skalweit, *Die Getreidehandelspolitik und Kriegsmagazinverwaltung: Preussens, 1740–1756.* Berlin, 1910.

Allardyce, A., ed. *Scotland and Scotsmen in the Eighteenth Century from the MSS of John Ramsay of Ochtertyre.* 2 vols. Edinburgh, 1888.

Argenson, René-Louis d'. *Journal du marquis d'Argenson.* Edited by E.-J.-B. Rathery. 9 vols. Paris, 1859–67.

Baltus, Jacques. *Annales de Baltus (1724–1756).* Edited by Abbé E. Paulus. Metz, 1904.

Barbier, E.-J.-F. *Journal historique et anecdotique du règne de Louis XV.* 4 vols. Paris, 1847–56.

Barker, John, M.D. *An Inquiry into the Nature, Cause and Cure of the present Epidemic Fever.* London, 1742.

Becmann, Johann Christoph. *Historische Beschreibung der Chur und Mark Brandenburg.* Edited by B. L. Bekmann. 2 vols. Berlin, 1751–53.

Berkeley, George. *The Works of George Berkeley, Bishop of Cloyne.* Edited by A. A. Luce and T. E. Jessop. 9 vols. London, 1956.

Berlin. *Statistisches Jahrbuch der Stadt Berlin* 34. 1915–19.

Bernier, T. "Notice sur l'origine et la tenue des anciens registres d'état civil dans la province de Hainaut." *Mémoires de la Société des sciences, des arts, et des lettres du Hainaut,* 4th ser., 9 (1887), 523–92.

Bock, Friedrich Samuel. *Versuch einer wirtschaftlichen Naturgeschichte von dem Königreich Ost- und Westpreussen.* 5 vols. Dessau, 1782–85.

Caledonian Mercury (Edinburgh). 1739–42.

Country Journal (England). 1740–43.

Desbordes, Jean-Michel, ed. *La Chronique villageoise de Varreddes (Seine-et-Marne): Un Document sur la vie rurale des XVIIe et XVIIIe siècles.* Paris, 1969.

Dunsford, M. *Historical Memoirs of Tiverton.* Exeter, 1790.

Duyn, Nicolaas. *Historische aanmerkingen van drie strenge winters (1709, 1740, 1742)*. Haarlem, 1746.

Faulkner's Dublin Journal. 1739–42.

Gentleman's Magazine. Vols. 5–14. 1735–44.

Gilchrist, Ebenezer, M.D., "Of Nervous Fevers." *Medical Essays and Observations*. Vol. V, pt. 2. 505–73. 5 vols. Edinburgh, 1733–44.

Gray, M., ed. *Memoirs of the Life of Sir John Clerk of Penicuik*. Edinburgh, 1892.

Hamel, M. du. "Observations botanico-météorologiques pour l'année 1740." *Histoire de l'Académie royale des sciences*. Paris, 1744.

Hanover. Edict by George II, King of Great Britain, Elector. Dated May 7, 1740. Broadside. Boston University, Mugar Library. Call no. 3198-#122.

Henderson, Ebeneezer, ed. *The Annals of Dunfermline*. Glasgow, 1879.

Henderson, J. A. *Annals of Lower Deeside*. Aberdeen, 1892.

Hering, J. H. *Tafereel van harde winters*. Amsterdam, 1784.

Huxham, John, M.D. *Observations on the Air, and Epidemic Diseases from the Beginning of the Year 1738, to the End of the Year 1748*. Trans. from the Latin by John Corham Huxham. 2 vols. London, 1759–67.

Kennedy, W. *Annals of Aberdeen*. Edinburgh, 1818.

Kundmann, Johann Christian. *Die Heimsuchungen Gottes in Zorn und Gnade über das Herzogthum Schlesien in Müntzen*. Leipzig, 1742.

Lachiver, Marcel. *Histoire de Meulan et da sa région par les textes*. Meulan, 1965.

La Mettrie, Julien Offray de. *Oeuvres de médecine*. Berlin, 1755.

Latimer, J., ed. *The Annals of Bristol in the Eighteenth Century*. Bristol, 1893.

London Advertiser. 1739–42.

London Daily Post. 1739–42.

Mackay, M. M. "A Highland Minister's Diary." *Cornhill Magazine* 152 (November 1935), 570–80.

Maitland, W. *The History of Edinburgh*. Edinburgh, 1753.

Mann, Theodore Augustin. *Mémoires sur les grandes gelées et leurs effets*. Ghent, 1792.

Maraldi, M. "Observations météorologiques faites à l'Observatoire royal pendant l'année 1740." *Histoire de l'Académie royale des sciences*. Paris, 1742.

Margary, I. D. "The Marsham Phenological Record in Norfolk, 1735–1925, and Some Others." *Quarterly Journal of the Royal Meteorological Society* 52 (June 1926), 27–52.

Marmoy, Charles F. A. "The Case Book of 'La Maison de Charité de Spittlefields,' 1739–41." *Proceedings of the Huguenot Society of London* 55 (quarto ser., 1981), 1–83.

Marshall, J. D., ed. *Autobiography of William Stout of Lancester, 1665–1752*. Manchester, 1967.

Maxwell, Robert, ed. *Select Transactions of the Honourable the Society of Improvers*. Edinburgh, 1743.

Mercure de France. 1740–42.

Messance, M. *Recherches sur la population des généralités d'Auvergne, de Lyon, de Rouen, et de quelques provinces et villes du royaume*. Paris, 1766.

Narbonne, Pierre de. *Journal des règnes de Louis XIV et Louis XV de l'année 1701 à l'année 1744 par P. Narbonne, premier commissaire de police de la ville de Versailles.* Edited by J.-A. Le Roi. Versailles, 1866.

Observations on the present epidemic Fever. London, 1741.

Pue's Occurrences (Ireland). 1740–41.

Réaumur, M. de. "Observations du thermomètre faites en 1740." *Histoire de l'Académie royale des sciences.* Paris, 1742.

Rutty, John, M.D. *A Chronological History of the Weather and Seasons, and of the Prevailing Diseases in Dublin.* London, 1770.

———. *An Essay Towards a Natural History of the County of Dublin.* 2 vols. Dublin, 1772.

Schenck, Heinrich C. F. *Die Wunder Gottes im Winter; oder, Historische Nachricht von dem sehr strengen, besonders merckwürdig- und ungewöhnlich-anhaltenden Winter des 1739 und 40. Jahres.* Arnstadt, 1741.

Scheppere, J. B. B., M.D. *Détail historique et curatif de la fièvre maligne qui règne actuellement en toute Flandre et ailleurs depuis l'an 1737 etc.* Ghent, 1741.

Scots Magazine (Edinburgh). 1740–41.

Short, Thomas, M.D. *A Comparative History of the Increase and Decrease of Mankind in England and Several Countries Abroad.* York, 1767.

———. *A General Chronological History of the Air, Weather, Seasons, Meteors, etc.* London, 1749.

———. *New Observations on City, Town, and Country Bills of Mortality.* London, 1750.

Sims, J., M.D. *Observations on Epidemic Disorders with Remarks on Nervous and Malignant Fevers.* London, 1773.

Sinclair, Sir John. *The Statistical Account of Scotland.* 21 vols. Edinburgh, 1791-98.

Smith, Charles. *The Antient and Present State of the County and City of Cork.* 2 vols. Dublin, 1750.

Southwell, T. "An Account of the Severe Winter of 1739–40 and of Its Effects in the County of Norfolk in the Year Following." *Norfolk and Norwich Naturalists Society, Transactions* 2 (1875), 125–30.

Süssmilch, Johann Peter. *Die göttliche Ordnung in den Veränderungen des menschlichen Geschlechts.* 4th ed. 3 vols. Berlin, 1775.

Targioni-Tozzetti, Giovanni. *Lettera.* Florence, 1741.

Trümpi, Christoph. *Neuere Glarner Chronik.* Winterthur, 1774.

Vanderlinden, Émile. "Chronique des événements météorologiques en Belgique jusqu'en 1834." *Mémoires de l'Académie royale de Belgique,* Classe des Sciences, 2d ser., 6 (1924), 1–329.

Wall. John, M.D. "Account of the Epidemic Fever of 1740, 1741, 1742." *Medical Tracts,* collected by Martin Wall, M.D. Oxford, 1780.

Walser, G. *Appenzeller-Chronik.* pt. 3 (1732–72). Edited by G. Nüesch. Trogen, 1830.

Wolff, Johann Philipp. *Consilium Medicum, welches über die dermahlen hier und dar anfangend und epidemicé grassirende Ruhr-Krankheit gestellet und mit getheilet hat.* Schweinfurth, 1743.

Secondary Works

Abel, Wilhelm. *Massenarmut und Hungerkrisen im vorindustriellen Europa.* Hamburg, 1974.

Alexander, B. W. "The Epidemic Fever (1741–42)." *Salisbury Medical Bulletin* 11 (1971), 24–29.

Altman, Laurence, M.D. "Unnoticed Loss of Body Heat Can Kill." *New York Times, Science Times,* December 25, 1979.

Anderson, Philip. "The Leeds Workhouse under the Old Poor Law: 1726–1834." *Publications of the Thoresby Society* 56 (pt. 2, 1980), 75–113.

Andrewes, C. H., and Walton, J.R., *Viral and Bacterial Zoonoses.* London, 1976.

Appleby, Andrew B. "Grain Prices and Subsistence Crises in England and France, 1590–1740." *Journal of Economic History* 39 (1979), 865–87.

——. "Nutrition and Disease: The Case of London, 1550–1750." *Journal of Interdisciplinary History* 6 (1975), 1-22.

Arnould, Maurice-A. "Mortalité et épidemies sous l'Ancien Régime dans le Hainaut et quelques régions limitrophes." In *Problèmes de mortalité,* edited by Paul Harsin and Etienne Hélin. Liège, 1965.

Ashton, T. S. *Economic Fluctuations in England, 1700–1800.* London, 1959.

——. *An Economic History of England: The Eighteenth Century.* London, 1955.

Aykroyd, W. R. "Definition of Different Degrees of Starvation." In *Famine: A Symposium Dealing with Nutrition and Relief Operations in Times of Disaster,* edited by G. Blix et al. Uppsala, 1971.

Barker, Sir Ernest. *The Development of Public Services in Western Europe, 1660–1930.* London, 1944.

Barker, F., M.D., and Cheyne, J., M.D. *An Account of the Rise, Progress and Decline of the Fever Lately Epidemical in Ireland.* 2 vols. Dublin, 1821.

Barnes, Donald C. *A History of the English Corn Laws from 1660 to 1846.* London, 1930.

Baulant, Micheline. "Le prix des grains à Paris de 1431 à 1788." *Annales: Economies, Sociétés, Civilisations* 23 (1968), 520–40.

——; Le Roy Ladurie, Emmanuel; and Demonet, Michel. "Une Synthèse provisoire: Les Vendanges du XVe au XIXe siècle." *Annales: Economies, Sociétés, Civilisations* 33 (1978), 763-71.

Baümler, D. G. "Medizinalstatistische Untersuchungen über Weiden (Oberpfalz) von 1551 bis 1800." *Archiv für Hygiene* 120 (1938), 195–243.

Bayne-Jones, Stanhope. "Epidemic Typhus in the Mediterranean Area during World War II." In *Rickettsial Diseases of Man,* edited by F. R. Moulton. Washington, D.C., 1948.

Beattie, J. M. "Crime and the Courts in Surrey, 1736–1753." In *Crime in England, 1550–1800,* edited by J. S. Cockburn. Princeton, 1977.

——. "The Pattern of Crime in England, 1660–1800." *Past and Present* 62 (February 1974), 47–95.

Beaudry, R. "Alimentation et population rurale en Périgord au XVIIIe siècle." *Annales de Démographie Historique* (1976) 41–59.

Beckwith, F. "The Population of Leeds during the Industrial Revolution." *Publications of the Thoresby Society* 41, Miscellany (1943–51), 118–96.

Behrens, Betty. "Government and Society." In *The Cambridge Economic History of Europe*, vol. v: *The Economic Organization of Early Modern Europe*. Cambridge, 1977.

Belletini, Athos. *La popolazione di Bologna dal secolo XV all'unificazione italiana*. Bologna, 1961.

Beltrami, Daniele. *Storia della popolazione di Venezia dalla fine del secolo XVI alla caduta della repubblica*. Padova, 1954.

Benenson, Abram, ed. *Control of Communicable Diseases in Man*. 12th ed. Washington, D.C., 1975.

Besdine, Richard, M.D. "Accidental Hypothermia: The Body's Energy Crisis." *Geriatrics* 34 (December 1979), 51–59.

Beveridge, Sir William, and Others. *Prices and Wages in England from the Twelfth to the Nineteenth Century*. Vol. I: *Price Tables: Mercantile Era*. London, 1939.

Beveridge, W. I. B. *Influenza: The Last Great Plague*. London, 1977.

Bielmann, Jürg. *Die Lebensverhältnisse im Urnerland während des 18. und ze Beginn des 19. Jahrhunderts*. Basel 1972.

Blayo, Yves. "Mouvement naturel de la population française de 1740 à 1829." *Population* 30, special no. (November 1975), 15–64.

Bloch, Camille. *L'Assistance et l'état en France à la veille de la Révolution*. Geneva, 1974.

Blockmans, F. "De Bevolkingscijfers te Antwerpen in de XVIIIe eeuw." *Antwerpen in de XVIIIe eeuw*. Antwerp, 1952.

Blum, Jerome. *The End of the Old Order in Rural Europe*. Princeton, 1978.

Boissonnade, P. *Essai sur l'organisation du travail en Poitou, depuis le XIe siècle jusqu'à la Révolution*. 2 vols. Paris, 1900.

Bondois, Paul. "Un Essai de culture exotique sous l'ancien régime: La 'Peste du riz' de Thiers (1741)." *Revue d'Histoire Economique et Sociale* 16 (1928), 586–655.

Bonenfant, Paul. *Le Problème du paupérisme en Belgique à la fin de l'ancien régime*. Brussels, 1934.

Bouvet, Michel. "Troarn: Etude de démographie historique (XVIIe–XVIIIe siècles)." *Cahiers des Annales de Normandie* 16 (1968), 17–202.

Boxer, C.R. *The Dutch Seaborne Empire, 1600–1800*. London, 1965.

Braudel, Fernand. *Capitalism and Material Life, 1400–1800*. Translated from the French by Miriam Kochan. New York, 1973.

—— and Labrousse, Ernest, eds. *Histoire économique et sociale de la France*. Vol. II: *1660–1789*. Paris, 1970.

Bricourt, Michel; Lachiver, Marcel; and Queruel, Denis. "La Crise de subsistance des années 1740 dans le ressort du Parlement de Paris (d'après le Fonds Joly de Fleury de la Bibliothèque Nationale de Paris)." *Annales de Démographie Historique* (1974), 281–333.

Bruneel, Claude. *La Mortalité dans les campagnes: Le Duché de Brabant aux XVIIe et XVIIIe siècles*. Louvain, 1977.

Bucher, S. *Bevölkerung und Wirtschaft des Amtes Entlebuch im 18. Jahrhundert*. Luzern, 1974.

Bull, G. M., and Morton, Joan. "Environment, Temperature, and Death Rates." *Age and Ageing* 7 (1978), 210–24.

Burckhardt, A. *Demographie und Epidemiologie der Stadt Basel während der letzten drei Jahrhunderte, 1601–1900.* Basel, 1908.

Burnet, Sir MacFarland, and White, David O. *Natural History of Infectious Disease.* 4th ed. Cambridge, 1972.

Burri, Hans-Rudolf. *Die Bevölkerung Luzerns im 18. und frühen 19. Jahrhundert.* Luzern, 1975.

Busvine, James R. *Insects, Hygiene, and History.* London, 1976.

Bynum, William F., ed. *Theories of Fever from Antiquity to the Enlightenment.* London, 1981.

Cage, R. A. *The Scottish Poor Law.* Edinburgh, 1981.

Cahill, George F., Jr., M.D. "Starvation in Man." *New England Journal of Medicine* 282 (March 1970), 668–75.

Cameron, Iain. *Crime and Repression in the Auvergne and the Guyenne, 1720–1790.* Cambridge, 1981.

Canard, J. "Les Mouvements de population à Saint-Romain d'Urfé de 1612 à 1946." *Bulletin de la Diana* 29 (1945), 118–55.

Carmichael, Ann. "Infection, Hidden Hunger, and History." *Journal of Interdisciplinary History* 14 (1983), 249–64.

Chambers, J. D. *Nottinghamshire in the Eighteenth Century.* 2d ed. New York, 1966.

———. *The Vale of Trent.* Economic History Review. Supp. 3. London, 1957.

Chandra, R. K., and Newberne, P. M. *Nutrition, Immunity, and Infection: Mechanisms of Infection.* New York, 1977.

Charbonneau, Hubert. *Tourouvre-au-Perche aux XVIIe et XVIIIe siècles (1668–1819).* Paris, 1970.

Charlesworth, Andrew, ed. *An Atlas of Rural Protest in Britain, 1548–1900.* London, 1982.

Charlot, E., and Dupâquier, J. "Mouvement annuel de la population de la ville de Paris de 1670 à 1821." *Annales de Démographie Historique* (1967), 511–19.

Christie, A. B. *Infectious Diseases: Epidemiology and Clinical Practice.* 3d ed. New York, 1980.

Cieślak, Edmund. "Aspects of Baltic Sea-borne Trade in the XVIIIe Century: The Trade Relations between Sweden, Poland, Russia, and Prussia." *Journal of European Economic History* 12 (1983), 239–70.

Coiffier, Joseph. *L'Assistance publique dans la généralité de Riom (au XVIIIe siècle).* Clermont-Ferrand, 1905.

Connell, K. H. *The Population of Ireland, 1750–1845.* London, 1950.

Corradi, Alfonso. *Annali delle epidemie occorse in Italia dalle prime memorie fino al 1850.* 8 vols. Bologna, 1865–94.

Creighton, Charles, M.D. *A History of Epidemics in Britain.* 2 vols. Cambridge, 1891–94.

Cullen, L. M. *An Economic History of Ireland since 1660.* London, 1972.

—— and Smout, T. C., eds. *Comparative Aspects of Scottish and Irish Economic and Social History, 1600–1900.* Edinburgh, 1977.

Daelemans, F. "Tithe Revenues in Rural South West Brabant, Fifteenth to Eighteenth Century." In *Productivity of Land and Agricultural Innovation in the Low Countries (1250–1800)*, edited by Herman van der Wee and Eddy van Cauwenberghe. Louvain, 1978.

Dalle, D. *De bevolking van Veurne-Ambacht in de 17e en 18e eeuw.* Brussels, 1963.

Dardel, P. "Crises et faillites à Rouen et dans la Haute Normandie de 1740 à l'an V." *Revue d'Histoire Economique et Sociale* 27 (1948), 53–72.

Daultrey, Stuart; Dickson, David; and Ó Gráda, Cormac. "Eighteenth-Century Irish Population: New Perspectives from Old Sources." *Journal of Economic History* 41 (1981), 601–28.

De Brower. "De demografische evolutie in de meierij Erembodegem en de heerlijkheid Oordegem gedurende de XVIIe en XVIIIe eeuw." *Cinq études de démographie locale (XVIIe–XIXe siècles.).* Brussels, 1963.

Del Panta, Lorenzo. "Cronologia e diffusione delle crisi di mortalità in Toscana dalla fine del XIV agli initi del XIX secolo." *Ricerche Storiche* 7 (1977), 293–343.

—— and Livi Bacci, M. "Chronologie, intensité et diffusion des crises de mortalité en Italie: 1600–1850." *Population* 32 (1977), 401–46.

Delumeau, J. "Démographie d'un port français sous l'ancien régime: Saint-Malo, 1651–1750." *XVIIe Siècle* 86–87 (1970), 3–21.

Deniel, Raymond, and Henry, Louis. "La Population d'un village du Nord de la France, Sainghin-en-Mélantois, de 1665 á 1851." *Population* 20 (1965), 563–602.

Desaive, J.-P., et al. *Médecins, climat, et épidémies à la fin du XVIIIe siècle.* Paris, 1972.

De Vos, J. "De omvang en de evolutie van het Eeklose Bevolkingscijfer tijdens de XVIIe en de XVIIIe eeuw." *Cinq Etudes de démographie locale (XVIIIe–XIXe siècles).* Brussels, 1963.

de Vries, Jan. "Histoire du climat et économie: Des faits nouveau, une interprétation différente." *Annales: Economies, Sociétés, Civilisations* 32 (1977), 198–226.

——. "Measuring the Impact of Climate on History: The Search for Appropriate Methodologies." *Journal of Interdisciplinary History* 10 (1980), 599–630.

Dixon, C. W. *Smallpox.* London, 1962.

Dobson, Mary Schove. "A Chronology of Disease and Mortality in Southeast England, 1601–1800." In chap. 7, "Patterns of Disease," in D. Phil. diss., University of Oxford, 1982.

Donazzolo, P., and Saibante, M. "Lo sviluppo demografico di Verona e dalla sua provincia dalla fine del sec. XV ai nostri giorni." *Metron* 6 (1926), 56–180.

Dorwart, Reinhold A. *The Prussian Welfare State before 1740.* Cambridge, Mass., 1971.

Drake, Michael. "The Irish Demographic Crisis of 1740–41." *Historical Studies* 6 (1968), 101–24.

——. *Population and Society in Norway, 1735–1865.* Cambridge, 1969.

Dreyfus, François G. "Prix et population à Trèves et à Mayence au XVIIIe siècle." *Revue d'Histoire Economique et Sociale* 34 (1956), 241–61.

Dupâquier, Jacques. "Les Caractères originaux de l'histoire démographique française au XVIIIe siècle." *Revue d'Histoire Moderne et Contemporaine* 23 (1976), 182–203.

——; Lachiver, M.; and Meuvret, J. *Mercuriales du pays de France et du Vexin français, 1640–1792.* Paris, 1968.

Dyrvik, Ståle; Mykland, Knut; and Oldervall, Jan. *The Demographic Crises in Norway in the Seventeenth and Eighteenth Centuries.* Bergen, 1976.

Easton, C. *Les Hivers dans l'Europe occidentale.* Leiden, 1928.

Ebeling, Dietrich, and Irsigler, Franz, eds. *Getreideumsatz, Getreide- und Brotpreise in Köln, 1368–1797.* Cologne, 1977.

Edwards, J. K. "Norwich Bills of Mortality—1707–1830." *Yorkshire Bulletin of Economic and Social Research* 21 (1969), 94–113.

Ehrhart, Wilhelm. "Die Sterblichkeit in der Reichsstadt Kempten (Allgäu) in den Jahren 1606–1624 und 1686–1870." *Archiv für Hygiene und Bakteriologie* 116 (1936), 115–30.

El Kordi, Mohamed. *Bayeux aux XVIIe et XVIIIe siècles.* Paris, 1970.

Elsas, Moritz J. *Umriss einer Geschichte der Preise und Löhne in Deutschland vom ausgehenden Mittelalter bis zum Beginn des 19. Jahrhunderts.* 2 vols. Leiden, 1936–49.

Eversley, D. E. C. "Mortality in Britain in the Eighteenth Century: Problems and Prospects." In *Problèmes de mortalité,* edited by Paul Harsin and Etienne Hélin. Liège, 1965.

Fedele, Salvatore. "Strutture e movimento della popolazione in una parrocchia della Capitanata, 1711–1750." *Quaderni Storici* 17 (1971), 447–84.

Ferrario, Giuseppe. *Statistica medica di Milano dal secolo XV fino ai nostri giorni.* 2 vols. Milan, 1838–50.

Flinn, Michael W. *The European Demographic System, 1500–1820.* Baltimore, 1981.

——. "The Stabilisation of Mortality in Pre-industrial Western Europe." *Journal of European Economic History* 3 (1974), 285–318.

—— et al. *Scottish Population History from the Seventeenth Century to the 1930s.* Cambridge, 1977.

Folge, William H. "Famine, Infections, and Epidemics." In *Famine: A Symposium Dealing with Nutrition and Relief Operations in Times of Disaster,* edited by G. Blix et al. Uppsala, 1971.

François, Etienne. "La mortalité urbaine en Allemagne au XVIIIe siècle." *Annales de Démographie Historique* (1978) 135–65.

——. "La Population de Coblence au XVIIIe siècle." *Annales de Démographie Historique* (1975), 291–341.

Frésel-Lozey, M. *Histoire démographique d'un village en Béarn: Bilhères-d' Ossau au XVIIIe–XIXe siècles.* Bordeaux, 1969.

Friberg, Nils. "The Growth of Population and Its Economic-Geographical Background in a Mining District in Central Sweden, 1650–1750." *Geografiska Annaler* 38 (1956), 395–440.

Friis, Astrid, and Glamann, Kristof. *A History of Prices and Wages in Denmark 1660–1800.* Vol. I: *Copenhagen.* London, 1958.

Ganiage, Jean. *Trois Villages d'Ile-de-France: Etude démographique.* Paris, 1963.

Gautier, Etienne, and Henry, Louis. *La Population de Crulai, paroisse normande.* Paris, 1958.

Gedrose, Judith, R.N., M.N. "Prevention and Treatment of Hypothermia and Frostbite." *Nursing* 10 (February 1980), 34–36.

Giacchetti, J. C., and Tyvaet, M. "Argenteuil (1740–90)." *Annales de Démographie Historique* (1969) 40–61.

Gille, H. "The Demographic History of the Northern European Countries in the Eighteenth Century." *Population Studies* 3 (1949), 1–65.

Glamann, Kristof. "The Changing Patterns of Trade." In *The Cambridge Economic History of Europe,* vol. V. *The Economic Organization of Early Modern Europe.* Cambridge, 1977.

Glonner, Stephan. "Bevölkerungsbewegung von Sieben Pfarreien im Kgl. Bayerischen Bezirksamt Tölz seit Ende des 16. Jahrhunderts." *Allgemeines Statistisches Archiv* 4 (1896), 263–79.

Godechot, Jacques, and Moncassin, S. "Démographie et subsistances en Languedoc du XVIIIe siècle au début du XIXe siècle." *Bulletin d'Histoire Economique et Sociale de la Révolution Française* (1964), 23–60.

Gordon, John. "Epidemiological Insights on Malnutrition: Some Resurrected, Others Restructured, a Few Retired." *American Journal of Clinical Nutrition* 31 (1978), 2,339–51.

———. "Louse-borne Typhus Fever in the European Theater of Operations." In *Rickettsial Diseases of Man,* edited by F. R. Mouton. Washington, D.C., 1948.

Goubert, Jean-Pierre. *Malades et médecins en Bretagne, 1770–1790.* Paris, 1974.

Goubert, Pierre. *The Ancien Régime.* Translated by Steve Cox. New York, 1974.

———. *Beauvais et le Beauvaisis de 1600 à 1730.* 2 vols. Paris, 1960.

———. *Cent Mille Provinciaux au XVIIe siècle.* Paris, 1968.

———. "Historical Demography and the Reinterpretation of Early Modern French History: A Research Review." In *The Family in History,* edited by T. K. Rabb and R. I. Rotberg. New York, 1973.

Goy, Joseph, and Le Roy Ladurie, E., eds. *Les Fluctuations du produit de la dîme.* Paris, 1972.

Gruffydd, K. L. "The Vale of Clwyd Corn Riots of 1740." *Flintshire Historical Society Publications* 27 (1975–76), 36–42.

Gutmann, Myron P. "Putting Crises in Perspective: The Impact of War on Civilian Populations in the Seventeenth Century." *Annales de Démographie Historique,* (1977), 101–28.

———. *War and Rural Life in the Early Modern Low Countries.* Princeton, 1980.

Haeser, Heinrich. *Lehrbuch der Geschichte der Medizin und der epidemischen Krankheiten.* 3d ed. 3 vols. Jena, 1875–82.

Hamilton, Henry. *An Economic History of Scotland in the Eighteenth Century.* London, 1963.

Hampson, E. M. *The Treatment of Poverty in Cambridgeshire.* Cambridge, 1934.

Hay, Douglas. "War, Dearth, and Theft in the Eighteenth Century: The Record of the English Courts." *Past and Present* 95 (1982), 117–60.

Helczmanovszki, Heimold, ed. *Beiträge zur Bevölkerungs- und Sozialgeschichte Österreichs.* Vienna, 1973.

Hélin, Etienne. *La Démographie de Liège aux XVIIe et XVIIIe siècles.* Brussels, 1963.

——. "Le Déroulement de trois crises à Liège au XVIIIe siècle." In *Problèmes de mortalité,* edited by Paul Harsin and Etienne Hélin. Liège, 1965.

——. *La Population des paroisses liègeoises aux XVIIe et XVIIIe siècles.* Liège, 1959.

——. "Les Recherches sur la mortalité dans la région liègeoise (XVe–XIXe siècles)." In *Problèmes de mortalité,* edited by Paul Harsin and Etienne Hélin. Liège, 1965.

Helleiner, Karl L. "The Population of Europe from the Black Death to the Eve of the Vital Revolution." In *The Cambridge Economic History of Europe,* vol. IV: *The Economy of Expanding Europe in the Sixteenth and Seventeenth Centuries.* Cambridge, 1967.

Helweg-Larsen, Per, et al. *Famine Disease in German Concentration Camps:* *Complications and Sequels.* Acta Medica Scandinavica, Supp. 274. Copenhagen, 1952.

Henne, A., and Wauters, A. *Histoire de la ville de Bruxelles.* 2 vols. Brussels, 1845.

Henry, Louis. "The Population of France in the Eighteenth Century." In *Population in History,* edited by D. V. Glass and D. E. C. Eversley. London, 1965.

Hofsten, E., and Lundström, H. *Swedish Population History.* Stockholm, 1976.

Hoskins, W. G. "Harvest Fluctuations and English Economic History, 1620–1759." *Agricultural History Review* 16, pt. 1 (1968), 15–31.

Houtte, G. van. *Leuven in 1740, ein krisisjaar: Ekonomische, sociale, en demografische aspekten.* Brussels, 1964.

Houtte, Hubert van. *Documents pour servir à l'histoire des prix de 1381 à 1794.* Brussels, 1902.

——. "La Législation annonaire des Pays-Bas à la fin de l'Ancien Régime et la disette de 1789 en France." *Vierteljahrschrift für Sozial- und Wirtschaftsgeschichte* 10 (1912), 96–119.

Hubatsch, Walther. *Frederick the Great of Prussia: Absolutism and Administration.* Translated from the German by Patrick Doren. London, 1975.

Hufton, Olwen H. *The Poor of Eighteenth-Century France, 1750–1789.* Oxford, 1974.

Imhof, Arthur E. "The Analysis of Eighteenth-Century Causes of Death: Some Methodological Considerations." *Historical Methods* 11 (1978), 3–35.

——. *Aspekte der Bevölkerungsentwicklung in den nordischen Ländern, 1720–1750.* Bern, 1976.

——. "Die nicht-namentliche Auswertung der Kirchenbücher von Giessen und Umgebung." In *Historische Demographie als Sozialgeschichte,* edited by Arthur E. Imhof. Darmstadt, 1975.

—— and Lindskog, B. I. "Les Causes de mortalité en Suède et en Finlande entre 1749 et 1773." *Annales: Economies, Sociétés, Civilisations* 29 (September–October, 1974) 915–33.

Joerger, Muriel. "The Structure of the Hospital System in France in the Ancien Régime." Translated by Elborg Forster. In *Medicine and Society in France,* edited by Robert Forster and Orest Ranum. Baltimore, 1980.

Jones, Colin. *Charity and "Bienfaisance": The Treatment of the Poor in the Montpellier Region, 1740–1815.* Cambridge, 1982.

Jones, E. L. *Seasons and Prices*. London, 1964.

Jörberg, Lennart. *A History of Prices in Sweden, 1732–1914*. 2 vols. Lund, 1972.

Jouan, M.-H. "Les Originalités démographiques d'un bourg artisanal normand au XVIIIe siècle: Villedieu-les-Poeles, 1711–1790." *Annales de Démographie Historique* (1969) 87–124.

Jungkunz, W. "Die Sterblichkeit in Nürnberg, 1714–1850." *Mitteilungen des Vereins für Geschichte der Stadt Nürnberg* 42 (1951), 289–352.

Jutikkala, Eino. *Die Bevölkerung Finnlands in den Jahren 1721–1749*. Helsinki, 1945.

Kahan, Arcadius. "Natural Calamities and Their Effect upon the Food Supply in Russia (An Introduction to a Catalog)." *Jahrbücher für Geschichte Osteuropas*, n.s. 16 (1968), 353–77.

Kaplan, Steven L. *Bread, Politics, and Political Economy in the Reign of Louis XV*. 2 vols. The Hague, 1977.

——. "The Famine Plot Persuasion in Eighteenth-Century France." *Transactions of the American Philosophical Society* 72 (pt. 3, 1982), 1–75.

——. "Lean Years, Fat Years: The 'Community' Granary System and the Search for Abundance in Eighteenth-Century Paris." *French Historical Studies* 10 (1977), 197–320.

Kark, Sidney L. *Epidemiology and Community Medicine*. New York, 1974.

Kass, E. H. "Infectious Diseases and Social Change." *Journal of Infectious Diseases* 123 (1971), 110–14.

Katsas, A. G. "Starvation Disease in Greece." *New England Journal of Medicine* 293 (October 1975), 881.

Kemp, D. D. "Winter Weather in West Fife in the Eighteenth Century." *Weather* 31 (December 1976), 400–404.

Keys, Ancel, et al. *The Biology of Human Starvation*. 2 vols. Minneapolis, 1950.

King, Lester S. *The Medical World of the Eighteenth Century*. Chicago, 1958.

Kington, J. A. "An Application of Phenological Data to Historical Climatology." *Weather* 29 (September 1974), 320–28.

Kisskalt, Karl. "Epidemiologisch-statistische Untersuchungen über die Sterblichkeit von 1600–1800." *Archiv für Hygiene und Bakteriologie* 137 (1953), 26–42.

Labrijn, Aart. *Het klimaat van Nederland gedurende de lastste twee en een halve eeuw*. Schiedam, 1945.

Labrousse, E. *Esquisse du mouvement des prix et des revenus en France au XVIIIe siècle*. Paris, 1932.

—— et al. *Le Prix du froment en France au temps de la monnaie stable, 1726–1913*. Paris, 1970.

Lachiver, M. "Une Etude et quelques esquisses." *Annales de Démographie Historique* (1969), 215–40.

——. *La Population de Meulan du XVIIe au XIXe siècle*. Paris, 1969.

Lamb, H. H. *Climate: Present, Past, and Future*. Vol. II: *Climatic History and the Future*. New York, 1978.

——. *The English Climate*. London, 1964.

Lebrun, François. *Les Hommes et la mort en Anjou aux 17e et 18e siècles*. Paris, 1971.

Lefebvre-Teillard, A. *La Population de Dôle au XVIIIe siècle*. Paris, 1969.

Le Goff, A. "Bilan d'une étude de démographie historique: Auray au XVIIIe siècle (vers 1740–1789)." *Annales de Démographie Historique* (1974), 197–229.

Lehners, Jean-Paul. "Die Pfarre Stockerau im 17. und 18. Jahrhundert: Erste Resultate einer demographischen Studie." In *Beiträge zur Bevölkerungs- und Sozialgeschichte Österreich,* edited by Heimold Helczmanovszki. Vienna, 1973.

Lelong, J. "Saint-Pierre-Église." *Annales de Démographie Historique* (1969), 125–35.

Le Roy Ladurie, Emanuel. *Les Paysans de Languedoc.* 2 vols. Paris, 1966.

——. *Times of Feast, Times of Famine: A History of Climate since the Year 1000.* Translated from the French by Barbara Bray. Garden City, 1971.

Lindsay, J. C. *Old Regime, 1713–63.* Cambridge, 1957.

MacArthur, Sir William. "Famines and Fevers in England and Ireland." *Journal of the British Archaeological Association,* 3d ser., 9 (1944), 66–71.

——. "Medical History of the Famine." In *The Great Famine,* edited by R. Dudley Edwards and T. Desmond Williams. New York, 1957.

——. "Old-Time Typhus in Britain." *Transactions of the Royal Society of Tropical Medicine and Hygiene* 20 (1926–27) 487–503.

McCloy, Shelby T. *Government Assistance in Eighteenth-Century France.* Durham, 1946.

McKeown, Thomas. *The Modern Rise of Population.* London, 1976.

——. and Record, R. G. "Reasons for the Decline of Mortality in England and Wales during the Nineteenth Century." *Population Studies* 16 (November 1962), 94–122.

——, ——, and Turner, R. D. "An Interpretation of the Decline of Mortality in England and Wales during the Twentieth Century." *Population Studies* 29 (1975), 391–422.

Maddalena, Aldo de. *Prezzi e mercedi a Milano dal 1701 al 1860.* 2 vols. Milan, 1974.

Mallet, Edouard. "Recherches historiques et statistiques sur la population de Genève: Son Mouvement annuel et sa longévité depuis le XVe siècle jusqu'à nos jours (1549–1833)." *Annales d'Hygiène Publique et de Médecine Légale* 17 (1837), 5–172.

Manley, Gordon. "Central England Temperatures: Monthly Means 1659 to 1793." *Quarterly Journal of the Royal Meteorological Society* 100 (1974), 389–405.

——. *Climate and the British Scene.* London, 1952.

——. "The Great Winter of 1740." *Weather* 13 (1958), 11–17.

Marshall, Dorothy. *The English Poor in the Eighteenth Century.* London, 1926.

——. "The Old Poor Law, 1662–1795." In *Essays in Economic History,* edited by E. M. Carus-Wilson, vol. I, 295–305. London, 1954.

Marshall, J. D. *The Old Poor Law, 1795–1834.* London, 1968.

Massachusetts General Hospital News 39 (December 1980), 1–4.

Mentink, G. T., and Woude, A. M. van der. *De demografische ontwikkeling te Rotterdam en Cool in de 17e en 18e eeuw.* Rotterdam, 1965.

Meuvret, Jean. "Les Crises de subsistance et la démographie de la France d'ancien régime." *Population* 1 (1946), 643–50.

——. "Demographic Crisis in France from the Sixteenth to the Eighteenth Century."

In *Population in History,* edited by D. V. Glass and D. E. C. Eversley. London, 1965.

——. *Etudes d'histoire économique.* Paris, 1971.

Mitchell, B. R., and Deane, Phyllis. *Abstract of British Historical Statistics.* Cambridge, 1962.

Mitchison, Rosalind. "The Making of the Old Scottish Poor Law." *Past and Present* 63 (May 1974), 58–93.

Molinier, A. *Une paroisse du bas Languedoc: Sérignan (1650–1792).* Montpellier, 1968.

Mols, Roger. *Introduction à la démographie historique des villes d'Europe du XIVe au XVIIIe siècle.* 3 vols. Louvain, 1954–56.

Morineau, Michel. *Les Faux-semblants d'un démarrage économique: Agriculture et démographie en France au XVIIIe siècle.* Paris, 1970.

Müller, Karl. *Geschichte des badischen Weinbaus.* 2d ed. Lahr, 1953.

Murchison, Charles. *A Treatise on the Continued Fevers of Great Britain.* London, 1862.

Murray, John, and Murray, Anne. "Suppression of Infection by Famine and Its Activation by Refeeding—A Paradox?" *Perspectives in Biology and Medicine* 20 (1977), 471–83.

Naudé, Wilhelm. *Die Getreidehandelspolitik der europäischen Staaten vom 13. bis zum 18. Jahrhundert.* Berlin, 1896.

Neveux, Hugues. "La Production céréalière dans une région frontalière: Le Cambrésis du XVe au XVIIIe siècle." In *Les Fluctuations du produit de la dîme,* edited by J. Goy and E. Le Roy Ladurie. Paris, 1972.

Olivier, E., M.D. *Médecine et santé dans le pays de Vaud.* 2 vols. Lausanne, 1962.

Oswald, N. C., M.D. "Epidemics in Devon, 1538–1837." *Devonshire Association* 109 (1977), 73–116.

Owen, David. *English Philanthropy, 1660–1960.* Cambridge, Mass., 1964.

Oxley, G. W. *Poor Relief in England and Wales, 1601–1834.* Newton Abbot, 1974.

Ozanam, J. A. F. *Histoire médicale générale et particulière des maladies épidémiques, contagieuses et épizootiques.* 2d ed. 3 vols. Paris, 1817–23.

Pearson, M. C. "The Winter of 1739–40 in Scotland." *Weather* 28 (January 1973), 20–24.

Perrenoud, Alfred. *La Population de Genève du seizième au début du dix-neuvième siècle: Etude démographique.* Vol. I: *Structures et mouvements.* Paris, 1979.

Perrot, Jean-Claude. *Genèse d'une ville moderne: Caen au XVIIIe siècle.* 2 vols. Paris, 1975.

Peter, Jean-Pierre. "Disease and the Sick at the End of the Eighteenth Century." Translated from the French by Elborg Forster and Patricia M. Ranum. In *Biology of Man in History,* edited by Robert Forster and Orest Ranum. Baltimore, 1975.

——. "Malades et maladies à la fin du XVIIIe siècle." *Annales: Economies, Sociétiés, Civilisations* 22 (1967), 711–51.

Pfaff, Christoph Heinrich. *Über die strengen Winter, vorzüglich des 18. Jahrhunderts und über den letzt verflossenen strengen Winter von 1808–1809.* Kiel, 1810.

Pfister, Christian. *Agrarkonjunktur und Witterungsverlauf im westlichen Schweizer Mittelland zur Zeit der ökonomischen Patrioten, 1755–1797.* Bern, 1975.

——. "Central European Thermal and Wetness Indices for Spring and for Summer from 1525 to 1825, Derived from a Body of Instrumental Measurements, Descriptive Evidence and Proxy-Data." Paper presented at the Conference on Climate and History, Harvard University, May 1979.

——. *Das Klima der Schweiz von 1525 bis 1860 und seine Bedeutung in der Geschichte von Bevölkerung und Landwirtschaft*. Bern, 1984.

——. "The Little Ice Age: Thermal and Wetness Indices for Central Europe." *Journal of Interdisciplinary History* 10 (1980), 665–96.

Pfister, Willy. "Getreide- und Weinzehnten, 1565–1798, und Getreidepreise, 1565–1770, im bernischen Aargau." *Argovia* 52 (1940), 237–64.

Phelps Brown, E. H., and Hopkins, Sheila V. "Seven Centuries of the Prices of Consumables Compared with Builders' Wage-Rates." In *Essays in Economic History,* edited by E. M. Carus-Wilson. 3 vols. London, 1962.

Pickard, Ransom. *The Population and Epidemics of Exeter in Pre-Census Times.* Exeter, 1947.

Piuz, Anne-Marie. "Climat, récoltes et vie des hommes à Genève XVIe–XVIIIe siècles." *Annales: Economies, Sociétés, Civilisations* 29 (May–June 1974), 599–618.

Poitrineau, A. *La Vie rurale en Basse Auvergne au XVIIIe siècle (1726–1789).* 2 vols. Paris, 1965.

Post, John D. "Climatic Variability and the European Mortality Wave of the Early 1740s." *Journal of Interdisciplinary History* 15 (1984), 1–30.

——. *The Last Great Subsistence Crisis in the Western World.* Baltimore, 1977.

Posthumus, Nicolaas W. *Inquiry into the History of Prices in Holland.* 2 vols. Leiden, 1946–64.

Pounds, N. J. G. "John Huxham's Medical Diary: 1728–1752." *Local Population Studies* 12 (Spring 1974), 34–37.

Pozos, Robert S., and Wittmers, Lorentz E., Jr., eds. *The Nature and Treatment of Hypothermia.* Minneapolis, 1983.

Pribram, Alfred Francis. *Materialien zur Geschichte der Preise und Löhne in Österreich.* Vienna, 1938.

Prinzing, Friedrich. *Epidemics Resulting from Wars.* Oxford, 1916.

Pyle, Gerald F. *Applied Medical Geography.* Washington, D.C., 1979.

Rebaudo, Danièle. "Le Mouvement annuel de la population française rurale de 1670 à 1740." *Population* 34 (1979), 589–606.

"The Relationship of Nutrition, Disease, and Social Conditions: A Graphical Presentation." *Journal of Interdisciplinary History* 14 (1983), 503–506.

Renbourn, E. T. *Materials and Clothing in Health and Disease.* London, 1972.

Richards, Toni. "Weather, Nutrition, and the Economy: Short-Run Fluctuations in Births, Deaths, and Marriages: France, 1740–1909." *Demography* 20 (1983), 197–212.

Risse, Guenter B. "Epidemics and Medicine: The Influence of Disease on Medical Thought and Practice," *Bulletin of the History of Medicine* 53 (1979), 505–19.

Robertson, George. *Rural Recollections.* Irvine, 1829.

Robson, John R. K., ed. *Famine: Its Causes, Effects, and Management.* New York, 1981.

Rogan, Francis, M.D. *Observations on the Condition of the Middle and Lower Classes in the North of Ireland As it Tends to Promote the Diffusion of Contagious Fever.* London, 1819.

Roller, Otto K. *Die Einwohnerschaft der Stadt Durlach im 18. Jahrhundert.* Karlsruhe, 1907.

Rose, John, ed. *Nutrition and Killer Diseases.* Park Ridge, N.J., 1982.

Rossi, Fiorenzo. "Storia della popolazione di Adria dal XVI al XIX secolo." *Genus* 26 (1970), 73–167.

Rudloff, Hans von. *Die Schwankungen und Pendelungen des Klimas in Europa seit dem Beginn der regelmässigen Instrumenten-Beobachtungen (1670).* Braunschweig, 1967.

Saint-Jacob, P. de. *Les Paysans de la Bourgogne du nord au dernier siècle de l'ancien régime.* Dijon, 1960.

Savitt, Todd. *Medicine and Slavery: The Diseases and Health Care of Blacks in Antebellum Virginia.* Urbana, 1979.

Schmoller, Gustav. "Die Epochen der Getreidehandelsverfassung und -politik." *Jahrbuch für Gesetzgebung, Verwaltung, und Volkswirtschaft im Deutschen Reich* 20 (1896), 695–744.

Schmölz, Franz, and Schmölz, Therese. "Die Sterblichkeit in Landsberg am Lech von 1585–1875." *Archiv für Hygiene und Bakteriologie* 136 (1952), 504–40.

Schofield, R. S. "Crisis Mortality." *Local Population Studies* 9 (Autumn 1972), 10–22.

Schreiber, A. "Die Entwicklung der Augsberger Bevölkerung vom Ende des 14. Jahrhundert bis zum Beginn des 19. Jahrhunderts." *Archiv für Hygiene* 123 (1939–40), 90–177.

Schürmann, M. *Bevölkerung, Wirtschaft, und Gesellschaft in Appenzell-Innerrhoden im 18. und frühen 19. Jahrhundert.* Appenzell, 1974.

Scrimshaw, N. S.; Taylor, C.E.; and Gordon, J. E. *Interactions of Nutrition and Infection.* Geneva, 1968.

Seitz, F. *Der Typhus, Vorzüglich nach seinem Vorkommen in Bayern geschildert.* Erlangen, 1847.

Sheppard, Thomas F. *Lourmarin in the Eighteenth Century.* Baltimore, 1971.

Slack, Paul. "Mortality Crises and Epidemic Disease in England, 1485–1610." In *Health, Medicine, and Mortality in the Sixteenth Century,* edited by Charles Webster. Cambridge, 1979.

Slicher van Bath, B. H. "Agriculture in the Vital Revolulation." In *The Cambridge Economic History of Europe,* vol. V; *The Economic Organization of Early Modern Europe.* Cambridge, 1977.

———. "Report on the Study of Historical Demography in the Netherlands." In *Problèmes de mortalité,* edited by Paul Harsin and Etienne Hélin. Liège, 1965.

Smith, Dale C. "Gerhard's Distinction between Typhoid and Typhus and Its Reception in America, 1833–1860." *Bulletin of the History of Medicine* 54 (1980), 368–85.

———. "The Rise and Fall of Typhomalarial Fever: Origins." *Journal of the History of Medicine and Allied Sciences* 37 (1982), 182–220.

Smout, T. C. *A History of the Scottish People, 1560–1830.* Glasgow, 1969.

Snell, W. E. "Measles and Its Complications Fifty Years Ago." *Public Health* 90 (1976), 211–17.

Sogner, Sølvi. "Aspects of the Demographic Situation in Seventeen Parishes in Shropshire, 1711–60." *Population Studies* 17 (November 1963), 126–46.

Sonderland, V. P. *Die Geschichte von Barmen im Wupperthale.* Elberfeld, 1821.

Spink, Wesley W. *Infectious Diseases: Prevention and Treatment in the Nineteenth and Twentieth Centuries.* Minneapolis, 1979.

Stanley, Neville F., and Joske, R. A., eds. *Changing Disease Patterns and Human Behavior.* New York, 1980.

Sticker, Georg. *Abhandlungen aus der Seuchengeschichte und Seuchenlehre.* 2 vols. Giessen, 1908–12.

Stratton, J. M. *Agricultural Records, A.D. 220–1968.* Edited by Ralph Whitlock. London, 1969.

Tapley-Soper, H., ed. *The Register of Baptisms, Marriages, and Burials of the Parish of Ottery St. Mary, Devon, 1601–1837.* 2 vols. Exeter, 1908–29.

Tate, W. E. *The Parish Chest.* 3d ed. Cambridge, 1969.

Taylor, Carl E. "Synergy among Mass Infections, Famines, and Poverty." *Journal of Interdisciplinary History* 14 (1983), 483–501.

Thomas, Michael. "The Rioting Crowd in Derbyshire in the Eighteenth Century." *Derbyshire Archaeological Journal* 95 (1975), 37–47.

Tilly, Charles. "Food Supply and Public Order in Modern Europe." In *The Formation of National States in Western Europe.* Princeton, 1975.

Tomasson, Richard F. "Millennium of Misery: The Demography of the Icelanders." *Population Studies* 31 (1977), 405–27.

Torfs, Louis. *Fastes des calamités publiques survenues dans les Pays-Bas.* 2 vols. Paris, 1859–62.

Tromp, S. W. *Medical Biometeorology.* Amsterdam, 1963.

Tucci, U. "Innesto del vaiolo e società nel Settecento veneto." *Annales Cisalpines d'Histoire Sociale* 1 (1973), 199–231.

Utterström, Gustaf. "Climatic Fluctuations and Population Problems in Early Modern History." *Scandinavian Economic History Review* 3 (1955), 3–47.

——. "Some Population Problems in Pre-industrial Sweden." *Scandinavian Economic History Review* 2 (1954), 103–15.

Van Assche–Van Cauwenbergh, D. "Deux Villages du Brabant sous l'ancien régime: Bierges et Overyse: Etude de démographie historique." In *Cinq Études de Démographie locale (XVIIIe–XIX siècles).* Brussels, 1963.

Verlinden, Charles, et al., eds. *Dokumenten voor de geschiedenis van prijzen en lonen in Vlaanderen en Brabant.* 5 vols. Bruges, 1959–73.

Wales-Smith, B. G. "Monthly and Annual Totals of Rainfall Representative of Kew, Surrey, from 1697–1970." *Meteorological Magazine* 100 (1971), 345–62.

Walton, K. "Climate and Famines in Northeast Scotland." *Scottish Geographical Magazine* 68 (1952), 13–21.

Watkins, Susan Cotts, and van de Walle, Etienne. "Nutrition, Mortality, and Population Size: Malthus' Court of Last Resort." *Journal of Interdisciplinary History* 14 (1983), 205–26.

Wearmouth, R. W. *Methodism and the Common People of the Eighteenth Century.* London, 1945.

Wee, Herman van der, and Cauwenbergh, Eddy van, eds. *Productivity of Land and Agricultural Innovation in the Low Countries.* Louvain, 1978.

Weikinn, Curt. *Quellentexte zur Witterungsgeschichte Europas.* 5 vols. Berlin, 1958–67.

Werveke, Hans van. "De Curve van het Gentse Bevolkingscijfer in de 17e en de 18e eeuw." *Verhandelingen van de Koninklyke Vlaamse Academie voor Wetenscheppen: Letteren en Schone Kunsten van Belgie* 10 (1948), 5–60.

Wiel, Ph. "Tamerville." *Annales de Démographie Historique* (1969), 136–89.

Woude, A. M. van der. *Het Noorderwartier.* 3 vols. Wageningen, 1972.

Wrigley, E. A., and Schofield, R. S. *The Population History of England, 1541–1871.* Cambridge, Mass., 1981.

Yeomans, Andrew. "The Symptomatology, Clinical Course, and Management of Louse-borne Typhus Fever." In *Rickettsial Diseases of Man,* edited by F. R. Moulton. Washington, D.C., 1948.

Young, Vernon R., and Scrimshaw, Nevin S. "The Physiology of Starvation." In *Food: Readings from "Scientific American."* San Francisco, 1973.

Zielinski, Herbert. "Klimatische Aspekte Bevölkerungsgeschichtlicher Entwicklung." In *Historische Demographie als Sozialgeschichte,* edited by Arthur E. Imhof. Darmstadt, 1975.

Index

Appleby, Andrew B., 26n, 78, 120–21, 126

Atmospheric variables and crop yields, model of, 78–81, 91–94

Austrian Succession, War of, 21, 25, 194, 196, 251–55, 266–67

Barbier, E.-J.-F., 159, 163

Barker, Dr. John, 236, 275

Beggars and vagrants: in England, 61–62, 183, 185, 192–93, 276; in France, 155–69, 250; in Germany, 197–200; in Ireland, 177–78, 244–46, 265–66; in Low Countries, 172–74; in Norway, 113, 180–81; in Scotland, 63, 74, 147–52, 263; in Sweden, 182–83, 259, 277–78

Berkeley, George, 177, 220, 264–65

Birth Statistics, 44–47

Brabant, See Low Countries

Braudel, Fernand, 17, 21

Bricourt, Michel, 99–100, 213

Bronchitis, 205–11. See also Respiratory diseases

Bruneel, Claude, 260–61

Cardiovascular disease, 205–8. See also Thermal stress

Carmichael, Dr. Ann G., 271

Celsius, Anders, 59, 66

Charitable relief contributions: in England, 186–88; in France, 152–68; in Ireland, 174–78; in Low Countries, 173–74; in Scotland, 146–52. See also Welfare and relief programs

Climatic regime of Western Europe, 20, 51–53, 61–64, 70–75. See also Weather patterns

Climatic variability and disease, 19, 23–27, 51, 76, 205–16, 228, 238–42, 252–54, 258–62, 267–70, 273–74, 276–78

Continued fevers, classification of, 228–33. See also Typhoid fever; Typhus fever

Cullen, Louis M., 87, 97

Dearth: in England, 89–93, 186–93; in Finland, 108–10, 113–14, 182–83; in France, 98–102, 153–69; in Germany, 195–99; in Ireland, 96–98, 174–78; in Low Countries, 102–4, 171–74; in Norway, 108–10, 113–14, 179–81; in Scotland, 93–96, 148–52; in Sweden, 108–10, 113–14, 182–83; in Switzerland, 106–7. See also Famine; Hunger

Death Statistics, 30–43. See also Dublin Bills of Mortality; Edinburgh Bills of Mortality; London Bills of Mortality; Mortality

Demographic crisis, definition of, 43–44

Demographic statistics. See Vital Statistics

Denmark: dysentery in, 267–68; grain harvests in, 85, 89, 112–14; grain prices in, 139–40; grain trade regulation in, 178–80; public granaries in, 180; typhoid in, 260, 268; weather patterns in, 67; welfare and relief programs in, 179–81

Diarrhea, famine, 217–18; in France, 223–24; in Ireland, 219–20; in Low Countries, 224; in Norway, 225–26. See also Dysentery

Dickson, David, 37–38, 245–46

Drake, Michael, 37, 87, 96, 124

Drought, 23, 55–57; in England, 55, 67–69, 74; in France, 75; in Ireland, 63–68, 75; in Low Countries, 55, 69–70, 75; in Scotland, 68. See also Precipitation; Weather patterns

Dublin Bills of Mortality, 211–12, 246. See also Vital statistics

Library of Congress Cataloging in Publication Data

Post, John D. (John Dexter), 1925–
  Food shortage, climatic variability, and epidemic disease in preindustrial Europe.

  Bibliography: p.

  1. Nutrition disorders—Europe—History—18th century. 2. Malnutrition—Europe—History—
18th century. 3. Food supply—Europe—History—18th century. 4. Climatic changes—Europe—
History—18th century. 5. Mortality—Europe—History—18th century. 6. Europe—Statistics,
Vital—History—18th century. 7. Europe—Statistics, Medical—History—18th century. I. Title.
RA645.N87P67 1985   363.8   85-4684
ISBN 0-8014-2773-2 (alk. paper)